《新概念英语自学导读丛书

主编　　　何其莘
顾问　　亚历山大（英）

新概念英语自学导读
NCE Study Guide
3

Developing Skills

孙玉荣 杜 建 编著

外语教学与研究出版社

PEARSON　LONGMAN

京权图字 01-2000-1345

图书在版编目(CIP)数据

新概念英语自学导读 3 / 孙玉荣，杜建编著. — 北京：外语教学与研究出版社，2000 (2014.6 重印)
(《新概念英语》(新版)辅导丛书)
ISBN 978-7-5600-1940-6

Ⅰ. 新…　Ⅱ. ①孙… ②杜…　Ⅲ. 英语—自学参考资料　Ⅳ. H31

中国版本图书馆 CIP 数据核字 (2000) 第 34958 号

出　版　人：蔡剑峰
出版发行：外语教学与研究出版社
社　　　址：北京市西三环北路 19 号 (100089)
网　　　址：http://www.fltrp.com
印　　　刷：北京市鑫霸印务有限公司
开　　　本：850×1168　1/32
印　　　张：20
版　　　次：2001 年 1 月第 1 版　2014 年 6 月第 29 次印刷
书　　　号：ISBN 978-7-5600-1940-6
定　　　价：24.90 元
＊　　　＊　　　＊
购书咨询：(010)88819929　电子邮箱：club@fltrp.com
外研书店：http://www.fltrpstore.com
凡印刷、装订质量问题，请联系我社印制部
联系电话：(010)61207896　电子邮箱：zhijian@fltrp.com
凡侵权、盗版书籍线索，请联系我社法律事务部
举报电话：(010)88817519　电子邮箱：banquan@fltrp.com
法律顾问：立方律师事务所　刘旭东律师
　　　　　中咨律师事务所　殷　斌律师
物料号：119400001

外研社 朗文 新概念英语 自学导读3

NEW CONCEPT ENGLISH (New Edition)

STUDY GUIDE 3: Developing Skills

English edition of *New Concept English* © L. G. Alexander 1967
Original English material © Addison Wesley Longman Ltd. 1997
This edition of New Concept English STUDY GUIDE 3
with the addition of Chinese material © Foreign Language Teaching and Research Press and
Pearson Education North Asia Ltd. , 2000. This edition is
published under the Longman imprint,
which is an imprint of Pearson Education Group,
and by arrangement with Pearson Education North Asia Ltd. , Hong Kong.

Licensed for sale in the mainland territory of the People's Republic of China only.

This simplified Chinese characters edition first published
in 2000 jointly by Foreign Language Teaching and Research Press
and Pearson Education North Asia Ltd.

合作出版人：李朋义(外研社)　沈维贤(朗文)
主编：何其莘　　　　顾问：亚历山大(英)
责任编辑：任小玫
执行编辑：周继东
封面设计：诸中英

外语教学与研究出版社
培生教育出版北亚洲有限公司 联合出版

《新概念英语》（新版）是《新概念英语》1967 年首次出版以来第一次推出的新版本。现在，由该经典教材的出版者外语教学与研究出版社和培生教育出版北亚洲有限公司独家授权、由原编著者何其莘教授亲自主持编写、亚历山大先生充任顾问的这套《新概念英语》（新版）辅导丛书涵盖自学导读、练习详解、词汇、语法以及录音练习等各方面的内容，是面向中国广大英语爱好者的一套权威的辅导用书，定能满足中国广大读者对《新概念英语》（新版）的全方位的要求，并使英语爱好者在学习过程中最大限度地发挥自己的潜能。

《新概念英语》（新版）辅导丛书包括：
《新概念英语自学导读 1》（NCE Study Guide 1：First Things First）
《新概念英语自学导读 2》（NCE Study Guide 2：Practice & Progress）
《新概念英语自学导读 3》（NCE Study Guide 3：Developing Skills）
《新概念英语自学导读 4》（NCE Study Guide 4：Fluency in English）
《新概念英语练习详解 1》（NCE Exercise Companion 1：First Things First）
《新概念英语练习详解 2》（NCE Exercise Companion 2：Practice & Progress）
《新概念英语练习详解 3》（NCE Exercise Companion 3：Developing Skills）
《新概念英语练习详解 4》（NCE Exercise Companion 4：Fluency in English）
《新概念英语语法手册》（An NCE Grammar Handbook）
《新概念英语词汇大全》（An NCE Complete Vocabulary List）
《新概念英语词汇自学手册》（An NCE Pocket Dictionary）
《新概念英语录音练习手册》（Recorded Drills for NCE）

Preface

This Study Guide is intended for all students of *Developing Skills*, but particularly for those working on their own.

Detailed notes are provided for each of the sixty texts. These consist of:

- Further notes on the text
- Grammar in use: further notes on the grammatical points in each text
- Word study: further notes on the vocabulary
- Key to written exercises

We believe that these additional notes will help students from all background to benefit from the course and to complete it successfully.

L. G. Alexander.

Louis George Alexander

前　　言

该《自学导读》专为所有使用《培养技能》的学习者而设计，特别适用于自学者。

书中，针对 60 篇课文中的每一篇均有进一步说明。其中包括：
- 课文详注；
- 语法：每课语法点详解；
- 词汇学习；
- 练习答案。

我们确信这些补充材料将使各种起点的学习者从中受益，并顺利学完本课程。

L. G. A......

L.G. 亚历山大

目　　录

Lesson 1
A puma at large
逃遁的美洲狮

📖 **课文详注 Further notes on the text**

1. A puma at large

此处 at large 为介词短语,作定语,修饰 a puma。在英语中,当介词短语作定语时,通常用于被修饰的名词之后,如:

The woman in black is his mother.

身着黑装的那位女士是他的母亲。

Experts from the Zoo began their investigation.

(来自)动物园的专家们开始了他们的调查。

at large 逍遥自在的,行动自由的;未捕获的。通常用来指具有危险性的人或事物未被控制的状态:

the escaped murderer at large 仍逍遥法外的在逃杀人犯

The disease is still at large.

此种疾病仍在蔓延。

2. Pumas are large, cat-like animals which...

cat-like 为派生词,由词根(名词)+后缀(-like)构成。后缀-like 表示"像……似的"、"有……特征的":

doglike 像狗似的

womanlike 女人似的

3. When reports came into London Zoo that a wild puma had been spotted forty-five miles south of London, they were not taken seriously.

(1)此 that 从句为同位语从句,作 reports 的同位语,进一步说明

1

报告的内容。此类结构通常直接用于某些名词(如 idea、fact、news、hope、thought、proof、message 等)之后,如:

There can be no doubt that she is qualified for the job.

毫无疑问,她胜任这项工作。

当 that 从句为主语的同位语,而谓语又较短时,为使句子更为紧凑,通常将谓语部分提前(如课文中句子),将主语同其同位语分开,如:

The thought came to him that she once told him so.

他突然想起她曾这样对他讲过。

(2) 主句中的代词 they 指前面时间状语从句中的主语 reports。

take sth. seriously 认真对待,如:

Nearly everyone had warned him of the danger, but he didn't take it seriously.

几乎每个人都警告过他有危险,但他并未把它当回事儿。

4. However, as the evidence began to accumulate, experts from the Zoo felt obliged to investigate, for the descriptions given by people who claimed to have seen the puma were extraordinarily similar.

(1) 并列连词 however 用来表示语义上的转折,如:

The task is a bit difficult. It is, however, not beyond their reach.

这个任务是有点难,但也并非他们无力来完成。

(2) 从属连词 as 在此处引导一时间状语从句,表示"随着"、"当……时",如:

As she talked on she got more and more worried.

她越说越焦虑。

(3) 动词 oblige 表示"迫使"之意时,其后通常跟随一表示人称的宾语和一动词不定式构成的复合宾语:oblige sb. to do sth. 迫使某人做某事。此动词,如文中那样,常用于被动语态:be /

feel obliged to do sth. 被迫做某事,如:

The police obliged the onlookers to leave.

警察迫使围观者离开。

He felt obliged to let her in.

他只得让她进来。

(4) 句中的 for 为一并列连词,可用来表示因果关系,通常用来引导一事后想到的原因,更类似于置于括号内的说明性文字。由于它的这些特征,因此在使用时不可直接用其引导一原因状语从句,或像原因状语从句那样置于句首,如不可说:

＊*For I was feeling quite hungry, I decided to stop and have lunch.*

而应说:

I decided to stop and have lunch, for I was feeling quite hungry.

我决定停下来吃午饭,因为我觉得非常饿。

(5) the description given by people 中的 given by people 为过去分词短语作定语,修饰 description。description 常与动词 give 或 make 搭配使用,在所描述的人或物前使用介词 of: give / make a description of sth. /sb. 对某事/某人进行描述,如:

She gave a vivid description of the match.

她对那场比赛作了生动的描述。

Could you make a detailed description of the thief?

您能详细描述那个小偷的模样吗?

(6) who claimed to have seen the puma 中的 who 引导一定语从句,修饰其前的 people。to have seen 为动词不定式的完成时结构,表示动词不定式的动作发生在谓语动词 claimed 之前。

5. ... a small village where a woman picking blackberries ...
此处 picking blackberries 为现在分词短语作定语,后置修饰 woman。现在分词/分词短语作定语时含有进行、持续和主动

3

的含义,因此可将其译为一位正在采摘黑莓的妇女,见下例:

Tell those children playing outside not to make so much noise.

让在外边玩耍的孩子别这么吵。

6. ... a puma will not attack a human being unless it is cornered.

(1) 此处 will 不是用来表示将来时的助动词,而是用来表示习惯性或动作特征的情态助动词,通常表示"就"、"就会"、"总是"之意,如:

He will never let anybody know what he is doing.

他从不让任何人知道他在干什么。

(2) unless it is cornered 为一条件状语从句,意即"除非它被逼得走投无路"。一般说来,unless 为 if ... not 之意,但语气较 if...not 重。在 unless 引导的从句中要使用现在时形式,而非将来时形式,如:

Come tomorrow unless I phone.

如果我没打电话,你明天就来。

此外,使用 unless 的句子含有"如果 B 未阻止,A 就会发生"之意,而不可用其表示"由于 B 未发生而 A 才发生"之意的句子,如:

I'll be surprised if he doesn't have an accident.

如果他不出意外我才感到吃惊呢。

上述句子中的 if...not 结构,不可用 unless 取代。

7. ... and at another place twenty miles away...

句中 twenty miles away 为定语,置后修饰 place。在英语中,一些常见的表示地点或时间的副词可用来置于名词之后作定语修饰这一名词,如:

表地点:

the way ahead　前面的路

his trip abroad　他的出国旅行

4

the sentence below 下面的句子

表时间:

the meeting yesterday 昨天的会议

their stay overnight 他们整夜的逗留

8.. . .it left behind it a trail of,. . .

behind it 为状语,由于句中宾语部分较长,为使句子结构更为紧凑,这样就将其置于宾语 a trail of 之前。leave sth. behind 把……留在身后;忘带;在……之后造成/产生,如:

She went out in a hurry and left the keys behind her at home.

她匆匆出去,把钥匙忘在了家中。

The storm left a heap of destruction behind it.

风暴过后,留下了大量毁坏物。

9. Paw prints were seen in a number of places and puma fur was found clinging to bushes.

(1) a number of 用来表示"若干"、"许多"之意,用于修饰可数名词,因此其后应使用复数名词或代词。当使用由其构成的短语作主语时,其谓语动词通常为复数形式,如:

An increasing number of students have made use of this newly-built library.

越来越多的学生利用了这座新建的图书馆。

(2) found clinging to bushes 中的 clinging to bushes 为现在分词短语,此处作主语 puma fur 的主语补足语。作补足语使用的分词结构常见于 see、hear、notice、watch、keep、find、get、have、feel、smell 等动词之后,如:

Do you smell something burning?

你闻到什么东西烧焦了吗?

She could feel her heart beating violently.

她可以感觉出自己心跳得厉害。

5

过去分词同样可用于此类结构中,如:

He acknowledged himself defeated.

他承认自己失败了。

现在分词或过去分词的使用主要取决于宾语同分词所表示的动作之间是主动还是被动的关系。此外,在上述动词后还可使用动词不定式(不带 to),其意义有所不同。使用动词不定式时,通常表示所做动作的全过程;使用现在分词时,往往表示动作的正在发生,即所做动作的部分过程,如:

I saw her cross the road.

我看到她穿过了马路。(从一边至另一边)

I saw her crossing the road.

我看到她正在过马路。(也许正在路中央)

当然,当无需作语义上的这种区分时,可使用任何一种结构,如:

I often heard him sing(ing) this song.

我经常听到他唱这支歌。

(3) cling 为不及物动词,其后通常使用介词 to + 宾语的形式,除表达文中"粘在……上"外,还常用来表示"坚持"、"萦绕于"之意,如:

cling tenaciously to one's opinion 固执己见

cling to the last hope 抱定最后希望

The odour clung to the great hall.

那气味在大厅里经久不散。

His friend's last words clung to his memory.

他朋友最后说的话一直萦绕在他的脑际。

10. Several people complained of 'cat-like noises' at night and a businessman on a fishing trip saw the puma up a tree.

(1) complain 报怨;诉苦。作不及物动词使用时,常见用法如下:

complain about / of 报怨/埋怨;complain to sb. about / of 向某

6

人报怨/埋怨,如：

You indeed have nothing to complain of.

你的确没什么可报怨的。

She's now complaining to the manager about the service.

她正向经理报怨服务质量不好。

作及物动词使用时,通常为 complain that 从句（即后跟宾语从句）结构,如：

She complained that he had always been rude to her.

她报怨说他一直对她很粗鲁。

（2）up a tree 作宾语补足语,说明 puma 的状况。

11. The experts were now fully convinced that the animal *was* a puma.

（1）convince 使……深信,常见用法有：convince sb. of 使某人深信；convince sb. + that... 使某人深信……,如：

I couldn't convince him of his mistake.

I couldn't convince him that he was mistaken.

我无法说服他认识错误。

句中 were now fully convinced that... 为被动语态结构,相当于 convinced themselves that...,即"使自己充分认识到……"之意。

（2）此处 was 用斜体,含强调之意,意即"确定是",需予重读。

12. As no pumas had been reported missing from any zoo in the country, this one must have been in the possession of a private collector and somehow managed to escape.

（1）as 在此处为从属连词,引导一原因状语从句,在使用中与 because、since 略有不同。使用 because 时,所表原因通常为句子中最重要的信息,通常用于句尾,如：

You want to know why I'm leaving? I'm leaving because I'm fed up!

你想知道我为什么离开？我离开是因为我受够了！

使用 as 与 since 时，所示原因一般已为人所知或地位次要于句中其他信息。since 较 as 略为正式些。as 与 since 引导的原因状语从句通常置于句首，如：

As you are busy, you need not go with me.

既然你很忙，你就不必和我一块儿去了。

Since you refuse to co-operate, I shall be forced to take legal advice.

既然你拒绝合作，那我只好听取律师的意见了。

(2) missing from any zoo 为现在分词短语作主语补足语（见本课课文注释 9 中 clinging to bushes）。

(3) must have been 这种在 must 后使用完成时的结构用来表示对过去事情的推测，如：

You must have seen him yesterday.

你昨天肯定见到了他。

The lights have gone out. A fuse must have blown.

灯灭了。肯定是保险丝烧了。

但在疑问句和否定句中表示对过去事情的推测时用 can 和 can't，如：

I don't think he can have heard you. Call again.

我想他肯定没听到你的声音，再喊他。

Where can John have put the matches? He can't have thrown them away.

约翰能把火柴放在哪儿呢？他不会把它们扔掉的。

(4) be in the possession of 属于；为……所有。含被动意味，其主语应为物；be in possession of 拥有，含主动意味，其主语应为人，如：

He was born in New York, while the city was still in the possession of the British troops.

他出生于纽约,当时该城还处于英军占领之下。

The chief was in possession of a large quantity of stolen property.

那个头目占有大量偷盗来的财产。

(5) 动词 manage 表示"设法"时,其后用动词不定式:manage to do sth. 含有"成功(设法)做成某事"之意,不可用其表达"设法做某事而未做成"之意的句子,如不可说:

* He managed to pursuade her but failed.

而应说:

He tried to pursuade her but failed.

他试图说服她,但未成功。

此外,manage 指一次性行为,因此不可用其表示经常性行为,如不可说:

* He was a terrific liar: he managed to make anybody believe him.

而应说:

He was a terrific liar: he could make anybody believe him.

他是个了不得的骗子,他能让任何人都相信他。

相反,不可用 can 的过去式表示一次性行为,如不可说:

* I talked for a long time, and in the end I could make her believe.

而应说:

I talked for a long time, and in the end I managed to make her believe.

我说了许久,最终设法使她相信了我。

13. It is disturbing to think that...

这里的 it 为先行词,在句中无实际语义,起形式主语的作用,而句子的逻辑主语是后面的动词不定式。当主语为动词不定

9

式、动名词短语或从句时,往往主语很长,为了避免句子显得头重脚轻,习惯使用先行词 it 作形式主语,而将这样的逻辑主语移至句子的后部,如:

It's difficult to understand what she's talking about.

很难弄明白她在说些什么。(动词不定式作逻辑主语)

It's no use talking to him about it.

跟他说这件事没用。(动名词作逻辑主语)

It was really astonishing that she refused to talk to you.

她拒绝同你谈话确实令人吃惊。(从句作逻辑主语)

语法 Grammar in use

简单句、并列句、复合句

1.简单句

(1) 简单句是英语中最小的句子单位,一般有一个限定动词,它有一个主语和一个谓语,如:

One of our aircraft   is missing.
　　　　(主语)　　　　　(谓语)

我们的一架飞机失踪了。

但可以用连词 and 将两个或两个以上的动词合并为一个简单句,如将:

We sang all night. We danced all night.

我们唱了一夜。我们跳了一夜。

合并为:

We sang and danced all night.

我们一整夜又唱又跳。

(2) 根据动词后所使用的不同成分,简单句可有 5 种基本句型。

　1)主语 + 动词:

　　　My head aches.

我头疼。

2)主语 + 动词 + 主语补足语：

Frank is clever/an architect.

弗兰克很聪明/是一名建筑师。

3)主语 + 动词 + 直接宾语：

My sister enjoyed the play.

我姐姐喜欢那出戏。

4)主语 + 动词 + 间接宾语 + 直接宾语：

The firm gave Sam a watch.

那家商行赠给萨姆一块手表。

5)主语 + 动词 + 宾语 + 宾语补足语：

They made Sam chairman.

他们使萨姆成了主席。

2. 并列句

(1) 将几个简单句连接起来构成并列句。在并列句中不存在单独的主句和从属于它的从句；各小句根据上下文的要求按逻辑次序排列，但各小句都同等重要并独立存在。我们常常把并列句中的各小句看成是并列主句。

(2) 可采用下列任何一种方式构成并列句：

1)用分号：

We fished all day; we didn't catch a thing.

我们钓了一整天的鱼，我们一条也没钓到。

2)用分号，后面跟一个连接副词(短语)，如 however、above all、in addition、as far as 等。

We fished all day; however, we didn't catch a thing.

我们钓了一整天的鱼，然而我们一条也没钓到。

3)用并列连词，如 and、but、so、yet 等，前面常加逗号：

We fished all day, but (we) didn't catch a thing.

我们钓了一整天的鱼，但是(我们)一条也没钓到。

3. 复合句

(1) 英语里很多句子是复合句,书面语尤其如此。复合句的构成方法可以是把简单句连接在一起,但复合句的各个组成部分并非同等重要(此点与并列句不同),其中总有一个独立小句(或称"主句")和一个或一个以上的从属小句(或称"从句");主句往往可以独立存在。

(2) 复合句的构成方法:

1) 用连词将从句与主句连接起来:

The alarm was raised(主句)*as soon as the fire was discovered*(从句).

一发现起火,警报器就响了起来。

If you're not good at figures(从句),*it is pointless to apply for job in a bank*(主句).

如果你不擅于计算,向银行求职就毫无意义。

2) 用动词不定式或分词结构。它们是非限定性动词,是短语而不是从句,但它们构成复合句(而非简单句)的一部分。之所以如此是因为它们可以用从句的形式表现出来。

To get into a university you have to pass a number of examinations.

进入大学你必须通过一系列考试。(= *if you want to get into a university*... 如果你想上大学的话……)

Seeing the door open, the stranger entered the house.

那个陌生人看见门开着就进了屋子。(= *When he saw the door open* ... 当他看见门开着……)

(3) 从句可分为以下 3 种:

1) 名词性从句:

He told me that the match had been cancelled.

他告诉我比赛取消了。

2) 关系/形容词从句:

12

Holiday resorts which are very crowded are not very pleasant.

那些拥挤的度假场所令人感到不很愉快。

3)副词从句:

However hard I try, I can't remember people's names.

不管我怎样用心,还是记不住人们的名字。

词汇学习 Word study

1. give (giving, gave, given) *vt.*

为可跟双宾语的动词。一般间接宾语为人,放在直接宾语的前面,如:

They gave us some advice.

他们给我们提了些建议。

也可将间接宾语放在直接宾语之后,但其前需有一个介词 to,特别是当直接宾语比间接宾语短的时候(如直接宾语为代词时)或想强调间接宾语时,如:

They gave some advice to us.

他们给我们提了些建议。

可以跟双宾语的动词还有 bring、grant、hand、leave、lend、offer、pay 等。

give 常用来表达下列各义:

(1) 赠送:

He gave his collection of antiques to the museum.

他将所收藏的古董赠送给了博物馆。

(2) 给予,授予:

Last year, 160 scientists were given the title of academician of the Academy of Science.

去年有160位科学家被授予科学院院士称号。

13

(3) 交给,托付:

Give your bags to the porter and he'll take them to your room.

把你的包交给门房,他会将它们送到你的房间。

2. leave (leaving, left, left)

可作及物动词、不及物动词和名词,常用来表达下列含义:

(1) *vt*. 留下:

The wound left an ugly scar on his forehead.

伤在他的前额留下了难看的疤痕。

(2) *vt*. 离开,脱离:

We left London at 9 in the morning.

我们于早上 9 点离开伦敦。

(3) *vi*. 离去,出发:

When does the train leave for Madrid?

火车何时驶往马德里?

(4) *n*. 准假,请假:

John asks for a ten-day leave.

约翰请 10 天的假。

Tom is on leave from the navy.

汤姆请假离开了海军。

3. complain

(1) *vi*. (about, of) 抱怨,发牢骚:

Go to his parents and complain of the boy's bad behaviour.

找这男孩的父母去抱怨他的劣行。

(2) *vi*. (about, of) 诉苦:

It seems to me that she always complains of a headache.

我觉得她总是在说她头痛。

(3) *vt*. 抱怨:

She complained that her boss had been unfair to her.
她抱怨老板一直对她不公平。

（4）*vt.* 诉说：

He complained that there was a pain in the chest.
他诉说胸部痛。

✍ 练习答案 Key to written exercises

1. 关键句型练习答案

A 1 at   2 to   3 to   4 in   5 on

B 1 He is the man we have heard so much about.

   2 The shelf you put those books on has collapsed.

   3 Who(m) did you receive a letter from?

   4 This is the road we came by.

   5 Where is the pencil you were playing with?

2. 多项选择题答案

1 d   2 a   3 c   4 c   5 d   6 b

7 d   8 d   9 c   10 b   11 b   12 a

Lesson 2
Thirteen equals one
十三等于一

📖 **课文详注 Further notes on the text**

1. Our vicar is always raising money for one cause or another, but he has never managed to get enough money to have the church clock repaired.

（1）is always raising money 所用的是正在进行时态的结构,但表达的是一般现在时态的内容。这样使用正在进行时态时,除可以表达出一般现在时内容外,往往还含有一定的感情色彩（如表明说话人的赞叹、厌倦等）,如:

How are you feeling today ?

你今天觉得怎样？（比 *How do you feel ?* 更显得亲切）

My daughter is doing fine work at school.

我女儿在学校学习挺不错。（比 *My daughter does fine work at school* 更有赞美之意）

He's always boasting.

他老爱吹牛。（表示厌烦）

一些副词常用于这样的结构中,以加强感情色彩。除文中 always 外,常见的还有 constantly、continually 和 forever,如:

He's continually asking me for money.

他总是不断问我要钱。

My father's forever losing his keys.

我父亲总是丢钥匙。

（2）enough 一词可作形容词或副词。作形容词修饰名词时,置于

16

此名词之前或之后均可,如:

> *He has money enough /enough money.*
> 他有足够的钱。

作副词修饰形容词或副词时,通常置于此形容词或副词之后,如:

> *We are strong enough to be able to resist aggression.*
> 我们很强大,完全能够抵抗侵略。
>
> *He did the job well enough.*
> 他把工作干得非常好。

此外,enough 一词常用于名词 /形容词 + enough + 动词不定式结构中,如:

> *He was fool enough to believe what the cheat said.*
> 他够傻的,竟会相信那个骗子说的话。
>
> *Are you brave enough to tell him what you think?*
> 你是否有足够的勇气把你的想法告诉他?

注意前一句中的名词前不可使用冠词。在此类用法中,名词更多表现出形容词的色彩,具有"有此名词特征/性质的"之意。

2. The big clock which used to strike the hours ...

used to 仅用来表示过去的习惯性动作或状态,而表达现在的习惯性动作或状态时通常使用一般现在时态就可以了,如:

> *He used to play cards a lot.*
> 他过去总是打牌。
>
> *He plays cards a lot.*
> 他总是打牌。

used 可作助动词(用于疑问句、否定句中),也可作一般性动词使用,如:

> *Did you use /Used you to play football at school?*
> 当学生时你总踢足球吗?

I didn't use / used not /usedn't to like opera , but now I'm getting interested .

我过去不喜欢歌剧,但现在我开始感兴趣了。

此外,不可将 used to 用于表示某事发生次数或时间长短意义的句子中,如不可说:

＊ I used to go to London seven times .

而应说:

I went to London seven times .

我曾去过伦敦 7 次。

不可说:

＊ I used to live there for three years .

而应说:

I lived there for three years .

我曾在那儿住了 3 年。

易与 used to do sth. 混淆的结构是 be used to (doing) sth.（习惯于〈做〉某事）。前者 to 后使用动词不定式,后者 to 后使用动名词;前者仅用于过去时,而后者则可用于过去时、现在时或将来时,如:

You can say whatever you like ! I'm used to being criticized .

你愿说啥就说啥,反正我已习惯挨批评了。

When I was younger I was used to walking long distances , but now I'm out of practice .

年轻时我惯于走长路,但现在已不习惯啦。

It's easy to be our secretary：you'll be used to it in a few days .

做我们的秘书很容易,用不了几天你就会习惯的。

3．One night，however，our vicar woke up with a start...

（1）however 然而,可是;仍然。并列连词,在句中的位置很灵活,

18

可将其用于句首、句中或句末，但应注意标点符号的使用。它不能像其他并列连词如 but 那样直接连接两个子句，此时应用分号将两个子句分开，并于 however 后标上逗号，或另起新句，如：

I would like to go ; however , I think I'd better not .

我愿意去，不过我想最好不去。

I feel a bit tired ; however , it's probably just the weather .

我觉得有点儿累，但很可能是天气的缘故。

用于句中时，通常用于主语或句首短语之后，并在其前后用逗号同句中的其他成分分开，如：

She has her weakness . That , however , doesn't mean she's not qualified for the job .

她有缺点，但这并不等于她不胜任这项工作。

用于句末时，在其前使用逗号，把它同句子的其他部分分开，如：

The essay is all right ; there is room for improvement , however .

这篇文章还行，但仍有改进的余地。

（2）with a start 作原因状语，修饰谓语动词，表明引发某一动作的原因，如：

The boy woke up from the bad dream with a start .

男孩从噩梦中惊醒。

4. Looking at his watch，he saw that it was one o'clock，but the bell struck thirteen times before it stopped .

（1）looking at his watch 为现在分词短语，作时间状语，说明主句动作发生的时间，如：

Turning around , she saw a blue car driving up .

转过身时，她看到一辆蓝色轿车开了过来。

(2) before 作表示时间状语的连词时,同其他用来表示时间状语的连词如 after、as soon as、until 等一样,从句中的谓语动词通常不用将来时态,如:

I'll tell you as soon as I know.

我一知道就通知你。

He'll be back before you've left.

你离开前他就会回来。

5. Armed with a torch, ...

armed with a torch 为过去分词短语,作方式状语。分词(短语)作状语时,其逻辑主语应与句中主语相一致。注意下列分词短语同句中主语的关系:

Not knowing what to do, I telephoned the police.

由于不知如何是好,我给警察打了电话。(表原因)

Putting down my newspaper, I walked over to the window and looked out.

放下报纸,我走到窗前向外望去。(表时间)

It rained for two weeks on end, completely ruining our holiday.

一连下了两个星期的雨,把我们的假日全毁了。(表结果)

Used economically, one tin will last at least six weeks.

如果省着用,一听罐头至少可用 6 个星期。(表条件)

6. In the torchlight, he caught sight of a figure whom he immediately recognized as Bill Wilkins, our local grocer.

(1) 名词 sight 常见的搭配如下:

- bear /stand the sight of ... 容忍(忍受)见到……,如:

  I really cannot bear the sight of that sloven woman.

  我连看也不想看那个邋遢女人。

- dread the sight of 害怕见到,如:

  Most of the staff in the company dread the sight of their

tyrant-like boss .

公司的雇员大都害怕见到他们暴君似的老板。

- hate the sight of 讨厌见到,如:

  I hate the sight of him , for he's always blindly boasting in face of others .

  我讨厌见到他,因为他总是在他人面前瞎吹牛。

- catch sight of 看到,发现;意识到,如:

  It was he , at that moment , who caught sight of the existing danger .

  在那一刻,正是他意识到了存在的危险。

- keep sight of 将……保持在视线之内,如:

  In order to prevent him from escaping , the police have been keeping sight of him for two weeks on end .

  为了防止他逃脱,警察把他监视了整整两个星期。

- lose sight of 不再看见;失去联系;忘记,忽略,如:

  In the fog , we lost sight of the boat , and didn't know what to do .

  在雾中,我们再也看不到那条小船,不知如何是好。

  We mustn't get so bogged down by details that we lose sight of our main objectives .

  我们决不能陷入琐碎细节之中而忽略了我们主要的目标。

  Unfortunately this may gradually be lost sight of .

  不幸的是,这会逐渐被人所遗忘。

在使用中,应注意在后 3 个动词短语的搭配中无冠词 a 或 the。

(2) recognize ... as ... 认出……是……介词 as 后的名词或代词为宾语补语。recognize 为一静态动词(stative verb),而非动态动词(dynamic verb),因此通常不用于正在进行时结构中,如不可说：

    * I was recognizing her while walking in the crowd.*

而应说：

    I recognized her while walking in the crowd.

    当我在人群中行走时,我认出了她。

此外,recognize 为一表示短暂时间概念的动词,因此不能同表示有延续时间概念的时间状语连用,或用于表示延续时间意义的句子中,如不可说：

    * I have recognized him for a long time.*

    I recognize him very well.

而应说：

    I have known him for a long time.

    I know him very well.

7.‘Whatever are you doing up here Bill?’asked the vicar in surprise.

（1）一般疑问代词或疑问副词 + ever 可用于表示语气强调,通常分开写,如：

    Who ever／Whoever broke the vase?

    到底是谁打坏了花瓶?

    Which ever／Whichever does she want?

    她究竟想要哪一个?

    Where ever／Wherever did you see him stealing?

    你到底在什么地方见他偷东西的?

（2）in surprise 惊异地,介词短语,作方式状语,修饰句中 asked。有时在名词 surprise 前使用某些形容词,说明以某种惊异的方式,如：

    On hearing the sudden news, they stared in dumb surprise.

    听到这突如其来的消息,他们惊得目瞪口呆。

At last she went away in grieved surprise.

最后她怀着悲伤并很意外的心情离开了。

8. I've been coming here night after night for weeks now...

I've been coming 为现在完成进行时结构,表示一定时间以来一直在进行的动作。完成时和完成进行时两者的强调点不同:

(1) 谈及更为固定不变的情况时,通常使用一般现在完成时;谈及更为暂时性行为和情况时,通常使用现在完成进行时,比较:

> *I haven't been working very well recently.*
> 近来我一直工作得不太好。
> *He hasn't worked for years.*
> 他已多年未工作了。

(2) 现在完成时一般用来表示动作的完成或动作所产生的结果;现在完成进行时通常用来强调动作仍在进行,比较:

> *I've painted two rooms since lunch time.*
> 午饭后我已油漆了两个房间。
> *Sorry about the mess—I've been painting the house.*
> 对不起,太乱了——我一直在油漆房子。

9. ...You see, I was hoping to give you a surprise.

(1) you see 作插入语,意即"你瞧"、"你听我说",如:

> *There, you see, the snow's stopped.*
> 瞧,雪停了。
> *Thus, you see, she saved me.*
> 听我说,她就这样救了我的命。

(2) I was hoping ... 为一种"试探性"语气,表示礼貌或尊敬,如:

> *I was hoping we could have dinner together.*
> 我是希望我们能一块儿吃饭。

10. 'You certainly did give me a surprise !' said the vicar.

助动词 do 可用来表示情感上的强调,如:

> *You do look nice today !*

你今天真的看起来很美!

She does talk a lot , doesn't she ?

她的确说了许多,不对吗?

当将 do 用于表示邀请的祈使句时,会使邀请听起来更为礼貌、真诚或友好,如:

Do come in !

快请进!

Do have another potato !

再吃个马铃薯吧!

助动词 do 的强调用法也可用于 be 祈使句中,如:

Do be quiet !

快安静下来!

Do be careful !

一定要小心!

11. '. . . Still, I'm glad the bell is working again.'

still 在这里为连词,表示与前文所述内容的对比,含"然而"、"但是"、"尽管如此"之意,如:

I did fail in the experiment—Still , I've learned a lot from it .

试验中我的确失败了——尽管如此,我还是从中学到了不少东西。

12. '. . . and there's nothing I can do about it.'

(1) I can do about it 为定语从句,修饰 nothing,之间省略了关系代词 that。当关系代词在定语从句中作补语、宾语或 there be 结构中的主语时,均可将其省略。这种省略在口语中更为常见,如:

She's no longer the girl（that）she was before she went to the countryside .

她已不再是去农村前的她了。(关系代词作从句中的

24

补语）

I'm not the fool（that）you thought me.

我不是你想像的那种傻瓜。（关系代词作从句中的宾语补足语）

Everything（that）he said seemed quite reasonable.

他说的话似乎都很有道理。（关系代词作从句中的宾语）

I must make full use of the time（that）there is left to me.

我要充分利用剩下的时间。（关系代词作从句中 *there be* 结构的主语）

(2) 当关系代词在介词之后时,只能使用 which,而且不能省略。但在口语中,这样使用的介词通常置于句末,这时可用关系代词 that,此关系代词通常予以省略,如:

> *The tool with which he is working is called a hand drill.*
>
> *The tool（that）he is working with is called a hand drill.*
>
> 他干活用的那个工具叫手摇钻。

> *This is the question about which we've had so much discussion.*
>
> *This is the question（that）we've had so much discussion about.*
>
> 这就是我们进行了大量讨论的问题。

13.'We'll get used to that,Bill,'said the vicar.

get used to 变得习惯于。to 为介词,后应使用名词、代词或动名词。参见本课课文注释2。

14.'Thirteen is not as good as one,...'

as good as 和……一样好,形容词比较级用法,如:

Her handwriting is as good as his.

她的书法和他的一样好。

但将其作副词短语修饰动词或形容词时,其意义通常为"和……几乎一样"、"实际上等于",当然全句意义也就未必表示好的或所希望的事物,如:

We are as good as ruined.

我们差不多完蛋了。

This old bike is as good as useless.

这辆旧自行车实际就等于废物一件。

语法 Grammar in use

1. 现在进行时、一般现在时表示习惯性的动作

在英语中,always、never 等表示非确定频度的副词,可以和现在进行时和一般现在时连用,表示习惯性的动作,即不断重复发生的事情,如:

I'm always hearing strange stories about him.

我常听说有关他的一些怪事。

They always stay up till midnight.

他们常到午夜才睡。

这类表示不断重复动作的非确定频度的副词有 always、constantly、continually、frequently、forever、hardly、ever、never、often、rarely、repeatedly 等。

2. 非确定频度副词的位置

(1) 当句子中只有一个动词 be 时,位于 be 之后,如:

I was never very good at maths.

我在数学方面从来就不很好。

(2) 当句子中有一个以上的动词时,位于第一个助动词之后,如:

You can always contact me on 6325642.

你可以常用 6325642 这个电话号码与我联系。

(3) 当句子中只有一个行为动词时,位于该动词之前,如:

Gerald often made unwise decisions.

杰拉尔德常常做出一些不明智的决定。

(4) 在疑问句中,则通常出现在主语之后,如:

Do you usually have cream in your coffee?

你常常在咖啡中放奶油吗?

(5) 在否定句中

1) not 必须用在 always 之前,而且也出现在 generally、normally、often、regularly 和 usually 之前,如:

Public transport isn't always very reliable.

公共交通并不总是非常可靠。

2) not 必须出现在 sometimes 和 frequently 之后,如:

Debbie is sometimes not responsible for what she does.

戴比有时对她所做的事不负责任。

(6) 表示肯定的副词可以用在句尾,如:

I get paid on Friday usually.

我通常在星期五领工资。

(7) 在特别强调和需要对比时,下列副词可用于句首:frequently、generally、normally、sometimes、usually 等,如:

Sometimes we get a lot of rain in August.

有时 8 月份雨水很多。

Very often the phone rings when I'm in the bath.

时常在我洗澡时来电话。

词汇学习 Word study

1. have（having, had, had）*v.*

英语中最常用的动词之一,具有多种用法。下面是常用的

27

几种：

（1）have to 不得不，必须（常用于表示某人不得不做某事）：

> We have to send these forms back before the end of the month.
>
> 我们必须在月底之前把这些表格送回去。

（2）用于名词性短语之前，代替动词表示某人做某事或参与某事，如 have a fight（打架）、have a look（看一看）、have a rest（歇一歇）、have a talk（谈一谈）、have a wash（洗一洗）：

> Can I have a ride in your car?
>
> 我可以坐一下你的汽车吗？
>
> Come and have a swim with us.
>
> 跟我们一起去游泳吧。

（3）have + 名词或代词宾语 + 动词的过去分词，构成使役式，表示使做成某事：

> I've just had my car repaired.
>
> 我的汽车刚修好。

（4）have + 名词 + 动词-ing 形式/过去分词，表示让某人做某事或使某人处于某种境地：

> John had me looking for that book all day.
>
> 约翰让我找那本书找了一整天。
>
> He had me utterly confused.
>
> 他把我全搞糊涂了。

2. look *vi.* 看，瞧

（1）look at 看，注视：

> Mike looked at his watch now and then.
>
> 迈克不时地看他的手表。

动词（短语）see、look at、watch 的区别如下所示：

see 看到：

> We saw the black smoke rising over the top of the

mountain.

我们看到黑烟从山头升起。

look at 看,瞧:

People looked at her in astonishment.

人们吃惊地看着她。

watch (因对发生或要发生的事感兴趣而)看,观看,注视:

She watched the whale with interest.

她饶有兴趣地观看那条鲸鱼。

see 和 watch 都可用来表示观看演出或体育项目。去电影院或剧院看电影或戏剧用 see 而不用 look at 或 watch:

I saw an American film yesterday afternoon.

我昨天下午看了一部美国电影片。

可以说 watch television (看电视),但不可说用 see,然而可以说 see 或 watch 某一电视节目。

He spends several hours watching television every day.

他每天看几个小时的电视。

We watched / saw a rugby match on television.

我们在电视上看了一场橄榄球赛。

同样,只可以说 watch football/volleyball (看足球/排球),但也可以说 watch/see 某场比赛:

More people are watching cricket than ever before.

与以前相比,有越来越多的人观看板球比赛。

Many people watched /saw yesterday's football match.

许多人观看了昨天的那场足球赛。

(2) look after 照看,照料:

Please look after the children while we're out.

我们外出时请照看一下孩子们。

(3) look forward to 盼望,期待:

I look forward to seeing you during the weekend.

我盼着周末见到你。

注:此处 to 是介词而不是动词不定式的一部分,其后使用动词的 -ing 形式。

3. recognize *vt*.

(1) 认出,认识:

She didn't recognize me at first.

她起初并未认出我来。

(2) 承认,确认,认可:

The government is beginning to recognize the problem.

政府开始承认这个问题的存在。

✍ 练习答案 **Key to written exercises**

1. 关键句型练习答案

1 Whatever *are you doing* up here, Bill? (*l*. 10)

2 *I'm trying* to repair *the bell*. (*l*. 11)

3 I'm glad *the bell is working* again. (*l*. 14)

4 *It's working* all right. (*l*. 15)

2. 难点练习答案

1 in a hurry   2 in the end   3 in sight

4 in ink, in pencil   5 in common   6 in tears

3. 多项选择题答案

1 d   2 d   3 c   4 b   5 d   6 b

7 c   8 a   9 b   10 a   11 a   12 c

Lesson 3
An unknown goddess
无名女神

📖 **课文详注 Further notes on the text**

1. Some time ago，an interesting discovery was made by ...

some time、sometime、sometimes 所表示的意义和使用方法有所不同。some time 一般含两种意义：较长一段时间；某一不定时间（如某一天等），如：

He left Beijing some time ago.

他前些日子离开了北京。

It will take me some time to read the whole book.

读完整本书要花费我不少时间。

在表达后一种意义时，some time、sometime 均可使用，无重复的含义，通常用于将来时态中，如：

Let's have dinner together sometime（one day）next week.

让我们下周（哪一天）什么时候一起吃饭吧。

When will I get married？ This year，next year，some time，never？

我什么时候能结婚？今年？明年？哪一天？永远不吗？

然而，sometime 也可作形容词，表示"从前的"之意，其他两个词则不行，如：

He was sometime professor of physics at the university.

他是那所大学的前物理学教授。

sometimes 为频率副词，含有在任何时间（过去、现在或将来）不十分经常之意，如：

We sometimes went hunting deer when I lived in Germany.

住在德国时,我们有时外出猎鹿。

I'll come back and see you sometimes, whenever I can manage it.

一得空儿我会回来常看你的。

discovery 一词常与动词 make 搭配使用,其后常见的介词有 about、in 或 of,如:

Many discoveries about the heavenly bodies have been made recently.

近来在天体方面有许多发现。

They made a new discovery in astronomy.

他们在天文学上有了新发现。

Dr. Fleming made his discovery of penicillin in 1928.

弗莱明博士于 1928 年发现了青霉素。

2. **The city at one time must have been prosperous, ...**

at one time 一度,曾经,注意此习语中要使用数词 one 来表示,不可使用不定冠词 a; at a time 表示"每次"之意。at one time 仅可用于过去时态中,如:

At one time we met every day.

我们一度每天见面。

Don't ask so many questions at a time.

每次不要问太多问题。

must have been 见第 1 课课文注释 12。

3. **Houses—often three storeys high—were built of stones.**

置于破折号内的 often three storeys high 为对 houses 的插入进行说明。在破折号内加入插入说明的形式常见于口语体裁中。如课文中那样。如这样的插入说明用于句中,其前后均需标注破折号;如用于句末,在其前用一破折号即可,表示后又想到或

要追加说明的内容,如:

We'll be arriving on Monday morning—at least, I think so.

我们将于星期一上午到达——至少我认为如此。

4. The city was even equipped with a drainage system,...

be equipped with 配备有,装备有(设备);具有(知识、能力等),如:

The army was equipped with up-to-date weapons.
军队配有最新式的武器装备。

He was equipped with sufficient knowledge for this job.
他具备从事此项职业足够的知识。

equipped with 还常作修饰名词的置后短语,如:

soldiers equipped with rocket launchers 装备有火箭筒的士兵们

a car equipped with air conditioning 一辆备有空调的小轿车

5. The temple which the archaeologists explored was used as a place of worship from the fifteen century B.C. until Roman times.

(1) 此处 which 从句为定语从句修饰 the temple。

(2) as a place of worship 在这里为主语补足语(在主动语态句子中为宾语补足语),补充说明 temple 是"被用来祭祀、祈祷的"。

除动词 use 外,还有若干常用动词可以用于这样的结构,如:

consider ... as ... 认为……是……

describe ... as ... 把……描述为……

recognize ... as ... 将……视为……

regard ... as ... 认为……是……

see ... as ... 把……视为……

treat ... as ... 把……当做……对待

这样的结构常用来表达如何看待/使用/描述某人或某物,如:

33

I see you as a basically kind person.

我认为你还算是个富有同情心的人。

She described her attacker as a tall dark man with a beard.

她把袭击者描述为一个高个、黝黑、留着胡子的男人。

此处 as 为介词,后面可使用动名词结构(通常为 being),如:

I don't regard you as being dangerous.

我认为你不是个危险人物。

但在动词 impress(给……留下印象)和 strike(使突然想起;使认为)之后,虽然也可使用 as 结构,但此 as 结构为主语补足语,而非宾语补足语,如:

He didn't impress me as /being very intelligent.

他给我的印象是他并非很聪颖。

It struck me as strange that nobody said anything.

使我感到不可思议的是没有任何人发表意见。

后一句中的 it 为形式主语,而逻辑主语是置后的 that 从句。

(3) from...until... 从……开始,直至。同样的结构还有 from... till... 和 from... to...。前两个除语气程度与 from... to... 不同外,而且只可用来表示时间,而 from... to... 则既可用于表示时间,也可用于表示地点,如:

We usually have our lunch-break from twelve-thirty to one-thirty.

我们通常从 12 点半至 1 点半午休。(也可用 *till* 或 *until*)

The puma haunted from one place to another at large.

美洲狮自由自在地出没于各地。(不可用 *till* 或 *until*)

6. In the most sacred room of the temple,...

为起到强调地点状语的作用,把它放在了句首。在英语中,一般在下述 3 种情况时使用倒装的地点状语:

(1) 由于体裁和所用动词原因使用的倒装:在叙事或描述体裁中,如谓语动词为 come、lie、stand、walk 等这类不及物动词,且地点状语较短时,为使句子更为紧凑,通常使用倒装形式,如:

On a hill in front of them stood a great castle.

在他们前面的一座小山上矗立着一座巨大的城堡。

Round the corner walked a large policeman.

就在拐角处走着一高大的警察。

(2) 用于强调的倒装:

Here in China we won't allow any form of discrimination against women.

在中国,对妇女任何形式的歧视都是不允许的。

(3) 用于加强与前文联系的倒装:

There are only a few people in the hall. On the right in front of the counter you could see a young lady speaking something to the reception personnel.

厅里只有几个人。在右边柜台前,你可以看到一位年轻的太太在同接待员说些什么。

7. The body of one status was found among remains dating from the fifteenth century B.C.

(1) remains 废墟;遗迹;遗体。此词必须用复数形式,但其动词有时可用单数形式,如:

The remains of the supper were /was taken away.

晚餐吃剩的东西被收走了。

(2) date from 追溯;始于。此动词短语无被动形式,如:

These stones dated from the days of the dinosaurs.

这些石头早在恐龙时代就存在。

8. Its missing head happened to be...

happen to 碰巧,恰巧。后用动词不定式,强调事件的偶发性,如:

I happened to be there when he arrived.

他到时我恰巧在那儿。

如 happen to 后为人或物,往往指某人/某物发生了不测或意外,如:

If anything happens to him, phone us as soon as possible.

如果他发生了什么意外,尽快给我们来电话。

9. ...they were amazed to find that the goddess turned out to be a very modern-looking woman.

(1) 此句中的动词不定式用来说明产生 amazed 的原因。这类动词不定式常用于作补语的形容词/过去分词之后,如:

They were really surprised to find him there.

看到他在那里他们的确感到很惊奇。

She was annoyed to hear them talk about him like that.

听他们那样议论他她很不高兴。

We were greatly grieved to learn of his sudden death.

听说他的突然去世我们深感悲痛。

可用于这种结构的形容词很多,且多以表示人的词为主语;然而在有些形容词如 easy、difficult、hard、comfortable 等后使用这类动词不定式时,主语往往为表示事物的词,如:

The experiment like that is as a rule hard to carry out.

像那类的实验一般都不易进行。

This room is comfortable to live in.

这房间住起来很舒适。

(2) turn out to... 证明是,原来是,结果是,后来成为。为系动词,其后的动词不定式可省略,直接将主语补足语放在其后,如:

He said he was a physician; but upon close investigation, he turned out (to be) a quack.

他自称是个医生,但仔细调查之后,证明他是个闯荡江湖的。

He has turned out（to be）a fine scholar.

他后来成为了很了不起的学者。

（3）modern-looking 为合成形容词,由形容词/副词 + 现在分词
   构成,常见的有:

   > *easy-going* 好相处的
   > *good-looking* 好看的
   > *far-reaching* 深远的
   > *well-meaning* 善意的
   > *hard-working* 工作努力的

10 . She stood three feet high...

句中 stood 为系动词,three feet high 作表语。当动词后的形
容词、名词等被用来描述和说明句子主语而非动词所表示的
动作时,这样的动词称作系动词。除动词 be 外,英语中常见
的可作系动词的动词还有 feel、seem、smell、sound、appear、
look、taste、lay、sit、fall、get、go、turn 等,举例如下:

> *The problem appeared impossible.*
> 这个问题似乎很棘手。
> *The soup tastes wonderful.*
> 这道汤味道很美。
> *My skin feels rough.*
> 我的皮肤摸起来很粗糙。
> *The valley lay quiet and peaceful in the sun.*
> 山谷安谧平静,沐浴在阳光之中。
> *She sat motionless, waiting for their decision.*
> 她坐着一动不动,等待着他们的决定。
> *Leaves go brown.*
> 树叶变成了褐色。

11 . She was wearing a full-length skirt...

在叙事体(故事等)中,过去正在进行时态常用于描述性文字

中,这样使描述显得更为生动,而一般过去时常用于对事件或行为的叙述,如:

> *The bride was wearing a white dress and carrying a bouquet of lilies. The bridegroom was trembling and looking pale. Suddenly a man stood up at the back of the church, 'Listen,' he said.*

新娘穿着白色连衣裙,手持一束百合花。新郎颤抖着,脸色苍白。突然,一个男人从教堂后面站起,"听着,"他说道。

12. ..., the archaeologists have been unable to discover her identity.

注意下面 3 个词 unable、disable、enable 的区分。这 3 个词的中心词均为 able,但由于每一词使用前缀的不同,其含义和用法也就不同。unable 为补语形容词,其后应使用带 to 的动词不定式补语,表示"不能"、"无法"之意,如:

> *I'm unable to go to Shanghai this summer, so you must go alone.*

今年夏天我不能去上海了,你只好自己去了。

disable 为动词,通常指由于疾病、事故等所致而失去做事的能力,如:

> *The war disabled him and now he has an artificial leg.*

战争使他成了残废,现在他的一条腿是假的。

enable 为动词,其后常跟人,再加动词不定式短语,表示"使……能够"之意,如:

> *The fast car will enable her to reach the company in time.*

这辆快车能使她按时赶到公司。

discover 同 invent 是易用错的两个词。一般用 discover 指"发现"原已存在但从未被人注意过的事物;invent 指"发明"新的从未存在过的东西,如:

Hargreaves invented the spinning-jenny.

哈格里夫斯发明了多轴纺纱机。

Columbus discovered America.

哥伦布发现了美洲。

但当表达"发明"某种新药或新疗法或"发现"一新的事实时，应用 discover；"发现"新的工作方法时，应用 invent，如：

Radium and penicillin were discovered.

发现了镭和青霉素。

Einstein discovered the theory of relativity.

爱因斯坦创立了相对论。

He and his colleagues invented a new method of applying artificial respiration.

他和同事们发明了进行人工呼吸的新方法。

语法　Grammar in use

must have ＋ 动词的过去分词

这种结构用来表示对过去某事的一种推测，如：

Here's a note from Colin. He must have called while we were out.

这儿有科林的一个留言。我们不在家时他一定来访过。

Where can Mum have put the keys? She can't have taken them away.

妈妈会把钥匙放在哪儿呢？她不可能把它们带走。

词汇学习　Word study

1. happen *vi.*

(1)（偶然）发生：

A strange thing happened.

发生了一件奇怪的事。

What's happened to Mary?

玛丽出了什么事?

计划好而发生的事不能用 happen,而应用 take place:

The first meeting of the committee took place on 9 January.

委员会的第 1 次会议于 1 月 9 日召开。

(2) 碰巧,恰巧:

He happens to be / It happens that he's at home at the moment.

此刻他碰巧在家。

There happened to be a policeman on the corner, so I asked him the way.

街角正好有一个警察,于是我就向他问了路。

2. find (found, found) *vt.*

(1) 找到,寻得,找回:

I eventually found what I had been looking for.

我终于找到了我在寻找的东西。

I'm sure I've already paid this bill, but I can't find the receipt.

我敢肯定我已经付了账单,可是我找不到收据了。

(2) 感受到,发觉,认为:

I find (that) three hours is long enough.

我觉得 3 个小时足够了。

I find it hard to keep a family on a single wage.

我觉得靠一份工资很难养家糊口。

(3) (out) 获悉,得知;查明:

What we have to do now is find (find out) why the accident happened.

我们现在必须得查明为什么会发生这起事故。

We found out that she was wrong.

我们查明是她错了。

3. equip *vt.*

(1) 配备,装备:

His car is equipped with air conditioning.

他的轿车配备了空调。

They will equip the park with a playground, a parking lot and a historical museum.

他们将在这座公园里设立一个游乐场、一个停车场和一个历史博物馆。

(2)(智力上、体力上)赋予;使有资格:

His spare time learning has equipped him for a career as an accountant.

他业余时间的学习使他能担任会计师的工作。

She is equipped with a deep sense of justice.

她具有强烈的正义感。

🖉 练习答案 Key to written exercises

1. 关键句型练习答案

Yesterday I...

left home early, *laid* the table for breakfast, *lay* in bed till 10 a.m., *chose* to stay at home, *raised* an important question, *rose* at dawn, *beat* Tom at chess, *bit* my tongue, *caught* a cold, *heard* the sad mews, *sang* in a concert, *thought* I would see you, *showed* Tom my stamp collection, *ran* a mile, *lost* my wallet, *began* my new job, *fell* down and *hurt* myself, *felt* really ill

2. 难点练习答案

A 1   She happened *to mention that it is your birthday today.*

    2   It happened *that I was abroad when I heard the news.*

    3   Tell me what *happened.*

    4   If you happen *to see Maggie, please ask her to phone me.*

B 1   Some hotels are more than thirty *storeys* high.

    2   Children love hearing *stories* from their parents.

    3   A church or a temple is a place of *worship.*

    4   Many *warships* were sunk in World War II.

3. 多项选择题答案

1 d   2 d   3 a   4 d   5 b   6 c

7 b   8 b   9 a   10 d   11 b   12 b

Lesson 4
The double life of Alfred Bloggs
阿尔弗雷德·布洛格斯的双重生活

📖 **课文详注 Further notes on the text**

1. **These days, people who do manual work often receive far more money than people who work in offices.**

在形容词或副词比较级前,常可使用一些程度副词来修饰比较级,以加强其程度或语气。常见的这类程度副词有 a bit、a little、a lot、lots、a good ／ great deal、any、no、rather、far、very much、much 等,如:

   a little less expensive 便宜一点

   a lot ／ a great deal happier 高兴得多

   very much nicer 漂亮得多

   Is your patient any more relaxed ?

   你的病人更松弛些了吗?

但应注意个别副词的用法:

(1) 不可在比较级前用 very 来加强程度或语气,应用 much 或 far,如:

   He's far more tolerant than she is .(而非 *very*)

   他比她更能忍让。

(2) quite 只能用于 better 前,指身体恢复状况,如:

   Are you feeling better ?

   你觉得好些了吗?

   Quite better .

   好多啦。

43

（3）在用 more 修饰的可数名词前可用 far 或 many,但不可用
　　much 来修饰,如:

> *many / far more opportunities* 多得多的机会
>
> *much / far more money* 多得多的钱

（4）在 less 和 fewer 前可用 much 或 far 来修饰,但不可用 many
　　来修饰,如:

> *much / far less time* 少得多的时间
>
> *far less / fewer mistakes* 少得多的错误

2. People who work in offices are frequently referred to as 'white-collar workers' for the simple reason that they usually wear a collar and tie to go to work.

（1）to refer to …as… 把……称作……as 后内容为宾语补足语,
　　见第 2 课课文注释 6 和第 3 课课文注释 5。

（2）white-collar workers 通常指脑力劳动者,与其相对 blue-collar
　　workers 指体力劳动者。用某人/某物所具的某种特征指代某
　　人/某物为生活或写作中常见的一种隐喻(metonymy)方法,
　　如用 crown (王冠)喻指"国王";fur and feather (皮毛和羽毛)
　　喻指"禽兽";The pen is mightier than the sword 这一句中,用
　　pen 喻指"文学的力量",而 sword 喻指"武力"。明确隐喻的
　　使用有助于更好理解所听所看内容。

3. Such is human nature, that a great many people are often willing to sacrifice higher pay for the privilege of becoming white-collar workers.

（1）代词 such 用于句首时起强调作用,后面通常使用倒装语序,
　　如:

> *Such were his words.*
>
> 他就是那么说的。
>
> *If such is the case, there will be no need to make any more investigation.*

如果情况就是这样,就不必再进行调查了。

(2) sacrifice...for... 为……牺牲……;为……而失去……也可用介词 to 代替句型中的介词 for,如:

He's just the kind of man that is willing to sacrifice his own personal interest to / for public good.

他正是那种乐意为公众利益而牺牲个人利益的人。

4. This can give rise to curious situations, as it did in the case of Alfred Bloggs who worked as a dustman for the Ellesmere Corporation.

(1) give rise to 引起,使发生;导致。如:

Such conduct might give rise to misunderstanding.

这种行为可能会导致误解。

(2) as it did 中的 it 指前文中 this 所指内容,即上一句中 that 从句所述情况,而 did 用来替代 gave rise to curious situations,因此这里的 as it did 意即"正如(过去曾)造成的怪现象那样"。

(3) in the case of ... 在……情况下。这一短语还含有"至于"、"就……来说"的意义,如:

Poverty depresses most people; in the case of my father it was otherwise.

贫困使多数人消沉,但我父亲却不一样。

但是短语 in case of (无冠词)则表示"以防"或"万一"、"如果"之意,如:

In case of fire, ring the alarm bell.

如遇火灾,即按警铃。

The wall was built along the river in case of floods.

为了防洪,沿河筑了堤。

5. When he got married, Alf was too embarrassed to say anything to his wife about his job.

Alf 为 Alfred 的昵称。too...to... 太……以致不能……。too 为副词,表示"太……"、"超过所能……的程度",其后使用形容词或副词原级形式, to 引导一个表结果状语的动词不定式。too...to...已含否定意义,如:

It's too good to be true.

太好了,让人不敢相信。

有时后面不用动词不定式,用"for + 名词"的结构也可表达否定含义,如:

These shoes are too large for him.

这双鞋他穿太大了。

但实际上,这种结构后均省略了动词不定式内容,如例中省略了 to wear。但如果在 too 前使用了副词 only,则往往不含否定意义,而相当于 very 之意,并且语气较 very 更强,如:

I'm only too glad to have someone to speak to.

能找人聊聊天我太高兴了。

6. Every morning, he left home dressed in a smart black suit.

dressed in a smart black suit 为过去分词短语,作方式状语,修饰 left,表明以何种方式 left。参见第 2 课课文注释 5。

7. ...and spent the next eight hours as a dustman.

动词 spend 可用来表示"花(钱)"、"用(时)"、"费(时)"等意。

(1)当用 spend 表示"用(时)于……"、"费(时)于……"之意时,如后面表用途的内容为名词,一般在 spend 后需使用介词 in;如为动名词,in 可有可无,如:

We spent more than three hours in discussion without reaching any agreement.

我们讨论了三个多小时仍未达成协议。

She used to spend the evening (in) reading.

她过去总把晚上的时光消磨在读书上。

(2)当用 spend 表示"花(钱)于"之意时,如后面表用途的内容为

46

名词,一般在 spend 后需使用介词 on;如为动名词,介词需用
in(也可不用),如:

A lot of money has been spent on the new factory.

建这家新工厂花了很多钱。

He spends nearly one third of his monthly income（in）
buying books.

他把每月近三分之一的收入都用来买书。

(3) 一般不可将表示"时间"、"金钱"、"精力"等之外的普通名词用
于 spend 之后作宾语;使用 spend 时,其主语(主动语态中)只
能是人,其后不能使用动词不定式,如:

The boy has used up all the ink in his pen.

男孩已用完了钢笔里的墨水。(不可使用 *spent*)

You're just wasting your time trying to persuade her.

你想说服她简直是在浪费时间。(不可使用 *spending*)

My father spent only five dollars on this book.

这本书只花了我父亲 5 美元。(不可用 *this book* 为主语
而 *spent* 为谓语的句式)

The author spent about an hour（in）tracing this
quotation.

这位作家花了大约一个小时找这句话的出处。(不可用
to trace)

8. Alf did this for over two years...

this 在此指前文所述内容。

9. ...and she never will,...

will 后承前省略了 discover that she married a dustman。

10. He will soon be working in an office.

将来进行时除可被用来表示谓语动词动作会在将来某一特定
时间进行和作为一种礼貌地询问某人计划/安排的方式外,也
可用来表示现已确定或决定的将来的某件事情,如:

Professor Gorb will be giving another talk on English literature at the same time next week.

乔伯教授将于下周同一时间进行另一次有关英国文学的演讲。

Shall I pick up your shopping for you?
我可以为你取回你所购买的东西吗?
Oh, I couldn't trouble you.
噢,我不能那样麻烦你。
It's all right, I'll be going past the shops anyway.
没什么,反正我也路过那些商店。

11. He will be earning only half as much as he used to, but he feels that his rise in status is well worth the loss of money.

(1) will be earning 这一将来进行时如前句中将来进行时一样表示已确定下来的将来的某件事情。见本课注释 10。

(2) half as much as he used to 为避免重复,在 to 后省略了 earn。half 在这里作状语,修饰 as much as。as...as...结构前常可用表示次数如 twice、three times 或表示数量如 half、one third 等的副词来修饰,如:

We got three times as many people as we expected.
来的人数是我们预想的 3 倍。
She's not half as clever as she thinks she is.
她还没她认为自己的一半那样聪明。

此外,在 as...as...结构前还可使用诸如(not) nearly、almost、just、nothing、like、every bit、exactly 这类表示程度的副词来修饰,如:

You're nothing like as critical as you used to be.
你一点儿也不像以前那样爱挑剔了。
She's every bit as beautiful as her elder sister.
她同她姐姐一模一样的漂亮。

48

（3）worth 值得,使用时应注意如下几点:

1）其后需使用名词或动名词,如:

The film is well worth seeing.

那部电影很值得一看。

He paid 20 dollars for the bag. Do you think it is worth the money?

他买那个包花了 20 美元,你觉得值吗?

worth 后一般使用动名词,在使用名词时,这一名词往往只为钱数或相当于"代价"的比喻性名词,如:

It's worth the time and effort we devoted to it.

我们在此事上花费的时间和精力是值得的。

2）其后使用动名词时,常用于两种句子结构中:

a. 用先行词 it 作主语的句子,如:

It's not worth getting angry with her.

同她生气不值得。

b. 用名词或代词作主语的句子,如:

The car /It isn't worth repairing.

这辆车/它不值得一修。

但用名词或代词作主语时,worth 后的动名词总是用主动形式表达被动意义,不可使用动词不定式或动名词的被动形式。

12. From now on, he will...

from now on 从现在起,从此。作时间状语。常见的相同结构还有:

from today / this week, this month, etc. on 从今天/这个星期/这个月等起

from this moment on 从此刻起

语法 Grammar in use

现在完成时与现在完成进行时

1. 现在完成时

现在完成时不能和表示过去时间的副词/副词短语搭配使用（如 ago、yesterday、a moment ago 等）。下列副词/副词短语、句型等常与现在完成时连用，因为它们明确表示出过去和现在的联系，如 before（now）(〈在此〉之前)；it's the first time（第一次）；so far（到目前为止）；so far this morning（到上午为止）；up till now（直到现在）；up to the present（直到目前）。ever、not...ever 或 never 也可同现在完成时连用,如:

> *I've planted fourteen rose bushes so far this morning.*
>
> 今天上午到现在为止,我已种了 14 株玫瑰。
>
> *It's the most interesting book I've ever read.*
>
> 这是我读过的最有趣的书。

since 和 for 常与现在完成时连用，表示直到现在的时段。"since + 时间"可作连词、副词、介词:

> *Tom hasn't been home since he was a boy.*
>
> 汤姆从小就不在家了。
>
> *I saw her in May, I haven't seen her since.*
>
> 我 5 月份见到过她,此后我就再未见到过她。
>
> *I've lived here since 1990.*
>
> 自 1990 年我就住在这儿。

since 作连词时,后面可跟一般过去时或现在完成时:

> *I retired in 1990 and came to live here. I've lived here since I retired.*
>
> 我于 1990 年退休后就搬到这里。自退休后我就一直住这儿。(即我退休的时间:1990 年)
>
> *I have lived here for several years now and I've made many*

50

new friends since I have lived here.

我已在这里住了好几年。自我在这里住下到现在已交了许多新朋友。(即一直到现在)

"for + 时段"常与现在完成时连用,但也可以和其他任何时态连用。试比较:

I've lived here for five years.

我在这里住了 5 年了。(我仍住在这里)

I lived here for five years.

我在这里住过 5 年。(我已不住在这里)

现在完成时还可以和下列副词连用,表示动作刚刚发生。just(刚刚)、recently(最近)、already(已经)、yet(已经)(用于疑问句和否定句)、still(还;仍)、at last(终于)、finally(最终),如:

I've just tidied up the kitchen.

我刚把厨房收拾干净。

Have you passed your driving test yet?

你已经通过驾驶考核了吗?

I haven't passed my driving test yet.

我还未通过驾驶考核。

现在完成时还可和表示频度的副词连用,表示反复和习惯性动作,如 often(经常)、frequently(屡次)、three times(3 次)等,如:

I've watched him on TV several times.

我在电视里看他好几次了。

2. 现在完成进行时

现在完成进行时表示并强调动作在某一段时间内一直在进行,通常动作有现在的结果。

(1)句中常用 all + 表示时间的词,如 all day(整天):

She is very tired, She's been typing letters all day.

她很累。她整天都在打信件。

（2）表示持续性的动词，如 learn（学）、lie（躺）、live（居住）、rain（下雨）、sleep（睡）、stand（站），可以同 since 或 for 副词短语连用，也可用于以 how long 开头的疑问句中：

I've been working for Exxon for 15 years.

我在埃克森公司工作了 15 年。

上述动词本身就表示持续性动作，所以也可以用现在完成时。惟一的区别是，进行时形式更强调动作的持续性。

（3）现在完成进行时还可表示经常重复的动作，如：

Jim has been phoning Jenny every night for the last week.

上星期，吉姆天天晚上都给詹妮打电话。

📂 词汇学习 Word study

1. say (said, said) *vt.*

（1）说，讲：

I didn't hear what you said.

我没听到你说的话。

I'd like to say a few words.

我想讲几句话。

（2）讲述，说明：

She says that you can't book a room in advance without paying a deposit.

她说你不付押金就不能预定房间。

注：通常不用 say a story / lie / joke，而说 tell a story / lie/ joke：

You're telling lies now.

你在说谎。

2. keep (kept，kept)

(1) *vt*. 保存，保留：

He would not be able to keep his job.

恐怕他保不住他那份工作了。

(2) *vt*. 保守；隐匿：

She is not the right person to keep a secret.

她可不是保守秘密的那种人。

(3) *vi*. 重复，持续：

My mother keeps asking questions.

我妈妈不停地问问题。

The bonfire is still burning. I think it'll keep going all night.

篝火还在燃烧。我想它会燃烧一整夜。

3. worth

(1) *prep*. 相当于……价值，值……钱：

His house is worth ＄550,000.

他的房子值55万美元。

a yacht worth ＄1.7 million 价值170万美元的游艇

(2) *prep*. 值得：

The book is worth reading.

这本书值得一读。

He put foward a proposal which was worth consideration.

他提出一项值得考虑的建议。

(3) *n*. 价值；作用：

They have salvaged a sunken boat and found in it 12 million pounds worth of gold and jewels.

他们打捞了一艘沉船，在里面发现了价值1,200万镑的黄金和珠宝。

You are involved in a project that could be of worth.

你参与了一项可能很有价值的项目。

练习答案 Key to written exercises

1. 关键句型练习答案

A　1　Alf's wife has never discovered. . . (*l* .13)

　　2　Alf has just found another job. (*ll* .13-14)

B　1　I've been living in this flat *since last April* .

　　2　How many postcards have you sent *up till now*?

　　3　Your mother has *just* phoned. Do you want to call her back?

　　4　Have you *ever* visited Xi'an?

　　5　I haven't been there *yet* , but I intend to go one of these days.

2. 多项选择题答案

1　a　　2　c　　3　d　　4　b　　5　d　　6　c

7　b　　8　c　　9　d　　10　b　　11　c　　12　a

Lesson 5
The facts
确切数字

📖 课文详注 **Further notes on the text**

1. **Editors of newspapers and magazines often go to extremes to provide their readers with unimportant facts and statistics.**

（1）go to extremes 走极端，采取极端手段。注意使用此短语时使用复数形式，而用动词 run 表达同样意义时通常用 an extreme 如：

> *Don't go to extremes/run to an extreme in everything.*
> 不要凡事都走极端。

在使用 go to the extreme of 表示"采取……极端手段"时，extreme 需为单数，其前需用定冠词，如：

> *The boss went to the extreme of dismissing most of his workers.*
> 那个老板居然采取了解雇大多数工人的极端手段。

（2）to provide their readers with 此动词不定式为目的状语。用 provide 表示"向某人提供某物"意义时，通常使用 provide sb. with sth. 或 provide sth. for sb.，置于动词 provide 之后的宾语不同，所用介词也不同，如：

> *The school provides the students with lecture sheets.*
> 学校免费供给学生讲义。

> *The bank has promised to provide money for us.*
> 银行答应了向我们提供资金。

但近来也可看到 provide 后使用双宾语的情况，即使用

55

provide sb. sth.,如：

We provided them board and lodging.

我们向他们提供膳宿。

但这样使用时,总是间接宾语(人)在前,直接宾语(物)在后。

2. Last year a journalist had been instructed by a well-known magazine to write an article on the president's place in a new African republic.

(1) had been instructed 为过去完成时的被动语态结构,为强调后来发生事件而使用的过渡性用法,在此没有强调动词 instructed 动作之意。一般说来,在谈及过去所发生的动作时,用过去完成时态描述这一过去动作之前发生的另一动作,如：

I explained that I had forgotten my keys.

我解释说我忘了带钥匙。(*forget* 动作发生于过去所发生的动作 *explain* 之前)

但是,在谈及过去不同时间发生的两个动作时,并非总要将最早发生的动作用过去完成时态表示。当按动作发生的顺序进行描述时,通常使用一般过去时即可,如：

Mary said some rather horrible things to me; I felt pretty upset, but tried not to think about them too much.

玛丽对我说了些很可怕的事情;我感到极为不安,但尽力试着不去过多地想。

然而,当我们要强调过去时间以后发生的动作,而只想将发生于此动作之前的动作作为临时性过渡时,这一动作通常用过去完成时表达。这样使用时,对用过去完成时表达的动作没有强调之意,如：

I felt pretty upset because of what Mary had said, but I tried not to think about it too much.

因为玛丽对我所说的话,我感到极为不安,但尽力试着不

56

去过多地想。

文中过去完成时 had been instructed 的使用正是为了更好地引出下文。

(2) write...on... 就……写……这里用介词 on 表达"有关"、"关于"之意,相当于介词 about 的含义,如:

You're wrong on all these issues.

在这些问题上你都错了。

She's been writing a paper on Shakespeare.

她一直在写一篇有关莎士比亚的论文。

3. The editor at once sent the journalist a fax instructing him to find out the exact number of steps and the height of the wall.

(1) at once 立即,马上。大多数副词既可置于句中又可置于句尾,如:

She angrily walked out of the room.
She walked angrily out of the room.
She walked out of the room angrily.
她生气地走出房间。

然而副词短语通常不可用于句中,如:

Mr. John called a meeting of the directors on Friday.

约翰先生星期五召开了一次董事会。(*on Friday* 不可置于主语之后)

但是,at once, very often 等很短小的常见副词短语可如文中那样置于句中,如:

I have very often wondered why people read advertisements.

我时常搞不明白人们为什么看广告。

(2) instructing him to ...,现在分词短语,作状语,对谓语动词 sent 作进一步说明。参见第 2 课课文注释 5。

4. The journalist immediately set out to obtain these important

facts, but he took a long time to send them.

动词 take 通常可以用 3 种不同的结构形式表达"花费多长时间做某事"之意：

(1) 主语为人,如：

I took three hours to get home last night.

我昨晚花了 3 个小时才到家。

(2) 主语为行为,如：

Painting the kitchen took me all week.

给厨房刷漆用了我一个星期。

(3) 主语为先行词 it,如：

It took her longer than she had expected to get a passport.

拿到护照所花的时间比她想像的要长。

5. Meanwhile, the editor was getting impatient, for the magazine would soon go to press.

(1) was getting impatient 中的动词 get 作系动词,impatient 作补语,对主语作补充说明。

(2) go to press 开印;付印。press 前也可有定冠词 the。

6. He sent yet another fax informing the journalist that if he did not reply soon he would be fired.

(1) yet another 又;更。此处 another 为形容词。除副词 yet 外, still 也可用于 another 前表示此意,如：

His latest novel, which has been translated into many languages, offers yet/still another proof that he is an author of great talent.

他最近的一部小说已经译成多种语言,这又一次证明了他是一个有才华的作家。

(2) informing the journalist that,现在分词短语,作状语。参见第 2 课课文注释 5。

7. When the journalist again failed to reply, the editor reluctantly

published the article as it had originally been written.

(1) 用于 fail 后的动词应为带 to 的动词不定式形式,如:

We could never fail to keep our promise.

我们决不会食言。

(2) as it had originally been written 按照原先写的样式,为从属连词 as 引导的方式状语从句,修饰 published,如:

He operated the machine as the instruction said.

他按照说明书操作机器。

8. Not only had the poor man been arrested, but he had been sent to prison as well.

not only...but (also)... 不仅……而且……使用此并列连词时,应注意以下 3 点:

(1) not only 与 but (also) 后所随成分应一致:

This young scientist is not only intelligent but (also) hardworking.

这位年轻的科学家不仅有才智而且勤奋。(*not only* 与 *but also* 后均为补语)

It concerns not only me but you as well.

此事不仅与我有关而且与你也有关。(*not only* 与 *but also* 后均为宾语)

(2) 两个连词后所表达语义与 as well as 正好相反,用于 as well as 前的内容为强调点,其后为非强调点;not only 后内容为非强调点,but (also)后内容为强调点,如:

{ *He can speak French as well as English.*
He can speak not only English but also French.
他不仅会说英语,而且会说法语。

(3) not only 用于句首时,如文中那样,其后需用倒装语序,如:

Not only is this young scientist intelligent, but hardworking.

这位年轻的科学家不仅有才智而且勤奋。

此外，not only... but also... 还可如下表达：

> *not only...but...*
>
> *not only...but also*
>
> *not only...but...as well*

9. **However，he had at last been allowed to send a fax in which he informed the editor that he had been arrested while counting the 1,084 steps leading to the fifteen-foot wall which surrounded the president's palace.**

(1) in which 引导一定语从句，修饰 a fax。此处介词 in 不能省略，相当于 in the fax。

(2) while counting... 为时间状语。当两个动作同时发生时，如文中 arrest 和 count，起说明性作用的这一动词(count)动作通常可用分词形式表示，其前可使用连词 when 或 while，强调两个动作发生时间的一致性，如：

> *Don't mention this while talking to him.*
>
> 和他谈话时不要提及此事。

这样使用时，分词的逻辑主语应同主语相一致。参见第 2 课课文注释 5。

(3) leading to... 此处为现在分词短语，作定语后置修饰 steps。

语法 Grammar in use

1.the，some，any

(1) the 与 some 都是限定词。the 具有"确定"的含义。在我们说 the library 、the shops 等的时候，可能有两种情况：受话者已知道我们所指的是哪个图书馆或哪些商店；或我们正要告诉受话者我们要指的是哪个图书馆或哪些商店，如：

> *The windows are dirty. I must wash them.*

窗子都脏了。我得把它们擦洗一下。(双方都知道是指哪些窗子)

Those are the girls who live next door.

那些是住在隔壁的姑娘们。(文中的定语从句说明这里指的是哪些姑娘)

(2) some 和 any 具有"非确定"的含义,此时与不定冠词 a/an 相同,只是它们被用来修饰不可数名词或可数名词的复数,试比较:

I haven't got a car.
我没有汽车。(单数可数名词)
I've got some books.
我有一些书。(复数名词)
Have you got any medicine?
你有药吗?(不可数名词)

不可数名词和复数名词常常不伴以 some/any 或者冠词,且含义不变,如:

Would you like(some)cheese?
你想来点奶酪吗?

Did you borrow(any)book?
你借书了吗?

(3) some 和 any 经常用于表示非确定的或未知的数目或数量,如:

You've got some great jazz records.
你有几张十分精彩的爵士乐唱片。

Is there any milk in the fridge?
冰箱里还有些牛奶吗?

(4) some 不用于否定句中,如:

I don't have any money.
我没钱。

而不说：

> * *I don't have some money.*

在疑问句中既可用 some 也可用 any,其区别在于,当询问某人以确认某事是否为事实时使用 some,但对某事并不确切地知道时使用 any,如：

> *Do you have some questions ?*
> 你是有几个问题要问吧？（知道或认为某人想要问几个问题）
>
> *Do you have any questions ?*
> 你有问题要问吗？（并不清楚某人是否要问问题）

2. 否定词用于句首时的倒装句

(1) 否定词或具有否定含义的副词如 never、rarely、seldom、little、on no account 等用于句首时,必须后接助动词(be、do、have、can、must 等) + 主语 + 句子的其他部分。这种倒装用于正式文体,尤其用于加强语气,如：

> *Never/Seldom has there been so much protest against the Bomb.*
> 如此强烈地反对原子弹的抗议活动从来/很少有过。
>
> *On no account must you accept any money if he offers it.*
> 如果他要给你钱,你可绝不能接受。

(2) 与 only 构成的词组置于句首时,句子往往也要倒装,如：

> *The pilot reassured the passengers. Only then did I realize how dangerous the situation had been.*
> 驾驶员再一次要乘客们放心。此时我才明白刚才的情况有多么危险。

(3) so + 形容词(...that...)和 such(...that...)引导的句子也需倒装,如：

> *So sudden was the attack (that) we had not time to escape.*

袭击来得非常突然,我们来不及躲避。

Such was his strength that he could bend iron bars.
他力气大得能把铁棍弯过来。

📁 词汇学习 Word study

1. send(sent，sent)

(1) *vt.* 发送,寄:

He used to send me a card at Christmas.
他过去每逢圣诞节就给我寄张贺卡。

(2) *vt.* 派遣,打发;令/请……去:

The government sent troops to suppress the rebellion.
政府派遣军队去镇压那场叛乱。

(3) send for 派人……去请,召唤;订购:

Leave this house now, or I'll send for the police.
现在离开这所房子,否则我就叫警察了。

You can send for the furniture at a very cheap price.
你可以很便宜地订购这些家具。

2. take(taking，took，taken) *vt.*

(1) 拿,取:

Don't forget to take your umbrella.
别忘了带伞。

(2) 后接名词,表示做一次动作:

She has the habit of taking a nap after lunch.
她有午饭后睡午觉的习惯。

(3) 占用(地盘);花费(时间):

This new washing machine doesn't take much room.
这台新洗衣机并不占多少地方。

It may take them several weeks to get back.

63

他们得用几周的时间才能返回。

3.provide

(1) *vt.* 提供,给予:

The hotel provides good breakfast.

这座饭店提供很好的早餐。

The Foundation provided him with funds.

基金会为他提供资金。

Most animals provide food for their young.

多数动物给它们的幼仔供以食物。

(2) *vi.* (for) 抚养,供养:

He managed to provide for a large family.

他尽力供养了一个大家庭。

✎ 练习答案 Key to written exercises

1.关键句型练习答案

B 1 What's the name of the person who first sailed up *the Hudson River*?

2 I wonder if you could give me *some information* about train times.

3 Why don't we go to *the cinema* this evening?

4 Film-making in Hong Kong is an important *industry*.

5 I need *flour and milk* to make cakes.

6 When you're out, please get me *a newspaper*.

2.难点练习答案

1 Not only has he made this mistake before but he will make it again.

2 Only then did I realize what was happening.

3 Never will I trust him again.

4　Seldom do you find traffic wardens who are kind and helpful.

3. 多项选择题答案

1　c　　2　b　　3　a　　4　b　　5　c　　6　d

7　b　　8　c　　9　c　　10　b　　11　d　　12　d

Lesson 6
Smash-and-grab
砸橱窗抢劫

📖 **课文详注** **Further notes on the text**

1. ...the arcade was almost empty.

empty 空无,空的。易于同此词混淆的形容词是 vacant（没有占用的,空着的）,如:

The house is empty.

房子里空无所有。

The house is vacant.

房子没有占用。

由于语义的不同,可用其修饰的词有所不同,有时虽修饰同一个词,但表达的意思也有所不同,如在 empty bottle（空瓶子）与 empty stomach（空腹）等短语中不能用 vacant 取代 empty,而在 vacant hours（没有事的时候）、vacant mind（茫然若失的心情）、vacant post（空着的职位）中,有时我们可以用 empty 取代 vacant,但意义不同,如:

empty mind 百无聊赖的心情

empty space 空无所有的空间

2. Mr. Taylor, the owner of a jewellery shop was...

the owner of a jewellery shop 为 Mr. Taylor 的同位语。一名词或代词后如跟随另一与此名词或代词作用相当并与句中其他句子成分的关系也相当的名词或名词性短语,对前一名词或代词作进一步说明或解释时称为同位语。在使用同位语时,应注意以下几点:

(1) 作同位语的部分通常需由逗号同句子的其他部分隔开,如:

> *Tolstoy, the novelist, wrote* War and Peace.
> 小说家托尔斯泰写了《战争与和平》这部小说。

(2) 在作同位语的名词特别是表示职业的名词前如文中那样通常需用定冠词 the。有时同位语前所用定冠词也表示读者认为知道所提及的人物、地点或事物,如:

> *Kobe, the Japanese port, is twenty miles west of Osaka.*
> 日本港口神户位于大阪以西 20 英里处。

(3) 表示职称或称号的同位语前的定冠词可以省略,如:

> *Mr. Black, (the) Secretary of the Art Society, had a long talk with me yesterday.*
> 美术协会秘书布莱克先生昨天同我进行了长谈。

3. **Two of his assistants had been working busily since eight o'clock and had only just finished.**

此句中的过去完成进行时态和过去完成时态的使用,均表明动作 work 和 finish 为发生在前句过去正在进行的动作 was admiring 之前的动作。下句中使用被动语态结构的过去完成时态 had been beautifully arranged 也是这样,以生动地描述事件发生前珠宝店的状态。

4. **... when a large car, with its headlights on and its horn blaring, roared down the arcade.**

with its headlights on and its horn blaring 为介词 with 引导的独立主格结构,在句中作方式或伴随状况状语。its headlights 和 its horn 为 on 和 blaring 的逻辑主语,如:

> *The day was bright, with a fresh breeze blowing.*
> 天气晴朗,吹来阵阵清风。

独立主格结构的使用往往使描述更为生动。

5. **It came to a stop outside the jeweller's.**

come to a stop 停住,停止,如:

The singing suddenly came to a stop .

歌声嘎然而止。

6. **While this was going on , Mr. Taylor was upstairs.**

while 为从属连词,引导一时间状语从句,说明伴随 Mr. Taylor was upstairs 时发生的另一动作。当我们谈及在同一时间发生的两个动作或情况时,我们通常可以使用 as、when 或 while,但在使用时应注意下述几点:

(1) 引导较长"背景"情况

引导的背景动作或状况发生于主句所述短暂时间概念动词动作之前,也许在其后仍在继续,如:

As / When / While I was walking down the street I noticed a police car in front of the shop .

当我沿街向那边走时,我注意到一辆警车停在那家商店前。

当从句中的动词为表示短暂时间概念动词时,通常只用 when,比较:

John arrived when / while I was cooking lunch .

我正做午饭时约翰到了。

When John arrived I was cooking lunch .

约翰到时我正在做午饭。

使用 when 和 while 时,"背景"事件通常用过去进行时表达,而使用 as 时,尤其在表达更为正式的书面体裁时,有时可使用一般现在时,如:

As I sat thinking about my life , I began to realize something I even didn't pay any attention to in the past .

当我坐着回顾我的生活时,我逐渐意识到我过去毫不在意的一些事情。

在用 as、while 和 when 引导的时间状语从句中,需用现在时态表达将来时态内容,如:

I hope you'll think of me as /when / while I'm entering the contest .

我希望在我参加比赛之际你会想到我。

（2）同时发生的延续性动作

说及同时发生的两个延续性动作/事件或情况时,通常使用 while。主从句中既可使用一般时态也可使用进行时态,如:

While John was sitting / sat biting his nails , I was working /worked out a plan to get us home .

约翰坐在那里束手无策时,我想出了能让我们回到家里的计划。

此时很少使用 when 和 as,但是 as 可被用来说明两个正在发展的或正在变化的情况,如:

As I get older I get more optimistic .

随着年龄的增长,我越来越乐观。

（3）同时发生的表示短暂时间概念的动作或事件

此时最常用的是 as 或 just as;也可使用 when,如:

Just as he caught the ball there was a tearing sound .

正当他接住球时,发出一声撕裂的声音。

7. Chairs and tables went flying into the arcade.

此处 flying 为现在分词,作伴随状语。动词-ing 为现在分词还是动名词（如 to go boating、hunting、shopping、skating、swimming 等)通常由句子主语决定。当主语指人时,go 后的 -ing 通常为动名词,如:

She likes to go shopping with her mother .

她喜欢和母亲一块儿去买东西。

8. ...but he was too busy helping himself to diamonds to notice any pain.

（1）be busy doing sth. 正忙于做某事。在使用形容词 busy 时,根据其后所用词的不同,它的用法也不同,但一般可分为下面两类:

1) 其后使用名词或代词时,其间可用介词 with、about、at 或 over,不可直接将名词或代词置于其后使用,均表示"忙于 ……"之意,如:

The high-ranking officials are busy with a complete shake-up in the government.

高级官员们正忙于政府内部的彻底大改组。

She is busy at her work.

她正忙于工作。

使用介词 with 的情况最为常见。

2) 其后使用动词-ing 形式时,可直接使用动词-ing 形式,也可在动词-ing 形式前使用介词 in,但不可在 busy 后直接使用动词不定式,如:

Tom is busy（in）repairing his bike.

汤姆正忙着修自行车。

(2) help oneself to ... 窃取;随意拿取。此处 to 为介词,后需使用名词或名词性短语,如:

The two thieves broke into the shop and helped themselves to the stock.

这两个小偷破门而入,随心所欲地窃取店里的货物。

9. The raid was all over in three minutes, ...

all over 通常表示:处处;浑身;十足,完全;全部结束。用于表示前 3 种意义时,all over 为副词性短语,作状语;用于表示最后一种意义时,如文中那样,与系动词 be 连用,构成系补结构,如:

She is looking for you all over.

她正到处找你。（作状语）

Her mother has a high fever and aches all over.

她母亲在发高烧,浑身酸痛。（作状语）

When they got there, the meeting was all over.

他们到达那里时,会议已全部结束。(作补语)

10. ...Mr. Taylor rushed out and ran ofter it throwing ashtrays and vases...

此现在分词短语为伴随状语,说明与动词 ran 同时进行的动作,如:

He stood there, reading the newspaper.

他站在那里看报纸。

11. They had got away with thousands of pounds worth of diamonds.

worth 值一定金额数量;相当于特定单位数量。在用 worth 表达上述意思时,如文中那样,后面通常使用介词 of + 某物结构。此外使用中应注意其前使用数量词时所属格的用法,如:

an hour's worth of work 一小时的工作

two yuan's worth of oranges 价值两元的橘子

$ 10 million worth of paintings 价值 1,000 万美元的绘画

注意前两例的数量词均需使用所属格形式,而最后一例的数量词不用所属格形式。

语法 Grammar in use

1. 构词

英语中有多种构词方式,最常使用的有转化(conversion)、派生(derivation)和合成(compounding)3 种形式。转化是由一个词类转化为另一个词类,如:

water 水(名词)

water 浇水(动词)

派生则是通过加前缀或后缀构成另一个词,如:

加前缀:

happy 高兴 → *unhappy* 不高兴

加后缀：

happy 高兴(形容词) → *happiness* 高兴(名词)

2. 前缀

前缀加在词干前,对基本词义进行修饰。前缀一般不构成词类的变化,只构成词义的变化。许多前缀构成反义词义。

常用的表示否定含义的前缀有：

un-:   *untrue* 不真实的

      unpack 打开

dis-:   *dislike* 不喜欢

      dishonest 不诚实

in-:   *informal* 非正式的

      inconvenient 不方便的

im-:   *impossible* 不可能的

      impolite 不礼貌的

ir-:   *irregular* 不规则的

      irresponsible 不负责任的

il-:   *illegal* 非法的

      illogical 不合逻辑的

表示其他含义的前缀有：

re-(重新):   *retell* 重述

      redesign 重新设计

ex-(前):   *ex-husband* 前夫

      ex-president 前总统

semi-(半):   *semi-circle* 半圆

      semi-final 半决赛

bi-(双):   *bicycle* 自行车

      bilingual 双语的

tri-(三):   *tricycle* 三轮车

	triangle 三角
pre-(之前的):	preschool 学前的
	pre-liberation 解放前的
post-(在……之后的):	post-war 战后
	post-election 大选后

📁 词汇学习 Word study

1.break（broke，broken）

（1）*vt*.打碎，折断：

I tried to break the pole，but with no success.
我试图折断那根杆子，可是没有成功。

（2）*vt*.破坏，违反：

His coming has broken the peace in the family.
他的到来破坏了家庭的和睦。

（3）*vi*.破碎，破裂：

She stepped backwards onto a cup，which broke into several pieces.
她向后退不小心踩到一个杯子上，杯子碎成了几片。

2.staff

n.全体职员，全体雇员，全体教员：

The police questioned me and all the staff.
警察询问了我和全体职员。

注：staff 后既可以跟单数动词又可以跟复数动词，但通常多用复数动词：

The staff in my office are/is very helpful.
我办公室的职员都很帮忙。

当说"某一职员"时不能用 staff，而应是 a member of staff：

There are two students to every member of staff.

每位教员负责两名学生。

3. move off/out

启程,出发:

The bus moved off/out before all the passengers had got on board.

没等全体乘客上车,公共汽车就开了。

4. upstairs

(1) *adv*. 在楼上,往楼上:

He went upstairs and pulled down the blind.

他上楼放下了遮帘。

注:upstairs 前不能用 to、at 或 in 等介词。

(2) *adj*. 楼上的:

Neighbours watched from their upstairs windows.

邻居们从楼上的窗户往外看。

The people upstairs are very friendly.

楼上的人们非常友好。

✍ 练习答案 Key to written exercises

1. 关键句型练习答案

A　See text.

B　1　*Just as* Mr. Taylor was opening the door of his shop, two men appeared and asked for money.

　　2　Mr. Taylor *used to* own a shop in Hatton Gardens before he moved to Piccadilly.

　　3　*While* I was waiting for a bus yesterday, a friend saw me and offered me a lift in his car.

2. 多项选择题答案

1	b	2	a	3	c	4	c	5	b	6	a
7	a	8	d	9	a	10	a	11	b	12	c

Lesson 7
Mutilated ladies
残钞鉴别组

📖 **课文详注 Further notes on the text**

1. Has it ever happened to you?

副词 ever 常用来表示某种强调,含有"在任何时候"之意,其反义词为 never(从未)。在使用 ever 中,有如下几点应注意:

(1) ever 主要用于疑问句、否定句、条件状语从句和含有否定意义词(如 hardly、stop 等)的句中,如:

> *Do you ever go to the opera?*
> 你有时去听歌剧吗?
> *No, never.*
> 不,从未去过。
> *Yes, sometimes.*
> 是的,有时去。

> *His mother hardly ever goes out.*
> 他母亲几乎不出门。

> *I'm going to stop him ever doing that again.*
> 我要去阻止他不再干那种事了。

虽然否定句可由 not ever 构成(如 I haven't ever been there),但通常用 never 来表示(如 I have never been there)。

(2) ever 用于现在完成时态时,通常表示"直至现在的任何时间"之意;用于过去时态或过去完成时态时,通常表示"直至过去某一时间点的任何时间"之意,如:

> *Have you ever seen a nuclear-submarine?*

你见到过核潜艇吗？

She asked him if he had ever been in trouble with the police.

她问他是否曾与警察有过麻烦。

（3）ever 可用于比较级结构中的 than 之后，进行时间上的强调，如：

You're looking lovelier than ever.

你比任何时候看起来都可爱。

（4）ever 有时用于疑问或假定句中表示愤怒或惊讶，如：

Has anyone of you ever heard such nonsense?

你们有谁听到过这种废话吗？

当然，在这样的用法中，ever 一词经常给予更强的语气强调。

2. When you rescued your trousers, did you find the note was whiter than white?

本句中，作者使用夸张的修辞形式，如使用较大的词 rescued 而非常用的 took/got...out；使用为人熟知的英国有关洗衣粉电视广告中常用的广告词 whiter than white 而非常用的 faded 描述一件小事，以达到全句的戏剧性效果，从而使全句更显生动，给读者留下更深印象。

3. People who live in Britain needn't despair when...

need 一词可作为完全变化动词（有时态、人称变化），也可作为特殊限定动词（无时态、人称变化）来使用，但应注意以下几点：

（1）作为完全变化动词使用时，其时态、人称变化与一般动词一样，如：

Does anybody need his help?

有谁需要他帮忙吗？（人称变化）

She didn't need to go to school yesterday, did she?

她昨天不必去上学，对吗？（时态变化）

（2）作为特殊限定动词使用时，need 后需使用不带 to 的动词不定

76

式,主要用于疑问句、否定句和 if 引导的从句中,而不可用于肯定句中,如:

Need he go to school yesterday ?

他昨天需要去学校吗?

I wonder if he need wait any longer .

我不清楚他是否需要再等下去。

(3) needn't 为 must 的否定式,意为"不必",如:

> *Must they all go now ?*
> 他们都必须现在去吗?
> *No , they needn't .*
> 不,不必了。

(mustn't 为"不准"之意)

(4) needn't 后如接动词不定式的完成时态形式,表示没必要做但已做过的事情,如:

They had a holiday yesterday , and Tom needn't have gone to school .

他们昨天放假,所以汤姆本没必要去上学。(实际汤姆去了)

4. Fortunately for them, the Bank of England has a team called Mutilated Ladies which deals with claims from people who fed their money to a machine or to their dog.

called Mutilated Ladies 为分词短语作定语,置后修饰 a team,意即"(被)称作 Mutilated Ladies 的小组"。后面由关系代词 which 和 who 各引导一定语从句,分别置后修饰 Mutilated Ladies 和 people。应注意的是,虽然 which 引导的是限定性定语从句,但由于全句中连续 3 个较长定语的使用,如简单地按限定性定语从句的译法处理此句,就会使定语变得极为复杂,因而应如译文中那样,将其大体按非限定性定语从句来译,这样更易于理解,也更符合中文的表达习惯。

5．Dogs，it seems，love to chew up money！

it seems 为插入语,为一种附加解释(或说明)方法。如将其置于全句之前,就可构成全句的主要成分(主语和谓语),而原来句子的主要成分就会被置于一个从句之中。与 it seems 类似的常用插入语还有: I think / hope / guess / believe / suppose /wonder 等;you see / know 等;don't you think / know 等;it seems、it seems to me、it is said、it is suggested、I'm afraid 等。这类插入语可以放在句尾,也可插在句中。但是由于其所置位置的不同,句子的中心也随之改变。置于句中时,其前为句子中心。置于句末时,全句所述内容则为句子中心,如:

The trees in that area，it is said，are mostly over thirty feet tall．

那一带的树据说多数都有三十多英尺高。

This，I suppose，will give you some idea of our stand on the question．

这一点我想有助于你们了解我们在此问题上的立场。

The progress they've made in this respect is marvellous，don't you think？

你不认为他们在这方面取得的进步是令人吃惊的吗?

6．A recent case concerns Jane Butlin whose…

concern 与……有关,涉及到。除文中之义外,concern 作动词时还可表示"使……关心"、"使……担心",通常用被动语态形式来表示,如:

In fact，people are always the ones who are mostly concerned about the world peace．

事实上,人民总是最为关心世界和平的人。

此外,在使用动词 concern 时,应注意以下几点:

(1) concern 可作"与……有关"、"涉及到"解,但不可用来作"是关于"、"讲的是"解,如不可将课文中的这个句子译作"最近的一个案例讲的是(是关于)简·巴特林(的)",而应如译文中那样将其译为"最近的一个案例与简·巴特林有关"。因为此案例的主体应为下文中被煮的钱包,而简·巴特林仅为客体即说明主体时所涉及到的人。再如:"这是一本反映改革后农民生活的小说"不可表达为:

    * This novel concerns peasant life after the reform.

而应说:

    This novel has to do with peasant life after the reform.

    This is a novel concerning peasant life after the reform.

    (此句中 concerning 为介词,而非现在分词)

(2) concern 后如使用反身代词时,通常表示"管……"、"忙于……"之意,且一般用于否定句中,如:

    She needn't concern herself with so much unimportant details.

    她无需去管那样多无关紧要的细节。

(3) 动词 concern 后使用不同的介词,往往表示出不同的意义,如:

    They were all concerned about the matter.

    他们都关心/担心此事。

    They were all concerned in the matter.

    他们都参与了此事。

    They were all concerned with the matter.

    他们都与此事有关。(或:他们都参与了此事)

(4) 用 be concerned with 通常可表达动词 concern 的含义,而用 concerned with 通常可表达 concerning (介词)的含义,如:

    The story is concerned with a national hero.

    The story concerns a national hero.

    本故事与一位民族英雄有关。

> *The article deals with some questions concerned with state-operated enterprises.*
>
> *The article deals with some questions concerning state-operated enterprises.*
>
> 本文探讨了有关国营企业的几个问题。

7．Then he and Jane went horse-riding.

在动词 go 后使用动词时,常见的使用结构有带 to 的动词不定式和名词化的动名词。选用时,应注意以下两点:

（1）其后如为不及物动词,通常使用动名词形式,如:

> *They have gone cycling / riding / shopping / hunting / skating / swimming etc.*
>
> 他们骑车／骑马／购物／打猎／滑冰／游泳等去了。

（2）其后如为及物动词,或说话者强调目的时,通常使用带 to 的动词不定式,比较:

> *All of them have gone to climb the hill across the valley.*
> 他们都去爬峡谷那边的山了。
>
> *All of them have gone climbing.*
> 他们都去爬山了。

> *When she met us there, we were going to swim across the river.*
> 她在那里遇到我们时,我们正打算游过河去。(强调目的)
>
> *When she met us there, we were going swimming.*
> 她在那里遇到我们时,我们正打算去游泳。

8．...and without realizing it,...

此介词短语在句中作原因状语,表示"由于没有意识到它"。根据上下文使用 without doing sth.结构可表示多种状语含义,如:

80

She left without saying good-bye to us.

她未告辞就走了。(方式状语)

One cannot obtain the tiger's cubs without entering its lair.

不入虎穴,焉得虎子。(条件状语)

They dropped three bombs without hitting any of the ships.

他们投下了 3 颗炸弹,但未炸着一条船。(结果状语)

9. Imagine their dismay when they found a beautifully-cooked wallet and notes turned to ash!

这里由副词 beautifully 同过去分词 cooked 构成的合成形容词为一种反语(irony)表达法,即用诙谐的或间接的语义表达形式使读者或受话者意识到在开玩笑或在言及其反义,往往可使语言更为生动、诙谐和幽默,从而给读者或受话者留下较深的印象。

10. 'So long as there's something to identify, we will give people their money back...'

从属短语连词 so / as long as 可用于比较状语从句和条件状语从句中,分别表示"(在时间或长度上)像(如)……那样长"和"只要"的含义,如:

> *The time she spent in Britain is not so long as that she had spent in Africa.*
>
> 她在英国度过的时间没有在非洲度过的时间长。(比较状语)
>
> *I shall lend you this book as long as you keep it well.*
>
> 只要你能把这本书保管好我就借给你。(条件状语)

在 as long as 引导的条件状语从句中应使用一般现在时态表达将来内容,如第 2 例。用 as/so long as 来表示"只要"含义的条件状语从句则具有较强的时间意义,意即:在从句的动作进行期间,主句可以成立;一旦从句的动作结束,主句即被推翻。这种主从句意义同时并存的概念是 as/so long as 条件状

语从句的主要特点,如:

Your problem will never be solved so / as long as you keep it to yourself.

你不把问题讲出来,你的问题是得不到解决的。

句中所强调的是:你一天隐藏不讲,问题就一天得不到解决。

语法 Grammar in use

1. 让步状语从句

让步状语从句含有使句子具有对比的因素,因此有时也称之为对比从句(contrast clause)。

引导让步状语从句的常用连词有:although (虽然)、considering (that)...(就 …… 而论,考虑到 ……)、though (虽然)、even though (即使)、even if (即使)、while (虽然)、whereas (鉴于)、no matter how ...(不管如何)、no matter how much ...(不管有……) 等,如:

Although / Though / Even though I felt sorry for him , I was secretly pleased that he was having difficulties.

虽然我为他感到惋惜,但对他的困难我却暗自高兴。

While I disapprove of what you say , I would defend to the death your right to say it.

尽管我不赞成你说的话,我还是要拼命维护你这样说的权力。

however 可与许多形容词和副词连用:

However far it is , I intend to drive there tonight.

不管有多远,我今晚也要开车到那儿去。

However brilliant you are / may be , you can't know everything.

不管有多么聪明,也不可能什么都知道。

no matter 可与疑问词 who、when、where 等一起引导让步状语从句,如:

I told him to report to me after the job was completed , no matter how late it was .

我让他无论多晚在这项工作完成后都要向我汇报。

带-ever 的复合词也可像 no matter 一样引导让步状语从句,如:

Whatever I say , I seem to say the wrong thing . (= No matter what . . .)

无论我说什么,似乎都说得不当。

2. 后缀

后缀可以分为两类:一类是用来表明词的功能的词形变化后缀,如 pencil—pencil + -s (区别单复数形式);look—look + -s, look + -ed, look + -ing (区别不同的动词形式);great—great + -er, great + -est;fast + -er, fast + -est (区别形容词与副词的级)。另一类起到派生作用,使词性得到变化。

(1) 构成名词的常用后缀有:

    -er: *thinker , teacher , worker*

    -or: *actor , sailor , transistor*

    -ness: *illness , happiness*

    -tion: *dictation , preparation , repetition*

    -ment: *movement , argument , government*

常用的还有 -ist、-ism、-ship、-th、-age、-ee 等。

(2) 构成形容词的常用后缀有:

    -ful: *beautiful , cheerful , useful*

    -less: *careless , homeless , fearless*

    -ish: *childish , selfish*

    -ive: *active , destructive*

    -like: *childlike , warlike , manlike*

常用的还有 -ous、-able、-ant、-ly、-some 等。

(3) 构成动词、副词和数词的常用后缀有：

    动词：-ize：　*realize*，*modernize*

       -en：　*broaden*，*hasten*

      -ify：　*beautify*，*simplify*

    副词：-ly：　*really*，*happily*，*terribly*

     -ward：*backward*，*homeward*

     -wise：*likewise*，*clockwise*

    数词：-teen：*fourteen*，*seventeen*

      -ty：　*thirty*，*seventy*

      -th：　*sixth*，*twelfth*

📁　词汇学习　Word study

1. put（putting，put，put）

(1) *vt*. 放，安置：

> *Please put these things on the table.*
>
> 请把这些东西放在桌子上。

(2) put on 穿上，戴上：

> *Whait a minute! I'm just putting on my coat / putting my coat on.*
>
> 等一会儿！我正在穿外衣。

(3) put up with 容忍，忍受：

> *Why should we put up with such terrible working conditions?*
>
> 我们为什么要忍受如此糟糕的工作条件?

2. run（running，ran，run）

(1) *vi*. 跑，奔：

> *There's the bus. We'll have to run!*

公共汽车来了。我们得跑几步！

(2) *vt*.经营,管理,开办;主持:

Who runs this company?

谁经营这家公司？

We'll run a training course for the local teachers this summer.

今年夏天,我们要为当地的教师办个培训班。

(3) *vi*.竞选,当候选人:

He then ran for Governor of New York.

他那时在竞选纽约州州长。

注:run 作"竞选"、"当候选人"解时限用于美国英语;英国英语用 stand:

She was invited to stand as the Liberal candidate.

她应邀作为自由党的候选人。

3.remember

(1) *vt*.记得,回想起:

I still remember the whole incident like it was yesterday.

对那事件的始末我仍然记忆犹新,宛若昨天的事一样。

I remember cabling home for more money.

我记得给家里发过电报再要些钱。

(2) *vi*.记住;有记忆力:

Some remember better than others.

有些人的记忆力比别人强。

注:remember 后既可以跟动词不定式又可以跟动词-ing 形式,但意义不同,如:

I remembered to post the letters.

我记住了要发信。

I remembered posting the letters.

我记得把信寄出去了。

前一句表示没忘记去做 post 这个动作,而后一句则表示记得曾做过 post 这个动作。

(3) *vt* . 代……问候:

Please remember me to your parents .

请代我向你父母问好。

注:更常用的表达方式是:Give my regards to your parents.

✍ 练习答案 Key to written exercises

1.关键句型练习答案

A   See text.

B   1   Firemen *rescued* the little boy who had climbed a tree and couldn't get down.

2   Jane *went* to find John and told him what had happened.

3   Jane *cooked* the next meal in an ordinary oven after her experience with the microwave.

4   The bank manager *sent* the remains of John's wallet to Newcastle.

5   The ladies at the bank *examined* the remains and found they could be identified.

6   The bank *paid* John all his money, so he was very pleased.

2.难点练习答案

1   painless   2   beautiful   3   daily   4   childish

5   athletic

3.多项选择题答案

| 1 | b | 2 | d | 3 | b | 4 | a | 5 | c | 6 | b |
| 7 | c | 8 | a | 9 | a | 10 | d | 11 | b | 12 | b |

Lesson 8
A famous monastery
著名的修道院

📖　**课文详注　Further notes on the text**

1. The Great St. Bernard Pass connects Switzerland to Italy.

connect...to... 把……与……连接起来。connect 通常指不紧密地"联系",被联系的仍然保持自己的特性,但中间建立起某种相关联系。可用于具体事物或抽象概念。介词 to 也可为 with,如:

> *The island is connected by a steamer service to / with the mainland .*
>
> 轮船航线把该岛同大陆联系起来。

2. At 2,473 metres, it is the highest mountain pass in Europe.

此介词短语在句中作原因状语,其前省略了表示原因的现在分词 being。全句意为"由于位于海拔 2,473 米,因而是欧洲最高的山峰"。

3. These friendly dogs, which were first brought from Asia, were used as watchdogs even in Roman times.

(1) 这里的 which 引导出一非限定性定语从句(non-restrictive attributive clause)。限定性定语从句(restrictive attributive clause)与其所修饰的词往往有着密不可分的关系,因此如果去掉它往往会使句子失去意义或意义不清。但是非限定性定语从句往往只是对其所修饰词的进一步说明,去掉后不会造成该句的意义不明。限定性定语从句通常紧随所修饰词之后,而非限定性定语从句同句子的其他部分通常用逗号隔开,

常译为一并列的句子,如:

> *A man who doesn't try to learn from others can't hope to achieve much.*
>
> 一个不向他人学习的人是不能指望取得多少成就的。(限定性定语从句)
>
> *This note was left by Mary, who was here a moment ago.*
>
> 这个条子是玛丽留的,她刚才到这儿来过。(非限定性定语从句)
>
> *The farm now has 30,000 hectares of land, more than two-thirds of which are under cultivation.*
>
> 现在这个农场拥有 30,000 公顷土地,其中三分之二已耕种。(非限定性定语从句)

(2) as watchdogs 为主语补足语。

4. Now that a tunnel has been built... whenever a traveller is in difficulty.

(1) now that 既然。为关系连词,引导一原因状语从句,用来说明一种新情况,如:

> *Now that it has stopped raining, let's go at once.*
>
> 既然不下雨了,我们立刻走吧。

应注意的是,用 now that 引导的原因状语从句必须说明一种新情况,如不是新情况时往往需用其他关系连词如 since 等引导从句,如:

> *Since no one has read the book, we can't discuss it.*
>
> 既然没有人读过此书,我们无法对此进行讨论。

因为"没有人读过此书"并非现在才发生的新情况,因此不可用 now that 代替 since。

(2) in difficulty 处境困难。为介词短语,起形容词作用,作补语。

注意与 difficulty in 同 in difficulty 为一对同音逆序词组,用法

88

与意义完全不同。前者表示"在……方面有困难",difficulty 只能是不可数名词,不能用其复数形式,其后如使用动词,则应用此动词的动名词形式,如:

> *They may have some difficulty in getting there by six.*
> 他们在 6 点以前到达那里可能有些困难。

in difficulty 通常作补语或后置定语,表示"处于困境"、"在困难中"之意,可以使用 difficulty 的单复数形式,但意义不同。用 difficulty 的复数形式时,一般指处于财政上、经济上的困境中或有财政、经济上的困难,如:

> *She's alway been willing to lend him a hand whenever he's in difficulty.*
> 每当他遇到困难时,她总是乐于帮他一把。

> *He's now in difficulties.*
> 现在他手头拮据。

5. Despite the new tunnel, there are still a few people who rashly attempt to cross the Pass on foot.

(1) despite 尽管;不顾。介词,用来引出让步状语,也可用介词短语形式 (in) despite of 来表示,与 in spite of 具有同样的功能和含义。需注意的是,它们均为介词(短语),不可作从属连词使用,即其后只可为名词或名词性短语,而不可引导让步状语从句。此外,一般说来,despite 和 (in) despite of 为较陈旧的表达方法,现在更常使用 in spite of,如:

> *In spite of all his riches, he's never contented.*
> 尽管他很富有,但他从来不感到满足。

> *The manager came to the meeting (in) despite (of) his serious illness.*
> 经理不顾重病仍然到会了。

(2) attempt 试图。作动词使用表达"试图"时,其后的动词可用动词不定式,也可用动名词形式,但动词不定式形式更常见。

6. During the summer months...

during 在……期间。为介词而非从属连词,因此其后只可使用名词或名词性短语,而不可使用从句。此外,在使用中,往往易与介词 for 和 in 混淆。在使用中应注意以下几个方面:

(1) during 和 for 均指一段时间,但 during 表示句中动词动作或状态发生于这段时间中的某一点或若干点,而 for 则指这一动作或状态贯穿整个这段时间,即 during 用来说明动作或状态发生的时间,而 for 则用来说明这一动作或状态所延续的时间,如:

> *There was a storm during the night : it rained for three or four hours .*

> 夜里下了场暴雨,大雨下了三四个小时。

在上两例中,during 和 for 不可互换使用。另外,during 后一般需用精确说明长度和始终点的时间,当为较含混意义的延续时间如 some time, a long time 等时,只可用 for,如:

> *I haven't seen him for some time/a long time .*

> 我有日子/很久没见到他了。

此句中的 for 不可由 during 取代。

(2) during 和 in 都可用来说明在某一特定时间段或在此时间段开始和结束之间某一点/若干点所发生的事情,如:

> *We'll be on holiday in/during August .*

> 我们 8 月份去度假。

但需确切说明某事在那段而不是其他段时间里发生时,通常使用 in,而非 during,如:

> *They usually go on holiday in July , but last year they went in September .*

> 他们通常 7 月份去度假,但去年他们是 9 月份去的。

during 多用于强调在某一特定长度的时段内所发生事情的持续性,如:

90

The shop's closed during the whole of August.

那家商店整个 8 月份都未营业。

当说明某一期间而非某一段时间时,只可用 during,如:

He had some amazing experiences during his military service.

他在服役期间有些令人吃惊的经历。

而在指一般一段时间时,往往两个均可使用,如:

He had some amazing experiences during / in his childhood.

他在儿童时期有些令人吃惊的经历。

7. As there are so many people about...

as 由于。从属连词,引导一原因状语从句。about 到处,副词,作地点状语。

8. The monks prefer winter to summer...

prefer...to... 宁愿……而不愿,喜欢……而不喜欢……这里的 to 为介词,其后需接同类名词、代词或动名词,含有两者相比较之意,如:

I prefer the original book to its sequel.

我觉得原书比续篇好。

Even on holidays, he preferred doing something to doing nothing.

即使在假日里,他也宁愿干点什么事而不愿闲呆着。

prefer to 宁愿;喜欢。这里的 to 为动词不定式符号,后需使用动词原形,如:

We should have preferred to leave on the 8th, but owing to some reason we didn't.

我们本来愿意 8 号走,但由于某种原因没走成。

prefer to...rather than... 宁可(愿)……也不…… 由 prefer to 延伸而成。由于 prefer to...中已含比较含义,因此这一结构

91

中的 rather 不可省掉,如:

They prefer to die fighting rather than live in enslavement.

他们宁可战死,也不肯活着受奴役。

句中 live 前的 to 一般都省去。由于这里是对两个动词不定式的比较,因此不能再简单使用 prefer...to... 的结构,需顾及 rather than 的使用。当然,用 prefer...to... 来表达也是可以的,但必须注意其结构上的不同,试比较:

They preferred to die rather than surrender to the enemy.
They preferred death to surrender to the enemy.
他们宁死也不愿向敌人投降。

第 1 句中 to 后使用了动词 die,因此 rather than 后的 surrender 为省略了 to 的动词不定式;第 2 句中使用 prefer...to... 结构,如上所述,在此结构中,prefer 和 to 后均需使用名词或名词性短语,因此在 prefer 后使用了 die 的名词形式 death,而 to 后的 surrender 此时则作为名词使用,而非前句中的动词,尽管其形式相同。

9．...for they are allowed to wander outside their enclosure.

句中 wander outside their enclosure 为主语补足语。在 allow sb. to do sth. 中,to do sth.为宾语 sb. 的补足语,但由于本句使用的是被动语态,宾语提前作了主语,因此本句中的动词不定式为主语补足语。

10．...who go there at Christmas and Easter.

Christmas 圣诞节,每年 12 月 25 日。

Easter 复活节,每年春分月圆后第一个星期日。

📑 语法 Grammar in use

1. 带 ever 的复合词: whatever、whoever、whenever、wherever、however

(1) 上述各词可以作连词,引导让步状语从句,表示:不管什么人 (whoever)、什么事情(whatever)、什么地方(wherever)等,表达 no matter who、no matter what、no matter where 等之意, 如:

> *Wherever (= No matter where) you go, you can't escape from yourself.*
> 无论你到哪里,都不可能摆脱你自己。
>
> *However (= No matter how) brilliant you are, you can't know everything.*
> 不管你有多聪明,也不可能事事都知晓。
>
> *Whoever (= No matter who) you vote for, prices will go on rising.*
> 无论你选谁,物价都要上涨。

(2) whatever 还可作代词或指示代词,表示任何事情或一切事情, 如:

> *He volunteered to do whatever he could.*
> 他自告奋勇要尽其所能去做。
>
> *She had to rely on whatever books were lying around.*
> 她只能依靠摆在她周围的任何的书籍。

作副词,置于否定词或词组之后,强调没有,如:

> *He knew nothing whatever about it.*
> 他对那事一无所知。
>
> *There is no scientific evidence whatever to support such a view.*
> 没有任何科学根据来支持这一观点。

93

whenever 作连词,引导时间状语从句,表示任何时候,如:

Whenever she had a cold , she only ate fruit .

每次感冒,她就只吃水果。

Come and see me whenever you feel depressed .

你觉得不愉快时就来找我。

whoever 作代词,表示任何人,如:

If death occurs at home , whoever discovers the body should contact the family doctor .

如果家里发生死亡事件,任何发现尸体的人都应该与家庭医生联系。

表示不确知的某人,如:

Whoever answered the phone was a very charming woman .

接电话的那个人是个非常可爱的女人。

however 作副词,表示"然而"之意,如:

Losing at games doesn't matter to some women . Most men , however , can't stand it .

在比赛中失利对某些女人来说算不了什么,然而多数男人却受不了。

2. 带 ever 的强调疑问句

ever 可用在除 which 和 whose 的疑问词之外所有疑问词的后面,构成强调疑问句,表示惊奇、赞美、愤怒、关切等。ever 通常与疑问词分开写,在句中要重读。what/where/when ever 在疑问句中也可连写成 whatever、wherever、whoever,但有些人认为是不正确的,如:

Where ever did you pick that up ?

你究竟在哪儿捡到它的?

Why ever did you go there ?

你究竟为什么要到那儿去?

How ever did you find me ?

你究竟是怎么找到我的?

📁 词汇学习 Word study

1. lie (lies, lying, lay, lain) *vi*.

(1) 躺,平卧:

The baby was lying on the table.

婴儿躺在桌子上。

(2) 被平放:

A dress lies on the floor.

裙子被平放在地板上。

(3) 位于:

The bridge lies beyond the docks.

那座桥坐落在码头的对面。

2. lie (lies, lying, lied, lied)

(1) *vi*. 说谎:

Why should he lie to me ?

他为什么对我撒谎?

He had lied about never going back.

他曾谎称永不回去。

(2) *n*. 谎言,谎话:

I have never told a lie to my pupils.

我从未对我的学生说过谎。

注:此处与动词 tell 搭配,不能说 say a lie。

3. bring (brought, brought) *vt*.

(1) 带来,拿来,取来:

If you're going to the kitchen , would you mind bringing me a glass of water , please ?

如果你去厨房,请你给我带杯水过来好吗?

(2) 把……引来:

Her screams brought the police.

她的喊叫声引来了警察。

(3) 导致,产生,招致:

The earthquake brought disaster.

地震酿成灾害。

This incident might bring them into a war.

这一事件可能会使他们卷入一场战争。

✎ 练习答案 Key to written exercises

1. 关键句型练习答案

A See text.

B 1 I first met Harry fourteen years *ago*.

2 I once stayed in Zurich *for six months* when I was a student.

3 *When* I got home, I found an urgent message on my answering machine.

4 I haven't seen Harry *since 1988*.

2. 难点练习答案

1 what*ever*   2 When*ever*   3 Who*ever*

3. 多项选择题答案

1	c	2	c	3	d	4	d	5	a	6	a
7	c	8	c	9	b	10	a	11	d	12	c

Lesson 9
Flying cats
飞　猫

📖 **课文详注　Further notes on the text**

1. Cats never fail to fascinate human beings.

否定词 never 同表示否定意义的动词 fail 构成的双重否定形式表示肯定意义。把 fail 一词仅译为或仅理解为"失败"是常见的错误。实际上 fail 往往表示出"不能"、"没有"或简单的否定。fail 的 3 种常见结构是：

(1) fail to do sth. 未能做成某事，如：

Don't fail to come to the concert on Saturday evening.
星期六晚上的音乐会你一定要来。

(2) fail in (doing) sth. 在(做)某事中失败，如：

She failed in everything she tried.
她所作的一切努力都没成功。

His colleague failed in persuading him.
他的同事未能说服他。

(3) fail + sb. 使某人失败，如：

At that crucial moment his courage failed him.
在紧要关头他却胆怯了。

2. They can be friendly and affectionate towards humans...

friendly 友好的，和睦的。为形容词，同 affectionate 一样，在句中作补语。在英语中，许多形容词后加后缀-ly 即可构成副词，如：

The engine's very quiet.

这台马达几乎没什么声音。

The engine runs quietly in the workshop.

这台马达在车间无声地转动。

但一些自身以-ly 结尾的常用形容词经常被误认为副词,如 friendly、lovely、lonely、likely、ugly、cowardly、silly 等。这些词不可作为副词使用,因此当需用副词形式表达其意义时,通常以短语形式或用其他词替代的形式来表示,如:

He spoke to me in a very friendly way.

他对我说话非常友好。

She sang beautifully.

她唱得很美。

另外还有一些以-ly 结尾的与时间有关的词,它们既可作形容词也可作副词,如 daily、weekly、monthly、yearly、early,如:

A daily paper is published daily.

日报每天出版发行。(其中第 1 个 *daily* 为形容词,而第 2 个则为副词)

We got up early to catch an early train.

为赶早班火车,我们起得很早。(其中第 1 个 *early* 是副词,而第 2 个则为形容词)

3. Most cats remain suspicious of humans all their lives.

(1) remain 保持不变。为不及物动词,因此不能在其后使用直接宾语,不可将其用于被动语态或将其过去分词形式作定语。用 remain 表示"把……留给"、"把……留下"的意义即将 remain 作及物动词是常见的错误,如:

They left us a lot of problems to solve.

他们给我们留下了许多需解决的问题。(不可用 *remained* 替代 *left*)

I won't detain you any longer.

我不再留你了。(不可用 *remain* 替代 *detain*)

remain 常被用来表示"尚有"、"仍旧"、"继续"之意,如:

His friends have done their best to point out his errors but he remains silent .

他的朋友们已尽力指出他的错误,但他仍沉默不语。

Language was , is , and will remain the chief means of exchange of ideas .

语言过去是、现在是、将来仍将是交流思想的主要工具。

(2) suspicious 猜疑的;多疑的。作补语用时,后面常接 of,如:

He became suspicious of her intention .

他开始疑心她用心不良。

suspicious 既表示"猜疑的"又表示"被猜疑的",如:

The policeman cast a suspicious look at the stranger .

警察用猜疑的目光瞟了陌生人一眼。(主动)

The stranger seems to be suspicious .

那个陌生人似乎很可疑。(被动)

4. One of the things that fascinates us most about cats is the popular belief that they have nine lives .

句中有两个以 that 引导的从句,但两个从句在句中的作用不同。that fascinates us most about cats 为定语从句,置后修饰 one of the things;that they have nine lives 则为同位语从句,置后对 the popular belief 作进一步说明。它们的主要区别在于,定语从句由关系代词/副词引导,其所指内容在从句中作某种成分;同位语从句由连接代词/副词引导,在从句中不作任何成分,如:

Any problem that remains unsolved should be discussed again .

所有尚未解决的问题还应再进行讨论。(定语从句,关系代词 *that* 所代 *any problem* 在从句中起主语作用)

This is the place where they first met .

这是他们初次见面的地方。(定语从句,关系副词 *where* 所代 *the place* 在从句中起地点状语作用)

We expressed the hope that they would come and visit China again.

我们表示希望他们再来访问中国。(同位语从句)

Then arose the question where we could get the money.

随之产生了这样一个问题:我们从哪儿能搞到这笔钱。

(同位语从句)

后两句中的 that 和 where 分别为连接代词和连接副词,在从句中不起任何成分作用,仅是对 hope 和 question 的进一步说明。

5. A cat's ability to survive falls is based on fact.

(1) to survive falls 动词不定式作定语,置后修饰 ability。survive 常用来表达"比……活得更长"之意,如:

His wife survived him by three years.

他妻子在他死后 3 年去世。

并由上义中引申出"经过危险、攻击、动乱等而仍然活着或完好无损"之意,如:

He was the only passenger that survived the aircraft crash.

他是此次飞机失事中惟一脱险的乘客。

(2) base sth. on 以……为某事根据,如:

I based my statement on newspaper reports.

我的发言是以报纸的报道为根据的。

6. All these cats had one experience in common:they had fallen off high buildings, yet only eight of them died from shock or injuries.

(1) in common 共同的,公有的。形容词短语,常用于置后修饰名词,如:

You two have got a lot in common.

你们两人有许多共同之处。

You and Mary had background in common.

你和玛丽有共同的背景。

in common with 与……一样,常作副词短语,如:

In common with many other companies, we advertise in local press.

像许多其他公司那样,我们也在地方报纸上登广告。

(2) yet 可作副词和连词,表达"然而"、"不过"、"可是"、"但是"之意。使用时,如 yet 用于两个形容词或副词之间时,其前不标注逗号,但作连词如文中那样用来连接两个句子时,其前应标注逗号,如:

The old man walks slowly yet steadily.

这位老人走路很慢,但是很稳健。

That might sound incredible, yet she said she had seen it with her own eyes.

那听起来也许令人难以置信,但是她说那是她亲眼所见。

(3) 在使用动词 die 时,应注意如下几个方面:

1) die 为表示终止性的不及物动词,不可同表示有连续时间概念的状语连用,如:

His father has been dead for three years.

他的父亲已死去 3 年了。(不可用 *died* 替代形容词 *dead*)

2) die 后常可与多个不同介词、副词搭配使用,表示"死于……"、"因……而死亡"、"为……而死亡"等意,大体用法如下:

a. 表示死于疾病、饥饿等时,常用介词 of,如:

Many of them died of starvation.

他们许多人死于饥饿。

b. 表示死于创伤、事故等时,常用介词 from,如:

The soldier died from a wound in the breast.

这名士兵因胸部受伤而死亡。

c. 表示死于一般性原因时，常用介词 through，如：

In some poorest regions many children died through lack of proper nourishment.

在一些极贫困地区，许多儿童因缺乏必要的营养而死去。

d. 表示"为……献身／牺牲／捐躯"时，常用介词 for，如：

Lots of them died for the cause of liberation.

他们许多人为解放事业而献身。

e. 表示相继死去时，通常与副词 off 搭配使用，主语必须为复数，如：

The flowers are dying off because there has been no rain.

由于一直没下雨，这些花正相继死去。

3) 此外，应注意当强调死于横祸或突发事件时，通常使用 kill 而非 die，如：

He was killed in a motor accident.

他死于一次车祸。

4) 有时 die of 和 die for 被用来表达某种极度渴望的心情，夸张用语使用，多见于口语中，且需用正在进行时态表达，如：

We are all dying of curiosity.

我们都好奇得要命。

7. There are plenty of high-rise windowsills to fall from!

(1) plenty of 足够的，很多的。既可用来修饰可数名词，也可用来修饰不可数名词，动词则视句中主语形式而定，如：

There's plenty of food in the kitchen.

厨房里有充足的食物。

There're plenty of books on the shelf.

书架上有许多书。

此外,plenty of 多用于肯定句中,在疑问句和否定句中通常用enough,如:

We have plenty of food for the holidays.
我们有充足的食物度假。

Have you enough food for the holidays?
你们有充足的食物度假吗?

(2) fall from 动词不定式作定语,置后修饰 windowsills。

8. ...yet only suffered from a broken tooth.

suffer from 患……,以……为患。suffer 一词可作及物动词或不及物动词。suffer 是指"忍受"精神或肉体的痛苦。作及物动词时为"受……之苦"、"遭受"之意,宾语一般均为不利的事,如pain、loss、defeat、punishment、hardship、torture 等,如:

Their factory suffered heavy losses in the accident.
他们的工厂在事故中遭受重大的损失。

作不及物动词使用时,后面常用介词为 from 或 for,但两者含义不同。suffer from 多指使人引起痛苦的疾病,但也可指对主语产生直接的不利的影响,如:

She suffered greatly from insomnia.
她深受失眠之苦。

Almost every country suffered from a serious economic crisis at that time.
那时,几乎每一个国家都遭受到严重的经济危机。

suffer for 多用来表示"因……而倒霉"、"受……之患",如:

She's sure to suffer for her stubbornness.
她这样顽固,将来一定会吃苦头儿。

9. It seems that the further cats fall, the less they are likely to injure themselves.

(1) the more..., the more... 表示"越……越……"之意,为形容词

103

或副词比较级的一种使用方法,即由两个定冠词(the)＋形容词/副词比较级＋句子的倒装结构构成,用来表示两个变化同时发生,如:

The more dangerous it is, the more I like it.

越危险我越喜欢。

The harder you work, the more you'll achieve.

要想更多地收获就要更勤奋地工作。

(2) be likely to 很可能会,如:

I'm likely to be very busy tomorrow.

我明天很可能会非常忙。

10. ...falling cats have time to relax.

to relax,动词不定式,置后修饰 time,意即"放松自己的时间"。

📑 **语法 Grammar in use**

1. 形容词和副词的两种比较形式:the...the...结构与-er and -er

(1) the...the...结构

将形容词和副词的比较级与 the 一同使用,表示当一方变化时另一方也随之变化,如:

The more expensive petrol becomes, the less people drive.

汽油越贵,开车的人就越少。

The more people you know, the less time you have to see them.

你认识的人越多,你见他们的时间就越少。

注:在上述句子中,不能去掉定冠词 the,同时不能把 more 和后面的副词,形容词与名词分开。

(2) -er and -er 结构

将形容词或副词的两个比较级形式用 and 连接,可以表达持续不断的变化,如:

104

Debbie is growing fast; she's getting taller and taller.

戴比长得很快,她个子越来越高。

Computers are becoming more and more complicated.

计算机变得越来越复杂。

注:在使用-er and -er结构时,不能重复使用其后的形容词或副词,如不能说 more complicated and more complicated。

2.so 与 such

这两个词用在句中都起强调的作用,区别在于 so 用于强调形容词,如:

I was so busy.

我真忙。

而 such 则用于名词前(名词前可有形容词)。单数名词前要用冠词 a 或 an,如:

It's such a cold day.

这是多冷的一天啊。

You really shouldn't tell such obvious lies.

你真不该说这种显而易见的谎话。

试比较:

> *It was such a nice party!*
> 那是一个多好的聚会!
> *The party was so nice!*
> 那个聚会多好啊!

试比较下面句子中的 so...a/an:

It was so important an occasion, we couldn't miss it.

这是个很重要的机会,我们不能错过。

当形容词前面有 the、this、that、these、those 或物主代词时,不能使用 so 或 such,如不可说:

* It was our first visit to this so old town.

而应说:

105

It was our first visit to this very old town.

这是我们第一次访问这座非常古老的小镇。

so 还可用于强调副词,如:

Time seems to have passed so quickly.

时间似乎过得太快了。

在口语中还可用 ever so 进行强调,如:

I'm ever so grateful to you for talking to me.

你同我谈话,我实在是太感谢了。

📂 词汇学习 **Word study**

1. seem *vi.*

(1) 后跟形容词或 to be:

Even minor problems seem important.

甚至微不足道的小问题似乎也重要。

They seemed to be good at reading.

他们好像擅长阅读。

(2) 后跟名词短语:

It seemed(to be)a long time before the food came.

好像过去了很长时间饭才上来。

What seems to be the trouble?

毛病可能是什么?

(3) 与动词不定式/从句连用:

The experiments seem to prove that sugar is not very good for you.

试验似乎证明糖对你并不非常有益。

It seemed as though the war had ended.

好像战争已经结束了似的。

106

2．survive

(1) *vt*. 比……活得长：

　　He was survived by his wife and three children.

　　他死后留下妻子和 3 个孩子。

(2) *vt*. 从……中逃生,经……后继续存在：

　　He was the only one in the family who had survived the 1976 earthquake.

　　在 1976 年地震中他是家里惟一的幸存者。

　　Many buildings survived the earthquake.

　　许多建筑物经受住了这次地震。

(3) *vi*. 活下来,幸存：

　　Four of their children had died as babies and the fifth survived.

　　他们的 4 个孩子都夭折了,第 5 个孩子活了下来。

3．suffer

(1) *vt*. 忍受,遭受(精神或肉体的痛苦),常与其搭配的名词有 pain(痛苦)、loss(损失)、defeat(失败)、punishment(惩罚)、wrong(冤屈)、hardship(困苦)、torture(折磨) 等：

　　He suffered a lot of discomfort.

　　他饱受不适之苦。

(2) *vi*. (from)患,以……为患：

　　The patient complained that he had been suffering from repeated stomach ache.

　　那个病人抱怨说他的胃一直在疼。

✍ **练习答案　Key to written exercises**

1．关键句型练习答案

　A　See text.

107

B See text.

2．难点练习答案

　　1 so　　2 such　　3 such an　　4 so　　5 such a

3．多项选择题答案

　　1 a　　2 d　　3 a　　4 c　　5 b　　6 d

　　7 b　　8 a　　9 b　　10 c　　11 c　　12 a

Lesson 10
The loss of the *Titanic*
"泰坦尼克"号的沉没

📖 **课文详注 Further notes on the text**

1. **The great ship, *Titanic*, sailed for New York from Southampton on April 10th, 1912.**

   sail for 驶往……, (船) 开往, 如:

   > *The ship sails for Qingdao tomorrow.*
   > 这艘船明天驶往青岛。

   动词 sail 同介词的常见搭配形式有:

   > *sail about* 在……驶来驶去
   >
   > *sail across* 横渡
   >
   > *sail along / down / up* 沿……向前 / 向下游 / 向上游驶 (去)
   >
   > *sail from . . . to . . .* 从……驶往……
   >
   > *sail into* 驶入
   >
   > *sail out of . . . toward . . .* 离开……驶往……

2. **She was carrying 1,316 passengers and a crew of 891.**

   (1) she 这里指 the great ship, 为拟人法 (personification)。英语中, 一般指人用 he 或 she, 指物用 it, 但常见如下 3 种例外情况:

   　　1) 当动物被以为有人性、头脑或感情时, 常用 he 或 she 称谓 (饲养宠物者常将其宠物以 he 或 she 称谓, 但他人一般不如此称谓), 如:

   > *I think Felicity's upset about something. She's not giving much milk these days.*

我想费利西蒂对什么感到很不安。这些天来她产奶可不多。

2）一些人用 she 称谓自己的汽车、摩托车等交通工具;船员通常用 she 称谓船只,如:

How's your new car?

你的新车怎么样?

Terrific, she's going like a bomb.

棒极了。她奔驰如飞。

3）she 多用来称谓国家,如:

France has decided to increase her trade with Romania.

法国已决定增加她同罗马尼亚的贸易。

(2) crew 为集合名词,指"全体船员",不用来指"一个船员"。与其搭配使用的动词可为单数形式,也可为复数形式。一只船只有一个 crew,两只船有两个 crews,如:

The crews of two boats are getting ready to sail off the harbour.

两只船的船员准备好离港。

3．Even by modern standards...

这里的介词 by 作"依照"、"按照"解,如:

Never judge a person by his looks.

千万别以貌取人。

By twentieth century standards, the journey wasn't at all a comfortable one.

用 20 世纪的标准来衡量,那次旅行根本不舒服。

4．At that time, however, she was not only the largest ship that had ever built, but was regarded as unsinkable, for she had sixteen watertight compartments.

at that time 在那时,当时。其句中所述内容只用过去/过去正

110

在进行时态,如:

> *At that time I was too young to know much about life.*
> 那时我还太年轻,对人生的事情懂得不多。
> *At that time I was cooking in the kitchen.*
> 当时我正在厨房做饭。

5．Even if two of these were flooded, she would still be able to float.

(1) even if 即使,尽管,纵然。意思与 even though 相同,用来引导让步状语从句。even if 多用于口语中,而 even though 多用于书面语中,如:

> *I will come even if I am tired.*
> 即使我累了,还是要来的。
> *He will never be dishonest even though he should be reduced to poverty.*
> 纵然他穷困了,也决不会不诚实。

使用中注意下面两点:

1) 上述例句中不可将 if 或 though 省略,仅用 even 表示。even 为一副词,不能作从属连词引导一从句。

2) 用 though (虽然)。引导的让步状语从句与 even if/though 引导的让步状语从句所表示的语义不同。even if/though (即使),引导的句子有退一步设想之意,因此是不肯定的;用 though 引导的句子表达的是一事实,比较:

> *He will not reveal the secret even if he knows it.*
> 纵使他知道这个秘密,他也不会说出来。
> *He will not reveal the secret though he knows it.*
> 虽然他知道这个秘密,但也不会说出来。

第 1 句中,他对这个秘密可能知道,也可能不知道;第 2 句中他肯定知道这个秘密。

(2) be able to... 能够。虽然情态助动词 can 同形容词短语 be

111

able to 均可用来表示"能够"之意,但在使用中应主要注意以下几点:

1)用 be able to 表达将来做某事的能力,而不用 can,如:

> *I'll be able to speak German in another few months.*
>
> 再过几个月我就能说德语了。

can 常用来表达现在的或一般的能力,如:

> *You can certainly cook, even if you can't do anything else.*
>
> 即使其他事你都不会做,你也肯定会做饭。

但是,当含有现在对将来能力做出决定的意义时,可以用 can,如:

> *We're too busy today, but we can repair your car tomorrow.*
>
> 我们今天太忙,不过我们明天能修你的车。

2)谈及过去特定场合能做某事时,通常使用 was/were able to,managed to 或 succeeded in,而不用 could。见第 1 课课文注释 12。

3)可以用 was/were able to 表达 could + 完成时态结构表达的句义,即用来表达过去本能做某事而未做之意,如:

> *I was able to marry anybody I wanted to, but I didn't. (= I could have married anybody I wanted.)*
>
> 我本能同我愿意的任何人结婚,但我没这样做。

6. ...for she went down on her first voyage with heavy loss of life.

went down 下沉。on her first voyage 为时间状语,修饰 went down。with heavy loss of life 为结果状语,修饰 went down。

7. ...the great ship turned sharply to avoid a direct collision.

此动词不定式作目的状语,修饰 turned。动词不定式根据谓语动词或句子语义等,常可起到多种状语作用,如:

> *We can send a car over to fetch you.*

112

我们可以派辆车去接你。（目的状语）

She has said something accidentally only to make him feel more upset .

她偶然说了些什么却使他感到更为不安。（结果状语）

They jumped with joy to hear the news .

他们听到这个消息高兴得跳了起来。（原因状语）

在动词 avoid 后需使用名词、代词、名词性短语或动名词形式，通常用来表示"（有意识地）躲避"不愉快的或可能发生危险的事物或情况，如：

He deliberately avoided seeing me .

他故意回避我。

The danger can be avoided if we lay our plan carefully .

如果我们计划定得周密，危险就可避免。

8. The *Titanic* turned just in time, narrowly missing the immense wall of ice...

（1）in time 及时。指句中的动作发生在所提到的或规定的时间之前，其后常接以 for 引导的短语或动词不定式表示的目的状语，如：

They were in time for the train .

他们及时赶上了火车。

The news came in time for us to send it to the press .

新闻到时正好来得及付印。

Cancer can be cured if discovered in time .

癌症若发现得及时可以治愈。

用 in time 还可表达"迟早（sooner or later）"、"总有一天（some day）"的意思，如：

You will find out in time the truth of what I say .

早晚你会明白我说的话是有道理的。

on time 的意思与 in time 很相似，但指句中的动作发生在所提到或规定的时间之内,即"准时(punctually)"、"按时(at the right time)"之意,美国人还常用其表示"以分期付款方式"的意思,如:

In spite of our late start, we managed to arrive on time.

尽管我们动身晚,但还是设法准时到达了。

Many people are never out of debt because they buy everything on time.

许多人永远欠债,因为无论买什么东西他们都采取分期付款的方式。

(2) narrowly missing 勉强避开。为现在分词短语,作结果状语。分词短语可作结果状语,通常置于句子后部。如:

Her husband died that year, leaving her with two children.

那一年她丈夫死了,给她丢下了两个孩子。

9. ... there was a slight trembling sound from below ...

from below 从下面,介词短语,作地点状语。在介词 from 后常可使用一个介词或副词,进一步说明方位,如:

The child was peeping at the guest from under the bedclothes.

孩子正从被子下偷看客人。(*under* 为介词)

Some fruits are often rotten from within.

一些水果经常从里面开始腐烂。(*within* 为副词)

10. The noise had been so faint that no one thought that the ship had been damaged.

so ... that ... 太……以致……关联连词,一般只用来引导结果状语从句(由于它们表示主句的动作或状态达到何种程度而引起结果,因此也有人将其称作程度状语从句)。so 为副词,that 为连词,引导一从句。副词 so 有 4 种搭配形式:(1) so+形容词/副词+that 从句;(2) so+形容词+a(n)+单数

114

名词 + that 从句;(3) so + 动词 + that 从句;(4) so many, few / much / little + 复数名词/不可数名词 + that 从句,如:

He spoke so fast that I could not follow.

他讲得太快,我听不懂。(*so* + 副词)

His manner was so bright that Jane felt at ease with him at once.

他的态度那样爽朗,简立刻觉得和他在一起毫无拘束。
(*so* + 形容词)

It was so easy a question that every one of us could answer it.

这样简单的问题,我们每个人都能回答。(*so* + 形容词 + *a〈n〉* + 单数名词)

The execution of the arrangement so thrilled him that he felt as though he were walking on air.

这事的安排使他打心眼里乐了起来,觉得浑身飘飘然的。
(*so* + 动词)

He fools away so much time on fishing that he never gets anything done.

他在钓鱼上浪费了太多的时间,因此一事无成。(*so* + *much* + 不可数名词)

11. Below, the captain realized to his horror that...

to his horror 为介词短语,作状语修饰 realized。"to one's + 感情名词"是英语中一种常见的介词短语结构,如:

to one's	*delight*		高兴的是
	horror		恐惧的是
	joy	使某人	高兴的是
	satisfaction		满意的是
	surprise		惊奇的是

有时为了强调感情表达程度,可在这类名词前用表程度的形容词如 great, extreme 等进行修饰,也可在介词 to 前用表程度

的副词如 greatly、much 等进行修饰,如:

To her great surprise, they saw eye to eye on the question.

使她大为惊奇的是,他们对那一问题的看法竟然一致。

Much to his surprise, none of them could tell the difference between them.

使他极为吃惊的是,他们竟没人能讲出这两者间的不同。

12. As there were not enough ...

as 在此为从属连词,引导一原因状语从句。参见第 1 课课文注释 12。

📖 语法 Grammar in use

过去完成时态的被动形式

过去完成时态的被动形式为:had + been + 过去分词,如:

When she came the room had already been cleaned.

她来时房间已经打扫过了。

He had been poisoned by his girlfriend.

他被他的女友毒死。

🗁 词汇学习 Word study

1. set out

(1)(for,on) 出发,启程:

He set out for work an hour ago. Hasn't he arrived?

他一小时前就上班去了。他还没到吗?

Having missed the last bus, we had to set out walking.

由于错过了末班车,我们只得步行动身。

(2)(as,in,on) 开始(从事某种职业):

Her mother helped her to set out as a professional singer.

她母亲帮助她步入专业歌手的行列。

116

Soon after the death of his father, he set out in business.

他父亲一去世,他就开始经商了。

(3)打算,试图:

He set out to be a doctor, but in the end he turned out to be a successful lawyer.

他原打算做个医生,可是他后来却成为一个成功的律师。

They had failed in what they had set out to do.

他们计划做的事落了空。

2．flood

(1)*n*.洪水,水灾:

The spring flood came early this year.

今年的春讯到得早。

The flood made thousands of people homeless.

那场洪水使成千上万的人流离失所。

(2)*vt*.淹没,灌满:

The dam collapsed, flooding an area of five thousand square miles.

大坝垮了,淹没了5,000平方英里的区域。

She left the water running and the kitchen was flooded.

她任凭水在流,使厨房灌满了水。

(3)*vt*.充斥,充满:

The New Year is coming and we are flooded with cards.

新年将至,我们收到大量的贺卡。

Cheap plastic bowls and buckets flood the market.

廉价的塑料碗、桶充斥了市场。

3．realize *vt*.

(1)明白,意识到:

Everybody realizes how vital it is to have clean drinking water.

人人都意识到清洁的饮用水有多么重要。

I hope you realize that you're making a big mistake.

我希望你认识到你在犯一个大错。

（2）实现（常与 hope〈希望〉、dream〈梦想〉、plan〈计划〉等连用）：

I have at last realized my dream of becoming an artist.

我最后终于实现了成为一名艺术家的梦想。

We'll try our best to realize the project.

我们将竭尽全力实现这一计划。

✎ 练习答案　Key to written exercises

1. 关键句型练习答案

A　See text.

B　1　At that time, she was the largest ship that *had* ever *been built*.

　　2　After the alarm *had been given*, the great ship *turned* sharply to avoid a direct collision.

2. 难点练习答案

1　physicist　　　　2　miner　　　　3　humanity

4　impression　　　5　originality

3. 多项选择题答案

1　d　　2　c　　3　a　　4　b　　5　d　　6　d

7　b　　8　d　　9　a　　10　c　　11　b　　12　a

Lesson 11
Not guilty
无　罪

📖　课文详注　**Further notes on the text**

1. Customs Officers are quite tolerant these days,but they can still stop you when you are going through the Green Channel and have nothing to declare.

（1）go through 穿过,通过。除文中之意外,此动词短语还常用来表达"完成(工作等)"、"遭受,经历(苦难等)"、"(法案)被通过"、"(计划)被批准"、"审查"、"检查"等之意,如:

> *They've gone through that dangerous and uninhabited desert.*
> 他们已通过了那个危险、荒无人烟的沙漠。
> *She went through her task just in time.*
> 她按时完成了任务。
> *You'll have to go through tremendous pain in treating the cancer.*
> 在治疗癌症中,你还得遭受极大的痛苦。
> *Her application went through and she was hired.*
> 她的申请获得通过,她被录用了。
> *They went through our luggage at the customs.*
> 海关人员检查了我们的行李。

（2）to declare 为作定语的动词不定式,置后修饰 nothing。前面课文中已多次出现动词不定式作定语的情况,现将作定语的动词不定式常见形式归纳如下:

1）当被修饰词指物时,动词不定式与其所修饰的词通常具有逻辑上的动宾关系,如:

That will be the only thing to do now, I'm afraid.
恐怕那是目前惟一可行的办法。

There are still a few more items to be included in the list.
还有几个项目应列入这张单子中。

正因为它们的这种动宾关系,因此当动词不定式为不及物动词时,其后就应跟有必要的介词,如:

She has a lot of things to attend to.
她有许多事要管。

There's nothing to worry about.
没有什么值得发愁的。

2）当被修饰词指人时,它同动词不定式通常具有逻辑上的主谓关系,如:

She's always the first to bear hardships, the last to enjoy comforts.
她总是吃苦在前,享乐在后。

3）用在一些名词之后,如 need、time、way、right、chance、opportunity、courage、reason、effort、decision、tendency、intention、wish 等,如:

I think that'll be the best way to solve the problem.
我认为那是解决问题的最好方法。

They finally made the decision to carry on the work themselves.
他们最终决定自己继续这项工作。

4）在一些后面常可使用动词不定式的动词和形容词的同源名词后,常可使用动词不定式作定语,如 attempt、promise、plan、ability、determination、anxiety、eagerness 等,如:

He's always making changes in his plans to do things.

他总是改变做事情的计划。

I think she has the ability to do the experiment alone.

我认为她具有独立进行此项实验的能力。

She expressed her anxiety to visit her Chinese friends.

她表达了她要拜访她的中国朋友的渴望。

2. **Even really honest people are often made to feel guilty.**

动词不定式 to feel guilty 在句子中作补语。在动词 make 后,常可使用复合宾语形式,即其后可使用一作宾语的名词(或代词),再于这一名词(或代词)之后使用一动词不定式结构。但是,在主动语态中,要使用不带 to 的动词不定式,如:

His speech made us feel nervous.

他的讲话使我们感到紧张。

这种后面可使用复合宾语结构,且需使用不带 to 的动词不定式的常用动词有 feel、have、hear、let、make、notice、see、watch,等,如:

Don't forget to have her come with you.

别忘了让她和你一起来。

He often hears her sing songs in the next room.

他常听到她在隔壁唱歌。

如文中所示,当这些动词用于被动语态时,其宾语后的动词不定式仍需使用 to,如:

Someone was heard to come into the room.

听到有人走进了这间屋子。

In the heavy rain, people were made to take shelter in the nearest possible shops.

大雨中,人们不得不在离自己最近的商店里避一避雨。

3. **The hardened professional smuggler, on the other hand, is never troubled by such feelings, even if he has five hundred gold**

watches hidden in his suitcase.

（1）on the other hand 另一方面；而。在句中作插入语。英语中有许多用来表明所说内容结构概念的表达方法。on the other hand 则表明"与前文相比"的概念。属此类的表达方法还有 all the same（同样；依然；毫无区别）、yet（而，然而）、and yet（然而，可是）、still（仍然，尽管如此）、however（然而，但是）等，如：

> *She's not doing a very good job. All the same, you've got to admit that she's doing her best.*
>
> 她工作干得不很出色。反正都一样，你得承认她在尽最大的努力。
>
> *He claims to be a socialist, and yet he has two houses and a Rolls-Royce.*
>
> 他声称自己是个社会主义者，但是他却有两所房子，一辆罗尔斯—罗伊斯轿车。

（2）hidden in his suitcase 藏在手提箱里的。为过去分词短语，置后修饰 watches，这样的结构相当于谓语为被动语态结构的定语从句，如：

> *watches hidden in his suitcase = watches which were hidden in his suitcase*

4．'Have you anything to declare?' he asked, looking me in the eye.

looking me in the eye 直盯着我的眼睛。为分词短语，在句中作方式状语。look sb. in the eye(s)/face，直视某人，多用于口语，通常用于否定式和一般时，如：

> *I wonder she can look me in the face after the way she's behaved!*
>
> 我纳闷她那样表现之后还敢面对我。
>
> *I knew he was lying when he couldn't look me in the eyes.*

由于他不敢正视我,所以我知道他在撒谎。

5.'Would you mind unlocking the suitcase please?'

mind 介意,在乎。一般只用于否定或询问句中,后使用名词或动名词作宾语,不可使用动词不定式,如:

Do you mind me making a suggestion?

我可以提个建议吗?

You shouldn't mind being criticized, so long as it is helpful in improving your work.

只要批评有益于改进你的工作,你不应太在意对你的批评。

此外,用 mind 表达的"你介意……吗?"是一个常用的口语句型。如不介意时,其回答应是 Certainly not、Not at all 或 Of course not,如介意(不同意)时,通常用表示某种推却的理由来回答,如 I'm sorry 或 I wish you wouldn't 等。用 Yes,I do 表示的回答等于拒绝,而且语气很不客气,如:

Would you mind me opening the window?

你不在意我开一下窗子吗?

I'm sorry, but you see I've got a bad cold.

对不起,你知道我得了重感冒。

6.The officer went through the case with great care.

(1) went through 检查。参见本课课文注释 1。

(2) with great care 十分仔细地,为英语中常用的"介词 with + 抽象名词"结构。除本课中的 care 外,常见的用于 with 后的名词有 difficulty、ease、joy、pleasure、reason、safety、satisfaction、shame、sorrow、speed 等。在此结构中,名词前无冠词,如:

He found the place with difficulty.

他好不容易才找到那个地方。

We won the football match with ease.

我们轻易地赢了那场足球赛。

He complained with reason that he had been treated unfairly.

他有理由抱怨受到了不公正的对待。

有时为了加强语气,在这类名词前可以使用表示程度的形容词如 great、much 等,如:

They reached there with great speed.

他们很快到达了那里。

I heard the news with much satisfaction.

我非常满意地听到了这个消息。

7．All the things I had packed so carefully were soon in a dreadful mess.

in a dreadful mess (处于)乱七八糟(的状态中),如:

Her hair was in a terrible mess.

她的头发乱糟糟的。

That country's economy is now in a mess.

那个国家的经济现在乱作一团。

8．Suddenly,I saw the Officer's face light up.

light up 露出得意的神情。为省略了 to 的动词不定式,在句中作补足语。动词 see 常用于 see sb. do sth. 和 see sb. doing sth. 结构中。

9．...and he pounced on it with delight.

(1) pounce (up)on 猛地抓住。常用于一般时态中。除本课意义外,它还被用来表示"突然袭击 / 逮住 / 扑住"和"喜欢挑(毛病)"之意,如:

After waiting by the hole for hours, the dog pounced on the rabbit as it came out.

在洞口等了几小时后,那条狗在兔子出来时猛地扑住了它。

This teacher pounces on spelling mistakes, so use your

124

dictionary.

这个老师喜欢挑拼写错误,所以要查查词典。

(2) with delight 高兴地。作状语,修饰 pounced。参见本课课文注释 7。

10. **'You should have declared that...'**

"should＋动词不定式的完成时态"可用来表达"本该做而未做的事情",如:

The tree's dead. Maybe I should have given it more water.

这棵树死了。也许我本应给它浇更多的水。

We should have got here earlier: the train's packed.

我们本该早些到这儿:火车太挤了。

11. **'... Perfume is not exempt from import duty.'**

exempt 被免除(责任、义务等)的;被豁免的。在此作形容词,常用于 be exempt from 结构中,如:

She's exempt from the examination.

她被免试。

Tom was exempt from military service.

汤姆被免除服兵役。

12. **... I was able to hurry away with precious chalk marks on my baggage.**

with precious chalk marks on my baggage 为独立主格结构。

语法 Grammar in use

大写字母

英语中大写字母的使用分两类,一是必须要大写,二是既可大写也可小写。

1. 在下述情况时必须用大写字母

(1) 句子或直接引语中第一个单词的首字母:

The train came into the station. It arrived at five o'clock.

火车进站了。它于 5 点钟到达。

'Have you anything to declare?' he asked, looking me in the eye.

"您有什么需要申报的吗?"他直盯着我的眼睛问。

(2) 人名、组织名、书名、电影名、剧名等中各单词的首字母(介词、连词等短小的词除外):

... Mr. Andrew Smith, head of management development at International Business Machines.

...安德鲁·史密斯先生,国际商用机器公司经营开发负责人。

Romeo and Juliet, *one of Shakespeare's famous plays, will be put on the stage during the next week.*

《罗密欧与朱丽叶》,莎士比亚的名剧之一,将要在下周公演。

(3) 地名:

Miss Helen Perkins was born in India in 1945.

海伦·帕金斯 1945 年生于印度。

Madison Avenue 麦迪逊大街

(4) 星期、月份、节日:

The trial continues on Monday.

审讯持续到星期一。

December 12 月

Easter 复活节

Spring Festival 春节

(5) 某国人:

126

This morning I interviewed two journalists—one an American, one a Chinese.

今早我会见了两位记者,一位是美国人,一位是中国人。

(6) 用以指某人所创作的艺术品、音乐和文学的人名:

In those days you could buy a Picasso £300.

那时你可以花 300 镑买一幅毕加索的画。

I listened to Mozart.

我听莫扎特的曲子。

(7) 产品名称:

Four armed men stopped his new car as it slowed down to make a turn, disabled the chauffeur with Mace spray, and pulled him into another car.

当他的新车减速拐弯时,4 名武装人员用梅斯气制服了司机后,把他拉进了另一辆车。

(8) 姓名前的头衔:

There has been no statement so far from President Bush.

到目前为止尚无布什总统的声明。

The tower was built by King Henry Ⅱ in the 12th century.

这座塔是亨利二世于 12 世纪建造的。

(9) 表明国名和地名的形容词:

an American author 一位美国作家

the Californian earthquake 加利福尼亚地震

(10) 表明与某人有关或相像的形容词:

his favorite Shakespeare sonnet 他最喜欢的莎士比亚十四行诗

in Victorian Times 在维多利亚时代

(11) 人称代词 I 在任何情况下都要大写:

I thought I was wrong.

我认为我错了。

2．在下述情况下大小写均可

（1）表示方向的单词的首字母：

It is cold in the north in winter .

冬天北方寒冷。

The home-ownership rate in the Southeast of England is higher than that in the North .

英格兰东南地区的住房拥有率高于北方。

（2）年代：

The movement of learning from Lei Feng started in the sixties .

向雷锋学习的运动始于 60 年代。

Most of it was done in the seventies .

大部分完成于 70 年代。

（3）季节名称：

He planted several trees in his garden last autumn .

去年秋天他在花园里种了几棵树。

In the Autumn of 1948 Caroline returned to the United States .

卡罗琳于 1948 年秋天回到了美国。

（4）用以指某一类人的头衔：

the great prime ministers of the past 过去伟大的首相们

He was one of the greatest Prime Ministers who ever held office .

他是历届执政的最伟大的首相之一。

（5）代词 he、him 和 his 指代上帝或基督时：

Some said they saw the son of God ; others did not see Him .

有人说见到了圣子；其他人没见到。

1．go through

(1) 通过：

> *The piano won't go through the narrow entrance; it will have to come in through the window.*
>
> 钢琴无法通过这个狭窄的入口,得从窗户进来。

(2) 搜查,查找：

> *The police have gone through the whole district, but no evidence has been found.*
>
> 警察搜查了整个区域,但是没找到任何线索。

(3) 遭受：

> *Since her husband died she has gone through such a lot.*
>
> 她丈夫去世后,她受了那么多的罪。

2．make *vt*.

(1) 使得,迫使：

> *What made her faint?*
>
> 什么使她昏了过去?(*to make* + 宾语 + 不带 *to* 的动词不定式)
>
> *He was made to change his mind.*
>
> 他被迫改变了主意。(被动语态时要用带 *to* 的动词不定式)

(2) 做某事：

> 此为 make 一词最常用词义之一,与某一名词搭配表示"做"之意,如 make a suggestion(提个建议)、make a promise(许一诺言)等。常与其搭配的名词有 arrangement(安排)、choice(选择)、decision(决定)、journey(旅行)、speech(讲话)、visit(参

观)、noise(噪音)、plan(计划)、remark(讲话)等,如:

> *He made the shortest speech I have ever heard.*
>
> 他做了一个我所听到的最简短的演讲。
>
> *I've realized I've made the wrong decision.*
>
> 我意识到我做出了一个错误的决定。

(3) 成为,变成:

> *He will make a good lawyer.*
>
> 他将成为一名好律师。
>
> *They make a good football team.*
>
> 他们组成了一个优秀的足球队。

✍ 练习答案 Key to written exercises

1. 关键句型练习答案

ll. 16-17：The Customs Officer told the writer he should have declared the perfume because it was not exempt from import duty.

ll. 18-19：The writer told the Customs Officer that it wasn't perfume, but it was hair gel. He said it was a strange mixture he made himself.

ll. 21：He told the Customs Officer to try it.

2. 难点练习答案

Because Tim Jones cannot speak French or German, he never enjoys traveling abroad. Last March, however, he went to Denmark and stayed in Copenhagen. He said he spent most of his time at the Tivoli, which is one of the biggest funfairs in the world. At the Tivoli, you can enjoy yourself very much, even if you don't speak Danish.

130

3. 多项选择题答案

| 1 c | 2 c | 3 a | 4 d | 5 c | 6 b |
| 7 a | 8 a | 9 c | 10 a | 11 d | 12 b |

Lesson 12
Life on a desert island
荒岛生活

📖　**课文详注　Further notes on the text**

1. We sometimes imagine a desert island to be a sort of paradise where the sun always shines.

(1) 尽管动词 imagine 可在"动词 + 宾语 + 动词不定式"结构中使用,如:

> *Our producers should constantly imagine themselves to be in the consumers' position.*
>
> 我们的生产单位要经常设身处地为用户着想。

句中动词不定式 to be 引导的短语在句中作宾语补足语,imagine 还常见于被动语态结构中,如:

> *He was imagined to be an excellent choice.*
>
> 他被人们想像为极佳的人选。

但是,这样的结构书本气很浓,人们更经常使用"imagine + that 从句"结构,如:

> *I had imagined that he was an excellent choice.*
>
> 我原猜想他是极佳人选。

此外,在 imagine 后还常使用动名词结构,如:

> *I can't imagine asking him for money.*
>
> 我简直不敢想像向他借钱。

(2) where the sun always shines 为定语从句,置后修饰 paradise。

2. Ripe fruit falls from the trees and you never have to work.

have to 得,需。常用来表示某种义务。在英国英语和美国英语的使用中略有不同。在英国英语中通常使用 have got to 形式,而在美国英语中通常使用 have to 形式。在语义表达上,通常将所要表述内容分为习惯性/重复性与非习惯性义务两种。而由于这种语义上的区分,在表达中通常使用不同的句子结构形式。在表达重复性/习惯性语义概念时,陈述句通过 have(got)to 形式表示,如:

He has(got)to travel on business once a month.
他每个月得出一趟差。

而否定或疑问句则使用 do,如:

I don't usually have to work on Thursday afternoon.
我星期四下午通常不必去工作。

Does she often have to speak French in her job?
她在工作中经常得说法语吗?

在表达非习惯性语义概念时,其否定或疑问句通常直接由 haven't(got)to 和 have(got)to 构成,如:

Has he got to go to school tomorrow?
他明天得去上学吗?

have got to 形式通常不用于过去时态中,需用一般的动词形式取代,如:

Did you have to go to school every Saturday afternoon when you were a school boy?
你上学时,每周六下午都得去学校吗?

have(got)to 和 will have to 均可用来表达将来时态,如:

I've got to / I'll have to get up early next week.
下周我得早起。

在美国英语中,可用一般的动词形式(疑问句中用不带 got 的助动词 do 形式)表达习惯性(或重复性)与非习惯性的义务。由于美国英语的影响,在英国英语中使用这种结构形式越来越普遍,如:

I have to leave now.

我现在得离开了。

在美国英语的口语中也常使用 have got to 结构,在极随意的口语中甚至将 have 省略,如:

I('ve) got to go.

我得走啦。

You('ve)just got to help me.

你可得帮帮我。

课文中 have to 前使用了否定词 never,表示出"根本/完全无需"之意。

3. You either starve to death or live like Robinson Crusoe,waiting for a boat which never comes.

并列连词 either...or... 用来指两种可能性之间的选择。

either 后所用句子成分应与 or 后所用句子成分相一致,如:

> *You may go with either boys or girls.*
> *You may go either with boys or with girls.*
> 你可以同男孩去,也可以同女孩去。

Either you leave this house or I'll call the police.

要么你离开这所房子,要么我叫警察。

当 either...or... 后的成分均为句子主语时,动词的形式应同 or 后的主语人称相一致,如:

Either he or you are to blame.

不是他的错就是你的错。

Either you or he is to blame.

不是你的错就是他的错。

4. ... but few of us have had the opportunity to find out.

have the opportunity to do /of doing sth. 表示"有机会做某事"之意。opportunity 通常指一般的"机会",或用来指对自己有利的机会。应注意 opportunity 同 possibility 在语义及结构用法

134

上的不同。possibility（可能性）。之后通常不使用动词不定式,且不同动词 have 搭配使用。它常与 there is 一同使用,其后跟随 of doing sth. 结构或由连词 that 引导的同位语从句,比较:

> *There's a possibility of his going to France.*
> *There's a possibility that he may be able to go to France.*
> 他有可能去法国。

> *He has the opportunity to go to France.*
> *He has the opportunity of going to France.*
> 他有机会去法国。

5. **Two men who recently spent five days on a coral island wished they had stayed there longer.**

had stayed there longer 在那儿再多呆些日子就好了。为虚拟语气结构。与动词 hope 不同,由于 wish 一般用于难以实现或不可能实现的愿望,在其后的宾语从句中通常使用虚拟语气结构:除过去完成时态外,一般按原应使用时态"推进一级"的形式构成,即一般现在时态→一般过去时态;现在进行时态→过去进行时态;一般过去时态→过去完成时态;现在完成时态→过去完成时态;表示将来时间概念的 be going to→表示过去将来时间概念的 be going to;表示将来时间情态概念的 will→表示过去将来时间情态概念的 would,如:

要表达内容 的时态条件	*wish* 后宾语从句中 虚拟语气的构成
a. *She's not nice.* 她不讨人喜欢。	*She wishes she was nice.* 她希望她能讨人喜欢。
b. *It's snowing heavily.* 雪下得很大。	*They wish it wasn't snowing heavily.* 他们希望雪没下那么大。

135

c. *The girl said some-*
thing unpleasant.

那个姑娘说了些令人
不愉快的话。

The girl wishes she hadn't
said it.

那个姑娘希望她没有说过
那样的话。

d. *He has lost his key.*

他把钥匙丢了。

He wishes he hadn't lost it.

他希望他没把它丢了。

e. *She's going to take an*
exam tomorrow.

她明天要考试。

She wishes she wasn't
going to do it.

她希望她不用去考试。

f. *The woman will talk*
all the time.

那个女人总说个没完。

They all wish she would
shut up.

他们希望她把嘴闭上。

在书面英语中,wish 后的宾语从句中可使用 I / he / she / it
were ... 结构,如:

She has to say she wishes the situation were a little better.

她不得不说她希望形势好一些。

要表达真实的将来愿望时,不能使用 wish...would... 结构,而
应使用 hope...will... 结构,如:

They all hope there will be a party tomorrow.

他们都希望明天有个聚会。

6. ... from the Virgin Islands to Miami to have it repaired.

动词 have + 宾语后的动词形式通常有 3 种:have + 宾语 + 动词
不定式(无 to);have + 宾语 + 动词-ing 结构;have + 宾语 + 动
词的过去分词。3 种结构中的每一种都可用来表达 3 种意思:

(1) 使/叫某人做某事;使某事得以做成,如:

The teacher had every student recite the text.

老师叫每个学生背课文。

Within five minutes, he had them all playing hide-and-
seek.

136

不到 5 分钟,他使他们所有人都玩起了捉迷藏。

He ordered them to get out of the store or he would had them all arrested .

他命令他们都滚出商店,否则他就叫警察把他们都抓起来。

(2) 经历一事件或行动,如:

It's lovely to have people say hello to you in the street .

人们在街上向你打招呼是件非常愉快的事。

I've never had such a thing happening to me before .

我以前还从未碰到过这种事。

The boy has his hair cut once a month .

那个男孩每月理一次发。

(3) 拒绝接受或允许某种局面(常与 will not 或 won't 连用),如:

They won't have him tell them what to do .

他们不会听凭他指挥的。

I won't have you speaking like that about your father .

我不会让你那样说你的父亲。

She'll never have her house turned into a market .

她决不会让她的家变成个市场的。

7. They quickly loaded a small rubber dinghy with food, matches, and cans of beer and rowed for a few miles across the Caribbean until they arrived at a tiny coral island.

(1) load...with... 把……装/摆到……,如:

The hostess loaded the table with delicacies .

女主人把餐桌上摆满了美味佳肴。

They loaded the ship with export goods .

他们把出口货物装到了船上。

有时还可用 load...with... 表达"使……承受/载……"之意,如:

The air is loaded with smoke and dirt.

空气中弥漫着烟雾和尘埃。

He went home loaded with honours.

他载誉归乡。

(2) until 直到。同 till 的意思一样。till 多用于口语, until 在口语和书面语中都使用。使用时,应注意以下几点:

1) until 和 till 只可用于表达时间,如:

He'll wait until/till he receives your letter.

他要一直等到收到你的来信。

当 until / till 作连词时,应用一般时态表达其后所要表达的将来时内容,如例中所示,不能用 he will receive... 取代句中 he receives... 形式。

不能用 until/till 表达指时间以外的"直到"含义,如不能用:

* *They walked until/till the edge of the forest.*

表达"他们一直走到树林边儿"之意,应当用 as far as 或 to。

2) until/till 为表达延续时间概念的连词/介词,因此当主句谓语动词为短暂时间概念的动词时,通常需用否定形式表达其肯定的内容,如:

He didn't leave until Friday morning.

直到星期五上午他才离开。

如上例所示,until/till 前所使用的否定结构只能用来表达根本未做出的动作,即 until 前的 leave 为未做出的动作,不可使用否定结构形式去表达做出的动作,如不能用:

* *She hadn't been waiting long until he returned.*

来表达"她没等多久他就回来了"之意,需用 before 替代句中的 until,构成:

She hadn't been waiting long before he returned.

3) 只能用 until/till 表达"现在正在进行而在将来某一时刻将

138

停止的事情或动作",不能像介词 by 那样被用来表达"将来某一时刻会发生或在此时刻之前会发生的事情或动作",如不能用:

　　* *Can you repair my radio until next Monday ?*

来表达"下星期一之前你能修好我的收音机吗?"之意,应用介词 by,再如:

> *Can I stay until/till the weekend ?*
> 我能呆到周末吗? (正在进行的动作)
>
> *Yes, but you'll have to leave by Monday midday at last.*
> 可以,但是你最迟必须在星期一中午以前离开。(将来某一时刻前发生的动作)

8．. . .and, as one of them put it 'ate like kings'.

(1) as 正如,像。为从属连词,引导一方式状语从句,用以说明人与人、物与物、动作与动作、状态与状态的相似之处。其后为一从句,其中有主语、谓语等,如:

　　She's behaving as her mother used to.

　　她的举止和她母亲过去一模一样。

as 也可用于介词词组之间,如:

　　In 1939, as in 1914, there was a great surge of patriotic feeling.

　　在 1939 年,同在 1914 年一样,爱国热情大大高涨。

在书面文体中,as 后有时跟倒装语序,如:

　　He was a novelist, as were most of his friends.

　　正像他的大多数朋友那样,他也是个小说家。

like 也可用来表达此义,但在一般情况下,like 为介词,其后使用名词或代词,如:

　　He's very like his brother.

　　他很像他哥哥。

但在美国英语的口语中,like 常代替 as 作连词,如:

Nobody loves you so dearly like I do , baby .

孩子,谁也不会像我这样疼你。

（2）put it 中,代词 it 指所说的话 ate like kings。这样使用时,根据
上下文内容,it 通常需有一特定的指代关系,如:

What I have seen here is so fantastic that it's hard for me
to put it in words .

我在这里的所见太离奇了,我很难用语言表达出来。

例句中 it 指前文中"What I have seen here"。

（3）eat like kings 吃得像国王一样好。常见与 eat like 搭配的名词
有 eat like a bird（吃得非常少）;eat like a horse（吃得非常多）
等。句中 ate 同 caught 为并列谓语,as one of them put it 为插
入语,对 ate 作进一步说明。

9. . . . both men were genuinely sorry that they had to leave.

that they had to leave 为原因状语从句,说明产生 sorry 的原因。
在一些表达个人对事件作出反应的形容词后,常可使用 that 引
导的原因状语从句。常见的这类形容词有 afraid(害怕的,担心
的)、ashamed(羞愧的)、content(满意的)、delighted(高兴的)、
disappointed(失望的)、glad(高兴的)、pleased(高兴的)、satisfied
(满意的)、surprised(惊奇的)等,如:

We're glad ∕ that ∕ you're all right .

你安然无恙,我们很高兴。

They were surprised that she could come .

她能来,他们感到惊奇。

语法 Grammar in use

wish 与 if only

在英语中可以用动词 wish 或短语 if only 表示愿望。两者往
往可以互换,但 if only 强调所希望的状况并不存在,而 wish 则表

140

示所希望的事情有可能发生。

在 wish 或短语 if only 后使用：

——过去时态表示现在；

——过去完成时态表示过去；

——与 would 和 could 连用时表示一般愿望或未来。

1. 指现在：

I wish/If only Tessa was/were here now.

要是特萨现在在这儿就好了。(单数代词或单数名词短语作主语时可用 *was* 或 *were*，但 *were* 比较正式，它使愿望显得更加渺茫)

wish 和 if only 后面还可以用过去进行时：

I wish/If only the sun was/were shining at this moment.

但愿此刻阳光灿烂。

2. 指过去：

I wish/If only you had let me know earlier.

要是你早点让我知道就好了。

3. 同 would 和 could 连用：

I wish you would/wouldn't.

我希望你要/不要。(因为这种愿望易于实现，所以一般不使用 *if only*)

I wish you wouldn't make so much noise.

我希望你别这么吵。

would 表示愿望，could 表示能够，在 I 和 we 后用 could 而不用 would，如：

If only we could be together.

要是我们能在一起就好了。

I wish I could be you.

我要是你就好了。

I wish he would come tomorrow.

141

我希望他明天会来。(即:我不知道他是否愿意来)

I wish he could come tomorrow.

但愿他明天能来。(即:我肯定他不能来)

4. 不能用 to wish + that 从句表示对将来的某一现实的愿望。如不能说:

　　* *I wish you'll have a nice time in Finland.*

而应说:

　　I hope you'll have a nice time in Finland.

　　I hope you have a nice time in Finland.

来表达"我希望你在芬兰过得愉快"之意。但可以使用"wish + 双宾语"结构表达对将来的某一现实的愿望,如:

　　May I wish you luck in writing your book.

　　祝你写书顺利。

　　I wish you every possible happiness.

　　我祝你万事如意。

📁　词汇学习　Word study

1. find (found, found)　*vt*.

(1) 找到:

　　I'm sure I've already paid this bill, but I can't find the receipt.

　　我肯定已经付过了这个账单,可是我找不到收据了。

注:find 用于此义时,后面不可跟 out。find out 后面不可跟具体名词。

(2) (偶然)发现,碰上:

　　Can you imagine what I've found in the attic?

　　你能想像我在阁楼上发现了什么吗?

(3) (out) 发现,找出:

142

What we have to do now is find out why the accident happened.

我们现在必须要做的是找出事故发生的原因。

（4）感觉到,认为,觉得:

The boy found it difficult to learn English.

那男孩认为学英语十分困难。

注:这类句子中,find 后面必须使用 it。不可说:

* *The boy found difficult to learn English.*

2．opposite

（1）*prep*. 在……对面:

There's a bank opposite my office.

我办公室的对面有家银行。

He drank off half his beer, still eyeing the Englishman opposite him.

他喝下去半杯啤酒,眼睛仍然盯着他对面的那个英国人。

（2）*n*. 相反的人或物,对立物,对立面:

He's the opposite of /to what I'd imagined.

他与我想像的恰恰相反。

如果相对照的人或物十分明显,可直接用 the opposite,而不需用 of,如:

It isn't bad news, It's just the opposite.

不是坏消息,恰恰是好消息。

（3）*adj*. 对面的;截然相反的,全然不同的,如:

We have opposite points of view.

我们的观点截然相反。

Too much pressure would produce overheating, whereas too little would produce the opposite result.

压力过大会产生过多的热量,而压力过小则产生相反的结果。

The house opposite is up for sale.

对面的房子要出售。

注:街对面的一所房子可以说 the house on the opposite side of the street 或 the house opposite。

（4）*adv.* 在对面:

They are building a supermarket opposite.

他们正在对面建造一座超级市场。

3. hardly *adv.* 几乎不,不十分:

He's so old now, he hardly works at all.

他现在太老了,几乎不工作了。

注:hardly 本身就是个否定副词,所以句子中不能再用否定词。如不能说:

* He's so old now, he doesn't hardly work at all.

The boy is eight years old and he can hardly read !

这男孩已经 8 岁了,可是他几乎不识字。

注:如与助动词或情态助动词连用,hardly 应放在助动词或情态助动词之后。不能说:

* *The boy is eight years old and he hardly can read !*

而可说:

John's got hardly any friends.

约翰几乎没有任何朋友。

hardly 可 与 when 连 用 表 示 一 件 事 紧 随 另 一 件 事 发 生。hardly 置于句首时句子要倒装。

The local police had hardly finished their examination when the CID arrived.

本地警察刚结束审问刑事调查部的人就到了。

Hardly had he got into the car when he began moaning.

他刚一进到车里就开始呻吟起来。

hardly ever 几乎从未:

144

We hardly ever go to the cinema these days.

这些日子我们几乎从不去电影院。

✍ 练习答案 Key to written exercises

1. 关键句型练习答案

A 1 *If you had told me earlier*, I would have telephoned you.

2 *If I were you*, I wouldn't do that.

3 *You will be disappointed if* it rains tomorrow.

4 *You would change your mind if* you could speak to him.

2. 难点练习答案

1 had   2 wouldn't   3 were't/wasn't

4 did   5 had   6 hadn't

3. 多项选择题答案

1 c   2 d   3 a   4 b   5 d   6 c

7 b   8 c   9 b   10 d   11 d   12 a

Lesson 13
'It's only me"
"是我，别害怕"

📖 **课文详注 Further notes on the text**

1. After her husband had gone to work, ...

过去完成时态常同表示时间状语的从属连词 after 一同使用，如：

> *After she'd written all her letters, she did some housework.*
> 她把信全写完后干了些家务活儿。

假如从句中先于主句谓语动词动作发生的那个动词动作很短暂，常可用一般过去时来代替过去完成时态，如：

> *After she put the cat out, it ran off into the bushes.*
> 她把猫放出去后，它就跑开钻进了灌木丛。

但是，当两个分句为同一主语时，更早发生的那个动作通常用过去完成时态来表示，如：

> *After he had seen her off, he locked the door and went to bed.*
> 他送走她后就锁上门，睡觉去了。

2. She was too excited to do..., for in the evening...

（1）too...to do... 太……以致不能……

（2）for 因为。是一个可用来表示因果关系的并列连词。

3. She intended to dress up as a ghost and as she had made her costume the night before, she was impatient to try it on.

（1）intend 打算。有关其用法及实例参见本课词汇学习部分。

（2）dress up as... 装扮成……，如：

146

The children dressed up as pirates and fought with each other in the yard .

孩子们装扮成海盗模样,在院子里相互厮打着。

(3) try on、have on 和 put on 这 3 个由动词＋副词构成的短语动词都有"穿"、"戴"之意,其后常接鞋、袜、衣、帽、手套之类的名词作宾语。宾语为代词时,如课文中那样,宾语需置于副词 on 之前。

1) try on 表示"试穿",可用于进行时,如:

Do you like them ? Try them on .

你喜欢这双吗? 穿上试试。

She's trying on a new hat .

她正在试一顶新帽子。

2) have on 表示状态或动作意味不强的持续性,不能用于进行时态,如:

They had their best suits on for the celebration .

他们穿着节日盛装去参加庆祝活动。

3) put on 动作意味很强,多用于祈使句中,一般不用于进行时态,如:

Take off your overcoat and put on your raincoat .

把大衣脱掉,穿上雨衣。

He put on his raincoat , went out and disappeared in the torrents of rain .

他穿上雨衣,走了出去,消失在倾盆大雨之中。

4．Though the costume consisted only of a sheet，it was very effective.

(1) 虽然 though 和 although 在作为从属连词引导让步状语从句这一点上用法基本相同,但两个词的具体使用中应注意其下述几点的区别:

1) though 多用于正式的口语或书面语中;although 用于各种

文体,如:

Although / Though the factory is small, its products are of very good quality.

这个工厂虽小,但产品质量却很高。

I'd like to go out for a walk, although / though it is a bit late.

虽然天有点儿晚了,但我还是很想出去走走。

2) 在如 even though(纵使,尽管) 和 as though(仿佛……似的) 短语性质的从属连词搭配中,even 和 as 只能同 though 而不能同 although 搭配使用,如:

Even though you make great progress in your work, you shouldn't be conceited.

即使你在工作中取得了很大进步,也不应骄傲自满。

(*even though* 同 *though* 的区别参见第 10 课课文注释 5)

He talks as though we were all stupid and he alone clever!

听他的口气就仿佛我们都是傻瓜,只有他一个人聪明似的!

3) though 可作副词,置于句子的末尾,表示"然而"、"不过"之意,但 although 则不能这样使用,如:

It was a quiet party; I had a good time, though.

这次聚会不热闹,不过我还是玩得挺痛快。

4) 与汉语的"虽然……但是……"用法不同,though 和 although 均不可同表示转折关系的连词 but(但是)连用,但可以用 nevertheless、still、yet 等副词对主句内容进行强调,如:

Though the water is deep, yet it is clear.

水虽深却清澈。

(2) consist of... 由……构成;包括。此短语动词为静态动词,同其他静态动词一样,通常不用进行时态表达(属于动态动词范畴的动词通常可用于进行时态)。其主语与宾语表明整体与部分的关系,如:

The apartment consists of three bedrooms and a kitchen.
那套房间包括 3 间卧室和 1 间厨房。

(3) only 仅,只。副词 only 在句中的位置很灵活,修饰主语时一般放在主语之前,如:

Only a woman like her could do such things.
只有像她那样的女人才能干这样的事情。

用 only 修饰句中的另一部分时,可将其置于句中动词之前,如:

He only talks like that when he's nervous.
只有紧张时他才那样说话。

They've only been to China once.
他们只去过中国一次。

由于它在动词前可以修饰主语外的其他任何成分,因此当主语成分为两个以上时,往往就可能使句子包含多种意义,如:

Our teacher only praised Tom in class.
往往可表达:

Our teacher did nothing else in class.
我们的老师在课堂上没做其他事情。

Our teacher didn't praise anybody else in class.
我们的老师在课堂上没表扬其他人。

It was in class that our teacher praised Tom.
我们的老师只是在课堂上表扬了汤姆。

在口语中,往往可以通过句子重音形式(即重读想要强调的部分),把含义准确地表达出来。虽然在书面语中也可通过上下文关系理解所要表达的含义,但也可将 only 直接置于所要修

149

饰的宾语、状语等成分之前,将意义更精确地表达出来,如:

Only she did some cotton-picking yesterday.

只有她昨天摘了点儿棉花。

She only did some cotton-picking yesterday.

她昨天不过摘了点儿棉花。

She did some cotton-picking only yesterday.

她只是昨天摘了棉花。

5. After putting it on, Mrs. Richards went downstairs.

分词短语可用于 after、before、on、once、since、until、when、whenever、while 等之后,同其一起构成时间状语,如:

After having made everybody angry, he went home.

他惹得每个人都生气后就回家了。

On being introduced to somebody, an Englishman often shakes hands.

英国人被介绍给对方时常和对方握手。

6. She wanted to find out whether it would be comfortable to wear.

在间接引语中,可用 whether 或 if 引导一个一般疑问句(即无疑问词引导的问句),如:

We're not quite sure whether/if we'll have enough time.

我们不敢完全肯定我们是否有足够的时间。

当为两种选择时常用 whether,特别是在书面表达中,如:

Some of them didn't know whether the plan would be carried out ahead of schedule or be put off.

他们中的一些人并不知道计划是否提前了还是被推迟了。

在动词 discuss(讨论)后只能用 whether,不能用 if,如:

They've discussed whether they should close the factory.

他们讨论了是否应关掉那家工厂。

在介词后或在带 to 的动词不定式前只能用 whether,如:

The question of whether she should go with us hasn't been

settled .

她是否和我们一块儿去的问题还未定下来。

Tom doesn't know whether to start the work or wait for them .

汤姆不知道是开始工作还是等等他们。

7. She knew that it must be the baker.

must 可用来表示"肯定"推论,如:

She must have some problem : *she keeps crying* .

她肯定有什么难处,她一直在哭。

疑问和否定推论需使用 can 或 can't,如:

Whom do you think this letter can come from ?

你认为这封信会是谁来的?

That can't be John——he promised to be here at 3 .

那不会是约翰——他答应 3 点到这儿。

must 与完成时态的动词不定式连用表示对过去事情或状况的肯定推论(疑问与否定推论用 can 和 can't),见第 1 课课文注释 12。

8. She had told him to come straight in if ever she failed to open the door and to leave the bread on the kitchen table.

(1) straight (笔)直的;直接地。此词的副词与形容词同形,如:

A straight road goes straight from one place to another .

一条直路从一处笔直地通往另一处。(第 1 个为形容词,第 2 个为副词)

课文 straight 作副词使用。

(2) if ever...中 if 为从属连词,引导一条件状语从句,ever 表示强调,可译作"在任何时候"。

(3) failed to open the door 不(能)去开门。fail + 动词不定式通常表示"不能"、"没有"或简单的否定含义,用法参见第 5 课课文注释 7。

(4) leave the bread on the kitchen 把面包放在厨房的桌上。此动词不定式同前面的 to come straight in(直接进来)为并列成分,同作动词 told 的宾语补足语。

9．**Not wanting to frighten the poor man,Mrs. Richards quickly hid in the small storeroom under the stairs.**

(1) Not wanting to frighten the poor man(因为或由于)不想去吓唬这个可怜的人。not wanting...构成分词短语的否定形式,作原因状语。分词短语可在句中起到原因状语的功能,如:

> *Being unable to help them in any other way,he gave them some money.*
>
> 由于不能以任何其他方式帮助他们,他就给了他们一些钱。
>
> *The doctor,not wishing to make her more nervous,didn't fully explain the seriousness of her condition.*
>
> 由于害怕她更紧张,大夫并未完全给她讲明她病情的严重性。

用分词短语表达原因状语时,应注意分词动作的逻辑主语与句中动词主语的一致性。

(2) under the stairs 楼梯下的。此介词短语在句中作定语,修饰 storeroom。有关用作定语的介词短语参见第1课课文注释1。

10．**She heard the front door open and heavy footsteps in the hall.**
open 为不带 to 的动词不定式,作动词 heard 的宾语补足语,heavy footsteps 作动词 heard 的宾语。

11．**She tried to explain the situation,saying 'It's only me,'...**
saying 'It's only me' 说了声"别怕,是我!"此分词短语作方式状语。有关作方式状语的分词短语用法参见第2课课文注释5及第6课课文注释10。

12．**The man let out a cry and jumped back several paces.**
let out a cry 大叫一声。这里 let out 表示"发出(声音)"之意。通常用一般时态表达此意义,如:

He let out a cry of pain as the nail went into his foot.

钉子扎进他脚里时,他疼得大叫一声。

13. **When Mrs. Richards walked towards him, he fled, slamming the door behind him.**

slamming the door behind him 把门砰地一声关上。此现在分词短语作时间状语,说明 fled 动作发生的时间。有关用法参见第 2 课课文注释 4 及第 5 课课文注释 9。

📖 语法 Grammar in use

形容词 + 动词不定式

1. 英语中许多形容词之后可跟动词不定式,表达各种含义。常见这样使用的形容词有 glad(高兴)、pleased(愉快的)、kind(仁慈的)、brave(勇敢的)、careless(不小心的)、generous(慷慨的)、good(好的)、polite(客气的)、right(正确的)、wrong(错误的)、rude(粗鲁的)、selfish(自私的)、silly(愚蠢的)等,如:

   She is easy to get on with.

   与她相处很容易。

   如上一例所示,当动词与介词连用构成"形容词 + 动词不定式"句子结构中的动词不定式时,常将其置于句尾。

2. 更常见的形式是把 it 作为先行主语。此用法中,用 of 短语表示所指的人。如果所指比较明确,可将此 of 短语省略,如:

   It was kind of her to help us.

   她真好,帮助了我们。

   It was silly (of us) to believe him.

   (我们)相信了他,真愚蠢。

3. enough 和 too 常与"形容词 + 动词不定式"结构连用。enough 放在形容词之后时,表示"达到必要的程度",如:

   He is strong enough to lift it.

他很壮,完全可以把它举起来。

He is too weak to lift it.

他太弱,举不起它。

The baby's too much for her to cope with.

照看这个婴儿对她来说可太难了。

📁　词汇学习　**Word study**

1. intend *vt.*

(1) 打算,计划:

> *He intended to come to our house yesterday.*
>
> 他昨天想来我家。
>
> *He had really intended staying longer.*
>
> 他确实曾打算多呆一段时间。

(2) 指望,打算使……成为:

> *The fund is intended for emergency use.*
>
> 这笔基金专供应急之用。
>
> *Everything they do and say is intended to promote sales.*
>
> 他们所做和所说的一切都是为了促销。

(3) 意指:

> *What do you intend by saying so?*
>
> 你说此话什么意思?
>
> *I don't think he intended any harm.*
>
> 我并不认为他有什么恶意。

2. hear (heard, heard)　*vt.*

(1) 听见:

> *I heard what you said.*
>
> 我听见了你说的话。
>
> *Below me I could hear the roar of a waterfall.*

我听到下面瀑布的咆哮声。

hear后面跟动词-ing结构时,表示听到该动作的一部分,或该动作的持续发生,如:

Did you hear him leaving ?

你听到他离开的声音了吗?

而hear后跟不带to的动词不定式时,通常表示听见整个动作的发生,如:

I heard him dash into the bathroom.

我听到他冲进了洗澡间。

当hear用于被动语态时,其后则使用带to的动词不定式结构,如:

He was heard to say,'I won't stand this behaviour any longer.'

有人听到他说:"我可再也忍受不了这种行为了。"

(2)听说,听到,得知:

We are happy to hear that the peace treaty has been signed by the two sides.

听说双方签署了和平条约我们十分欣慰。

(3)听(演讲、音乐会、广播等):

We heard some wonderful music at last night's concert.

在昨天晚上的音乐会上,我们听到了一些优美的音乐。

听现场音乐会要用hear,而不用listen to;表示习惯性动作时,可用listen to,也可用hear,如:

I listen to/hear the 9 o'clock news every evening without fail.

我一天不误地听晚上9点的新闻。

✍ 练习答案 Key to written exercises

1．关键句型练习答案

A　See text.

B　1　I'm late already so I *must go* now. I *must be* at the office by nine. (necessity)

Compare: John is late. He *must be* in a traffic jam. (deduction)

2　You *mustn't speak* to your father like that. I've written to you but you *needn't answer* my letter.

3　I was late for work because I *had to go* to the bank. I *ought to have told* you, but I forgot.

2．难点练习答案

A　1　glad to hear　　2　sorry to have　　3　sad to hear

B　1　I'm *pleased to* tell you that you have been promoted.

2　We're *proud to* announce that we've just have a son.

3　I'm *delighted to* be here again.

4　I was *shocked to* learn that she is in hospital.

3．多项选择题答案

1	d	2	c	3	c	4	c	5	b	6	b
7	b	8	c	9	a	10	d	11	a	12	b

156

Lesson 14
A noble gangster
贵族歹徒

📖　**课文详注　Further notes on the text**

1. There was a time when the owners of shops and businesses in Chicago had to pay large sums of money to gangsters in return for 'protection'.

（1）when 为关系副词,在这里引导一定语从句(即从 when 至
　　'protection'部分),置后修饰名词 time。在指时间或地点的名
　　词之后,可用 when 和 where 表达定语从句中 at which 或 in
　　which 的含义,如:

　　　　*Can you suggest a time when ／ at which it will be
　　　　convenient for both of us to meet ?*
　　　　你能否提出一个对我们双方都方便的会面时间吗?
　　　　*She knows a wood where ／ in which we can find wild
　　　　strawberries .*
　　　　她知道一处我们可在那儿找到野草莓的树林。

　　只有当指时间或地点的名词／先行词在从句中起到时间状语
　　或地点状语作用时,才可使用关系副词 when 或 where 引导的
　　定语从句,如:

　　　　*That's the time（which）she's found to be convenient for
　　　　both of us to meet .*
　　　　那是她所能找到的对我们双方都方便的会面时间。
　　　　*He told her the hidden place（which）the children found
　　　　while playing hide-and-seek .*

他告诉了她孩子们玩捉迷藏时发现的那个藏身之处。

虽然上两例中的先行词指时间和地点,但由于它们在定语从句中起到的是宾语作用(即指 she's found the time to be convenient for both of us to meet 和 the children found the hidden place while playing hide-and-seek),因此只能使用关系代词 which / that 引导这两个定语从句。

(2) 在英语中,可以用 have (got) to(不得不,得⋯⋯)和 must(必须)谈论义务,但它们的意思不同。must 多用来指说话者或受话者主观认为"有必要"去做的事情;have (got) to 一般用来指"外界"(客观)的义务要求去做的事情,比较:

I must try to finish it in time.

我必须尽量按时完成这件工作。(我要求自己这样做)

I have to finsh it in time.

我不得不按时完成这件工作。(客观或他人要求我这样做)

由于情态助动词 must 无其过去形式,因此讲过去的一项义务时,通常用 had to 来表达,如:

When your mother was your age she had to get up before 5 every morning.

你母亲在你这个岁数时,每天早晨 5 点以前就得起床。

但 must 可用在间接引语中,以说明一种过去的义务,如:

The boss told him he must make a decision before the meeting.

老板对他说,他必须在会前做出决定。

此外,must 同 have (got) to 的否定式所表达的意思极为不同,试比较:

You mustn't tell her about it.

你不许告诉她这件事。(= *Don't tell her about it.*)

You don't have to tell her about it.

158

你不必把此事告诉她。(= *You can if you like to but it isn't necessary*.)

但在英国英语中常用 needn't 形式而非 don't have to 或 haven't got to 形式。

有关 have to 与 have got to 的用法与不同,参见第 12 课课文注释 2。

(3) large sums of money 大笔的钱。sum 作"款项"、"金额"解时,既可用单数形式,也可用复数形式,用单数形式时表示"一笔款项"之意,如:

The government has laid out a large sum of money in purchasing safety devices.

政府拨了一大笔钱购买安全设备。

(4) in return(for...) 作为(……的)回报;作为(……的)交换。通常指被看作有同等价值或同等意义上的回报/交换,如:

What did he do in return for your kindness?

对你的好意,他做了些什么呢?

They have helped us a lot, but we really feel sorry that we have nothing to give them in return.

他们给予了我们极大的帮助,但我们真为拿不出什么来报答他们而感到遗憾。

2. ...the gangsters would quickly put a man out of business by destroying his shop.

(1) put...out of business 使……失败/垮台等,如:

This slow trade will soon put me out of business.

这项进展缓慢的交易很快就会让我破产。

(2) by destroying his shop 用捣毁他的商店的方法。在句中作方式状语,修饰动词 put。介词 by 在这里为"以……方式"之意。

3. Obtaining 'protection money' is not a modern crime.

Obtaining 'protection money' 榨取"保护金"。为动名词短语,

159

在这里作主语。由于动名词(动词-ing 形式)保留着动词与名词的基本特征,因此在使用时,一方面就像动词那样,其后可跟随宾语、状语等(动名词同其后跟随的其他成分一起构成动名词短语),而另一方面,则又可像名词那样,在句中可以起到如主语、宾语、补语的作用,如:

Beating a child will do more harm than good.

打孩子弊多利少。(作主语)

She hates writing letters.

她讨厌写信。(作宾语)

Her job is taking care of children.

她的工作是照看孩子。(作主语补足语)

4. **As long ago as the fourteenth century, an Englishman, Sir John Hawkwood, made the remarkable discovery that people would rather pay large sums of money than have their life work destroyed by gangsters.**

(1) as long ago as 追溯到……,早在……作时间状语,说明动作 made 发生的时间,如:

   I knew him as long ago as the year 1960.

   我早在 1960 年就认识他了。

   在使用中应注意:在短语后表示时间、年代的词前不能使用介词 in;不可将 ago 置于表示时间、年代的词之后;在使用中,应将 as long ago as...同引导条件状语从句的从属连词 as long as...(只要)区分开来。

(2) would rather...than... 宁可……也不……此结构中的 than 是连词,引导省略部分内容的状语从句,如:

   We're all sure she would rather die than give up.

   我们都深信她一定会宁死不屈。(此句实际为 *We're all sure she would rather die than she would give up* 的省略形式)

160

用 prefer to...rather than...结构也可表达 would rather...than...结构的意义,如:

She prefers to work rather than remain idle.

她宁愿工作而不愿闲着。

但只有当 prefer 后的宾语为动词不定式时,才可在其后使用 rather than 结构,如 prefer 后的宾语为名词或动名词形式时,只能用于 prefer...to...结构。有关动词 prefer 的用法参见第 8 课课文注释 8。

(3) have their life work destroyed by gangsters 将他们毕生的心血毁于歹徒之手。有关"have + 宾语 + 动词形式"的用法参第 12 课课文注释 6。

5. He soon made a name for himself and came to be known to the Italians as Giovanni Acuto.

(1) make a name for oneself 使自己成名。多用于口语中,如:

It's difficult to make a name for yourself on the stage, where the competition is so fierce.

你要在舞台上出人头地很难,那儿的竞争太激烈了。

(2) came to be known 渐渐被知晓/称作。come/get + 动词不定式结构表示一种情况的变化过程,表示出"逐渐"的含义。在汉语译文中,有时并不一定译出来,如:

She will come to be ashamed of what she has done today.

总有一天她会为她今日所做所为而感到羞愧。

Soon they're getting to have a better understanding of the problem.

他们对这一问题逐渐有了较深的了解。

be known to sb. 为某人所知。当 to 后为"某地"时则表示"闻名于某地"之意,如:

Your neighbour's known to the police, so you'd better keep an eye on him.

161

你的邻居是警察熟悉的人物，所以你最好对他留神点。

The family is quite known to the area.

这家人在这一地区很出名。

在 be known 后还可以使用介词 as 和 for，虽然都可用来表示"以……而出名"的意思，但它们在含义和用法上有所不同。be known as...后的介词宾语与主语为同位语成分，而 be known for...后的介词宾语则为主语的所属内容。

1）当主语为表示人的名词时，be known as...表示"以某种身份而出名"，而 be known for...则表示"以某种技能、作品或特征等而出名"，比较：

> *Edison was known as a great inventor.*
>
> 爱迪生以一位伟大的发明家而著称。
>
> *Edison was known for his inventive talent.*
>
> 爱迪生以其发明天赋而闻名。

2）当主语为表示地点的名词时，be known as...表示"以……的产地或地方而出名"，be known for...则表示"以……特产而出名"，比较：

> *The area is known as a green tea producing region.*
>
> 这个地区是以绿茶产地而出名。
>
> *The area is known for its green tea.*
>
> 这个地区以其绿茶而闻名。

3）当主语为事物名词时，be known as...表示"以……形式而出名"，be known for...则表示"以……内容、特征、价值等而为人所知"，比较：

> *This book is known as a reference book.*
>
> 这本书作为参考用书使用。
>
> *This book is known for its practical usage.*
>
> 这本书以其实用性而为人所知。

句中 be known to the Italians as Giovanni Acuto 是 be known

to...和 be known as...两种结构的组合形式。

6. Whenever the Italian city-states were at war with each other, Hawkwood used to hire his soldiers to princes who were willing to pay the high price he demanded.

(1) whenever 每次,每当。除句中之意外,引导时间状语的从属连词 whenever 还可用来表示"无论什么时候"、"任何时候"之意,如:

Whenever she saw him she felt nervous.

她只要见到他就感到紧张。

(2) be at war with... 与……处于战争状态。

(3) be willing to do 愿意做,如:

I was still willing to marry her.

我仍愿意同她结婚。

He's quite willing to pay the price I ask.

他很乐意照我索要的价付钱。

7. In times of peace, when business was bad, Hawkwood and his men would march into a city-state and, after burning down a few farms, would offer to go away if protection money was paid to them.

(1) in time(s) of 在……时期,如:

He was still enthusiastic for the scheme even in times of difficulty.

即使在困难的时期,他仍对那项计划很热情。

(2) when business was bad 和 after burning down a few farms 在句子中作时间状语,分别说明发生 march 与 offer 动作的时间。

(3) if 如果,为从属连词,引导条件状语从句。if 可用来引导两类不同的条件状语从句:真实性条件状语从句和非真实性条件状语从句。这里仅就前者用法举例说明。由 if 引导的条件状语从句既可置于句首,也可置于句尾,并可使用多种时态,如:

If that was Mary, why didn't she stop and say hello?

假如那人是玛丽,她怎么也不停下来打个招呼?

Give my love to Lawrence if you see him.

如果见到劳伦斯,请代我问个好。

但在 if 从句中应使用一般时态表达将来时的内容,如:

If you've got exams tomorrow, why aren't you studying?

如果你明天考试,现在为什么还不学习?

She said if she had enough money the next year, she would go to Japan.

她说如果明年有足够的钱,她将去日本。

此外,在 if 从句中既可使用 some(包括 something、somewhere 等),也可使用 any(包括 anything、anywhere 等)。使用 some 或 some 结构的词时,"肯定"的意味略强些,但区别并非很大,如:

She'll go with us if she has some/any spare time.

假如她有空闲,她会同我们一起去。

If I find it somewhere/anywhere, I'll tell you.

如果我在哪儿找到它,我会告诉你的。

8. Hawkwood made large sums of money in this way.

(1) made large sums of money 赚了大笔的钱,make money 赚钱,如:

It's really an interesting occupation, but you'll never make money at it.

这的确是个有趣的行当,但你绝不会赚钱。

(2) in this way 用这种方法/方式。为介词短语,作方式状语,修饰 made。在口语中,此短语中的 in 经常省略。同样,在类似介词短语中,如 in the same way(以相同的方式)、in another way(以另一种方式)中的介词 in 也常被省略,如:

I did it (in) the same way he had done it.

164

我用和他相同的方法做的这件事。

She's managed to have the work done (in) quite another way.

她用完全不同的方法做好了这件工作。

但在强调方式状语时,如将其置于句首位置时,介词 in 不可省略,如:

Wash them in soap water. In this way you can get rid of the dirty marks.

把它们放在肥皂水中洗涤,这样你就可以除去这些污迹了。

9. In spite of this, the Italians regarded him as a sort of hero.

(1) In spite of this 尽管如此。介词短语作状语,修饰整个句子。this 指上文中所述内容。

(2) a sort of 类似……的人物/东西,如:

A sort of coughing noise could be heard in the next room.

能听到隔壁房间有类似咳嗽的声音。

10. When he died at the age of eighty, the Florentines gave him a state funeral and had a picture painted which was dedicated to the memory of...

(1) at the age of 在……岁时。

(2) be dedicated to... 为 dedicate...to... 的被动语态形式,作"(被)奉献给……"解。这一结构中的 to 为介词,后需使用名词、代词或动名词,不可使用动词不定式,如:

The monument is dedicated to the memory of those who died in the defence of the country.

这座纪念碑为纪念为国捐躯者而建造。

Mornings were dedicated to reading and afternoons to writing. That's the way of his life.

上午一心读书,下午专事写作,那就是他的生活方式。

would rather 与 would sooner(宁愿)

1．would rather/would sooner + 没有 to 的动词不定式

表示个人的选择,或谈论他人的选择,可以指现在:

> *I'd rather work on the field than work in a factory.*
>
> 我宁愿在田里干活,不愿在工厂工作。
>
> *He'd rather (not) go by car.*
>
> 他宁可(不)坐汽车。

也可指过去:

> *If she'd had the chance, she'd rather have lived 100 years ago.*
>
> 如果可能,她宁愿生活在 100 年前。

作否定回答时,可省略动词不定式:

> *Are you coming with us?*
>
> 你和我们一起去吗?
>
> *I'd rather not.*
>
> 我不想去。

可以用 far 和(very) much 修饰 would rather/sooner,如:

> *I'd far / much rather be happy than rich.*
>
> 我宁可要幸福,不要财富。

2．would rather/sooner + 从句

would rather/sooner 可以跟一个自身带主语的从句,其主语与主句的主语不同,用以表示"宁愿某人做什么或是什么",如:

> *I'd rather/sooner Jack left on an earlier train.*
>
> 我宁愿杰克乘前一班火车走。

此结构中,从句用过去时指现在或将来:

> *I'd rather she sat next to me.*

我宁愿她挨着我坐。

表示否定的选择时,可以用 didn't 表示现在或将来含义,以避免主动词的重复,如:

You always go without me and I'd rather you didn't.

你总是不带我去,我可不愿意你这样。

用过去完成时指过去:

I'd rather he hadn't told me about it.

我宁愿他没有告诉我这件事。

其否定式用 hadn't,如:

Katie went by car and I'd rather she hadn't.

凯蒂是坐汽车去的,我倒宁愿她不坐汽车去。

此结构中,动词不定式常用被动形式:

I'd rather be told the truth than be lied to.

我宁愿听真话,不愿被欺骗。

📁 词汇学习 Word study

1. pay(paid,paid)

(1) *vt.* 支付,付钱给:

    How much did you pay for that dress?

    那条裙子你付了多少钱?

注:为某件东西或某项服务付钱用 pay for。

    How much did you pay the plumber?

    你付给水管工多少钱?

    Let me pay you for the repair.

    我来付你修理费。

注:付某人钱用 pay sb.,为某事付某人钱时用 pay sb. for sth.。但付账单时用 pay a bill,如:

    I have paid the bill.

我已付了账单。

(2) *vi*. 付款,交款:

I'll pay by cheque.

我将用支票付款。

Willie paid for the drinks.

威利付了饮料钱。

(3) *n*. 工资,薪金:

The pay is good.

酬金不少。

She lost 3 weeks' pay.

她失去了 3 周的薪水。

2. offer

(1) *vt*. 给予,提供:

No alcohol was offered at the party.

晚会上不提供含酒精的饮料。

They offered him one thousand dollars for his horse.

他们出价 1,000 美元要买他的马。

(2) *vt*. 表示愿意,提议:

I offered to answer any questions they might have.

我愿意回答他们可能提出的任何问题。

(3) *n*. 提供(物),提议:

He accepted my offer.

他接受了我的提议。

I made him an offer of food and drink.

我主动提出给他吃的和喝的。

3. regard *vi*.

(1)(as) 看待,认为,把……看作:

I regard her as the best person for the job.

我认为她是干这项工作的最佳人选。

Parents are regarded as being responsible for the control of their children .

人们认为父母有责任管教他们的子女。

注:regard + 宾语 + as 结构中,as 后可跟名词,也可跟动词的 -ing形式,但不能跟动词不定式,如不可说:

* *Parents are regarded as to be . . .*

(2)尊重,敬重,看重:

I regard Mr . Smith highly .

我很尊重史密斯先生。

✍ 练习答案 Key to written exercises

1. 关键句型练习答案

A   See text.

B   1   He leaves the room any time he wants to *have a smoke* .

2   If you *have got a headache* (you *have a headache*) , you should take an aspirin.

3   I had some damage to my car, but I *have* now *had* it *repaired* .

2. 难点练习答案

1   go   2   left   3   didn't speak

4   not speak   5   settled   6   didn't tell

3. 多项选择题答案

1	b	2	b	3	a	4	a	5	c	6	b
7	a	8	c	9	b	10	d	11	d	12	c

Lesson 15
Fifty pence worth of trouble
五十便士的麻烦

📖　课文详注　**Further notes on the text**

1. Fifty pence worth of trouble

worth of 值一定金额数量的;相当于特定单位数量的。worth
为名词,常同介词 of 搭配使用,构成以上意义。有关 worth 的
其他用法参见第 6 课课文注释 11。

2. Children always appreciate small gifts of money.

appreciate 欣赏;领会;感激。后接名词、代词或动名词,不可使
用动词不定式,如:

Not many of us can appreciate Beijing opera.
我们当中没有几个能真正欣赏京剧。

The players really appreciate having time to relax.
运动员极为珍惜能有空休息一下。

appreciate 通常指对事物的深刻理解后的"欣赏"。文中使用了
"大"词表达出一般意义上的 like(喜欢)含义。暗示出"孩子们
深知其(零花钱之)所用"基础上的"喜欢"。appreciate 不用于
表达一般意义上的(即非来自较深刻理解或领悟意义上的)"欣
赏",如一般不用:

＊ *Most of us didn't appreciate Professor X's lecture.*

＊ *I appreciated very much this film.*

在上述对 appreciate 一词误用的两个例句中,应使用 like 或
enjoy。

3. ... provide a regular supply of pocket money, ...

170

provide 提供,provide a regular supply of 定期供应/提供,如:

The government used to provide a regular supply of relief grain for that backward area.

过去政府总是定期向那一落后地区提供救济粮。

如 appreciate 一样,这里使用了"大"词来表达 give(them) pocket money regularly 按时给(他们)零花钱的一般意义,以达到幽默的效果。

4.With some children,small sums go a long way.

(1) with 对于,就……来说。介词 with 可用来表示与所谈话题看起来相关的事物,如:

Everything was going on well with them.

(对)他们(来说)一切都进行得很顺利。

With those who don't hope to make any progress,it's the same.

对那些不思进取的人来说都一样。

句中将作状语的介词短语 with some children 提前,起到强调和使上下文显得更为紧凑的作用。介词 to 也常用来表示"对于"、"就……而言"之意,如:

He's awfully nice to us.

他对我们真是太好了。

To him it's really a great blow.

对他来说,这的确是一个巨大的打击。

但这里不能用 to 取代 with,否则会造成同动词 go 搭配后产生的歧义(即 Small sums go a long way to some children)。

(2) go a long way 耐用,经用。通常用来指食物或钱财能维持很长时间,如:

The food the two men saved from their sinking boat could really go a long way.

那两个人从他们正在下沉的船上打捞的食物的确能维持

不少时日。

此外,go a long way 还常被用来表示"有很大作用"、"大有帮助"之意,如:

Goodwill and cooperation can go a long way to(wards) smoothing your way to the success.

好的意愿与协作有益于你顺利取得成功。

5. **If fifty pence pieces are not exchanged for sweets,...**

exchange...for... 以(用)……换(取)……,如:

I'd like to exchange this dress for one in a larger size.

我想把这套裙子换号大些的。

如用介词 with 则表示"同……换……"之意,如:

Mary exchanged seats with John.

玛丽同约翰换了座位。

6. **Only very thrifty children manage to fill up a money box.**

fill up 填满,如只用动词 fill,则仅表达"填"之意。副词 up 同某些动词搭配使用时,通常表示出"完全"、"彻底"之意,如 tear up(撕碎)、eat up(吃光)、drink up(喝光)、use up(用光)等,如:

Drink up, then I'll refill your glass.

把杯子里的水喝光,然后我再给你倒上。

Who's used up all the milk? There's none to put in my coffee!

谁把牛奶都倒光了? 我没有加到咖啡里的牛奶了!

7. **For most of them, fifty pence is a small price to pay for a nice big bar of chocolate.**

(1) for most of... 对大部分/多数……来说。介词 for 在这里表示"就……而言"、"对……来说"之意,如:

He's a bit short for a basketball player.

就篮球运动员而言,他矮了点儿。

(2) pay for 为……付钱;付……钱。为动词加介词型短语动词,后

172

接表示物件或东西的名词,或接 wh-引导的宾语从句,如:

> *Do you have to pay for their schooling?*
> 你得为他们上学付学费吗?
>
> *Have you paid for these books?*
> 你付这些书的书钱了吗?
>
> *Have you paid for what you've eaten?*
> 你吃这些东西付钱了吗?

不应将表示物件的名词直接置于动词 pay 后作宾语,如不应说:

> * *I have paid the book.*

表达"我已付了这本书的钱"之意时而应在 paid 之后加上介词 for。此外,pay for 还可用于借喻中,表示"得到……报应"、"因……而受到惩罚"之意,如:

> *Sooner or later you'll have to pay for your carelessness.*
> 早晚有一天你会因粗心大意而自食其果的。

8. Very few of the fifty pence pieces and pound coins I have given him have found their way there.

have found their way there 被放进那里边,find one's way to... 常用来表达:

1) 设法到达;努力达到,如:

> *Take it easy. She's able to find her way to your house by herself.*
> 放心吧,她能自己找到你家的。

2) (由于外界力量而)进入;流入,如:

> *That beautifully-knitted carpet found its way to the auction room.*
> 那块编织美丽的地毯最终被送进了拍卖行。
>
> *That long river finds its way to the sea.*
> 那条大河流入大海。

173

3) (意外地)被发现在,如:

> *Here are your cigarettes in the refrigerator.*
>
> 这不,你的烟在冰箱里。
>
> *Good God! How on earth did they find their way there?*
>
> 天啊! 它们怎么竟会跑到这儿呢?

9 . ... and advised him to save it.

advise...to do... 劝/让……做……,如:

> *Some of the consultants strongly advised him to accept the suggestion.*
>
> 有些顾问竭力劝他接受这一建议。

10 . Instead he bought himself fifty pence worth of trouble.

instead 而,却,为副词,常用于句首或句末。用于句首时,起连接上下文的作用,通常表达出与前一句相反的或不同的情况。用于句末时,常用于两个独立的句子或一并列句中后一句的句尾,表达"本应……却……"的含义,如:

> *He never keeps his mind on his work. Instead, he plays all day.*
>
> 他从不安心工作,整天就是玩。
>
> *She had expected him to say 'Yes', but he said 'No' instead.*
>
> 她原以为他会答应,没想到他却没答应。
>
> *I was supposed to go myself, but she went instead since I was tied up with so many things.*
>
> 我本想亲自去,但许多事缠身,她就去了。

11 . ... and then disappeared down a drain.

down 向……底部。这里作介词,同 a drain 构成介词短语作状语,修饰 disappeared,意即"掉进了阴沟里",再如:

> *They went in high spirits down the mountain.*

174

他们情绪高涨地下了山。

The old man climbed down the ladder with his legs trembling.

老人颤抖着双腿爬下了梯子。

12. . . . and what is more, he could not get his arm out.

what is more 而且;更糟的是。作插入语,用以通过新的附加信息对前文所述作进一步的强调。应注意的是 what is more 为一固定结构,用于任何时态结构的句子中均需使用 is,如:

'What's more', he added, 'There are no signs of any change.'

"而且,"他接着说,"没有丝毫要改变的迹象。"

They missed the train, and what is more, they lost all their belongings.

他们不仅误了火车,更糟的是,他们把行李还都丢了。

13. . . . because the lady who owns the sweet shop heard about his trouble and rewarded him with a large box of chocolates.

(1) heard about 听说,用以表达间接地如通过第三者、书报等听说有关某人或某事的一些话,如:

We've heard of /about the arrival of some new teachers.

我们听说来了几位新老师。

Have you ever heard of such a thing!

你哪儿听说过这种事!(气愤)

(2) reward 报答,酬谢。通常指因做了某一具体事情而得到报答或酬谢。其后只能以指人或人的行为的词语作宾语。报答或酬谢的物品前需使用介词 with;如为报答或酬谢的原因则使用介词 for,如:

Those who find it will be rewarded with 100 dollars.

谁找到它将得到 100 美元的酬金。

I rewarded her with 10 dollars for taking me to the

station .

因为她把我领到了车站,我付给她 10 美元作为酬谢。

由于本文以幽默文体写成,作者对 George 用 50 便士引来的这次麻烦所得到的回报感到惊奇,因此这里的 reward 具有某种反语味道,即"还倒赏给了他"之意。

🗐 语法 Grammar in use

could,was able to 和 managed to

1. could 和 was able to 都可用来表示过去的能力,如:

    He could/was able to swim five miles when he was a boy.
    他小时候能游 5 英里。

2. was able to do sth. 表示不但有能力做某事,而且做到了,但 could 只表示有能力,但并不表示做到了。因此在下列句中不能用 could 取代 was able to:

    After treatment he was able to return to work .
    经治疗后他得以回去工作。

3. couldn't 和 wasn't able to 通常可以互换:

    I couldn't / wasn't able to finish the job yesterday.
    昨天我未能把工作做完。

    可以用 could have done sth. 表示过去有能力做某事但没有做,如:

    You could have been a little bit tidier .
    你完全可以稍微整齐一些。

4. managed to do sth. 表示设法做成了某事,如:

    I managed to finish the job yesterday.
    昨天我设法完成了这项工作。

📁 词汇学习 Word study

1. appreciate *vt.*

(1) 向……表示感谢,感激:

> *We appreciate your help.*
>
> 对你的帮助我们表示感谢。
>
> *We appreciate having such good friends at this difficult time.*
>
> 我们非常感激在这么困难的时候有这么好的朋友。

(2) 欣赏,赏识:

> *They really appreciate the peace and quiet of rural Wales.*
>
> 他们确实欣赏威尔士平和、宁静的农村生活。

(3) (充分)意识到,体会:

> *I appreciate the reasons for your anxiety.*
>
> 我知道令你焦急不安的原因。

2. buy (bought, bought) *vt.*

(1) 买,买得:

> *They bought us a present / they bought a present for us.*
>
> 他们给我们买了一件礼物。
>
> *Let me buy you a drink.*
>
> 我请你喝杯饮料。

(2) 赢得,获得:

> *They tried to buy time by saying that it would be ready next week.*
>
> 他们说下周事情就会办妥,以此来赢得时间。

(3) 行贿,贿赂:

> *They could not believe that the official was so easily bought.*

177

他们简直不敢相信这样轻而易举就收买了那个官员。

3．gather *vt*.

（1）聚集，集拢：

> They managed to gather hundreds of people for the demonstrations.
>
> 他们为示威召集了成千上万的人。

（2）采摘，收集：

> The children are out in the field gathering wild flowers.
> 孩子们在外面的田野里采野花。
>
> It's taken me a lifetime to gather all these books.
> 收集这些书花费了我一生的时间。

✍ 练习答案 Key to written exercises

1．关键句型练习答案

A　See text.

B　1　John is very busy, but I *was able to* speak to him on the phone yesterday.

　　2　*Could* you help me with this suitcase please?

　　3　I got a taxi and just *managed to* catch the last train home.

2．难点练习答案

1 save	2 sailed	3 buttoned/did	4 Eat
5 went	6 wrapped	7 wind	8 do

3．多项选择题答案

1 c	2 d	3 a	4 b	5 b	6 d
7 a	8 c	9 a	10 c	11 b	12 b

178

Lesson 16
Mary had a little lamb
玛丽有一头小羔羊

📖 **课文详注 Further notes on the text**

1. She kept it tied to a tree in a field during the day...

(1) 动词 keep 的宾语后可使用形容词、现在分词和过去分词这样的结构,来表达"使……处于某种状态、条件、姿势"等意义的句子中,如:

She's holding her arms like that to keep her warm.
她那样抱着双臂以使自己暖和些。

All the night we were kept awake by wolves.
狼使我们整夜无法入睡。

I'm sorry to keep you waiting long.
对不起,让你久等了。

It seemed that those doors were kept permanently locked.
那些门似乎总是锁着。

在这样的结构中,宾语后的形容词、现在分词和过去分词作动词 keep 的宾语补足语。

(2) tie...to... 把……拴/系在……,如:

The cowboy jumped off his horse, tied it to a tree and went into the inn.
牛仔跳下马,把它拴在一棵树上,走进了小酒店。

2. ...so it was obvious that the lamb had been stolen.

句中 it 为先行词,起到形式主语的作用,that 引导的从句在句中为逻辑主语。有关先行词 it 的用法参见第 1 课课文注释 13。

3. **When Dimitri came in from the fields, his wife told him what had happened.**

(1) came in 回到家里。副词 in 着重"进入"之意。

(2) what 为关系代词,在此用来引导一宾语从句。由 what 引导的名词性从句同...that/which 引导的定语从句往往可用来表达同样的语义。试比较:

> *The parents gave her everything that she needed.*
> *The parents gave her what she needed.*
> 父母亲给她所需的一切。

> *Can you follow the words that/which she says?*
> *Can you follow what she says?*
> 你能听明白她说的什么吗?

that/which 为引导定语从句的关系代词,分别代表各自句中的 everything 和 the words,在从句中起到宾语的作用。而 what 不仅起到连接主句与从句的作用,而且还包含着一个名词的含义,因此 what 可被理解为起到名词/代词 + that/which 的句法作用。what 的这一用法只限于表达名词/代词 + that/which 的含义,不能用其代替句子 + 关系代词(which)结构,如:

> *You tore up her photo, which upset her.*
> 你撕掉了她的照片,这使她很不高兴。

由于 which 指前一句整个内容,而非 photo 一个词,因此不可说用 what upset her 替代。

4. **... and angrily accused him of stealing the lamb.**

accuse...of 因……指控/指责,用 accuse 表达的"指责/指控"通常比较直接、尖锐,但所指控/指责的事情也可能并不是很严重,如:

> *She accused me of being careless in my work.*

180

她指责我工作中粗枝大叶。

在"指控"较严重的事情上,accuse 类同于 charge,但后者更强调有"正式的法律程序"之意。此外,这两个词在结构使用上不同,比较:

He was accused of taking bribes.

因受贿他被指控。

The merchant was charged with jacking up prices.

那商人因哄抬物价被指控。

注意应使用 accuse...of...或 charge...with...结构。

5. He told him he had better return it...

he had better return it 他最好归还它/羊。间接引语,省略了连词 that。had better 最好,其后需使用不带 to 的动词不定式,用于指现在和将来,不指过去。虽然用了 better(比较级形式),但并不用来表达比较意义,只用于表达"应该"之意,如:

We'd better hurry up if we want to get home before dark.

要打算天黑前到家,我们就得加快点。

had better 为固定搭配形式,在任何情况下不可将 had 改作 have。此外,其否定形式是将否定词 not 置于 better 之后,而非 had 之后,如:

You'd better not wake him up when you come in.

你进来时最好不要弄醒他。

6. Aleko denied taking it and...

denied taking it 不承认偷了羊。句中 taking it 为动名词短语,作动词 deny 的宾语,其后不可使用动词不定式作宾语。常见的此类用法的动词还很多,如:admit(承认)、appreciate(欣赏)、avoid(避免)、consider(考虑)、deny(否认)、enjoy(欣赏,喜欢)、excuse(原谅)、finish(完成)、give up(放弃)、can't help(忍不住)、imagine(想像)、mention(提及)、mind(在意)、put off(推迟)、can't stand(不能忍受)、suggest(建议)等,如:

She's been considering getting a job abroad.

她一直在考虑到国外找个工作。

Excuse my interrupting your work, but...

原谅我打扰了您的工作,但……

有关动词 deny 的用法参见本课词汇学习有关部分。

7. It was true that he had just bought a lamb, he explained, but *his* lamb was black.

(1) he explained 作插入语成分,起到附加说明的作用。

(2) his 他的。文中为斜体,表示对此词的强调,读时需重读。正是这一词的强调为下文打下了伏笔。

8. Ashamed of having acted so rashly, Dimitri apologized to Aleko for having accused him.

(1) Ashamed of having acted so rashly(由于)为刚才鲁莽的行为感到惭愧。可被视为省略了分词 being 的短语形式,在句子中作原因状语(有关用作原因状语的分词短语用法参见第 13 课课文注释 9)。实际上,英语中单独使用形容词或形容词短语构成各类状语的情况很常见,如:

1) 表示原因:

Afraid of getting into the rain, he took the raincoat with him when he went out.

由于担心被淋雨,他出去时带上了雨衣。

Modest and unassuming, the manager soon put his staff completely at ease.

由于很谦逊随和,经理很快就使他的员工们完全轻松下来。

2) 表示情况或方式:

Flushed and breathless, he rushed into the house.

他满脸通红、气喘吁吁地跑进了屋子。

3) 表示时间:

182

High in spirits, she is very talkative.

情绪好时,她是很健谈的。

(2) be ashamed of 为……感到羞愧,如:

She's much ashamed of what she has done.

她为她所做的事情感到极为羞愧。

(3) apologize to...for... 因……向……道歉,如:

The boy apologized to his neighbour for having broken the window.

男孩因打碎了邻居家的窗户玻璃向他们道歉。

Has Mary apologized to you for her rudeness last night?

玛丽昨天晚上对你不礼貌,她道歉了吗?

10. Its wool, which had been dyed black, had been washed clean by the rain!

(1) which had been dyed black 原被染成黑色的(羊毛)。为非限制性定语从句,表明与主句较为松散的结构关系,起到类似插入说明的作用,有关其用法及同限制性定语从句的区别参见第8课课文注释3。

(2) 由于使用的是被动语态结构,因此从句中的形容词 black 同主句中的形容词分别作主语 which 和 its wool 的补足语,分别说明主语被 dyed 和 washed 后的状态。在主动语态的句子中,这样使用的形容词为宾语补足语,如:

They pulled the rope tight.

他们把绳子拉紧。

She always writes her words big.

她总是把字写得很大。

上述两个例句中的形容词 tight 和 big 分别为各自句中宾语的补足语,说明宾语的状态。

📑 语法 Grammar in use

had better 的用法

1. had better 用于建议在将来某一具体场合采取行动,而不同于一般情况。它常常带有警告、告诫或催促的意味,语义较 should 和 ought to 更为强烈。中国学生一定要注意这个短语的这种内在涵义,切不可不分场合地滥用。had better 之后跟不带 to 的动词不定式:

   I had better introduce myself.

   我最好自我介绍一下。

2. had better 的否定形式是将 not 置于 better 之后,而不可将其置于 had 之后,如:

   You had better not be late tomorrow.

   你明天可不要迟到了。

3. 但是在疑问句中可以使用 hadn't + 主语 + better 的形式,如:

   Hadn't we better sum up our experience before going on ?

   我们是不是在继续工作之前最好先总结一下呢?

📂 词汇学习 Word study

1. fetch *vt.*

(1) 拿来:

   I don't want you to fetch anything for me.

   我不想让你去给我拿任何东西。

   I went and fetched another glass.

   我又去拿了一个杯子。

   注:fetch 是去某处去拿某物,而 bring 是将某物带到你所在的地方。试比较:

   If you're going to the kitchen, would you mind bringing me a glass of water please ?

如果你去厨房,请顺便给我带杯水过来,行吗?

Please fetch me a glass of water.

请给我倒杯水。

而 take 则是将某物从此处拿到另一处:

Take this glass of water to your father.

把这杯水拿给你父亲。

(2) 请来,接:

Every afternoon he fetches her on her way home.

每天下午他都在她回家的路上接她。

2. deny *vt.*

(1) 否认:

The Rosenbergs denied all the charges brought against them.

罗森堡夫妇否认对他们的全部指控。

He denied that he was responsible for the accident.

他否认他应对那一事故负责。

Green denied doing anything illegal.

格林否认做过任何违法的事情。

注:从上述例句中可以看出,在 deny 一词后面可跟名词宾语、that 从句或动词-ing 结构。

(2) 拒绝给予,拒绝某人的要求:

He was denied a fair and open trial.

他未能得到一个公正、公开的审判。

注:从上述例句中可以看出,用于此意时,deny 后面跟双宾语。

3. apologize *vi.*

道歉,认错:

Afterwards George apologized to him personally.

事后乔治亲自向他道了歉。

She apologized to me for being late.

她为迟到而向我认错。

The principal apologized to Mr. Green for the conduct of a few pupils in the school.

校长为学校几个学生的行为而向格林先生道歉。

✍ 练习答案 Key to written exercises

1. 关键句型练习答案

A   See text.

B   1   *We continued* asking/ to ask questions about what had happened.

2   *Let's go* swimming this afternoon.

3   *This shirt needs* ironing.

4   *Excuse my* asking, but how much did you pay for those shoes?

2. 难点练习答案

1   We'd better have lunch.

2   She'd better renew her passport.

3   You'd better not ask so many questions.

4   We'd better not stay any longer.

5   The children had better get an early night.

6   I'd better consult my solicitor.

3. 多项选择题答案

1	c	2	b	3	b	4	d	5	d	6	c
7	d	8	b	9	a	10	b	11	c	12	a

Lesson 17

The longest suspension bridge in the world
世界上最长的吊桥

📖 **课文详注** **Further notes on the text**

1. Verrazano, an Italian about whom little is known, sailed into New York Harbour in 1524 and named it Angoulême.

（1）about whom little is known 鲜为人知的。定语从句,修饰 an Italian。动词 know 同 about 组成一种固定的搭配形式。常同诸如 little、a little、much、a great deal、a lot、everything、something、nothing 等词或词组一同使用,表明知道或听说的程度。使用 to know about/of...通常指间接地知道或听说之意,与在 know 后直接跟随人作宾语的结构在意义上有所不同,如可以说:

> *I've known about/of him, but I don't know him.*
>
> 我听说过他,但我对他不了解。

这里应注意 know sb. 与 know about/of sb. 之间的区别。像动词 know 与介词 about/of 搭配那样,在英语中许多动词、形容词和名词常与特定的介词一起连用,这就经常出现介词被置于句子末尾的情况,在非正式文体中更是如此,如:

> *Naturally, many of them like being looked at.*
>
> 很自然,他们中的许多人都喜欢被人注意到。(动词＋介词)

> *Don't be nervous, but I don't know what on earth you're afraid of?*
>
> 别紧张,我不明白你到底怕什么?(形容词＋介词)

Maths, I'm sure, is one of the subjects he has a lot of difficulties with.

我敢肯定,数学是他深感困难的科目之一。(名词＋介词)

如文中所示,在 wh-词引导的句子中,也可将置后的介词提前到 wh-词前,这在正式文体中更常使用,如:

Do you remember the boy with whom I used to go out?

你记得我过去总一块儿出去的那个小男孩吗?

但是在使用这种结构中,要注意以下 3 点:

1) 这种结构不用于以 be 为主动词的句子里,如:

I wonder who it is for.

我想知道这是给谁的。

2) 使用这种结构后,原来应该使用 who(主格)引导的,由于之前使用了介词,因此需使用 whom(宾格)的代词形式,试比较:

She asked you who you intended to go with.
She asked you with whom you intended to go.
她问你想和谁一起去。

3) 当此结构用于定语从句时,介词后只能使用 whom 或 which,不能使用 that,比较:

He's the man (that) I like to talk with.
He's the man with whom I like to talk.
他就是我喜欢与之谈话的人。

(2) and named it Angoulême 并将其命名为安古拉姆。Angoulême 为动词 name 的宾语补足语。it 指 New York Harbour。在英语中,一些常见动词,如 appoint(任命)、call(称呼)、consider(认为)、elect(选举)、find(发现)、leave(留下)、make(使)、name(命名)、nominate(提名)、think(认为)后可使用宾语＋宾语补足语结构。在这种结构中,宾语补足语通常被用来补充说

明宾语的状态、特性、身份等,如:

We've found her a very nice person to get along with.

我们发现她是个极好相处的人。

Not long after that, her parents died one after the other, leaving her a helpless orphan.

自那之后,她的父母亲相继去世,使她成了个无依无靠的孤儿。

2. He described it as 'a very agreeable situation located within two small hills in the midst of which flowed a great river'.

in the midst of which flowed a great river 一条大河从其间流过的……定语从句,修饰 two small hills。此定语从句使用了倒装结构,其自然语序为:a great river flowed in the midst of...,which 代表 two small hills。这里倒装语序的使用可使句子更平衡。参见第 3 课课文注释 6。在定语从句中,常可见到"表示时间、地点的名词 + 介词 + 关系代词"搭配使用,但有如下几点需注意:

1) 这样的结构通常都用于正式文体中,而在非正式文体中常使用"表示时间、地点的名词 + 关系副词"这样的定语从句结构,比较:

> *This is the place in which I grew up.*
> *This is the place where I grew up.*
> 这是我长大的地方。

2) 这样的结构也可用于非限定性定语从句中,比较:

> *The summer of 1969, (the year) in which man first set foot on the moon, will never be forgotten.*
> *The summer of 1969, (the year) when men first set foot on the moon, will never be forgotten.*
> 1969 年夏是人们永远不会忘记的,这一年人类第一次登上月球。

3）在这样的结构中,介词后只可使用关系代词 which,不可使
用关系代词 that;如使用关系代词 that 时,需将介词置于句
末,这时 that 也可省略,比较:

> This is the place that/which I grew up in.
> This is the place I grew up in.
> 这是我长大的地方。

4）只有当表示时间或地点的名词作先行词,在定语从句中分
别起到时间状语或地点状语的作用时才能使用“表示时间、
地点的名词 + 介词 + 关系代词”或“表示时间、地点的名词
+关系副词”这两种结构,否则不能使用,如:

> She offered me her time (that) she had often used to
> play tennis.
> 她把过去经常用于打网球的时间提供给了我。
> That's the place (that) we first visited.
> 这是我们第一次访问的地方。

在以上两个例句中,由于先行词 time 和 place 分别在各自从
句中起到宾语作用,而非时间状语和地点状语作用,因此不
能用 ... her time in which... 或 ... her time when...
和...the place in which... 或 ...the place where... 表达
这两个句子。

**3. Though Verrazano is by no means considered to be a great
explorer, his name will probably remain immortal, for on
November 21st, 1964, the longest suspension bridge in the world
was named after him.**

（1）by no means 决不,在任何情况下都不。介词短语,在句中作
状语,如:

> He advised me by no means to get in touch with them.
> 他劝我决不要同他们接触。

当将其用于句首时,句子要部分倒装,如:

190

By no means can teaching in school be separated from practice.

学校的教学决不能脱离实践。

(2) be named after 以……的名字命名,如:

Harvard University was named after its founder, John Harvard.

哈佛大学以其奠基人约翰·哈佛的名字命名。

4. The Varrazano Bridge, which was designed by Othmar Ammann, joins Brooklyn to Staten Island.

join...to... 把……与……连接起来,如:

Join this pipe to the other one.

把这根管子同那一根连起来。

The house is joined to the one next door by a wall.

这所房子同隔壁那一所以一道墙相连。

有关动词 join 的用法,参见本课后词汇学习部分。

5. The bridge is so long that the shape of the earth had to be taken into account by its designer.

(1) so...that... 太……以至于……从属连词,引导结果状语从句。根据所修饰成分的不同,so(副词)后既可跟随形容词(原级)也可跟随副词(原级),如:

His reactions are so quick (that) no one can match him.
He reacts so quickly (that) no one can match him.
他的反应如此敏捷(以至于)无人比得上他。

有关用法参见第 10 课课文注释 10。

(2) be taken into account by... 被……考虑到。动词不定式的被动语态结构。take...into account 考虑……,如:

We must take local conditions into account while carrying out the policy.

在执行此项政策时,我们必须考虑当地条件。

6. These alone took sixteen months to build.

These alone... 仅仅这些……英语中有些常见的以字母 a-开头的形容词或副词,如 aboard(在船、飞机、车上)、abroad(在国外)、adrift(漂浮着的)、alike(同样的,相像的)、ahead(前面的)、alive(活着的)、alone(仅有的)、around(周围的)、asleep(睡着的)、afire(燃烧的)等,作定语修饰名词时一般置于被修饰的名词之后,如:

You can see a baby asleep in the bed.
你可以看到床上有一个睡着的婴儿。

They saw a house afire while on their way home.
在回家的路上,他们见到一所失火的房子。

7. It has been estimated that if the bridge were packed with cars, it would still only be carrying a third of its total capacity.

(1) It has been estimated 据估计。it 为形式主语,全句的逻辑主语为 that 引导的名词性从句。有关先行词 it 的用法参见第 1 课课文注释 13。

(2) 句中 that 引导的名词性从句由一个以从属连词 if 引导的非真实性条件状语从句构成。这种非真实性条件状语从句由从句中 if + 主语 + 动词的过去时和主句的主语 + 情态助动词的过去时构成。在使用这种非真实性条件状语从句时,需注意以下几点:

1) if 条件状语从句中单数主语后的 be 动词可使用 were 或 was,两者在意义上没有区别,但使用 were 时句子显得更为正式;在陈述有怀疑的事情或纯粹想像中的事情时更倾向于使用 were,如:

If I was/were better qualified, I'd apply for the job.
如果我的条件好一些,我就申请那份工作了。

2) if 条件句中的主句中,除可使用 would 外,还可使用 could、might、ought to 或 should 等情态助动词,表达能力、可能

性、义务等意义,如:

If he were here, he could help us.

如果他在这儿,他能够帮助我们。(能力)

If he were here, he might help us.

如果他在这儿,他可能帮助我们。(可能性)

If he failed, he ought to/should try again.

如果他失败了,他应当再干。(责任)

3) if 条件句中,主句的情态助动词可与动词的进行时和完成时形式连用,如:

If she were here now, she could be helping us.

如果她在这儿,她会帮助我们的。

If they were in the army, they would have been fighting in the jungle most of the time.

如果他们在服兵役,他们大部分时间一定一直是在丛林里作战。

4) 在 If I were you/If I were in sb.'s position/If it were not for...结构中,只能使用 were,不能使用 was,如:

If I were you/ in your position, I'd accept this offer.

如果我是你,我就接受他们的建议。

If it were not for your help, I would still be homeless.

没有你的帮助,我仍无家可归。

在正式文体中,常用 Were it not for... 或 Were it not for the fact that... 取代 If it were not for... 结构,如:

Were it not for your help/for the fact that you helped me, I would still be homeless.

没有你的帮助,我仍无家可归。

参见 14 课课文注释 7。

(3) pack...with... 把……装满,如:

The train was packed with passengers.

193

火车上挤满了旅客。

It's really a day packed with events.

这可真是多事的一天。

8. ... it is both simple and elegant, fulfilling its designer's dream to create an enormous object drawn as faintly as possible.

fulfilling... as faintly as possible 为现在分词短语,在句子中作结果状语,其逻辑主语为前面的整个句子。在这类分词前使用副词 thus(这样)或 thereby(因此)后,分词短语的这种表达功能就更为明显,如:

She hasn't come yet, thereby making it necessary for them to choose someone else instead.

她还没有来,因此他们必须另选一个人取代她。

🗐 **语法 Grammar in use**

动词 + 宾语 + to be(或其他动词不定式)

英语中有些动词可以跟宾语 + to be(或少数几个诸如 to have 这类表示状态的动词不定式)。在此结构中,动词的宾语往往是动词不定式的主语。这类动词有:acknowledge(承认)、assume(假定)、believe(相信)、calculate(估计)、consider(认为)、declare(声称)、discover(发现)、estimate(估计)、fancy(设想)、feel(感觉)、find(发现)、guess(猜想)、imagine(想像)、judge(判断)、know(知道)、maintain(主张)、proclaim(宣告)、prove(证明)、reckon(估计)、see(理解)、show(表明)、suppose(假设)、take(认为)、think(想)、understand(理解)。这些动词经常用于被动语态中,而且其后常跟动词不定式被动形式:

I consider him to be one of the best authorities in the field.

我认为他是这个领域中最有权威的人士之一。

She is believed to have gone to the U.S.A.

人们确信她已去了美国。

He is thought to have been killed in an air crash.

人们认为他已在一次空难中丧生。

I estimate them to have made more than a million.

我估计他们已挣了一百多万。

所有这些动词(除了 take, I take it〈that〉...之外)也可直接带 that 从句,如:

I estimate (that) they have made more than a million.

我估计他们已挣了一百多万。

We suppose that he is at work today.

我们认为他今天在工作。

📁 词汇学习 Word study

1. join

(1) *vt*. 连接,接合:

The newly built bridge joined the island to the mainland.

新修建的大桥将这座岛屿与大陆连在了一起。

(2) *vt*. 加入,参加:

How many countries can join the European Union?

多少国家能加入欧盟?

Will you join me for a drink?

来和我一起喝一杯好吗?

(3) *vi*. (in) 参加(某项活动):

The whole audience joined in singing the popular song.

全体观众加入进来一起唱起了这首流行歌曲。

2. be made of/out of、be made from、be made with、be made up of

(1) be made of/out of 表示"由……材料制成"的含义,但是制成物

195

仍能看出原材料。of 后一般接不可数名词：

> *Our new garden gate is made of/out of wrought iron.*
> 我们花园的新大门是由锻铁制成的。

(2) be made from 也表示"由……原材料制成"的含义。但制成物已看不出原材料。from 后通常接不可数名词：

> *Beer is made from hops and other ingredients.*
> 啤酒是由啤酒花和其他成分制成的。
>
> *Nylon is made from air, coal and water.*
> 尼龙是由空气、煤和水加工制成。

(3) be made with 表示"使用了……而制成"：

> *This cake is made with fresh cream.*
> 这个蛋糕用新鲜奶油制成。

(4) be made up of 含有"由……成分构成"的含义。of 后通常接可数名词：

> *The committee is made up of seven members.*
> 委员会由 7 名委员组成。

3．each

(1) *adj.* 各,各自的,每：

> *Each child in the school was questioned.*
> 学校里的每个孩子都受到了询问。
>
> *Each province is subdivided into several districts.*
> 每个省又细分为几个地区。

(2) *pron.* 各个,每个：

> *Each of these phrases has a different meaning.*
> 这些词组中的每个词组都有不同的含义。
>
> *If there is more than one comfortable hotel, you could spend a few nights at each.*
> 如果有不止一个舒适的旅店,你可以在每个旅店度过几个晚上。

196

注:each 不能用于否定结构,也不能将 almost、nearly 等与 each 连用,不可说:

* *Almost each house in the street is for sale .*

而应说:

Almost every house in the street is for sale .
这条街上几乎所有的房子都在出售。

不可说:

* *Each of the boys did not enjoy football .*

而应说:

None of the boys enjoyed football .

(3) *adv*.对各个,对每个:

They each chose a word from the list .
他们每人都从表中选了一个词。

They each have a share .
他们每个人都有一份。

注:在此用法中,主语为复数代词或名词时,动词也应用复数动词形式。如不可说:

* *They each has a share .*

表示数量时,each 一般放在句末,如:

They cost eight pounds each .
它们每个 8 镑。

✍ 练习答案 **Key to written exercises**

1. 关键句型练习答案

See text.

2. 难点练习答案

1 He is believed to have owned...

2 The Minister declared the treaty to be...

197

3 I know him to be...

4 I guess him to be...

5 We estimate this picture to be...

3. 多项选择题答案

1	d	2	a	3	a	4	a	5	a	6	b
7	d	8	d	9	a	10	c	11	c	12	d

Lesson 18

Electric currents in modern art

现代艺术中的电流

📖 **课文详注** **Further notes on the text**

1. **Modern sculpture rarely surprises us any more.**

    rarely 很少,极少。副词,含基本否定的含义,同 any more 搭配使用后表示出"几乎再也不"、"几乎再没有"含义。any more 需同表示(基本)否定的副词连用。另一表示相似概念的副词短语是 no more(不再)。由于 no more 已有否定含义,因此用于肯定句结构之中。这两个副词短语用于修饰终止性动词(terminative verb),可用于表示将来和过去时态的句子。no more 更常用于书面语中,而(基本)否定词... + any more 结构多见于口语中。此外,它们在句子中的使用位置不同,如:

    Lost time won't come back any more.

    失去的时间将一去不复返。

    The great ship, Titanic, *rapidly sank and was seen no more.*

    巨轮"泰坦尼克"号很快沉没,再也见不到了。

2. **The idea that modern art can only be seen in museums is mistaken.**

    由于 that 从句表达 idea 的具体内容,idea 在 that 从句中不具有任何功能作用,因此 that 是 idea 的同位语。有关同位语用法参见第 6 课课文注释 2 及第 9 课课文注释 4。

3. **Even people who take no interest in art cannot have failed to notice examples of modern sculpture on display in public places.**

(1) 关系代词 who 引导的定语从句修饰先行词 people。take no interest in... 对……不感兴趣。take 与 interest 之间可根据语义需要使用适当的表示程度的形容词(短语),如 little、a little、more、a great deal、much、great、considerable 等,以修饰 interest,如:

Most of the students in Class 4 take little interest in physics.

4 班的多数学生都对物理没多大兴趣。

She really takes great interest in such things.

她的确对这类事情很感兴趣。

(2) cannot have failed to notice 不至于没注意到。cannot have + 动词的过去分词结构表示对过去事情的否定推测。

4. We have got quite used to them.

have got quite used to 已十分习惯于。所用 got 为系动词,to 为介词,其后应跟随名词、名词性从句或动名词形式,如:

They have got used to such things.

他对这种事已司空见惯了。

He has got quite used to what people say about him.

他已对人们对他的议论习以为常。

She has got used to being treated like that.

她已习惯人们那样对待她。

5. ... some people—including myself—were surprised...

用破折号隔开的 including myself 在句中为插入语,对 some people 作进一步追加说明。

6. The first thing I saw when I entered the art gallery was a notice which said...

when 引导的时间状语从句修饰定语从句中的谓语动词 saw,说明 saw 这一动作发生的时间。

7. Oddly shaped forms that are suspended from the ceiling and

200

move in response to a gust of wind are quite familiar to everybody.

(1) oddly shaped 为过去分词短语作定语,修饰 forms。forms 在此指(展品)种类,意即"奇形怪状的(展品)种类"。

(2) that are...a gust of wind 为定语从句,置后修饰 forms。从 oddly 至 a gust of wind 构成句子的主语部分。

(3) in response (to) 作为回答,作为对……的反应,如:

He murmured something in response.

他咕哝着回答了些什么。

The quick recovery was truly in response to medication.

这次迅速康复确是药物治疗的结果。

(4) be familiar to... 为……所熟悉。使用时应注意它同 be familiar with...的区别。familiar to 和 familiar with 这两个形容词短语均有"熟悉"、"通晓"之意,均可用作主语补足语和后置定语。使用时 familiar to 的主语可为人或事物,但宾语只能为人(如文中那样),表示某人或某事物对某人来说是熟悉的之意,如:

There are faces not familiar to her.

有几张面孔她不熟悉。

Those woods were so familiar to both of them.

他们俩都对那些树林如此熟悉。

familiar with 的主语只能为人,宾语可为人或事物,表示某人熟悉某人或某事物之意,如:

Before you leave home for the United States, you should be familiar with the American English.

在你出国赴美之前,你应首先熟悉美国英语。

这两个短语的主语和宾语的位置正好相反,除所要强调的语句成分的不同外,其语义不变,如:

He's familiar with the subject. (= The subject is familiar

201

to him .）

他熟悉这个题目。

8．Lined up against the wall，there were long thin wires attached to the metal spheres．

（1）lined up against the wall 为过去分词短语作状语，说明主语 wires 的状况。

（2）attached to the metal spheres 为过去分词短语作定语，后置修饰 wires。attach...to... 把……同……连/结/系在一起，如：

The driver attached the trailer to the car .

司机把拖车挂在汽车后面。

Most of them are foolishly attached to old customs .

他们中的大多数人都愚昧地追随旧风俗。

9．The spheres had been magnetized and attached or repelled each other all the time．

all the time 不停地，经常，总是。副词短语，作时间状语修饰句中动词。注意 all the time 与 at all times 和 at times 的区别。at times 表示"有时"、"偶尔"，即 sometimes 之意，如：

At times，they play tennis in the afternoon .

他们有时下午打网球。

在表示"不停地"、"经常"、"总是"之意，即 continuous 和 always 时，at all times 比 all the time 更常用，如：

His mother talks about her trip to America all the time ／ at all times .

他母亲总是谈论她的美国之行。

然而，在表达"不论什么时候"即 at any time 之意时，则只能使用 at all times，如：

We must be ready at all times to stand up for the truth .

我们必须随时准备坚持真理。

10．These lights flickered continuously like traffic lights which

have gone mad.

which have gone mad 为定语从句,修饰 traffic lights。go mad 原意为"发疯"、"发狂",这里用来表示"失控"之意。此处用 to go mad 来描述 lights 为拟人手法,go 为系动词。

11. **Sparks were emitted from small black boxes and red lamps flashed on and off angrily.**

on and off 断断续续地,间歇地,修饰动词的副词短语,如:

It rained on and off all day yesterday.

昨天断断续续地下了一整天雨。

on and on 则为"继续不断地"、"不停地"之意,如:

They walked on and on until they got to the destination.

他们不停地一直走到目的地。

angrily 为副词,修饰 flash,同 go mad 一样,作者使用了拟人手法。

12. **These peculiar forms not only seemed designed to shock people emotionally, but to give them electric shocks as well!**

not only...but (also)... 不仅……而且……连词,为了避免不必要的重复,but 与 to 之间省略了 seemed designed。此用法参见第 5 课课文注释 8。seemed designed 中的 seemed 为系动词,相当于 were designed,构成被动语态结构。

📖 语法 Grammar in use

以-y 结尾的单词加-s 的拼写规则

在英语中,可数名词变复数时的拼写规则与规则动词一般现在时第 3 人称单数的变化是一致的。以-y 结尾的名词变成复数时的规则如下:

1. 以辅音写母-y 结尾时,变 y 为 i,再加-es,如:

lorry—lorries　　*country—countries*

factory—factories   study—studies

2．以元音字母-y 结尾时,直接加-s,如:

day—days   play—plays
key—keys   boy—boys

📁 词汇学习 Word study

1．used to(+动词不定式)

过去常……(指过去的习惯),如:

She used to tell me stories about people in India and Egypt.
她过去常给我讲有关印度和埃及人的故事。

注:used to 不常用于否定结构。在口语中可以说 didn't used to,如:

They didn't used to mind what we did.
他们过去常常不在意我们做什么。

也可用 never used to 或 used not to,但后一种太正式,如:

You never used to smoke.
你从不习惯抽烟。

It used not to be taxable, but now it will subject to tax.
过去对它不征税,可是现在要对它征税了。

在疑问句中可用助动词 did,如:

Did you use to play with your brothers?
你过去常跟你的兄弟们一起玩吗?

当疑问词 what 等为句子主语时,不用 did,如:

What used to annoy you most about him?
他过去什么行为令你最讨厌?

2．be used to ⟨sth. / doing sth.⟩

熟悉,习惯于:

I'm used to getting up early.

204

我习惯早起。

注:除了 be 动词之外,used to 还常与 get 连用:

I was beginning to get used to the old iron bed .

我开始习惯那张旧铁床了。

注:be accustomed to 与 be used to 表达同一种意思,但在口语中更常使用 be used to。前者也可与 become、get、grow 等动词连用,与 be used to 一样使用时 to 后不能使用动词不定式,如:

We are used to queueing .

我们习惯于排队。

I'm not accustomed to being interrupted .

我不习惯被人打断。

✍ 练习答案 Key to written exercises

1. 关键句型练习答案

See text.

2. 难点练习答案

ladies, supplies, valleys, qualifies, stories, days, says, replies, marries, ways, chimneys, hurries, stays, enjoys, buys, bodies, buries, fries

3. 多项选择题答案

| 1 | d | 2 | c | 3 | d | 4 | c | 5 | c | 6 | b |
| 7 | a | 8 | d | 9 | d | 10 | a | 11 | b | 12 | c |

Lesson 19

A very dear cat

一只贵重的宝贝猫

📖 **课文详注 Further notes on the text**

1. A very dear cat

根据文中所述内容,作者在篇名中以双关语形式使用了 dear 一词,即取其具有的"亲爱的"和"昂贵的"双重意义,很好地勾画出文章的主题。

2. Kidnappers are rarely interested in animals, but they recently took considerable interest in Mrs. Eleanor Ramsay's cat.

(1) be interested in 对……感兴趣;对……关心,如:

You know how interested I am in everything you do.

你知道我对你所做的一切多么感兴趣。

这个短语还可以用来表示"同……有利害关系"之意,如:

Being interested in the matter, he cannot arbitrate.

由于他与此事有利害关系,因此不能裁决。

如课文中那样,在形容词 interested 之前可使用相应的程度副词进行修饰。

(2) take interest in 对……感兴趣。如文中那样,在名词 interest 之前可使用相应的表示程度的形容词进行修饰。

3. Mrs. Eleanor Ramsay, a very wealthy old lady, has shared a flat with her cat, Rastus, for a great many years.

(1) 在英语中,如果某一名词由若干形容词来修饰,通常要有一定的顺序。其排列顺序的几条主要规则如下:

　1) 说明用途的形容词 + 名词,如:

206

a cheap tennis racket 一只便宜的网球拍

a small dining room 一个小餐厅

2）说明制造物的形容词＋说明用途的形容词＋名词,如：

a small wooden dining room 一个木制小餐厅

a plastic garden chair 一把塑料制花园用椅

3）说明来源的形容词＋说明制造物的形容词＋名词,如：

a pair of Spanish leather boots 一双西班牙皮靴

a Chinese writing desk 一张中式写字台

4）说明颜色的形容词＋说明来源的形容词＋其他,如：

a pair of black Spanish leather boots 一双黑色的西班牙皮靴

a dark brown Chinese writing desk 一张深褐色的中式写字台

5）说明年龄、形状、大小、程度等的形容词＋说明颜色的形容词＋其他,如：

a pair of old black Spanish leather boots 一双破旧的黑色西班牙皮靴

a big dark brown Chinese writing desk 一张宽大的深褐色中式写字台

在实际使用中,形容词的排列顺序十分复杂,而且中英文中的形容词顺序的排列有所不同,还应在学习中多加体会。

（2）share...with... 与……分享,与……共有,与……分担,如：

They generously shared it with us.

他们慷慨地与我们一同分享它。

He hated having to share the room with a stranger.

他讨厌非得同一个陌生人同住一个房间。

（3）Rastus 为 cat 的名字,作 cat 的同位语。

4. She looked everywhere for him but could not find him.

everywhere 为副词,作地点状语,修饰动词 look。正常语序为

207

She looked for him everywhere。这里将 everywhere 提前,起强调的作用。这里的 him 指 cat,为拟人格形式。

5．**The writer stated that Ratus was in safe hands and would be returned immediately if Mrs. Ramsay paid a ransom of £1,000.**

in safe hands 在可靠人手中。此处 hands 用来指人。常见的此类短语有:

$$in \left\{ \begin{array}{l} bad \\ good \\ green \\ new \\ old \end{array} \right\} \quad hands \qquad 在 \left\{ \begin{array}{l} 笨人 \\ 能人 \\ 生 \\ 新 \\ 老 \end{array} \right\} 手中$$

在使用中,应注意同介词短语 in hand 的区别。in hand 在句中可作状语、定语、补足语,主要用来表达以下几种含义:在手中(的);在控制中(用此义时常同动词 have、keep、take 等连用);(通常指工作)在进行中,如:

As the matter in hand was urgent, we dealt with it at once.

由于手中的问题紧迫,我们马上就把它解决了。

Can you have the situation well in hand?

你能完全控制住这种形势吗?

We should finish the work we have in hand before we begin something new.

开始新的工作之前,我们应完成我们正在进行的工作。

6．**Mrs. Ramsay was instructed to place the money in a cardboard box and to leave it outside her door.**

在 instruct...to do...(指示/命令/吩咐……做……)中,动词不定式在句中作宾语补足语,如:

The doctor instructed the patient to go to bed and rest.

208

大夫嘱咐那个病人上床休息。

但当用于被动语态时(如文中),由于宾语提前作了主语,动词
不定式则成为主语的补足语,如:

He's been instructed to take her to New York.

他奉命把她带到纽约。

因此课文中 to place the money in a cardboard box and to leave it
outside her door 的两个动词不定式短语均作句中主语的补足
语。

**7. At first, she decided to go to the police, but fearing that she
would never see Rastus again—the letter had made that quite
clear—she changed her mind.**

(1)动词 decide 后可使用动词不定式构成的宾语形式,如:

He decided to go on Tuesday instead of Thursday.

他决定在星期二而不在星期四去。

在表达"决定不做"含义时,否定词应置于动词不定式之前,即
构成 decide not to do... 形式,而不应置于动词 decide 之前,
如:

They decided not to tell him the truth.

他们决定不告诉他事实真相。

(2) fearing that she would never see Rastus again 由于害怕会再也
见不到拉斯特斯。为现在分词短语在句中作原因状语,说明
she changed her mind 的原因。

(3) the letter had made that quite clear,此句置于破折号内,作插入
语,应弱读。quite clear 作插入语部分的宾语补足语。

**8. ... but Mrs. Ramsay was sure that the kidnapper would keep
his word.**

keep one's word 信守诺言。使用时 word 用单数形式,如:

They failed to keep their word.

他们未能遵守诺言。

9. Considering the amount she paid,he was dear in more ways than one!

(1) considering 就……而论;考虑到。就此类词的词类划分,大体有 3 种意见。一种认为是连词,用其引导一让步状语从句或对比从句(contrast clause);一种认为是分词,同其后内容构成分词短语,作原因状语;再一种则认为是介词。这 3 种解释方式各有其道理,为讲解方便,现将若干常见的用于此类结构的动词-ing 均作介词处理,如 according to(根据)、concerning(关于)、considering(就……而论,考虑到)、regarding(关于)、respecting(关于,鉴于),如:

> *According to what you said just now ,John is quite right .*
> 根据你刚才所说的,约翰是完全正确的。
>
> *It seems that he knows nothing regarding the case .*
> 似乎他对此事一无所知。
>
> *Respecting these important facts ,a special committee is to be appointed .*
> 鉴于这些重要事实,马上要指定一个特别委员会。

(2) in more ways than one 不仅如此,还有别的意思/方面/方式等,多方面的,如:

> *The topic can be dealt with in more ways than one .*
> 此论题可以不仅仅以一种方式论述。

📖 语法　Grammar in use

逗号的用法(1)

1．下述情况必须用逗号

(1) 在呼语的后面或前面,如:

> *Hey ,James ,what's going on ?*
> 嘿,詹姆斯,怎么了?

210

(2) 在所列的几项事物之间,但在 and 或 or 之前不用逗号,如:

We had eggs , milk , bread and coffee for breakfast .

我们早餐吃的是鸡蛋、牛奶、面包和咖啡。

They were in love , in harmony and in Paris in spring .

他们相爱、和谐并于春天到了巴黎。

(3) 修饰某个名词的几个形容词之间,但在 and 连接时不用逗号,如:

He announced the news in a cool , light voice .

他用冷静而轻松的口气宣布了这个消息。

注:但是在 young、old 和 little 等形容词前一般不用逗号,如:

a charming little town 一个美丽的小镇

a kind old lady 一位善良的老妇人

(4) 在名字或名词短语之后,在描述语或进一步说明的文字之前,如:

a broad-backed man , baldish , in a fawn coat and brown trousers 一个背部宽阔的男人,秃顶,身着浅黄褐色外套和棕色的裤子

(5) 地名之间,如县、州和国家之间,如:

She was born in Princeton , New Jersey .

她出生于新泽西州的普林斯顿。

(6) 与主句分开的形容词之前或之后,分词之后,如:

She nodded , speechless .

她张口结舌地点了点头。

Laughing and singing , they left the classroom .

他们又笑又唱地离开了教室。

(7) 非限定性定语从句之前,如:

The government , which promises to cut taxes , will be popular .

这个政府保证要减税,它将会是得人心的。

（8）附加疑问句的前面，如：

  John was annoyed , wasn't he ?

  约翰生气了，不是吗？

（9）用于大数目之间，如：

  His personal fortune was estimated at $10,000,000.

  他个人的财产估计有 1 千万美元。

  They travelled 2,000,000,000 miles .

  他们旅行了 20 亿英里。

（10）信件中的称呼之后，如：

  Dear Sir ,

  尊敬的先生：

  Dear John ,

  亲爱的约翰：

📁 词汇学习 Word study

1．share

（1）*vt .* 分享，分担，合用：

  Mary and her sister , Louise , shared a room upstairs .

  玛丽和她的妹妹路易丝同住楼上的一个房间。

  I shared my food and drink .

  我与他人分享了我的食物和饮料。

（2）*vi .* 分担：

  You should encourage your husband to share in the care of your children .

  你应该让你的丈夫也分担一些照顾你们的孩子的事。

（3）*n .* 一份，份；股份：

  It does help when a father does his share at home .

  父亲承担一部分家庭责任确实是有益的。

He has shares in many companies.

他在许多公司里拥有股份。

2. lead (led, led)

（1）*vt.* 为……带路；领（路），指引，引路：

The guide led us to a spot in the desert where there was water.

向导领我们来到沙漠中一处有水的地方。

（2）*vt.* 致使，使得：

Gambling led him deep into debt.

赌博使他负债累累。

（3）*vi.* 通向：

The path leads directly to the farmhouse.

那条小路直通那座农舍。

3. follow *vt.*

（1）跟随；接在……之后：

The dog followed me all the way home.

那条狗一直跟着我到了家。

（2）听从，遵照：

He refused to follow the policeman's instructions and was fined.

他不服从警察的指示而被罚款。

（3）听懂，理解，领会：

They were having some difficulties in following the new teacher.

他们听这位新教师的讲课有些困难。

✎ 练习答案　Key to written exercises

1．关键句型练习答案

See text.

2．难点练习答案

Before going home, I went to the grocer's. Bill Smith, the man who always serves me, was very busy. This, however, did not worry me. On the contrary, it gave me the opportunity to look round for several things I wanted. By the time my turn came, I had already filled a basket with packets of biscuits, cans of fruit, bars of soap and two large bags of flour.

3．多项选择题答案

1	a	2	b	3	a	4	b	5	d	6	a
7	b	8	d	9	d	10	b	11	c	12	a

Lesson 20
Pioneer pilots
飞行员的先驱

📖 **课文详注　Further notes on the text**

1. **In 1908 Lord Northcliffe offered a prize of ￡1,000 to the first man who would fly across the English Channel.**

   动词 offer 如同 bring、buy、give、lend、make、pay、promise、refuse、send、take 等动词,其后可使用双宾语,即一个间接宾语(通常指人)和一个直接宾语(通常指物)。间接宾语经常置于直接宾语之前,如:

   He kindly offered us the suggestions.
   他友善地向我们提出了这些建议。

   They offered her two thousand dollars for her horse.
   他们出价 2,000 元要买她的马。

   间接宾语也可置于直接宾语之后,但其间通常需使用介词 to。当直接宾语比间接宾语短得多(如文中所示)、或当直接宾语为一代词、或当想对间接宾语进行强调时,经常这样使用,如:

   He offered his life to the country.
   他把生命献给了祖国。

   但在这样使用时,往往需根据所用动词的不同而使用不同的介词(如 for),如:

   Mother bought the ice-cream for you, not for me.
   妈妈是给你买的冰激凌,而不是给我。

   当两个宾语均为人称代词时,在英国英语中,直接宾语通常置于间接宾语之前,其间的介词 to 有时省略,如:

Give it（to）me.

把它给我。

2. Over a year passed before the first attempt was made.

（1）before 为一连词，引导一时间状语从句，表示"在……之前"，通常含有"在时间上前于"之意，如：

I'll be back before you have left.

在你离开前我就回来。

如文中所示，before 作连词使用时，有时可表示出"才"的含义，如：

The meeting was over before he arrived.

会开完了他才到。

此外，有时还可用 before 表示出"宁可……也不……"的含义，如：

She's determined to work herself to death before she gives up.

她决心宁可累死也不放弃这个工作。

英语中，在以 before 引导的时间状语从句中往往只有肯定形式，不用否定形式，因为 before 常常可以表示出从句的否定含义。因此当用 before 来表达"在……没有……之前"的含义时，应注意其用法，如：

He ran out of the room before they could stop him.

他们还没来得及阻止他，他已经跑出了屋子。（注意，此句不可表达为：* *Before they could not stop him, he ran out of the room.*）

将 before 和 until 同终止性动词（terminative verb）、延续性动词（durative verb）一起使用时，注意其用法上的不同：

1）before 可与终止性动词使用，而 until 在与终止性动词一同使用时，则需使用其否定形式，试比较：

216

$$\left\{\begin{array}{l} \textit{I woke up before she came back.} \\ 她回来前我就醒了。 \\ \textit{I didn't wake up until she came back.} \\ 她回来后我才醒。 \end{array}\right.$$

2) 它们均可同延续性动词的否定形式一同使用,但使用 before 时强调"在⋯⋯之前"的事实;使用 until 时则强调"对⋯⋯之前的情况的改变",如:

They didn't know any French before they came here.
他们来此之前根本不懂法语。

They didn't know any French until they came here.
他们来此之后才开始懂点法语。

第 1 例中用 before 陈述以前不懂法语这一事实;第 2 例中用 until 强调改变了以前的情况。(参见第 2 课课文注释 4)

(2) make an attempt $\left\{\begin{array}{l} \text{at...} \\ \text{to do...} \end{array}\right.$ $\left\{\begin{array}{l} 试图(尝试)某事 \\ 试图(尝试)做某事 \end{array}\right.$

如:

The prisoner made an attempt $\left\{\begin{array}{l} \textit{at escaping.} \\ \textit{to escape.} \end{array}\right.$

那个犯人企图逃跑。

有关 attempt 的动词用法参见第 8 课课文注释 5。

3. ...Hubert Latham took off from the French coast in his plane the 'Antoinette IV'.

take off from... 从/由/自⋯⋯起飞,如:

The helicopter took off from the terrace and soon disappeared.
直升机从露天平台起飞,很快就消失了。

4. He had travelled only seven miles across the Channel when his engine failed and he was forced to land on the sea.

217

(1) 就逻辑而言,此句的结构排列应为:

> *When he had travelled only seven miles across the Channel , his engine failed and . . .*

时间状语从句通常从逻辑上提供主句所述事件发生或出现的时间,在使用中通常可置于句首,也可置于句末,如:

> *I'll cook you a nice meal when you come back home .*
> 你回家后,我给你做顿美餐。

> *When she came into the room , she saw nobody but John .*
> 进屋时,除约翰外她谁也没见到。

在正式叙述体句子中,有时将逻辑上应用来引导时间状语从句的连词 when 置于主句之前,表明主句所要描述事件的意外性和突发性,以产生较强的戏剧性效果,如:

> *He felt his way in the dark when suddenly a horrible scream came from upstairs .*
> 他在黑暗中摸索着路,就在这时突然从楼上传来骇人的尖叫声。

(2) force. . . to do. . . 强迫……做……,如:

> *You can't force her to make a decision——she's got to do it on her own .*
> 你不能强迫她做决定——她得自己拿主意。

> *Hospitals are being forced to close departments because of lack of money .*
> 由于缺少资金,医院正被迫关掉某些科室。

5. The 'Antoinette' floated on the water until Latham was picked up by a ship.

(1) until/till 为同义词,既可作连词也可作介词使用,往往根据主句所使用动词的终止性或延续性性质,分别表示"到……为止"、"直到……才……"的含义。until 多用于较正式的场合,till 则更常用于口语文体之中,如:

Those boys played the football until/till six o'clock.

那些孩子们踢足球一直踢到 6 点钟。

（*until/till* 作介词,句子的主动词为延续性动词）

The parents waited for the boys until/till it got dark.

父母亲等那些孩子一直等到天黑。（*until/till* 作连词,
主句动词为延续性动词）

They won't begin their meeting until/till Friday.

到星期五他们才开始他们的会议。（*until/till* 作介词,
句子的主动词为终止性动词）

*She didn't go to bed until/till she had made sure that
everything was in order.*

直到她确信一切都井然有序后才去睡觉。（*until/till* 作
连词,主句动词为终止性动词）

由于 until/till 含有延续性时间概念,因此当与终止性动词使
用时,应将该终止性动词构成否定形式表达肯定意义(如上述
3、4 两例)。此外,在使用中还应注意下述 3 点:

1）当用于句首时,通常使用 until,而不用 till,如:

> *Until the last minute of the match, the players kept on
> playing.*
>
> 直到比赛的最后一分钟,运动员们仍在奋战。

2）在句首使用其否定形式时,除应使用 until(而非 till)外,句
子还应使用倒装语序,如:

> *Not until he finished his work did he go to bed.*
> 直到干完工作他才去睡觉。
>
> *Not until then shall we meet again.*
> 直到那时候我们才会再见面。

3）应在 until/till 引导的从句中使用一般时态(而非将来时
态)表达将来时态含义,如:

> *They will wait there till she returns.*

他们将一直等到她回来。(而不可说 *till she will return*)

（2）pick up 的基本意思是"拾起"、"拿起",但除文中表达的"(从水中)救起"外,还可表达如"开车接"、"学会"等意义,如:

> *The boys were asked to pick up the ears of rice on the ground.*
>
> 要男孩们把地上的谷穗拾起来。
>
> *The manager asked me to pick her up there and sent her home directly.*
>
> 经理吩咐我在那里接上她,并把她直接送回家。
>
> *Some of the young are picking up quickly.*
>
> 其中一些年青人正在很快地掌握。

6. Two days later, Louis Bleriot arrived near Calais with a plane called 'No. XI'.

with a plane called 'No. XI' 驾驶一架名为 11 号的飞机。介词 with 同其后的复合结构一起构成方式状语,如:

> *Now he could walk only with someone supporting him.*
>
> 现在他只能在别人的搀扶下才能行走。

7. Bleriot had been making planes since 1905...

had + been + 动词-ing 构成过去完成进行时的结构,用于叙述过去某一时刻之前一直继续着的历时较长的动作或情况,如:

> *When they arrived I had been waiting for three days.*
>
> 他们到达时我已等了 3 天。

例句中的 arrived 说明该动作为发生在过去时刻的动作,而 wait 动作为此过去时刻之前一直持续的动作,因此用过去完成进行时态表达。

8. Latham, however, did not give up easily.

短语动词 give up 既可作及物动词,也可作不及物动词使用。作及物动词时,其后使用名词或动名词作宾语,表示"放弃"、

220

"对……让步"之意；作不及物动词时,通常表示"投降"、"认输"之意,如：

Having heard the medical report, he soon gave up smoking.

听了那个医学报告后,他很快就把烟戒了。

When the enemy saw that they were surrounded, they gave up.

当敌人看到被包围时,他们就投降了。

9. **It looked as if there would be an exciting race across the Channel.**

as if/though 均表示"好像"、"似乎"、"仿佛……似的"之意,as if 更为普遍。英语中常用 as(像,如)或 as...as...(像……一样)结构的句子进行实际比较,如：

He thought English was as difficult to learn as Chinese.

他认为英语同汉语一样难学。

而通常用 as if/though 进行非事实的比喻或夸张,因此它们引导的从句中通常使用虚拟语气(如课文中 would be...结构),再如：

The old machine runs as if it were a new one.

这台旧机器如同新机器般运转。

He works very hard as if he never intended to sleep.

他工作非常努力,就仿佛他永远不打算睡觉似的。

此外,as if/though 常用于 it looks/seems/is 的系补结构中,并且当它们引导的从句表示一种实现可能性较大或说话人认为接近事实时,往往也用陈述语气,这在口语或非正式文体中更为常见,如：

It looks as if we're going to have trouble with Mrs. Jenkins again.

看来我们又会同詹金斯夫人发生争执。

221

在 as if/though 引导的从句中,有时可直接使用省略的不定式(短语)、分词(短语)、形容词(短语)等形式,如:

> *Some flowers shut up at night as though（they were going）to sleep.*
>
> 有些花晚间合起,仿佛睡觉似的。
>
> *The boy was holding her hand tightly as if（he were）afraid she would leave.*
>
> 男孩紧紧抓着她的手,仿佛怕她离开似的。

也可用 as if 表达惊讶、不满、气愤等语气,如:

> *He talks as if he were a hero!*
>
> 他讲话的口气,俨然像个英雄!
>
> *As if we were all stupid and he alone clever!*
>
> 哼,就仿佛我们全都是傻瓜,只有他一个人聪明似的!

此外,由于 as if/though 本身就有连词的功能,因此其前不可再加 that,如:

> *I felt as if my heart were bursting with enthusiasm.*（不应为 * . . . that as if . . .）
>
> 我感觉满腔热情仿佛炸开了似的。

10. . . . but Latham failed to get up early enough.

(1) 由于为已知内容,因此可将此句作为 . . . failed to get up early enough to take off on that day 的省略句,即省略了前文已给的 enough 之后的动词不定式短语部分。

(2) 除第 2 课课文注释 1 中所述 enough 用法外,还应注意 not . . . enough to 所表示的语义。在此结构中 not 为谓语动词的否定词,enough 为后置修饰语,修饰其前的形容词或副词,通常具有双重否定的含义,既否定 enough 前的形容词或副词,又否定 to 后的不定式,表示出"不/没能/没有/……不……"的含义。虽然文中未使用否定词 not,但由于动词 fail 本身包含了否定的意义,因此该句也具有双重否定的含义,即"但是莱瑟

222

姆起晚了(即起得不够早),未能在那一天起飞"。再如:

> *I don't know him well enough to ask him for help.*
> 我对他了解不够,不便请他帮忙。

而在 enough not to 的结构中,not 在形式和意义上都只能否定其后的动词不定式,因此通常仅表达出"很／太……不能……"、"如此……以致不……"这样单一否定的含义,如:

> *He's sensible enough not to do such a silly thing.*
> 他很明智,不会干这种蠢事。

11. His great flight lasted thirty-seven minutes.

last 持续,延续。为不及物动词,因此其后的 thirty-seven minutes 不是宾语,而只作时间状语。

12. ... and got within half a mile of Dover, ...

介词 of 在此句中表示距离,如:

> *a mile east of London* 伦敦以东 1 英里
> *within a mile of the town* 距离镇子不到 1 英里

语法 Grammar in use

逗号的用法(2)

2. 在下述情况下可用逗号表示强调

(1) 对主句加以补充说明部分的前后,如果这部分出现在句末,则其后不用逗号,如:

> *Hopefully, they'll arrive at an agreement.*
> 希望他们能达成协议。

> *They were, in many ways, very similar in character and outlook.*
> 他们在许多方面,在性格和观点上都非常相似。

(2) 列举一系列事物或在并列句中的 and、or、but 或 yet 等词之前,如:

We fished all day , but we didn't catch a thing .

我们钓了一天鱼,但是一条鱼也没钓着。

. . . remarks which shocked audience , yet also enhanced her reputation as a woman of courage .

……令听众震惊的讲话,然而也更加巩固了她是个有勇气的妇女的名声。

(3) 从句之后,如:

Even if the boxer survives surgery , he may be disabled permanently .

即使这个拳击手挺过这次手术,他也可能永远残废了。

注:一般从句前不用逗号,但是当从句用来进行对比或补充说明,或表示例外时用逗号:

The poor man was no threat to her any longer , if he ever really had been .

那可怜的男人对她再也构不成威胁了,假如以前他曾是的话。(补充说明)

(4) 分词之前,如:

They left the classroom , laughing and singing .

他们笑着唱着离开了教室。

(5) 用于名字前的名词之后,如:

She had married the marvellous singer , Jessy Norman .

她嫁给了那位了不起的歌手杰西·诺曼。

📁 词汇学习 Word study

1. offer *vt*.

(1) 给予,提供;出示:

No alcohol was offered at the party .

晚会上不提供任何烈性酒。

He turned , and offered his identity card .

他转过身来，出示了他的身份证。

（2）主动提出；表示：

He offered to lend me a sum of money .

他主动提出借给我一笔钱。

The new Premier offered to answer any questions the journalists might have at the press conference .

新任总理在记者招待会上表示愿意回答记者们提出的任何问题。

（3）出价，开价：

I'll offer you 5 pounds for this skirt .

我出 5 镑买这条裙子。

He offered the painting to me at a reduced price .

他愿削价把那幅画卖给我。

2．travel （travelling , travelled *BrE*）

（traveling , traveled *AmE*）

（1）*vi*．旅行，长途旅行：

I often travel to Brussels .

我常去布鲁塞尔。

I travelled to work by train .

我乘火车上班。

（2）*vt*．经过，通过，走过：

Nowadays you do not need to travel a long way to buy that machine . The only thing you have to do is to make a phonecall and soon they'll send it to you .

现在你不用到很远的地方去买这种机器了。你只需打个电话，他们就会很快把机器给你送来。

（3）*n*．（不可数）旅行，系列的旅行游览；（只能用复数形式）漫游：

They arrived after four days of hard travel .

他们经过四天艰苦的旅行后到达。

After she returned , she told us all about her travels .

她回来之后给我们讲述了有关她旅行的全部事情。

3. give up

(1) 放弃,终止,停止,辞去:

The doctor told him to give up smoking .

医生让他戒烟。

After she got married she gave up her job .

婚后她就辞去了工作。

(2) 交出,让出:

They fought bravely for about a week , but they had to give up their arms to the enemy at last .

他们勇敢地战斗了近一周,可是最后不得不向敌人缴械投降。

(3) 献出生命、时间:

When he was only a small boy , he decided to give himself up to football .

当他还是个小男孩的时候,他就决定把一生献给足球事业。

✍ 练习答案 Key to written exercises

1. 关键句型练习答案

A　1　What are you looking *at* ?

　　2　We have received fifty applications *in* all.

　　3　I happened to *meet your friend Tom this morning .*

　　4　It happened that *we were both travelling on the same train .*

　　5　I suppose *you've travelled by plane lots of times .*

6 He is supposed *to arrive here by 9*.

7 I wish you *had told me you were going to be late*.

8 I'd rather he *pretended he didn't know anything about it*.

9 If I can save up enough money, *I'm going to buy a car*.

10 You had better *leave now if you want to catch the next train*.

11 I find him to *be highly intelligent*.

B 1 John explained the position to me.

2 I described the film to my aunt.

C 1 *Not only* has he made this mistake before, but he will make it again.

2 *Only then* did I realize what was happening.

D 1 impolite   2 disagree   3 illegible
   4 inaccurate   5 unlocked   6 irregular

2. 多项选择题答案

1 c   2 b   3 b   4 c   5 a   6 c
7 d   8 a   9 c   10 d   11 a   12 d

Lesson 21
Daniel Mendoza
丹尼尔·门多萨

📖 **课文详注 Further notes on the text**

1. Boxing matches were very popular in England two hundred years ago.

ago 和 before 作副词时均可表达"在······(时间)以前"的概念，但是它们所指的时间段不同。用 ago 时，其时间段指"从现在起到过去某一点"的时间段，而用 before 时，其时间段通常指"从过去或将来某一点起到其前某一点"的时间段。由于它们所表达概念不同，因此使用 ago 时常与过去时连用，而使用 before 时常与过去完成时或将来完成时连用，如：

Several million years ago, our earth was covered by thick forests.

几百万年前，我们的地球被茂密的森林所覆盖。

John went abroad in June, 1997. I had met him two months before.

约翰 1997 年 6 月出国，在那之前两个月我见到过他。

I know she'll have then left her hometown two days before.

我知道她那时已于两天前离开她的家乡了。

但是，如果时间状语为 since + 时间 + ago 或句子谓语中使用了情态助动词、动名词、虚拟语气等时，ago 也可同完成时或现在时连用，如：

He has been there since two weeks ago.

两周来他一直在那儿。

You must have seen her two days ago.

你两天前一定见到过她。

I remember meeting you somewhere two years ago.

我记得两年前在哪儿见到过你。

2. In those days, boxers fought with bare fists for prize money.

fought with bare fists 赤拳搏斗。这里 fight (...) with... 表示"用……搏斗"之意。除此含义外,它还可表达出"在……帮助下战斗"、"同……战斗"之意,如:

A long time ago, people used to fight with swords.

过去,人们总是用剑搏斗。

In World War II, the Americans fought with the British and French against the Germans.

二战中,美国人同英国人和法国人一起并肩同德国人作战。

Try to stop the children from fighting with each other.

设法让孩子们别互相打斗了。

3. Because of this, they were known as 'prizefighters'.

because 和 because of 均作"因为"解,但 because 为连词,后须使用从句,表示原因,而 because of 则为介词,后应使用名词、代词或名词性从句,如:

He was worried because his daughter was late.

他感到担心,因为他女儿很晚还没来。

She was late because of the traffic.

因为交通的缘故,她来晚了。

She felt sorry because of what she had said.

她为自己所说的话感到后悔。

4. ... for there were no rules and ...

for 为并列连词,可用来表示因果关系,通常引导事后想到的原因,类似于置于括号内的说明性文字。具体用法参见第 1 课课文注释4。

5．The use of gloves was not introduced until 1860，when the Marquis of Queensberry drew up the first set of rules．

(1) 在包含 until(无论作介词还是连词)的句中主句动词为否定形式时，通常强调"对……之前的情况的改变"。

(2) Marquis 侯爵。英国贵族爵位封号有 Duke(公爵)、Marquis(侯爵)、Earl(伯爵)、Viscount(子爵)和 Baronet(男爵)。

(3) draw up 在此表示"制定"、"草拟"、"写出"之意，如：

The general has drawn up a plan to defeat the enemy.
将军已制定出打败敌人的计划。

Draw up a list of the guests for the dinner, please.
请列出一份参加宴会的客人名单。

6．... Mendoza did much to change crude prizefighting into a sport，for he bought science to the game．

(1) change . . . into . . . 把……变成……，如：

School has changed the boy into a coward.
学校把这个孩子变成了懦夫。

I should like to change these pounds into dollars.
我想把这些英镑换成美元。

(2) bring . . . to . . . 把……引进，把……加入到……，如：

How much experience does he bring to this specialised work?
他做这件专门工作有多少经验呢？

We must bring the rest of the villagers to our help in finding the missing child.
我们必须让其他的村民们来帮助我们一起找到这个失踪的孩子。

7．In his day，Mendoza enjoyed trememdous popularity．

in one's day 在某人年轻有为/兴旺发达/鼎盛时期，如：

She was really lovely in her day.

她年轻时的确很漂亮。

He produced numerous excellent works in his day.

他在鼎盛时期写出了无数优秀作品。

此时 day 需用单数形式,并且其前要有 his、her、their 等物主代词。

8. He was adored by rich and poor alike.

(1) 通常在某些表示抽象概念的形容词和某些表示人的形容词构成的名词前需使用定冠词,如:

You're asking me to do the impossible.

你在要我干不可能的事情。

In those days he had to take the rough with the smooth.

那时候他得逆来顺受。

这类表示抽象概念的形容词构成的名词通常与单数动词形式搭配使用,如:

The beautiful and realistic is what he is always longing for.

美好和现实的事物是他一直梦寐以求的。

然而这类表示人的群体的形容词却通常与复数动词形式搭配使用,如:

The poor of the city are often standing there begging.

城里的穷人们经常站在那里乞讨。

但是,在用 and 或 or 连接 rich 和 poor 表示"不论贫富(人)"时,其前通常不加定冠词 the,如:

Rich and poor live side by side but in conditions of extraordinary disparity.

富人穷人相邻而居,可是居住条件却天壤之别。

(2) 这里的 alike 为副词,修饰动词 adore,表示"同样地"之意,如:

'Write' and 'right' differ widely in meaning but are

231

pronounced exactly alike.

"write"和"right"两个词意义大不相同,而读音则完全相同。

alike 也可作补足语或后置定语形容词,其前可用 much、very much、somewhat、exactly,如:

The twins are very much alike.

那对双胞胎非常相像。

They are somewhat alike in appearance.

他们在外表上有些相像。

9. Mendoza rose to fame swiftly after ...

rise to fame 成名,如:

He rose to fame as an architect in 1950's.

他于 20 世纪 50 年代一举成为一名著名的建筑师。

10. In fact, Mendoza soon became so successful that Humphries turned against him.

turn(...)against ... (使……)转而反对,如:

Why did you turn against the party which had given you your first chance in politics?

你为什么转而反对曾给你第一次政治机会的政党呢?

The speaker's words were turned against himself.

演讲人的话自相矛盾。

11. The public bet a great deal of money on Mendoza, ...

bet on ... 对……下赌、bet sb. on ... 与某人打……的赌、bet...on... 在……上下……赌注,如:

Americans are fond of betting; they bet on horse races, baseball and football games and even on the election.

美国人喜欢打赌,他们对赛马、棒球和足球比赛,甚至选举都打赌。

He bet me on the black horse.

他和我赌那匹黑马。

I've bet all my money on the game.

我把所有的钱都压在了这场比赛上。

12. It was not until his third match in 1790 that he finally beat Humphries.

这是由先行词 it 引导的部分强调句,对正常句中的时间状语进行强调。这种句子由 it is / was...that...结构构成。在 is/ was 后放入正常句子中要被强调的部分,在 that 之后放入句子的其他部分。这种结构几乎可以用来强调除动词之外句子中的任何部分,如:

My mother threw an egg at the Minister of Education yesterday.

我母亲昨天向教育大臣扔了个鸡蛋。(正常句式)

It was my mother that threw an egg at the Minister of Education yesterday.

是我母亲昨天向教育大臣扔了个鸡蛋。(强调主语)

It was an egg that my mother threw at the Minister of Education yesterday.

我母亲昨天向教育大臣扔的是一个鸡蛋。(强调宾语)

It was yesterday that my mother threw an egg at the Minister of Education.

我母亲是在昨天向教育大臣扔了个鸡蛋。(强调时间状语)

It was the Minister of Education that my mother threw an egg at.

我母亲昨天是向教育大臣扔了个鸡蛋。(强调介词宾语)

当使用这种结构强调用人表示的主语时,可以用 who 取代 that,如:

It was my mother who threw an egg at the Minister of

233

Education yesterday.

是我母亲昨天向教育大臣扔了个鸡蛋。

当使用这种结构强调用人称代词表示的主语时,既可用该人称代词的主格形式,也可用其宾格形式。在非正式文体中,常常使用宾格形式,如:

$$\left\{\begin{array}{l} \textit{It was she who} \ldots \\ \textit{It was her that} \ldots \\ \text{正是她……} \end{array}\right.$$

13. Despite this,he was so extravagant that he was always in debt.

(1)despite 尽管。介词,同其后的名词(或代词等)构成的介词短语在句中作让步状语,通常与句子的主观意图无关。有关用法参见第 8 课课文注释 5。

(2)be in debt 负债,如:

He's head over ears in debt.

他债台高筑。

He's in debt to the extent of 10,000 dollars.

他负债已达 1 万美元。

14. He was sent to prison for failing to pay his debts and ...

for failing to pay his debts 因为还不起债。为介词短语,作原因状语,如:

Excuse me for not having answered your letter.

请原谅未给你回信。

语法 Grammar in use

1. ago 的用法

ago 用以指某事从发生至现在为止的一段时间,多与一般过去时连用,而不用于完成时态中,如:

That happened a long time ago.

那件事发生在很久以前。

I did it just a moment ago.

我刚刚才做了这件事。

如果表示某事从发生到现在之前的某一时刻,则不用 ago,而用 before 或 previously,并且用于过去完成时态句中,如:

He said that the supermarket had been opened some years before.

他说那家超市是几年前开张的。

在下述句式中,ago 不能同 since 同时使用,如不可说:

* *It is five years ago since we first met.*

而应说:

It is five years since we first met.

自我们初次相识已过去五年了。

ago 在"since + 时间 + ago"结构中的使用,见本课课文注释 1.

2. could 与 was/were able to

它们都用于表示过去的能力。通常 could 表示过去一般能力,而 was/were able to 表示过去做某一特定事情的能力,如:

He could run faster than anyone else.

他比任何人都跑得快。

I wasn't able to pass the exam.

我未能通过考试。

was/were able to do sth. 表示过去有能力做某事,并且做了某事。could 并不表示做了某事,如:

I was able to get two tickets for the World Cup Final yesterday.

我昨天搞到了两张世界杯赛的决赛票。

He said he could get two tickets for the World Cup Final.

他说他能搞到两张世界杯赛决赛的票。

could not 可以同 wasn't able to/was unable to 一样表示过去做

某一特定事情的能力,如:

I tried to ring you yesterday, but I couldn't/was't able/ was unable to get through.

昨天我给你打电话,可是没能打通。

could 可以表示目前或将来的可能性,如:

300,000 jobs could be lost.

可能会有 30 万人失业。

There could be something wrong in the plan.

计划中可能有误。

could 可以和 see、hear 和 smell 这类词连用,表示通过感官了解某事,如:

I could smell gas in the room.

我能闻到房间里有煤气的味道。

I could only see a few stars in the sky.

我在天空中只看到几颗星星。

📁 **词汇学习 Word study**

1. fight

(1) *n*. 战斗,打架,斗争:

John and his wife are always having fights.

约翰和他的妻子总是打架。

They have just had a severe fight.

他们刚刚经历了一场激烈的战斗。

(2) *vi*. 战斗,打架,斗争,奋斗:

Some men fight for glory; some fight for wages.

有些人为荣誉而奋斗;有些人为金钱而奋斗。

Words and facts are the weapons with which business battles are fought.

话语与事实是进行商战的武器。

(3) *vt*. 与……战斗,与……决斗,同……斗争:

For six years she fought a disease stubbornly.

她与一场疾病进行了 6 年顽强的斗争。

2. introduce *vt*.

(1) 介词,引荐:

Louise introduced Tom to her friends.

路易丝将汤姆介绍给她的朋友们。

He introduced her as his daughter.

他向大家介绍说她是他的女儿。

(2) 引进,传入,推行:

I wonder when tomatoes were introduced into Europe.

我想知道蕃茄是何时引进到欧洲的。

The new government will introduce new economic measures.

新政府将推行新的经济政策。

(3)（初次）提出:

The teacher introduced a question for debate.

老师提出一个问题让大家讨论。

A new budget will soon be introduced.

很快就会有一项新的预算出台。

3. draw up

(1) 起草,制定,拟定:

A report is now being drawn up.

正在起草一份报告。

He is now busy drawing up the project plan.

他正忙于起草那份项目计划书。

(2) 停住,使停住:

A police car drew up at our doors.

一辆警车停在了我们门前。

(3)(with)赶上,追上:

> *The Oxford crew began slowly but steadily drawing up with the Cambridge crew.*

牛津队开始缓慢但平稳地追上了剑桥队。

✍ 练习答案 Key to written exercises

1.关键句型练习答案

(Possible answers)

1   I went to the cinema *three days ago*.

   I had been to see the same film two days *before* that.

2   We *could* not see the game very well.

   We *were able to* see it when we stood on a bench.

3   He *did not* go abroad *until* he was twenty.

4   She was praised *by* the newspapers for her work with poor people.

   He was arrested *by* the police.

5   When the actor came of stage, the whole audience *rose* to cheer him.

   The girl *raised* her hand to ask a question.

6   We were *pleased to* hear your news.

   I was *sorry to* learn that you had been ill.

7   It is *clear* to me that they are not interested in the subject.

   When we set off, it was a beautiful *clear* day.

   When the road was *clear*, he crossed.

   She always keeps the kitchen very *clear*.

8   I am *afraid of* flying./He did the exercise *without* looking anything up in a dictionary./I must *apologize for* sending

238

you the wrong book. /They *congratulated* her *on* passing her
exam.

2. 多项选择题答案

| 1 | b | 2 | d | 3 | c | 4 | a | 5 | a | 6 | b |
| 7 | b | 8 | b | 9 | c | 10 | a | 11 | a | 12 | d |

Lesson 22
By heart
熟记台词

📖 **课文详注　Further notes on the text**

1. Some plays are so successful that they run for years on end.

on end 连续地,不断地。副词短语,可用来指人的行为或任何事物的延续性,如:

> *Some were made to work even for twelve hours a day on end.*
>
> 有些人被迫每天甚至连续工作 12 个小时。

此外,on end 还可表示"竖着"之意,用来指任何物体竖立放着,有时也可用来形容人因惊讶、害怕等而汗毛倒立,如:

> *He placed the box on end and made it for a tall stool.*
>
> 他把箱子竖着放,把它当个高凳使用。

> *The ghost story set their hair on end.*
>
> 那个鬼的故事使他们毛骨悚然。

2. ...,this is unfortunate for the poor actors who are required to go on repeating the same lines night after night.

(1) 这里 for 引导一个介词短语作状语,表示"对……而言"之意。who 为关系代词引导一定语从句,后置修饰 actors。意思为"对那些需要夜复一夜地重复同样台词的可怜演员来说是很不幸的"。

(2) go on doing 表示继续/接着做一直在做的事情,如:

> *You oughtn't go on living like that.*
>
> 你不应当继续这样生活。

240

She nodded , smiled , and went on stitching .

她点了点头,笑了笑,继续缝衣服。

在动词短语 go on 后,除了可使用动词的-ing 形式外,还可使用动词不定式形式,即 go on to do sth. 的形式,但表达继续／接着做另一件事的概念,如:

She went on to tell us about her life in America .

她接着给我们谈了谈她在美国的生活。

在动词后可使用动词-ing 形式,也可使用动词不定式形式,但语义不同的其他几个动词是 remember(记住)、forget(忘记)、stop(停止)和 regret(遗憾)等。上述这些动词后使用动词的-ing形式时,通常指该动作发生在上述动词之前,而使用动词不定式时,通常指该动作发生在上述动词之后。

3. **One would expect them to know their parts by heart and never have cause to falter.**

(1) 这里的 one 用来指泛指的人,意即"任何一个人"之意。

(2) 这里的 would 不是用来表示过去将来时,而是用来表示重复性和习惯性的行为。这种用法除可用来指过去外,有时还用来作为"will"这一用法(参见第 1 课课文注释 6)的委婉说法,表示"就会"、"往往会"、"总会",如:

Whenever Sunday came , we would get everything ready and go fishing .

每当星期天来临,我们都会把一切准备好去钓鱼。

He would never let anybody know what he was doing .

他决不会让任何人知道他在干什么。

(3) 介词短语 by heart 作方式状语,表示"通过记忆"的含义,常与动词 learn、know、get 等连用,组成习惯用语,如:

Soon he learnt the text by heart .

他很快就把这篇课文背了下来。

(4) have no cause to do 没有任何理由做。文中使用了表示否定的副词 never。句中的 to falter 作名词 cause 的定语,意即"结巴的理由"。有关作定语的不定式用法参见第 11 课课文注释 1。

4. A famous actor in a highly successful play was once cast in the role of an aristocrat who had been imprisoned in the Bastille for twenty years.

(1) be cast in the role of 被安排/分配扮演……角色。其中的介词短语 in the role of 为"以/作为……角色"之意。

(2) 关系代词 who 引导一定语从句,后置修饰 aristocrat。

5. In the last act, a gaoler would always come on to the stage with a letter which he would hand to the prisoner.

(1) in the last act 在最后一幕中。在戏剧中,act 为"幕"之意,scene 指"场"。a play in two acts 是"两幕剧";Act 1, Scene Ⅲ 是"第 1 幕第 3 场",如:

> *Hamlet kills the king in Act Ⅴ Scene Ⅱ.*
> 哈姆雷特在第 5 幕第 2 场中杀死了国王。

(2) gaoler = jailor。英国人常用 gaoler,美国人常用 jailor。

(3) come on 在戏剧表演或体育比赛中常用来表示"轮到上场/上台"之意,如:

> *The next player came on.*
> 轮到下一个运动员出场了。

(4) hand 作动词使用时可用作双宾语动词,构成 hand sb. sth. 或 hand sth. to sb.(把某物交给/递给某人)的结构,如:

> *I want that dictionary, would you please hand it to me?*
> 我想用那本词典。你能把它递给我吗?
> *He handed me the book, not even looked at me.*
> 他把那本书递给我,几乎连看都没看我一眼。

6. Even though the noble was expected to read the letter at each performance, he always insisted that it should be written out in

242

full.

(1) even though 连词,引导一让步状语从句,表示"尽管"、"即使"之意,如:

Even though you make great progress in your work , you shouldn't be conceited .

即使你在工作中取得了很大进步,也不应该骄傲自满。

有关用法参见第 10 课课文注释 5。

(2) 动词 insist 后所接的宾语从句中的 it should be written out...
为虚拟语气用法。在诸如 order(吩咐)、command(指示)、insist(坚持)、demand(要求)、request(要求)、ask(要求)、recommend(建议)、propose(建议)、suggest(建议)等动词后所接的宾语从句中,通常需使用 should + 动词原形构成的虚拟语气形式,如:

We insist that a meeting（should）be held as soon as possible .

我们坚持应尽快开会。

They demanded that they（should）be told the truth .

他们要求将实情告诉他们。

在英国英语中,常使用 should + 动词原形这样的虚拟语气结构,而在美国英语中,则直接使用动词原形这样的虚拟语气结构,特别是用于正式文体中。无论使用哪一种虚拟语气结构,这时从句中动词所表达的动作通常发生在主句动词动作之后。但是,当 suggest 表示"认为"、"表明",insist 表示"坚持说"、"坚持认为",而从句的动词动作又发生在这两个动词动作之前,或与之同时发生时,从句中还应使用正常的时态结构,如:

I insisted that he was wrong .

我坚持认为他是错的。

I suggest that you're not telling the truth .

243

我认为你没有说实话。

(3) in full 全部地,全数地,完全地。副词短语作状语,如:

> *They always accomplish each task in full.*
> 他们总是圆满地完成每次任务。

7. One night, the gaoler decided to play a joke on his colleague to find out if, after so many performances, he had managed to learn the contents of the letter by heart.

(1) play a joke on 拿……开玩笑,如:

> *Teachers often wonder what jokes the children will play on them next.*
> 老师们经常搞不清那些孩子们下面又会开他们的什么玩笑。

(2) to find out if...by heart 这一动词不定式在句中作目的状语。

(3) if 作连词,也可使用连词 whether 引导一个没有疑问词的问句,即表示"是否"之意的宾语从句,如:

> *He struck a match to see whether /if there was anybody in the room.*
> 他划了根火柴,看看屋子里是否有人。

当提出两种选择时,需采用 whether (...) or not 或 whether...or... 的结构,特别是在正式文体中,如:

> *They haven't decided whether they'll recommend or cancel the proposal.*
> 他们还未决定是提出还是取消这项提案。

当在介词之后或不定式之前使用时,则只能使用 whether,而不能使用 if,如:

> *I haven't settled the question of whether I'll go back home.*
> 我还没决定是否回家。

> *She doesn't know whether to get married now or wait.*
> 她不知道是现在就结婚还是等等再说。

有关用法参见第 13 课课文注释 6。

（4）after so many performances 这一作时间状语的介词短语,提到了 he had... by heart 之前,起到对此时间状语的强调作用。

8．The curtain went up on the final act of the play and revealed the aristocrat sitting alone behind bars in his dark cell.

（1）on the final act of the play 作时间状语,修饰动词 went up.

（2）sitting alone...cell 为现在分词短语,作 aristocrat 的定语。有关作定语的分词（短语）,参见第 1 课课文注释 5。

9．He entered the cell and presented the letter to the aristocrat.

present sth. to sb. 把某物交给（送给）某人;向某人提出某事。

使用时,通常将直接宾语放在动词之后,后面跟 to sb. 如:

They've presented a petition to the authorities.

他们已向当局递交了一份请愿书。

All this presents a grave threat to world peace.

所有这些都对世界和平构成严重威胁。

当将间接宾语置于 present 之后时,通常使用 present sb. with sth.的结构,如:

They presented the Queen with a bouquet of flowers on behalf of the women students.

她们代表女学生向女王献花。

10．The gaoler looked on eagerly, anxious to see if his fellow actor had at last learnt his lines.

anxious to see if...lines 为一形容词短语,在句中作伴随状况状语。形容词（短语）常可单独在句中起到多种状语的作用,多用于正式文体中,使文字显得更为生动,如:

Afraid of difficulties, they prefer to take the short cut.

由于害怕困难,他们宁愿走那条容易的路。（原因状语）

Overjoyed, she dashed out of the house.

她高兴极了,急步跑出屋外。(伴随状况状语)

Enthusiastic, they are quite co-operative.

热心的时候,他们相当合作。(时间状语)

有关用作状语的形容词(短语),参见第 16 课课文注释 8。这样使用形容词时,它们通常都被用来说明主语的情况。

11. **Then, squinting his eyes, he said...**

squinting his eyes 眼珠一转。这里为现在分词短语,作方式状语,表明做出 said 动作时的方式。

12. **Finding that he could not remember a word of the letter either, the gaoler replied:...**

(1) 这里为现在分词短语作原因状语,表明做出 replied 动作的原因。有关用法参见第 13 课课文注释 9。

(2) finding 后的 that 引导一宾语从句。

13. **Much to the aristocrat's amusement,... the letter which he proceeded to read to the prisoner.**

就结构而言,这里的关系代词 which 引导一限定性定语从句。但实际上,限定性和非限定性定语从句往往不因结构而定,而主要以该定语从句与先行词的语义关系而定。当它们之间的关系密不可分时,通常为限定性定语从句,反之则为非限定定语从句。由于就语义而言,句中 the letter 与 which 引导的定语从句关系比较松散,因此可视作非限定性定语从句来翻译。有关用法参见第 8 课课文注释 3。

📖 语法 Grammar in use

so...that...; such...that...; such a...that...

1. 这类从句描述结果。so 后面可跟形容词或副词,由 that 引导结果状语从句,that 可以省略,如:

His reactions are so quick(that)no one can match him.

他的反应如此敏捷(以致)无人比得上他。

We were so angry（that）we asked to see the manager.

我们如此生气而要求见经理。

such（a）后面跟名词(或形容词+名词)，由 that 引导结果状语从句，that 可以省略，如：

He is such a marvelous joker（that）you can't help laughing.

他是一个如此好开玩笑的人,(以致)弄得你不能不笑。

They are such wonderful players（that）no one can beat them.

他们都是出色的运动员,没有人能战胜他们。

2. 在书面语中,为了表示强调,可以将 so + 形容词置于句首,如：

So rapid is the rate of progress in the project that new one discovery seems to be followed by another on almost a monthly basis.

项目的进展如此之快,以致月月都有新的突破。

3. 也可用 so、and so 或 so that 表示结果,如：

He speaks very little English, so I talked to him through an interpreter.

他几乎不会说英语,所以我通过一个翻译与他交谈。

She was having great difficulty getting her car out, and so I had to move my car to help.

她费劲地想把她的车开出去,于是我不得不移动我的车而帮她。

My suitcase had been damaged on the journey home, so that the lid would not stay closed.

我的箱子在回家途中被摔坏了,所以箱盖关不严。

247

📁 **词汇学习　Word study**

1．expect *vt.*

（1）预计……可能发生；预料；期待：

> *I expect that the meeting will be postponed.*
>
> 我预计会议将会推迟召开。

注：在此义中，动词后可以用动词不定式，但所表达的意思与 that 从句略有不同，如：

> *I expect that Johnson will come to the meeting.*
>
> 我预料约翰逊会出席这次会议。
>
> *I expect Johnson to come to the meeting.*
>
> 我希望约翰逊出席这次会议。

前者仅表示一种单纯的预计，而后者则表示说话人希望约翰逊出席会议，如果他不来，说话人会不高兴或感到失望。再如：

> *I did not expect to find detectives waiting at home.*
>
> 我可没想到会看到侦探等在家里。
>
> *I don't expect it will be necessary.*
>
> 我没想到它是必不可少的。

注：表示预料或盼望某事不发生时用 do not expect it will happen，而不可说 expect something will not happen。

（2）认为：

> *I expect you've heard about the resignation of the chairman.*
>
> 我认为你已听说主席辞职的事了。
>
> *I expect they've gone.*
>
> 我想他们已经走了。
>
> *John should have reached home by now.*
>
> 约翰这会儿应该到家了。
>
> *I expect so.*
>
> 我也这么想。（而不用 *I expect it*）

248

（3）等待,期待,盼望:

> *They were expecting Wendy and the children.*
> 他们盼望着文迪和孩子们的到来。

> *I'm expecting an important letter from France.*
> 我正等待一封重要的法国来信。

注:不要将 expect 与 wait for 相混淆。wait for 表示等在某地或推迟做某事直到某人到来或某事发生,而 expect 则表示确信某人要来或某事要发生,如:

> *He sat on the bench and waited for his coffee.*
> 他坐在凳子上等他的咖啡。

> *We all have to wait for a kettle to boil.*
> 我们全都得等着一壶水烧开。

2. remember *vt.*

（1）牢记,记住,不忘记:

> *I remembered long passages from Shakespeare.*
> 我记住了大段莎士比亚的诗剧。

> *She tried hard to remember the poem.*
> 她竭力背下了那首诗。

（2）记起,回想起:

> *He remembered posting the letter.*
> 他记得已把那封信寄出去了。

注:remember 不能用进行时态。remember + 动词不定式与 remember + 动词-ing 形式所表达的意思不同。前者表示记得需要做某事,而后者表示记得已经做了的事。试比较:

> *I remembered to turn the gas off.*
> 我记住了要关掉煤气。

> *I remember calling home for more money.*
> 我记得曾打电报回家再要些钱。

（3）代……问候:

Remember me to your parents.

请代我向你父母问好。

✍ 练习答案 Key to written exercises

1.关键句型、难点练习答案

1 It was *so* hot *that* we all went swimming.

It was *such* glorious weather *that* we went to the beach.

It was *such a* hot day *that* we all went swimming.

2 We could use *used to* instead of *would*.

Mt grandfather *would* always read me a story when he came to visit us.

I *used to* enjoy the stories he told me.

3 See text *ll*.8-9.

4 *He suggested that* we should go for a walk.

He insisted that I should stay to lunch.

He demanded that we should give him his money back.

5 I *couldn't* swim very well, but *I managed to* swim across the small stream.

She *couldn't* speak English very well, but she managed to make herself understood.

6 See text *l*.13.

7 The girl *threw* a snowball *at* me.

He *pointed at* the building and said "That's the town hall".

8 We could say *have to* or *have got to* in place of *must*.

2.多项选择题答案

1 a   2 c   3 c   4 c   5 a   6 c

7 c   8 a   9 d   10 d   11 b   12 c

Lesson 23

One man's meat is another man's poison
各有所爱

📖 **课文详注　Further notes on the text**

1. **People become quite illogical when they try to decide what can be eaten and what cannot be eaten.**

   动词 decide 后为由关系代词 what 引导的两个并列宾语从句。用关系代词 what 与用关系代词 that/which 引导的从句不同，前者包含了关系代词 that/which 与"先行词"在内的含义。因此，当句中已有先行词时，其后不能使用 what。（有关用法参见第 16 课课文注释 3）如：

   * *You can have everything what you like.*
     你喜欢什么就要什么。
   * *That's all what I have.*
     那就是我所有的一切。

   应将以上两个错句中的 everything what 和 all what 分别改为 everything（that）和 all（that），或分别将错句中的 everything 和 all 去掉，只使用 what。

2. **If you lived in the Mediterranean, for instance, you would consider octopus a great delicacy.**

   a great delicacy 作宾语补足语，对 octopus 作补充说明。动词＋名词/代词＋名词的结构。一般而言，当动词后的两个名词间的关系可以通过"主语＋系动词＋主语补语"的结构从语义上予以说明时，这两个名词则为宾语和宾语补足语的关系；当从语义上不能予以说明时，则为双宾语（间接宾语和直接宾语）的

251

关系。如本句中 octopus 与 a great delicacy 间的关系可通过
Octopus is a great delicacy 结构予以解释,因此以上结构是宾语
同宾语补语的关系。试比较:

> *She made him a hero.*
> 她使他成为一名英雄。(复合宾语结构)
> *She made him a cake.*
> 她为他做了个蛋糕。(双宾语结构)

就语义而言,第 1 例中动词 made 后的代词 him 和名词 a hero
间的关系可解释为 he was a hero,而在后一例中则不能解释为
he was a cake。

3. **...to understand why some people find it repulsive.**

这里的 it 指前句中所提及的 octopus, repulsive 与前句中 a
great delicacy 一样,作宾语补足语,只是前者为一个名词作宾
语补足语,而此为一形容词作宾语补足语。动词后的名词/代
词和形容词之间的关系,同动词后的名词/代词和名词之间的
关系一样,均可用"主语＋系动词＋主语补足语"的结构予以说
明。

4. **On the other hand, your stomach would turn at the idea of
frying potatoes in animal fat——the normally accepted practice in
many northern countries.**

(1) 在"较长"的谈话或文章中,有许多词语可以表示出话语的结
构,说明话语与话语间的各类不同关系。这类语句的使用不
仅使所要表达的话语显得更为自然流畅,更富有逻辑性,而且
更易于受话者对所表达话语的理解。on the other hand 另一
方面,可是,而……却……,即为这类的话语,表明所说话语同
前文已说话语间的比较,如:

> *Food here is cheaper than in Britain; clothing, on the
> other hand, is dearer.*
> 这儿的食品比英国便宜,而衣服却比那儿要贵。

与之相类似的其他话语有 all the same(同样,仍然)、(and)yet
(然而)、still(仍然)、howerer(然而)等。

（2）at the idea of 一想到。类似的结构还有 at the mention of(一提
到)、at the sight of(一看到)、at the thought of(一想到)等,如:

> *She wept bitterly at the sight of his distress.*
>
> 一看到他那痛苦的样子,她就伤心地哭了起来。
>
> *The old man would brighten up at the mention of his grandsons and granddaughters.*
>
> 一提及孙子、孙女们,老人就会喜形于色。

（3）the normally accepted practice in many northern countries 破折
号后这部分为说明性内容,是对 frying potatoes in animal fat
这一做法的进一步说明。这种形式多用于表示对一人/事物
的表述后又想到或要追加说明的内容。当这样的说明性语句
出现在句中时,通常需在其前后各标注一破折号。有关用法,
见第 3 课课文注释 3。

5. The sad truth is that most of us have been brought up to eat certain foods and we stick to them all our lives.

（1）that 引导一名词性从句,在句子中作主语补足语。因为从句
中使用了被动语态,因此动词不定式短语 to eat certain foods
在该从句中作主语 most of us 的补足语。

（2）bring up 在本文中作"养育"、"抚养"之意,如:

> *The old woman has brought her up as her own child.*
>
> 那位老妇人把她当作亲生闺女一样抚养成人。
>
> *Their father believed in bringing them up the hard way.*
>
> 他们的父亲主张对他们管教要严。

（3）stick to 具有"坚持(立场、观点、原则、方法、规定等)"、"坚守
(岗位)"、"信守(诺言、合同)"、"忠于(某人)"等含义。其后一
般接名词或代词,如:

> *He always sticks to his own opinions.*

他总是坚持己见。

You should stick firmly to this principle.

你应坚决地坚持这一原则。

（4）句中 all our lives 为副词短语作状语,表示"一生"、"一辈子"之意。all one's life 中的 one's 根据句子主语的不同,其形式也有 our、their、your 等形式的不同,而其后的 life 也会有复数 lives 形式。该短语也可作名词词组,可以在句子中作宾语,表示"整个/全部生命"、"一生"之意。无论将其用作副词短语还是名词词组,句子中的动词均需使用延续性时间概念动词,如:

He has worked sincerely and hard all his life.

他热情努力地工作了一辈子。（*work* 为延续性动词,*all his life* 为状语）

They devoted all their lives to the cause of science and technology.

他们把全部生命都贡献给了科技事业。（*devote* 为延续性动词,*all their lives* 为宾语）

6．**No creature has received more praise and abuse than the common garden snail.**

more...than... 中的 more 之后可接名词（如句中）、形容词、副词和动词（修饰动词时,通常置于该动词之后）。这种结构通常用于表达事物之间的差别。当 more 后接名词时,more 为形容词;当为其他词性时,则为副词。than 为从属连词,引导出比较状语从句。本句中的 than 后是一省略的从句,为避免重复,省略了 has received。整个结构有"比……要……"、"与其说……倒不如说……"之意,如:

His new book is much more interesting than his last.

他新出的书比前一本要有趣得多。

More people like to drink green tea than black tea.

喜欢喝绿茶的人要比喜欢喝红茶的人多。

*The book he has recently written seems to be more a
dictionary than a grammar book .*

他最近写的书看上去与其说是语法书倒不如说是词典。

**7 . There are countless people who , ever since their early years ,
have learned to associate snails with food .**

（1）ever since their early years 在本定语从句中作时间状语，一般
置于句末。这里将其提至谓语动词 have learned 之前，表示对
该时间状语的强调。

（2）associate … with 将……与……联系起来，同……交往，与
……结交，如：

*People naturally associate Darwin with the doctrine of
evolution .*

人们很自然地把达尔文同进化论学说联系在一起。

Never associate with bad companions .

千万别同坏人交往。

8 . As his flat is in a large town , …

as 为从属连词，在此引导一原因状语从句，表示"由于"、"既然"
之意。由其引导的从句所表示的原因通常为已为人所知或次
要于句中其他信息。有关用法参见第 1 课课文注释 12。

**9 . The idea never appealed to me very much , but one day , after a
heavy shower , I happened to be walking in my garden when I
noticed a huge number of snails taking a stroll on some of my
prize plants .**

（1）appeal to… 对……有吸引力，投合……的兴趣/心意，如：

Does she say anything that appeals to you especially ?
她常说些你特别感兴趣的事情吗？

The Observer *does not appeal to emotion but to reason .*
《观察家报》不激发情感但激发理性。

（2）句子中的连词 when 为倒装用法，即就逻辑而言，它应置于 I

happened to be walking in my garden 之前, 而 I noticed... 为其主句。when 的这种倒装用法通常用来描述事件的意外性或突发性。有关用法参见第 20 课课文注释 4。

(3) 句中 taking a stroll（在散步）是以拟人法来形容蜗牛做出的动作。

10．Acting on a sudden impulse, I collected several dozen...

(1) acting on a sudden impulse 为一分词短语, 作原因状语。有关该用法的分词短语说明参见第 13 课课文注释 9。act on 常用来表示"按照/根据/凭藉……行动"、"对……起作用"之意, 如:

> *The police are acting on the information received.*
> 警察正根据得到的情报采取行动。
> *The medicine acted on his fever at once.*
> 这药使他立即退了烧。

(2) dozen 后省略了 of snails。当 dozen 同数词或 many、several、some 等形容词连用时, 复数不加 -s。

11．Robert was delighted to see me and equally pleased with my little gift.

(1) 在 be delighted to do 中, 动词不定式作原因状语, 说明使产生 delighted 情绪的原因。动词不定式的这一用法, 常用于作主语补足语的形容词（或过去分词）之后。

(2) be pleased with... 对……感到满意/高兴。介词 with 后一般接名词、代词或以 what 引导的名词性从句, 如:

> *They felt pleased with the gifts we had sent to them.*
> 他们对我们送的礼物感到满意。
> *She's very much pleased with what he's done for her.*
> 她对他为她所做的事情感到非常高兴。

12．...and had taken complete possession of the hall!

take possession of 占据（占有）; 获得, 如:

The soldiers took possession of the enemy's fort .

士兵们占领了敌人的要塞。

You can't take possession of the house until all the papers have been signed .

在各类文件签字以前,你不能住进那所房子。

📖 语法 Grammar in use

most 的用法

1. 用于构成形容词或副词的最高级

在英语中,除单音节或部分双音节形容词外,都用 the most + 形容词构成形容词最高级形式;而副词除个别副词外,通常都用 most + 副词构成最高级,如:

The head is the most sensitive part of the body .

头是身体中最敏感的部位。

These are the works I respond to most strongly .

这些是引起我最强共鸣的作品。

2. most 或 most of 用于谈论某群人或某些东西中的大多数或某物的大部分

most + 泛指名词,如:

Most doctors don't smoke .

大多数医生都不抽烟。

Most wine is imported .

大量的酒是进口的。

Most people lead unadventurous lives .

多数人过着平淡的生活。

most of + 特指名词,如:

She had drunk most of the wine .

大部分酒是她喝的。

Most of us have our own views on politics.

我们中多数人对政治都有自己的看法。

3. most 有时用于形容词或副词前表示非常

此时与 very 同义,以表达对某事的看法。但是不用于常用词 good 或 big 之前,如:

The car is most reliable.

这辆车性能非常可靠。

The film is most disturbing.

这部电影非常令人不快。

注:此用法过于正式,口语中可用 really 一词代替,如:

It was really good, wasn't, Tom?

真棒,对吧,汤姆?

We're doing really well actually.

我们的确干得不错。

📁 **词汇学习　Word study**

1. consider

(1) *vt.* 考虑,细想:

I'm seriously considering leaving the company.

我正认真地考虑离开这家公司。

注:consider 之后用 -ing 形式,在其后不能使用动词不定式,如:

He was considering taking the bedside table downstairs.

他在考虑把那个床头柜搬到楼下去。

He had no time to consider the matter.

他没有时间考虑这件事。

(2) *vt.* 认为,把……看作:

Professor Heinz is considered (to be) an expert in

political science.

海因兹教授被看作是政治学方面的专家。

I consider that the problem is now solved.

我认为那个问题现在已经解决了。

(3) *vi*. 考虑,细想:

Consider carefully before doing anything.

三思而后行。

2. bring up

(1) 养育,教养:

My aunt brought up four children.

我姑姑养育了4个孩子。

Your children have been well brought up.

你的孩子们很有教养。

注:在美国英语中可以用 raise 代替 bring up,如:

Henry and his wife May have raised ten children.

亨利和他的妻子梅养育了10个孩子。

(2) 提出:

Your suggestion will be brought up at the next meeting.

你的建议将在下次会议上提出。

At the court they brought up fresh evidence.

在法庭上他们提出了新的证据。

(3) 把……举高,使升上,拿到高处:

When the doctor arrives, bring him up.

医生来到之后,把他领上楼来。

This path will bring you up to the top of the cliff.

这条小路会将你带到这个悬崖的顶部。

3. collect *vt*.

(1) 收集,采集,聚集:

Once a year I volunteer to collect money for cancer

259

research .

我每年一次自愿为癌症研究集资。

(2)（去）取,接:

As soon as he came back from his holiday he went to his office to collect his own post .

他刚度假回来就到办公室去取他自己的信件。

(3) 聚集,积聚:

A blue layer of cigarette smoke collected near the office ceiling .

办公室天花板下聚集了一层蓝色的香烟烟雾。

A crowd collected in the square .

广场上聚集了一群人。

✍ 练习答案 Key to written exercises

1. 关键句型、难点练习答案

1 I was *quite* sure that the boy was innocent.

You must keep *quiet* during the concert.

2 *If you had lived* in the Mediterranean, you would have considered octopus a great delicacy.

3 When you are learning to play the piano, you need a lot of *practice* .

You need to *practise* a lot when you are learning to play the piano.

4 *Most* people hated the play.

This is *the most* interesting exhibition I've been to.

5 I've been learning English *since* I was ten.

I've been learning English *for* four years.

I started learning English four years *ago* .

6   *As* here means *because* or *since* :

    She often appears on the stage *as* a young girl.

    I saw her *as* she was coming out of the bank.

    You should do *as* you are told.

7   She *has been asking* me questions all day.

    She *has asked* me three questions in the past 5 minutes!

8   *He happens* to be a friend of mine.

    It happened that we were in the town on holiday.

    Nothing much *happened* at the meeting. It was boring.

2. 多项选择题答案

1	d	2	a	3	d	4	a	5	b	6	c
7	a	8	c	9	d	10	d	11	b	12	b

Lesson 24

A skeleton in the cupboard

"家丑"

📖 **课文详注 Further notes on the text**

1. A skeleton in the cupboard

是英语中一个成语,有"家丑"之意,直译为"柜中的骷髅",也称之为 a skeleton in the closet。

2. We often read in novels how a seemingly respectable person or family has some terrible secret which has been concealed from strangers for years.

(1) how 为连接副词,引导一个宾语从句。which 为关系代词,引导一个定语从句,置后修饰先行词 secret。

(2) conceal ...(from...)(对/向……)隐瞒……在语义上,与 hide 略有不同。除了较 conceal 更常用外,hide 可指偶然的隐蔽,不一定含有"故意"之意,如:

The sun is hidden by the clouds.

太阳被云遮没了。

此外,hide 一词可作不及物动词使用,而 conceal 只能作及物动词,如:

Let's hide behind the door.

我们藏在门后吧。

而 conceal 常指故意巧妙地"藏匿"、"隐瞒"之意,如:

The thief tried to conceal the stolen money in his shoes.

那个小偷想把偷来的钱藏在他的鞋里。

The driver tried to conceal from the police the fact that he

262

had drunk before driving.

那个司机想向警察隐瞒酒后驾车这一事实。(本句中 *the fact* 及其后由 *that* 引导的同位语从句为 *conceal* 的宾语，由于较长，为使句子紧凑和平衡，将其放在了 *from the police* 之后)

3. The English language possesses a vivid saying to describe this sort of situation.

possess 为"静态动词(stative verb)"，而静态动词不能用于正在进行时结构中，即使表示说话时正在进行的事情也如此，如：

I like this wine.

我喜欢这种酒。(不可说：* *I'm liking*...)

Do you believe what he says?

你相信他的话吗？(不可说：* *Are you believing*...?)

然而，还有一些动词，既可用作静态动词，也可用作"动态动词(dynamic verb)"，但表达不同的语义。只有用作表达动态动词的语义时，方可使用正在进行时态结构，试比较：

What is he thinking about?
他在想什么？
He thinks you're right.
他认为你是对的。

I'm just tasting it.
我只不过尝尝它。
It tastes wonderful.
这味道好极了。

We're seeing the manager tomorrow.
我们明天要见经理。
I see what you mean.
我明白你的意思。

在英语学习中，要特别注意动词的这种"静态"和"动态"的区

263

分,尤其具有静态动词特征的这类动词。

4. At some dramatic moment in the story, ...

句中 some 为"某一个"含义,而非"一些"含义。当用 some 表达此义时,其后名词须用单数形式,如:

> *I read about this in some magazine.*
>
> 我在某本杂志中读到过此事。

at some dramatic moment 是时间状语。单独使用介词短语 at the moment 时,只能作状语,往往具有两个意思:(1)此刻,目前,(2)当时,那时。用于前者时,通常使用现在时;用于后者时,通常使用过去时,如:

> *I know the phone number well enough, but I just can't think of it at the moment.*
>
> 我非常熟悉那个电话号码,可此刻一时就是想不起来了。
>
> *She didn't buy the ticket, because she had no money on her at the moment.*
>
> 她没买票,因为当时她没带钱。

5. The reader's hair stands on end when he reads in the final pages of the novel that the heroine, a dear old lady who had always been so kind to everybody, had, in her youth, poisoned every one of her five husbands.

(1) The reader's hair stands on end 读者感到毛骨悚然。这里 on end 为介词短语作状语,表示"倒立着"、"竖着"之意。类似的表达法还有 one's blood runs cold/turns to ice(某人被吓僵了)、one has goose-flesh(某人被吓得起了一身鸡皮疙瘩)等。

(2) that 为连接代词,引导一宾语从句,作动词 read 的宾语。一般情况下,由 that 引导的宾语从句应紧跟在动词之后,如:

> *The letter says that they are leaving on the 16th.*
>
> 信上说他们 16 号动身。

但由于本句中该宾语从句较长,而地点状语 in the final pages

264

相对较短,如将其置于句末,句子显得头重脚轻,缺少平衡感。为使句子更为紧凑,故将该宾语从句放到了地点状语之后。在口语中,that 经常省略,如:

> *I don't think you're right.*
> 我想你是不对的。
>
> *I don't suppose he cares, does he?*
> 我看他不在乎,对吧?

(3) in her youth 为时间状语,其正常结构是置于全句之后。现提前插入句中,主要起到对此时间状语的强调作用。

6. It is all very well for such things to occur in fiction.

it 在句中为形式主语,而全句的逻辑主语是带 for 结构的动词不定式。在英语中,"形容词 + for + 宾语 + 动词不定式"这样的结构中的形容词,常为下述 3 类形容词:

(1) 表示重要性或紧迫性的形容词(important、essential、vital、necessary、pointless、unimportant、unnecessary 等),如:

> *It's essential for the rooms to have plenty of light.*
> 室内光线要充足,这点很重要。

(2) 表示程度的形容词(common、normal、unusual、rare 等),如:

> *I think it's normal for a child to feel tired after the exercises.*
> 我想这样的练习后,孩子感到累是很正常的。

(3) 表示个人对将来情况的反应的形容词(anxious、eager 等),如:

> *We'll be delighted for the Johnsons to come and stay with us.*
> 我们对约翰逊一家能来并同我们住在一起感到很高兴。

It's all very well for...to do...、it's all right for...to do...和 it's natural for...to do...这样的结构还常同 but 连接的句子连用,往往表示某种失望或不满,如:

> *It's all very well/all right、natural for them to suggest*

265

buying a large colour TV set, but where can we get the money?

他们建议买一台大彩电是很自然的事儿,但我们到哪儿去弄钱呢?

7. To varying degrees, we all...

to varying degrees 在不同程度上。表示"在……程度上"时,常使用介词 to(而不可从汉语出发,误用介词 on),如:

to a certain degree 在某种程度上

to a considerable degree 在很大程度上

而 to a degree 往往表示"非常"、(美语中)"有点"之意,如:

He's insolent to a degree.

他有点傲慢。

此外,degree 通常用来指"质"的程度,而不表示"量"的程度,如不可用 That newly-published dictionary is to a great degree made up of second-hand knowledge 来表达"那本新出的词典的内容在很大程度上都是抄袭他人的"。由于该中文句中的"程度"指篇幅所占比重,是量的概念,因此应用 to a great extent 取代 to a great degree。

8. The only person I know who has a skeleton in the cupboard is George Carlton, and he is very proud of the fact.

(1) I know 为定语从句,省略了关系代词 that。who 也为关系代词,引导一定语从句,均修饰同一个先行词 person,意即"我所知道的惟一有柜中骷髅的人"。

(2) be proud of 为……而自豪,为……而骄傲。介词 of 后可使用名词、代词或动名词,在句中用作主语补足语。这一用法通常具有褒义,如:

We are proud of our country.

我们为自己的祖国感到自豪。

They are proud of being so successful.

他们对自己取得的巨大成功而自豪。

9. Instead of becoming a doctor, however, he became a...

instead of,短语介词,往往表示出一正一反,即肯定一面而否定另一面,有时含有"本应……而没……"的含义,有时根据上下文情况译作"而不(是)"、"不是"、"并非"、"反而"等,如:

They finally found themselves in Birkenhead instead of Liverpool.

最终他们发现他们是在伯肯黑德,而不是在利物浦。

The rain, instead of bringing any good as expected, caused a lot of harm to the crops.

那场雨非但没有给农作物带来什么好处,反而造成了极大灾害。

虽然 instead of 为一短语介词,但其后除了可以像如上例句中那样使用名词或名词性短语外,还可以使用形容词、介词短语、副词等,如:

Taking exercises every day makes him look younger intead of older.

每天锻炼身体使他显得年轻而不见老。(形容词)

In warm weather she often reads under that old tree instead of at home.

天气暖和时,她常在那棵老树下读书,而不是在家中读书。(介词短语)

Production increases quickly instead of slowly.

生产增长很快,而不是很慢。(副词)

10. I once spent an uncomfortable weekend which I shall never forget at his house.

which 为关系代词,引导一定语从句,修饰 weekend。at his house 作地点状语,修饰动词 spent(而非修饰从句中的动词 forget),意即"在他家度过的我永远不会忘记的那个周末"。

11. **..., I decided to hang one of the two suits I had brought with me in the cupboard.**

one of the two suits...me 作动词 hang 的宾语。I had brought with me 为定语从句,修饰先行词 one of the two suits。在此定语从句前省略了关系代词 that/which,意即"我随身带来的两套衣服中的一套"。

12. **... and then stood in front of it petrified.**

句中动词 stood 表示处于某种状态,起到系动词的作用。英语中,除 be 动词外,还有许多其他动词也可作系动词,其后常接形容词、名词、分词等,表示主语处于某种状态中的特征,可将其视作主语补语,如:

This remains a controversial topic.

这仍然是一个有争议的话题。(名词)

She sat there still without a word for hours.

她一动不动,静静地坐在那儿几个小时。(形容词)

Time has become more and more pressing.

时间变得越来越紧迫。(分词)

参见第 3 课课文注释 10。

13. **... and it gave me the impression that it was about to leap out at me.**

(1) 这里的 that 为连接代词。由于 impression 在从句中不承担任何成分,因此 that 引导的是一个同位语从句。

(2) be about to do...用于表达"即将做……"、"就要做……"或"正要做……"之意,表明现刻或马上的将来,而非长久的将来,因此通常不可同表示将来时间的状语连用,即便像 immediately (立即)、very soon(很快)、at once(立即)这类表示时间状语的词或短语也不可使用,如:

They are about to leave China for home.

他们就要离开中国回国了。

Don't go out now—we're about to have lunch .

不要出去了,马上就要吃中午饭了。

在美国英语里,not about to 可以表示"不愿意"之意,如:

I'm not about to pay 30 dollars for a dress like that .

我不愿意花 30 美元买这样一件衣服。

14.'That's Sebastian...'

Sebastian 即 Saint Sebastian,罗马基督教殉道者,早期基督教徒,罗马军官。他引导士兵信奉基督教,皇帝发现后命令用乱箭射杀,侥幸不死,后被乱棒打死。他经常出现在文艺复兴时期的绘画中。这里说话人将医科学生所用的人体骨骼比作绘画常用人物,是作者使用的暗喻(metaphor)修辞手法。

📖 语法 Grammar in use

few,a few;little,a little

1. few 与 a few 均用于可数名词前面,但所表达的意思不同。a few 表示"一些"、"几个"之意;few 则表示"几乎没有"、"没几个"等基本否定的含义,常与 very 连用,试比较:

> *I have a few friends .*
> 我有一些朋友。
> *I have few friends .*
> 我没几个朋友。

> *I'd like to ask a few questions .*
> 我想问几个问题。
> *I have few questions .*
> 我没什么问题。

few 和 a few 还可作代词,词义同上,如:

Each volunteer spent one night awake in the cathedral . A few spent two .

每位志愿者在教堂里呆一个晚上。有几个人呆两个晚上。

Many are invited but few are chosen.

许多人得到邀请,但几乎没人被选中。

注:在口语中很少用 few,多数情况下用 not many,如:

I don't have many visitors.

我没有多少来访者。

2. little 和 a little 均用于不可数名词前,但所表达的意思不同。a little 表示"有一些"、"有点儿"之意;little 则表示"几乎没有"、"没什么"等基本否定的含义,常与 very 连用,试比较:

> *I have a little money.*
> 我有点钱。
> *I have little money.*
> 我没什么钱。

> *I have made a little progress.*
> 我取得了一点进步。
> *He has very little hope of winning this race.*
> 他几乎无望在这场比赛中获胜。

little 和 a little 还可作代词,词义同上,如:

He knows a little of everything.

他什么都懂点儿。

Little has changed.

几乎没什么改变。

注:在口语中很少用 little,多数情况下用 not much,如:

I haven't got much money.

我没有多少钱。

词汇学习 Word study

1. learn (learned 或 learnt, learned 或 learnt)

(1) *vt*. 学,学习,学会:

I learnt how to knit when I was eight.

我8岁时学会了编织。

He had never learnt to read and write.

他从没学会读书写字。

(2) *vt*. 发现,得知,认识到:

He learnt that the plot had been exposed.

他知道阴谋已被揭穿。

People learnt that honesty paid.

人们认识到诚实有好报。

(3) *vi*. (from)从……知悉,向……学习:

We should learn from our own mistakes.

我们应该从我们自己的错误中接受教训。

I learnt it from John.

我从约翰那里听说的这件事。

2. spend (spent, spent) *vt*.

(1) 花(时间)做某事:

She woke early, intending to spend all day writing.

她起得很早,打算用一整天的时间写作。

He spends more time on sports than on studies.

他花在体育运动上的时间超过花在学习上的时间。

注:当在一段时间里自始至终做某事时,应使用 spend time doing sth., 而不说 spend time in/on doing sth. 或 spend time to do sth.。

(2) 度过,消磨:

She has spent all her life in this small town.

她已在这个小镇上度过了一生。

We found a hotel where we could spend the night.

我们找到了一个可以过夜的旅店。

271

(3) 用(钱),花费：

> *I can't spend any more money on this car.*
> 我不能在这辆车上花费更多的钱了。
> *Her husband had spent all her money.*
> 她丈夫花光了她所有的钱。

3. hang

(1) *vt.*（hung, hung）悬挂：

> *Would you mind helping me to hang the picture on the wall?*
> 你能帮我把这幅画挂在墙上吗？

(2) *vt.*（hanged, hanged）吊死,绞死：

> *In the 19th century, people were hanged for minor crimes.*
> 在 19 世纪,人们因轻微的罪而被绞死。

(3) hang up 挂断电话：

> *She was so angry that she hung up on him.*
> 她气得挂断了他的电话。

✐ 练习答案 Key to written exercises

1. 关键句型、难点练习答案

1 We *frequently* eat at that restaurant.

He *rarely* gets up before 11 o'clock.

She *always* catches the 8 o'clock bus to work.

They *never* get up early on Sundays.

2 She *taught* me to speak English.

He *allowed* us to park behind his house.

3 We invited 50 people to the barbecue, but *very few* came—only 5 in fact.

The next time we had a barbecue, *quite a few* people came—about 45.

When everybody had finished eating, there was *very little* (food) left.

There's *a little* meat left if you'd like some.

4 aware of, ready for, patient with, afraid of, fortunate in, curious about, dependent on, different from, skilful at, familiar with, close to

5 She *made* me do some extra exercises for homework.

The other teacher often *lets* me hand in my assignments late.

6 'You must see *Arsenic and Old Lace* again,' Tom said. 'It's a wonderful film.'

'No, thank you,' I answered. 'I don't think I could stand it.'

'I saw it years ago,' said Tom. 'I shall never forget those dear old ladies.'

'And I shall never forget the dreadful moment when Boris Karloff suddenly appeared at the window,' I said. 'I nearly jumped out of my seat.'

2. 多项选择题答案

1 a	2 c	3 a	4 a	5 d	6 b
7 c	8 b	9 d	10 a	11 d	12 a

Lesson 25
The *Cutty Sark*
"卡蒂萨克"号帆船

📖 **课文详注** **Further notes on the text**

1. She stands on dry land...

这里的 she 指 the *Cutty Sark* 号帆船，为拟人法（personification）。

2. She serves as an impressive reminder of...

serve as 充当,用作。这里 an impressive reminder of...为主语补足语,如:

His unpunctuality served as an excuse to dismiss him.

他不遵守时间被作为撵走他的借口。

It serves as a lesson to him.

这对他来讲是个教训。

动词 serve 后也可有一宾语,构成 serve sb. as 被某人用作;为某人充当,如:

He was sitting at the plain table that served him as a desk.

他正坐在那张被他当作办公桌使用的简易餐桌前。

3. The only other ship to match her was the *Thermopylae*.

这里的动词不定式短语 to match her 作定语,修饰 ship。动词 match 这里为"比得上"之意,作及物动词使用。在表达"在……比得上"、"在……相称"时,通常使用介词 in,如:

You can't match him in knowledge of American Literature.

在有关美国文学的知识方面,你无法同他相比。

274

No one can match her in singing.

论唱歌谁也比不上她。

在表达"与……相比"、"与……相一致"时,通常使用介词 with,如:

Your jacket doesn't match with your trousers.

你的短上衣与你的裤子不相配。

4. **Both these ships set out from Shanghai on June 18th, 1872 on an exciting race to England.**

(1) both these ships 与 both ships 意思相同。这里使用 these 表示对所指两条帆船的进一步强调。

(2) set out 出发/动身(旅行等)。该词组为"动词 + 副词",作不及物动词使用。在表达"出发/动身去"之意时,通常需使用介词 on/for,其后的 on/for 介词短语在句中作目的状语,如:

The children were always excited to set out on a camping trip.

孩子们对出发去野营旅行总是非常激动。

5. **The first of the two ships to reach Java after the race had begun was...took the lead.**

(1) 这里动词不定式短语 to reach Java 为定语,修饰 first,意即"两艘船中到达 Java 的第一艘船"。

(2) after 为连词,引导一时间状语从句,说明动词 reach 发生的时间。

(3) take the lead 领先,居首位,如:

Being the head of the team, you should take the lead in everything.

作为一队之长,你应事事带头。

与此相类似的搭配形式,如:

gain / have the lead 领先;获得领先位置

hold the lead 保持领先(位置)

275

lose the lead 失去领先位置/地位,落后

6. It seemed certain that she would be the first ship home, but during the race ...

(1) 这里的 it 为先行词 it 的使用方法,无实际语义含义,起到形式主语的作用,其后由 that 引导的从句为该句的逻辑主语。有关先行词 it 的用法参第 1 课课文注释 13。

(2) 这里的副词 home 指美国,在句中起定语作用,修饰 ship。有关用作定语的常见副词参见第 1 课课文注释 7。

(3) during 在……期间。为介词,其后使用名词或名词性短语,不可将其作连词使用。

7. ... a very heavy storm during which her...

这是由介词 during + 关系代词 which 构成的定语从句。关系代词代替了先行词 storm,介词 during 同其一起构成从句中的时间状语。有关此类定语从句的用法参见第 17 课课文注释 2。

8. The *Cutty Sark* rolled from side to side and it became impossible to steer her.

(1) from side to side 从一边到另一边,从左至右。类似的短语搭配形式很多,如 from day to day (天天,一天一天地)、from house to house (挨家挨户地)、from door to door (挨门挨户地)等,如:

We were being thrown from side to side of the carriage.
我们在马车中左右颠簸。

He sells books from door to door.
他挨门挨户地卖书。

这样的在 from 和 to 后使用相同名词的表达形式,通常表示"从一个至另一个"、"从一个至下一个"的含义,在句子中作状语,强调其所修饰动词的重复性。

(2) it became impossible to steer her 中 it 为先行词,作形式主语,动词不定式短语 to steer her 为逻辑主语,也可构成 to steer

her became impossible。有关用法参见第 1 课课文注释 13。

9. **A temporary rudder was made on board from spare planks and it was fitted with great difficulty.**

（1）介词短语 on board 在句中作地点状语。正常语序是将其放在 from spare planks 之后。现提前起到使文字更为紧凑和对该地点状语加以强调的作用。

介词短语 from spare planks 与句中动词 make 搭配使用,构成词组 be made from...（由……制成）。

（2）with great difficulty 为"介词＋抽象名词"构成的短语,在句中作状语。

10. **... for there was a danger that if she travelled too quickly, this rudder would be torn away as well.**

（1）for 为并列连词,引导一并列从句,对主句作原因上的追加(补充)说明。有关用法参见第 1 课课文注释 4。

（2）that 为连词,在此引导一同位语从句,对 danger 作进一步说明（解释）,有关用法参见第 9 课课文注释 4。

（3）if 在同位语从句中引导一条件状语,说明 this rudder would be torn away 的条件。

11. **Because of this, the *Cutty Sark* lost her lead.**

（1）because of 因为。其后应使用名词、代词或名词性从句。

（2）lost her lead 失去了其领先地位。有关动词同名词 lead 的搭配用法参见本课课文注释 5。

12. **..., the captain called in at a port to have a new rudder fitted, but by now the *Thermopylae* was over five hundred miles ahead.**

（1）call in 短暂访问,短暂停留。为动词＋副词搭配的短语,常用于一般时态,如:

Please call in any time you're in town, I shall be glad to see you.

进城时请随时来,我将很高兴见到你。

(2) 动词不定式短语 to have a new rudder fitted 为目的状语,表明将该船停靠在那一港口的目的。动词 have + 宾语 + 动词过去分词(即 to have sth. done)这种复合宾语结构表示"使某事处于完成的状态"的含义,但通常不指明动作的执行者,而过去分词表示出的动作由他人来完成。复合宾语的逻辑主语为动作的承受者,如:

You'd better have that tooth pulled out.

你最好把那颗牙拔掉。

The parents intended to have their daughter educated in America.

父母亲打算让他们的女儿在美国读书。

(3) by now 到此时(刻),到现在为止。当然,这里的 now 并非指说话人说话的那一时刻,而指"到当时的那一时刻为止",即为 by then 的含义。文中的这种使用方法拉近了事件发生的时间同读者之间的距离,因而使描述显得更为真实生动。在使用介词 by + 表时间的名词介词短语时,如果句中使用的是行为动词,该行为动词通常用完成时态来表达,如:

They had completed the test by the time they left the lab.

他们离开实验室时已完成了那项实验。

(4) ahead 为副词,作 miles 的定语。

13. Though the new rudder was fitted at tremendous speed, it was impossible for the *Cutty Sark* to win.

(1) though 尽管,虽然。从属连词,引导一让步状语从句。

(2) it was...to win 中 it 为形式主语,to win 为带 for 的动词不定式。

14. Even this was remarkable, considering that...delays.

(1) even 为副词,不是连词,因此不能单独用其引导一从句。有关用法参见第 10 课课文注释 5。

(2) considering that... 考虑到,就……而言。有关 consider 等动词-ing 的用法参见第 19 课课文注释 9。

15. **There is no doubt that if she had...she would....**

no doubt 常用来表示"大概"、"很可能"、"我料想"、"我推测"之意,如:

No doubt it'll rain soon.

我看很快就要下雨了。

You're tired, no doubt. I'll make you a cup of tea.

你大概累了,我给你沏杯茶。

课文例句中的 that 为关系连词,引导一同位语从句。这里的 if 为关系连词,在同位语从句中引导一"非真实性"条件状语从句。

📖 **语法 Grammar in use**

very 与 too

这两个词均可用于形容词和副词之前,起强调作用,但所表达的意思不同。

(1) very 用于加强语气,具有正面含义,如:

Tom's very clever.

汤姆非常聪明。

This train's going very slowly.

这列火车非常缓慢地离开。

(2) too 则用于表示过分或过多,具有反面意义,如:

Don't be too proud to ask for help.

不要太骄傲而不寻求帮助。

I realized my mistake too late.

我意识到我的错误太晚了。

试比较:

> *I arrived very late at the airport and just caught my flight.*
>
> 我很晚才到达机场,刚刚赶上我的航班。
>
> *I arrived too late at the airport and missed my flight.*
>
> 我到达机场太晚了,误了我的航班。

由于 too 所表达的是超出了人们所想像的,所以不可说:

   * *I'm too pleased with my new car.*

   * *I'm too happy when I heard about your promotion.*

而应说:

   I'm very pleased with my new car.

   我非常满意我的新车。

   I'm very happy when I heard about your promotion.

   听到你升职的消息我非常高兴。

但有人在 kind 前用 too 以表达感激之情,如:

   You're too kind.

   你太好了。

注:too 前不能用 very,但可用 much、far、rather、slightly 或 a bit 进行修饰,如:

   The eyes were far too deeply set.

   那双眼睛陷得太深了。

   The dress was rather too small for her.

   那条裙子她穿太小了。

不能将 too 置于修饰一名词的形容词之前,如不可说:

   * *These are too big boots.*

而应说:

   These boots are too big.

   这双鞋太大了。

📁 词汇学习 Word study

1. serve

(1) *vi*. 起……作用,有用:

It served as a clue to a criminal's tracing.

它是追踪罪犯的一条线索。

This will serve as a model.

这个可作为一个范例。

(2) *vi*. 服务;服役;供职:

He served some time as a waiter in a restaurant.

他有段时间在餐馆里当招待。

He served in the navy for thirty years.

他在海军服役 30 年。

(3) *vt*. 侍候……进餐;为……端上(食物或饮料等):

Soup is first served.

先上汤。

When everybody had been served, the meal began.

每个人的饭菜都摆好后,就开始进餐。

2. match *vt*.

(1) 敌得过,比得上:

They are trying to upgrade their cars to match the foreign competition.

他们在努力提高他们汽车的档次,以便适应外国的竞争。

(2) 和……相似;和……相称;适应:

The lampshade matched the curtains.

灯罩与窗帘十分相配。

(3) 使较量,使相抗,使比赛:

The chessplayer has tried matching his brain against the computer.

那位象棋手曾试图以他的智力同电脑较量。

3．fit　(fitted 或 fit,fitted 或 fit)

(1) *vt*．安装,容纳(用于此义时,其过去时常用 fitted)：

> *Philip fitted his key into the lock．*
>
> 菲利普将他的钥匙插进了锁孔。

(2) *vt*．(衣服、鞋等)合身;合适(用于此义时,英语过去时多用 fitted,而美语多用 fit)：

> *The boots fit Rudolph perfectly．*
>
> 这双鞋鲁道夫穿上正合适。

(3) *adj*．健康的,强健的：

> *We came back from our cycling tour suntanned and fit．*
>
> 我们骑车旅行回来了,晒得黑黑的,身体十分健康。

✍　练习答案　Key to written exercises

1．关键句型、难点练习答案

1　*I use* my bicycle every day.

　I am used to getting up early.

　I used to walk to school, but now I usually cycle.

2　He can run very *fast*.

　He can run *faster than* I can.

3　We *set off* at 7 o'clock yesterday morning.

　That girl *has* just *set up* a new world record.

4　The engine has lost *its* power.

　It's warmer today than it was yesterday.

5　I've got *a lot of* books.

　I've got *a great many* books.

　This will cost *a great deal of* money.

6　*on fire*, *in ink*, *in common*, *in tears*, *on foot*, *on purpose*,

282

in love, *in a hurry*

7   I arrived *very* late, but I caught the train.

    I arrived *too* late to catch the train.

8   He *is having* a house *built*.

    She *had had* his suit *cleaned*.

9   He *won* the competition.

    He *beat* all the other competitors.

2．多项选择题答案

1 c   2 a   3 d   4 c   5 b   6 d

7 a   8 d   9 b   10 a   11 a   12 c

Lesson 26
Wanted: a large biscuit tin
征购大饼干筒

📖 **课文详注** **Further notes on the text**

1. wanted

征求,征购。广告常用语。

2. No one can avoid being influenced by advertisements.

在动词 avoid 避免之后,只能用名词或动名词作其宾语,不能用动词不定式作其宾语。该词具有"(有意识地)躲避/避免"不愉快的或可能发生危险的事物或情况,如:

She has avoided seeing him since their last quarrel.

自他们上一次吵嘴后,她一直回避见到他。

The danger can be well avoided if they plan earnestly and thoroughly.

如果他们认真周密地制定计划,危险就能完全避免。

由于句中主语为动词 influence 的承受者,因此其后应使用动名词的被动语态形式 being influenced。

3. Much as we may pride ourselves on our good taste, we are no longer free to choose the things we want, for advertising exerts a suitable influence on us.

(1) as 为从属连词,在此引导一让步状语从句,主要用于正式文体中,表示"尽管"、"虽然"之意。虽然 as 表达的意义与从属连词 although/though 相同,但其主从句语义间的对比更为强烈。它通常可以使用下述两种结构的语序形式:

1) 当从句主动词为系动词时:

284

主语补语 + as + $\left\{\begin{array}{l}\text{主语}\\\text{系动词}\end{array}\right\}$ 或 $\left\{\begin{array}{l}\text{系动词}\\\text{主语}\end{array}\right\}$ + 主句,如:

Cold as it was , we went out . (cf. Although it was so cold , . . .)

尽管天气很冷,我们还是出去了。

Tired as was Professor Wilson , they couldn't stop him from doing the experiment late at night . (cf. Although Professor Wilson was very tired , . . .)

尽管威尔森教授很累,但是他们还是无法阻止他把实验一直做到深夜。

当从句中的主语为代词时,系动词需置于该主语之后(如第 1 句);当从句中的主语为名词时,系动词需置于该主语之前(如第 2 句)。

2)当从句中的主动词为行为动词,或该动词被一副词修饰时,使用"动词原形或副词 + as + 主语... , + 主句"这一结构,如:

Fast as you read , you can't finish the book in two days .

尽管你读得很快,但你也不能在两天内读完这本书。

Try as he might , John couldn't get out of the difficulty .

虽然约翰很努力,他仍不能摆脱困境。

由于从句主语后通常跟随 might、could、would 等情态助动词,因此置于 as 之前的动词需为动词原形。从属连词 though 同样也可使用这种特殊的语序,表示让步状语从句,如:

Bravely though they fought , they had no chance of winning .

虽然他们打得很勇敢,但是仍无获胜机会。

（2）pride oneself（up）on 以……自夸；自夸，如：

> *He prides himself（up）on his skills as a pianist.*
>
> 他对自己弹钢琴的技巧感到自豪。

（3）no longer 不再；已不。用于肯定句中，表达否定意义，通常用于行为动词之前或 be 动词之后，多在书面语中使用，如：

> *Some of the experts no longer consider the discovery of great value.*
>
> 其中一些专家不再认为这个发现很有价值。
>
> *They are no longer living in Beijing.*
>
> 他们已不住在北京了。

在口语中多使用 not...any longer，意思与 no longer 相当，但需将 not 置于 be 动词或助动词之后，而将 any longer 置于句末，如：

> *Mr. Smith is not living in the shabby hut any longer.*
>
> 史密斯先生已不住在那个破旧的小屋里了。

而单独使用 any longer 时，只能将其用于疑问句中，置于句末，表示"还"的意思，如：

> *Does he work there any longer?*
>
> 他还在那里工作吗？

no longer、not...any longer 和 any longer 在句中起状语作用，通常与表示延续性时间概念的动词搭配使用。由于含有将现在同过去进行比较之意，因此虽可用于过去时或将来时，但更多是用于现在时。

（4）be free to do 可允许／准许做；自由地做，如：

> *You're free to leave at any time.*
>
> 你随时都可以离开。

（5）exert an influence on 对……有影响；对……施加影响。名词 influence 常可同诸如 have、exercise、produce 等动词搭配使用，后面使用介词 upon 或 on，分别表达"对……有影响"、"对……

286

施加影响"、"对……产生影响"等,如:

> *The moon exerts an influence on the tides.*
>
> 月球对潮汐有影响。
>
> *The new theory of his has produced a telling influence on the new technological development.*
>
> 他的这一新理论已对新的技术开发产生了有力的影响。

4. In their efforts to persuade us to buy...

动词 persuade 说服,劝服,使相信。其后可以使用"宾语 + (作宾语补足语的)动词不定式"这样的结构,构成 persuade sb. to do sth. 这样的用法,如:

> *That stubborn man has been artfully persuaded to drop his foolish plans.*
>
> 那个固执己见的人已被巧妙地说服放弃了他那些愚蠢的计划。

persuade 可作不及物动词,含有"被说服"、"被劝服"之意,如:

> *Most of the boys persuade easily.*
>
> 大多数孩子们都容易被说服。

persuade 后除可用于上述结构外,其后也可用"宾语 + (介词) into + 动名词",即 persuade sb. into doing sth. 的结构,如:

> *The owner of the jewellery shop persuaded the customer into buying a diamond.*
>
> 那位珠宝店的店主说服那位顾客买了一颗钻石。

当 persuade 的宾语后不使用动词不定式,而使用名词时,通常跟介词 of,如:

> *I persuaded him of its truth.*
>
> 我使他相信这是真的。

在表达"说服某人不去做某事"时,其宾语之后通常使用"(副词) out + (介词) of",即 persuade sb. out of (doing) sth. 这样的结构,如:

Can you persuade her out of her foolish plans ?

你能劝说她放弃那些愚蠢的计划吗?

She persuaded me out of continuously carrying out the project .

她说服我不再继续进行那个项目。

persuade 表示"说服"、"劝服"、"使相信"。即表示劝说者使被劝者接受了所劝内容的含义,因此当仅仅表示"劝"的含义时,通常使用 try to persuade 或 advise,如:

We tried to persuade him , but he just wouldn't listen to us .

我们劝他,但他就是不听。

I advised him to drop the plan .

我劝他放弃那个计划。

5．Advertisers discovered years ago that all of us love to get something for nothing.

（1）years ago 为时间状语,如放在较长的宾语之后,则使句子结构显得松散,有头重脚轻之感,因此放到了句中。此外这里还有对这个时间状语强调的含义。应该注意的是,当这类时间状语所修饰的成分容易引起误解时,更应注意它们在句中的位置,如:

He discovered that they begun unlawful activities years ago .

他发现数年前他们就开始了非法活动。

She decided to go to the place where the accident took place a few days ago .

她决定去那个几天前发生过事故的地方(看看)。

由于状语被用来修饰句中的动词,说明动词动作所发生的时间,因此在以上两个例子中置于句末的时间状语就可能产生不同的理解:即用来修饰主句中的谓语动词,或修饰从句中的谓语动词。当时间状语用来修饰主句谓语动词时,为了避免产生这样的误解,应将时间状语提至主句之中,如 He discovered years ago that... 和 she decided, a few days ago, to...,也可将它们直接置于主句句首。

(2) to get something for nothing 免费得到;白拿东西。动词不定式短语,在从句中作宾语。动词 love 后可用动词不定式作宾语,构成"love to do sth.(喜欢做某事)"的句型结构。这里的介词 for 表示"以……为交换","以……为代价"等含义,如:

> *I'll give you my watch for your camera.*
> 我愿拿我的表换你的相机。

6. An advertisement which begins with the magic word FREE can rarely go wrong.

(1) begin with 以……开头,如:

> *They began with entreaties and ended with threats.*
> 他们先是请求,到最后是恐吓。

> *Education, in the largest sense, begins with a man's birth and does not end until he dies.*
> 从广义上讲,教育始于人出生之初,直至其死亡。

(2) rarely 很少,难得。副词作状语。英语中有若干副词,如 seldom、rarely、scarcely、hardly、barely 等,构成句子的"基本否定"形式,而且这些词在使用方法上有很多相似之处,如:

a. 与否定词 not 一样,需同 any(而非 some)一同使用,如:

> *She hardly eats anything.*
> 她几乎什么都不吃。

b. 在反意疑问句中,通常使用肯定的附加疑问句,如:

> *You seldom panic, do you?*
> 你很少惊慌,是吧?

c. 用于句首时,通常需使用倒装语序(较正式的用法,一般英语中不常使用),如:

Rarely had she been faced with so difficult a choice.

她很少碰到这样两难的局面。

Barely were they able to stand firm in the torrent.

她们在急流中几乎无法站稳。

7. Radio and television have made it possible for advertisers to capture the attention of millions of people in this way.

代词 it 在句中作形式宾语,而 for...in this way 为带 for 的动词不定式结构,作句子的逻辑宾语。当动词不定式、动名词短语或以连接代词引导的从句为句子的逻辑宾语时,通常需在主动词之后用 it 作形式宾语,而将逻辑宾语置于句末,如:

(1) 动词不定式作逻辑宾语:

I find it difficult to talk to you about anything serious.

我觉得很难同你谈任何严肃的话题。

All these worries made it impossible for her to concentrate on her work.

种种烦恼使她不能专心工作。

(2) 动名词短语作逻辑宾语:

He thought it absolutely senseless attempting the impossible.

他认为想做不可能做到的事是完全没道理的。

I don't think it worthwhile going to such a place.

我看去这样一个地方是不值得的。

(3) 连接代词引导一从句作逻辑宾语:

I thought it peculiar that she hadn't writeen any letter.

我觉得她没来信有点奇怪。

I want to make it clear whether she's related to him or not.

我想搞清楚她是否与他有亲属关系。

8. The response to this competition...

介词短语 to this competition 为 response 的定语,意即"对这一竞赛的反响"。response 常与 to 搭配使用,如:

He was unable to get any response to his tapping.

他轻声敲门,但无人答应。

No one made any response to his inquiry.

没人对他的询问给予答复。

9. Before long, biscuit of...

before long 不久。介词短语,在句中作时间状语,如:

I hope to see you before long.

我希望不久即可见到你。

Don't go too far; the train will arrive before long.

别走远了,火车不久就要到站了。

10. A little later, a man came along with a biscuit which...

come along 用来表示"到来"之意,如:

You go now, and I'll come along in a few minutes.

你这就去,我一会儿就来。

He went to London whenever the chance came along.

他一有机会就去伦敦。

come along with... 表示"同……一道来"、"带……来到"之意,如:

John wants to come along with us to the movie.

约翰想同我们一道去看电影。

He came along with a big bundle on his shoulder.

他扛着一个大包裹走来。

11. All the biscuits that were sent were carefully weighed.

that 为关系代词,引导一定语从句。该句的主语 biscuits 无论在主句中还是从句中都是动词 send 和 weigh 的承受者,因此主句和从句都使用了被动语态结构。

12. ...for they bought...for ＄24,000.

这里的介词 for 表示"以……为代价"之意。有关用法参见本课课文注释 5。

📖 语法 **Grammar in use**

动名词与现在分词的区别

1. 动名词和现在分词的形式相同,均由动词-ing 构成。一般来讲,动词-ing 形式作名词时叫动名词,作形容词时叫现在分词。然而这两种功能之间却有一些重叠,故往往难以作出有效的区别。

2. 就广义而言,尽管像动词那样,动名词可以带宾语,但它们可以代替名词,如:

$$
John\ likes \begin{cases} planes. \\ flying. \\ flying\ planes. \end{cases}
$$

$$
约翰喜欢 \begin{cases} 飞机。 \\ 飞行。 \\ 驾驶飞机。 \end{cases}
$$

现在分词可以代替形容词,如:

$$
This\ is\ a \begin{cases} wide \\ running \end{cases} stream.
$$

$$
这是一条 \begin{cases} 宽宽的 \\ 奔流的 \end{cases} 小河。
$$

动词-ing 形式作为动名词在一般陈述句中相当于不带冠词的不可数名词。它可用 it 来替代,如:

Dancing is fun. I love it.

跳舞有趣。我爱跳舞。

3. 动名词可以放在 a、the、this、a lot of 和 some 这样的限定词以及

292

物主代词和形容词之后,如:

The sinking of the Titanic *has never been forgotten.*

"泰坦尼克"号的沉没从未被遗忘。

I did some/a lot of/a little shopping this morning.

今天上午我去买了一些/许多/一点东西。

动名词也具有动词的特点,例如:

(1)它可带副词或副词短语:

Walking quickly is difficult.

快走很难。

(2)它可以有宾语:

Washing the car seems to be your main hobby.

擦洗汽车似乎是你的主要爱好。

(3)它可以有完成时和被动式:

I'm sorry for having wasted your time.

我很抱歉浪费了你的时间。

I can't forgive myself for having been taken by surprise.

我不能原谅自己被弄得措手不及。

4.现在分词表示正在进行的行为时,如在进行时里一样,应与动词连用。分词短语常可替代从句,如:

Walking in the park the other day, I saw a bird building a nest.

几天前我在公园散步时,看见一只鸟在筑巢。

5.现在分词和动名词均可作形容词,如:

Here are your running shoes.

这是你的跑鞋。(意即 *shoes for running* 为动名词)

I love the sight of running water.

我喜欢看流水。(意即 *water which is running* 为现在分词)

📂　词汇学习　Word study

1．persuade　*vt*．说服，劝服

(1)（＋*obj*．＋动词不定式）：

He is trying to persuade local and foreign companies to invest in the project．

他企图说服本地和国外的公司为这个项目投资。

(2)（＋*obj*．）

If she doesn't want to go，nothing you say will persuade her．

如果她不想去，你说什么都说服不了她。

(3)（＋*obj*．＋that 从句）

A higher gasoline tax might persuade consumers that small cars are the best option．

较高的汽油税可能会使消费者认为小型汽车是最佳选择。

2．discover　*vt*．

(1) 发觉；知道，了解到：

He has discovered that his statement was wrong．

他已经意识到他的声明是错误的。

(2) 找到(用于此义时与 find 同，但较 find 正式)：

I eventually discovered what I had been looking for．

我终于找到了我在找的东西。

(3) 发现：

Columbus discovered the largest island in the Caribbean．

哥伦布发现了加勒比海最大的岛屿。

3．bring

(1) *vt*．带来，拿来，取来：

We can bring the goods to you this afternoon．

今天下午我们就能把东西给你带来。

He would have to bring Judy with him.

他必须得把朱迪带过来。

(2) *vt.* 导致,引起,使得:

Her presence has brought us so much happiness.

她的出席令我们非常高兴。

The explosion brought the whole building to the ground.

爆炸使得整座大楼坍塌。

(3) bring in 拿进来;引进,推出:

Bring the washing in, it's raining outside.

把洗的衣服拿进来,外面在下雨。

The police brought several young men in for questioning.

警察把几名年轻人带进来进行询问。

📝 练习答案 Key to written exercises

1. 关键句型、难点练习答案

1 *He* enjoys *playing tennis*.

Imagine *going on holiday to England*!

It's no use *complaining now*: it'too late.

It's not worth *waiting any longer*: *they're not coming*.

Would you mind *opening* the window?

2 These apples *have gone bad*.

The leaves on these trees *turn yellow* or red in autumn.

When the teacher entered the classroom, the students *grew quiet*.

3 This chair is *in the way*: can you move it?

I met John *on the way* here this afternoon.

By the way, I wanted to ask you something.

4 I *lent* a book to my friend. /She *gave* some money to her children.

5 There was only *one* book on the table. /I bought *a* book from the bookshop.

6 See text.

2. 多项选择题答案

| 1 | d | 2 | a | 3 | c | 4 | c | 5 | b | 6 | a |
| 7 | c | 8 | d | 9 | c | 10 | d | 11 | b | 12 | a |

Lesson 27
Nothing to sell and nothing to buy
不卖也不买

📖 **课文详注** **Further notes on the text**

1．Nothing to sell and nothing to buy.

两个动词不定式均起到定语作用,修饰各自前面的不定代词 nothing。

2．It has been said that everyone lives by selling something.

（1）that 从句在句中为逻辑主语,it 为形式主语。当谓语动词为"想"、"说"之类的动词,而主语又为 that 或 whether 引导的主语从句时,通常可将这样的谓语动词构成被动语态结构,其前使用先行词 it 作形式主语,而将该主语从句置于全句的末尾,试比较:

That witches communicated with the devil was widely believed.

It was widely believed that witches communicated with the devil.

过去人们普遍认为巫婆与魔鬼来往。

Whether there was gold left in the mine was not known.

It was not known whether there was gold in the mine.

不知道矿里是否还有黄金。

这类常见的动词有 believe、feel、presume、report、say、understand 等,如:

It is generally understood that this will be a good chance to exchange experience.

297

大家都明白,这将是交流经验的一个好机会。

以从句作主语的句子结构常用于正式文体之中,而以先行词 it 作形式主语的句子结构,常用于口语之中。

(2) live by... 以……为生。动词词组中的介词 by 表示"以……方式/手段"之意,其后多接动名词,也可接名词,如:

John lives by writing for a small magazine.

约翰靠给一家小杂志社写稿来维持生计。

3. In the light of this statement, teachers live by...

in the light of 按照,根据,考虑到,如:

In the light of recent discoveries their previous theory should be revised.

根据最近的发现,他们先前的理论应予修正。

He reviewed his decision in the light of recent developments.

根据近来的发展,他重新审视了自己的决定。

介词短语 in (the) light of 还可用来说明原因,表示"鉴于"、"考虑到"、"由于"之意,如:

It is to be regarded as excusable in the light of circumstances.

考虑到具体情况,这将被看作可以原谅的。

有时该短语还用来表示"当作"、"视为"之意,如:

He views progress in the light of scientific achievement.

他认为进步就是科学的成就。

4. Though it may be possible to measure the value of material goods in terms of money, it is extremely difficult to estimate...

(1) it may be possible to measure... 及后面的 it is extremely difficult to estimate... 中的 it 均为先行词 it,作形式主语,其逻辑主语分别为 to measure... 和 to estimate... 动词不定式短语。有关用法参见第 1 课课文注释 13 及第 24 课课文注

释6。

（2）in terms of 根据；从……方面（来说），如：

> *It is difficult to express it in terms of science.*
> 很难从科学的角度来表达它。

> *Let each child read in terms of his own taste and choice.*
> 让每个孩子根据自己的兴趣爱好和选择来读书。

5．There are times when we would willingly give everything we possess to save our lives, yet we might grudge paying a surgeon a high fee for offering us precisely this service.

（1）time 的复数形式通常在下述情况时使用：

1）指"时期"、"时代"时，如：

> *in ancient/modern times* 在古/近代

> *in these technically and culturally advanced times* 在此技术、文化都先进的时代

> *Times have changed.*
> 时代变了。

2）指"日子"、"生活"时，如：

> *Times are hard.*
> 时世艰难。

> *Bad times have vanished like a nightmare.*
> 苦日子就像一场噩梦一样消逝了。

3）指"多种具体的不同时间"、"一些具体的零星时间"时，如：

> *She's likely to drop in at all times.*
> 她随时都可能进来拜访。

> *He often does some carpentry work at odd times.*
> 他经常零星地干点木匠活。

4）指"次数"时，如：

> *I've seen her a few times.*
> 我见到过她几次。

I've told you a dozen times not to do that.

我已屡次告诫你不要做那件事。

5) 指"倍数"时,如:

This is three times the size of that one.

这个是那个的 3 倍大。

It is running at ten times normal speed.

它正以正常速度的 10 倍运转。

6) 作介词指"乘以"时,如:

Two times three is/are six.

2 乘 3 等于 6。

(2) grudge doing sth. 在动词 grudge 之后通常可使用名词或动名词作宾语,或使用双宾语结构,如:

We had to pay £5 for lunches of which I grudged them every penny.

我们得付 5 镑的午餐钱,我极不情愿地掏给他们每一个便士。

She will not grudge doing a bit extra when it's really needed.

如果需要的话,她会乐意多干点的。

6. The conditions of society are such that skills have to be paid for in the same way that goods are paid at a shop.

in the same way that... 以与……相同的方式。由于 that 相当于 in which,在从句中起状语作用,因此这里的 that 作关系副词。这一用法是因为使用了 the same 所决定的。通常使用 same 时,除其前必须使用定冠词 the 外,需在紧随其后的名词或代词之后使用 as,表示"像……一样",如:

Her hair's the same colour as her mother's.

她头发的颜色同她母亲的一样。

I like the same music as you.

你喜欢的音乐我也喜欢。

但是当在 same 后的名词或代词之后为一从句时,在该从句前应使用 that,如:

He was wearing the same shirt（that）he'd had on the day before.

他穿的那件衬衫是他前一天穿过的同一件衬衫。

That's the same man that asked me for money yesterday.

那个人跟昨天向我要钱的是同一个人。

在上述两例中,由于 that 在从句中分别起到宾语和主语的作用,因此均为关系代词。当从句用于 way 之后时,that 可以省略,如:

I went out the same way I'd got in.

我顺着进来的路走了出去。

7. Tramps seem to be the only exception to this general rule.

使用 exception 表示"对……例外"时,后面通常需使用介词 to,如:

It forms an exception to the general rule.

这构成了一般规则的一个例外。

My short brother was an exception to our family tradition of tall men.

我们家的男子历来长得高大,我那矮小的兄弟则是个例外。

8. He has deliberately chosen to lead the life he leads and is fully aware of the consequences.

形容词 aware(意识到)一般更强调感官可及的外界事物。当所意识到的内容为一名词或代词时,其后通常使用介词 of 再加该名词或代词的结构,如:

We are fully aware of the gravity of the situation.

我们完全明白形势的严重性。

Presently she became aware of footsteps hurrying after her.

她突然发觉身后有脚步声匆匆追来。

aware 后面也可使用 that 引导的从句。这样使用时,应去掉介词 of,如:

The driver was perfectly aware that he was driving at seventy miles an hour.

这个司机完全清楚他正在以每小时 70 英里的时速开车。

当其后为 wh-引导的从句时,通常保留介词 of,如:

She was not aware of what was going on around her.

她不知道周围发生了什么事情。

It was several minutes before I was aware of what had happened.

过了好几分钟我才明白发生了什么事情。

9 . ... but he is free from the thousands of ...

be free from 不受……影响;没有;免于,如:

The city is free from thieves.

这个城市没有盗贼。

It's a day free from wind.

这是个无风的日子。

其后通常使用表示危险、困难、影响等的名词,如:

We should be free from arrogance and rashness.

我们应该戒骄戒躁。

She's now free from troubles.

她现在没有了烦恼。

10 . His few material possessions make it possible for him to move from place to place with ease.

(1) 代词 it 在句中作形式宾语,而带介词 for 的动词不定式结构作句子的逻辑主语。有关用法参见第 26 课课文注释 7。

(2) with ease 为"介词 + 抽象名词"结构,在句中作状语。这样用时,抽象名词前不加冠词。

11. By having to sleep in the open, he gets far closer to the world of nature than most of us ever do.

(1) by having to sleep in the open 为介词短语,在句中作原因状语,意即"由于不得不露天睡觉"。这里的介词 by 表示"由于"之意。

(2) get far closer to... than... 比……接近……得多。在形容词比较级前通常可以直接使用除 very、quite(仅可用于表示身体康复时,如 quite better)以外的表示程度的副词(短语)。

(3) do 代替 get close to the world of nature,以避免重复。

12. We often speak of tramps with contempt and put them in the same class as beggars, but how many of us can honestly say that we have not felt a little envious of their simple way...?

(1) speak of (一般性地)提起,提到,说起,如:

We've heard him speak of it.

我们听到过他提及此事。

I've never spoken of these things to anyone before.

我从未向任何人提到过这些事情。

当表示较详尽地"谈论"、"谈及"时,常用 speak about/on,如:

They didn't want to speak about this before us.

他们不愿意在我们面前谈及此事。

(2) put...in... 在句中为"把……归入……"之意。

(3) feel / be envious of 羡慕,虽可用于表示"嫉妒"之意,但一般情况下用来表示对他人的好运、成功等不含恶意的羡慕,如:

The weak are often envious of the strong.

弱者常常羡慕强者。

He's never envious of others for their wealth.

他从不羡慕他人的富有。

📑 语法 Grammar in use

so as to, in order to, in order that, so that

1. so as to 与 in order to 是带 to 的不定式变体,不是连词。它们不能引导一个从句,用来表示目的。由于这种结构较为简单,所以比较常用。也可直接使用动词不定式表示目的,如:

> *I went to live in France to / in order to / so as to learn French.*
>
> 我去法国居住,以便学习法语。
>
> *She was sent to England to / in order to / so as to be educated.*
>
> 她被送到英国去受教育。

so as not to/in order not to 可用来表示"反面的目的",如:

> *I shut the door quietly, so as not to wake the baby.*
>
> 为了不惊醒宝宝,我轻轻地关上门。

如果主语改变,可以用"for... +动词不定式"结构,如:

> *I bought a second car (in order) for my son to learn to drive.*
>
> 我买了第 2 辆车,以便让我的儿子学开车。

2. so that/in order that 可以引导目的状语从句。其他可用来引导目的状语从句的连词有 in case、lest、for fear (that)等,如:

> *He has to earn lots of money so that he can buy his children nice food and clothes.*
>
> 为了能给孩子们买好的食物和衣服,他不得不挣许多钱。
>
> *I bought a new car in order that my wife might have a car of her own.*
>
> 我买了一辆新车,以便我妻子有一辆自己的汽车。

当主句中的动词为现在时、现在完成时或将来时,so that 和 in order that 后面可以跟 may、can 或 will。在使用中,so that 比 in order that 更为普遍,如:

> *I've arrived early so that/in order that I may/can/will get a good view of the procession.*

> 我到得很早,以便我可以/能/将会好好看看那行进的队伍。

so that 和 in order that 之后也可以跟现在时,如:

> *Let us spend a few moments in silence so that/in order that we remember those who died to preserve our freedom.*

> 让我们默哀片刻,以缅怀那些为维护我们的自由而牺牲的人们。

当主句中的动词为一般过去时、过去进行时或过去完成时,so that 和 in order that 后面跟 should、could、might 或 would,如:

> *I arrived early so that/in order that I should/could/might/would get a good view of the procession.*

> 我到得很早,以便我可/能/会好好看看那行进的队伍。

注意在 so that/in order that 后面的否定形式,如:

> *I arrived early so that/in order that I might not miss anything.*

> 我到得很早,以免错过什么。

这种否定形式并不常用,更常用的是不定式结构,如:

> *I arrived early so as not to miss anything.*

> 我到得很早,以免错过什么。

so that 既可引导目的状语从句,也可引导结果状语从句。对其的判断需根据主句同从句的逻辑关系进行。so that 引导的目的状语从句,一般表示尚未实现的目的或意图,主句与从句的关系为结果与目的的关系。so that 引导的结果状语从句,则为主句所导致的结果,主句与从句为原因与结果的关系。如:

> *We arrived early so that/in order that we could/should/might/would get good seats. (i.e. We arrived early for*

305

that purpose.)

我们到得很早,以便找到好座位。(表示目的,即我们是为该目的而早到的)

We arrived early, so (that) we got good seats. (i.e. We got good seats as a result of arriving early.)

我们到得早,因此找到了好座位。(表示结果,即我们找到好座位是到得早的结果)

📂 词汇学习 Word study

1. live

(1) *vi.* 活,生存:

He was so badly injured in the accident that the doctors did not expect him to live.

他在事故中受伤十分严重,医生们认为他活不了了。

(2) *vi.* 居住:

Many people want to live in the country.

许多人想住在乡下。

She has been living in France now for almost two years.

到现在她已在法国住了近两年。

(3) *vi.* (by, on, upon, off)(靠……)生活:

For several years she lived by begging.

有几年她靠乞讨为生。

The natives live on a diet of fruit and occasionally meat.

当地人靠吃水果,偶尔吃些肉生存。

(4) *adj.* 活的(用于名词前):

There was a tank of live lobsters in the restaurant.

饭馆里有一箱活龙虾。

The cat was playing with a live mouse.

那只猫正在玩弄一只活老鼠。

2. pay （paid, paid）

(1) *vi*. 付钱,交款:

How much did you pay for the tickets?

这些票你花了多少钱?

Pupils would be paid for any work they did.

孩子们所做的任何工作都会得到报酬。

注:如果为别人付饮料或饭钱,不能说 * pay them the drink 或 meal,应当说:buy them the drink/meal 或者 treat them to lunch,如:

I'll buy you lunch.

我请你吃午饭。

She offered to treat them to dinner.

她提出请他们吃晚餐。

(2) *vt*. 付钱给,给报酬;出钱雇;支付:

If you go to the bank, will you pay/deposit these cheques for me?

如果你去银行,能帮我付一下这些账单吗?

I paid the plumber (with) cash.

我给水管工付现金。(双宾语)

(3) *n*. (不可数)工资,薪金:

Can you lend me ten dollars until I get my pay?

在我发工资前你能借给我 10 美元吗?

As expected, the management said the workers' pay claim was too high.

正如所料,管理部门说工人要求增加的工资太高了。

注:pay 一般指工作所得,而 income 则指工作和其他各种收入,如:

Have you any income apart from your pay?

307

除工资外,你有其他收入吗?

a salary 指按月付给专业人员的薪金。wages 指按周或日付给的酬金(特指付给体力劳动者的酬金)。fee 指付给某项专业服务(如律师)的费用。

3. aware *adj.*

(1)(of)意识到的,知道的:

> *He said that the government was acutely aware of the problem.*

> 他说政府完全清楚这个问题。

(2)有觉悟的;(在某方面)有知识的(用于副词后):

> *She's so politically aware because she always reads newspapers.*

> 她很有政治头脑,那是因为她总在看报纸。

> *Much to my surprise, the old driver was so artistically aware.*

> 令我大为吃惊的是那位老年司机竟然那么懂艺术。

✍ **练习答案 Key to written exercises**

1.关键句型、难点练习答案

1 He is said *to be very rich.*

   It is said that *he is very rich.*

2 I'd like some *information.*

   The *news* from home is very good.

   I've done a lot of *work* today.

   How much *luggage* have you got?

3 They say *it will be* a fine day tomorrow.

   There was a terrible storm in the night.

   There has been another burglary in the village.

308

4　I opened the door quietly *so as not to* disturb the baby.

　I worked hard *in order that my mother* might be proud of me.

　She screamed loudly *so that* someone would hear her.

5　He never expected his bicycle *to be found*.

　Their house will have *to be sold*.

6　Who was this book written by?

　This is not the sort of book (which) I am interested in.

7　See text.

2. 多项选择题答案

1	a	2	d	3	b	4	b	5	b	6	b
7	d	8	c	9	c	10	a	11	b	12	c

Lesson 28

Five pounds too dear

五镑也太贵

📖 **课文详注 Further notes on the text**

1. **Small boats loaded with wares sped to the great liner as she was entering the harbour.**

(1) loaded with wares 为过去分词短语,在句中作 boats 的定语,意即"满载着货物的小船"。

(2) as 为从属连词,引导一时间状语从句。有关用法参见第 1 课课文注释 4 及第 6 课课文注释 6。

(3) she 指 liner,为拟人用法。参见第 10 课课文注释 2。

2. **Before she had anchored, the men from the boats had climbed on board and the decks were soon covered with colourful rugs....**

be covered with... 被……覆盖。covered 一词常被视为形容词,用来表示一种状态。如:

The pathway across the field was covered with thick snow.
穿过旷野的那条小径被厚厚的雪覆盖着。

The dead body was covered with a white sheet.
尸体上盖着白被单。

3. **It was difficult not to be tempted.**

not to be tempted 为动词不定式的否定形式(注意否定词 not 应置于动词不定式之前),在句子中作逻辑主语。it 为先行词,在句子中作形式主语。

4. **Many of the tourists on board had begun bargaining with the tradesmen, but I decided not to buy anything until I had**

310

disembarked.

(1) bargain with sb. 同某人讨价还价;同某人交易,在表示"为……讨价还价"时,其后常使用介词 for;表示"就……(价格)而讨价还价"时,其后常使用介词 about,如:

> *I bargained with the producer for a constant supply of the articles.*
>
> 我与厂家就不间断地供货讨价还价。
>
> *They are bargaining with her about the price.*
>
> 他们正在就价格同她讨价还价。

(2) not to buy anything 为动词不定式的否定形式,作动词 decide 的宾语。

(3) until 为从属连词,引导一时间状语从句。该句也可译为"……但我打定主意上岸之后再买东西"。

5. I had no sooner got off the ship than I . . .

no sooner . . . than . . . 刚……就……,一……就……在句中引导一时间状语。使用中 no sooner... than... 需分开写,no sooner 引导的动词动作发生在 than 引导的动词动作之前。在从句中需使用过去完成时,主句则需使用过去时;当 no sooner 置于句首时,其从句中应使用倒装语序,如:

> *We had no sooner reached the airport than the plane took off.*
>
> 我们刚到机场,飞机就起飞了。
>
> *No sooner had they arrived than they begun to work.*
>
> 他们刚一到就开始干了起来。

6. I had no intention of buying one, but I could not conceal the fact that I was . . .

have an/the intention of doing sth. 有意/想/打算做某事。在此用法中,intention 后多使用介词 of + 动名词(短语)的形式,如:

He has the intention of visiting his native land next year.

他想明年访问他的祖国。

She doubted whether he had any intention of marrying her.

她怀疑他是否有意同她结婚。

7. The man went to great lengths to prove that ...

go great lengths to do sth. 竭力做某事。在表达此意中,也可使用其他表示程度的形容词修饰 lengths,如:

He said he would go to any lengths to be revenged.

他说他要尽一切努力报仇。

They went all lengths to persuade him to give up the plan.

他们不遗余力地说服他放弃那项计划。

8. As we were walking past a shop, he held a diamond firmly against the window and made a deep impression in the glass.

(1) hold...against... 这里表示"把……按在……"之意。

(2) make a deep impression 表示"留下一道深深的痕迹"。

9. It took me over half an hour to get rid of him.

(1) it 为先行词,在句子中作形式主语。该句的逻辑主语为动词不定式短语 to get rid of him。

(2) it takes sb. some time to do sth. 这一句型常用来表示"某人用多少时间做某事"的含义,如:

It took me more than three hours to get home last night.

昨晚我花了三个多小时才到家。

(3) get rid of 摆脱;去掉;除去,如:

You should get rid of your mental burden and concentrate on your new task.

你应摆脱精神负担,把精力集中在你的新工作上。

Such criminals like him ought to be got rid of.

像他这样的罪犯应当除掉。

10. **... the words 'made in the U.S.A.' ...**

made in the U.S.A.(美国制造)为 the words 的同位语,意即"美国制造这几个字"。

11. **The man said that the pen was worth £50, but as a special favour, he would let me have it for £30.**

(1) be worth...值……;值得……就用法而言,worth 一词应视为介词。

(2) as a special favour 作为一种特别优惠。这里的 as 作介词使用,表示"作为"之意。

(3) let sb. do sth. 让某人做某事。用于主动语态时,动词 let 后的动词不定式应使用没有 to 的动词不定式结构。

(4) for £30 中的介词 for 作"以……为代价"、"以……为交换"之意。

12. **... held up five fingers indicating that ... £5.**

indicating that... £5 为现在分词短语,在句中作目的状语。

13. **Gesticulating wildly, the man acted as if he found my offer outrageous, but he eventually reduced the price to £10.**

(1) gesticulating wildly 为现在分词短语,在句中作方式状语。

(2) as if/as though 为从属连词。引导一方式状语从句,这样的从句经常用于动词 be(是)、act(行动)、appear(显现)、behave(举动)、feel(感到)、look(看起来)、seem(好像)、smell(闻)、sound(听起来)、taste(尝起来)等动词之后,如:

I feel as if/though I'm floating on the air.
我感到好像漂浮在空中一样。

It sounds as if/though the situation will get worse.
听起来好像情况会恶化似的。

(3) reduce...to... 把……减少到……,把……降低到……当 reduce 一词用来指量的变化时,它通常指"人为地减少/降低"之意,多数情况下都作及物动词,如:

They set themselves the task of reducing the amount of waste to a minimum.

他们给自己确定的任务是把浪费降低到最小限度。

Good designing reduced actual construction to only one year.

由于设计工作搞得好,实际建设时间缩短到了一年。

如果 reduce 用来指质的变化,它往往具有"使……变成……"之意,如:

After the battle, the whole village was reduced to ruins.

那次战斗之后,整个村子都变成了废墟。

After the illness, she was reduced to skin and bone.

病后她变得骨瘦如柴。

14. Though he kept throwing up his arms in despair, ...

(1) keep doing sth. 可用于表示在较短的一段时间里"不断／总是做某事"的意思,doing 为分词,如:

Alice kept waving to us.

爱丽丝不断向我们招手。

People kept coming to the hospital to see him.

人们不断到医院去看望他。

也可用于表示在较长一段时间里不断做出的动作或持续的状态,如:

They kept hoping that you would have a chance to visit China some day.

他们一直希望你会有机会到中国访问。

(2) in despair 绝望地。介词短语作状语,如:

He finally gave up the attempt in despair.

他最终在绝望中放弃了这种尝试。

15. No matter how hard I tried, it was impossible to fill this beautiful pen with ink and ...

(1) no matter how 不管怎样。为从属连词,引导一让步状语从句。在 no matter 之后可同 who、what、which、where、when、how 连用,构成这类让步状语从句,如:

No matter what you say, nobody will believe you.

不管你说什么,都没人会相信你的话。

No matter where you go, you'll never find a job like this.

不管你去哪儿,你都不会找到像这样的工作。

虽然从句中的含意为将来时,但在表达中需用一般现在时。

当意义比较明确时,有时将 no matter when 或 no matter what 置于句末,其后不加动词,如:

She'll always love him, no matter what happens.

不管发生什么事,她都始终如一地爱他。

(2) it is impossible to fill this beautiful pen with ink 中,it 为先行词作形式主语,其逻辑主语为后面的整个动词不定式短语。

📋 语法 Grammar in use

1. no sooner ... than ...

这一短语常用于书面语中,意指某件事紧随另一件事而发生。一般多用于前句的主动词之前,这一主动词常用过去完成时。类似的短语还有 hardly...when...、scarcely...when、barely...when...。当这些短语用于句首时,从句需使用倒装语序,如:

Mrs. Winthrop had no sooner left the room than they began to gossip about her.

温斯罗普太太刚离开房间,她们就议论起她来了。

No sooner did I reach the surface than I was pulled back again.

我刚露出水面就又被拉了回去。

Mr. Jenkins had hardly/scarcely/barely begun his speech

315

when he was interrupted.

詹金斯先生刚开始讲话就被人打断了。

Hardly had the game begun when it started raining.

比赛刚开始就下起雨来。

注:no sooner 后跟随的连词是 than;hardly、scarcely 和 barely 后跟随的连词是 when。

2. as...as...与 not as/so...as...

将某人或某物同另一人或另一物进行比较,表示"像……一样"、"同……一样"时,用"as + 形容词原级/副词原级 + as"这一结构表达,如:

You're just as bad as your sister.

你和你姐姐一样坏。

The meal was as awful as the conversation.

这顿饭就跟这次谈话一样糟糕。

连词 as(即后一个 as)后面可以跟一个名词 + 动词,也可只加名词,如:

You are as old as I am.

你和我年龄一样大。

He answers as quickly as his sister(does).

他回答得和他妹妹一样快。

如果连词后面只有一个代词的话,一般都用代词的宾格(如 him、her 等),如:

Jane was as clever as him.

简和他一样聪明。

但是,如果代词后跟动词的话,必须用代词的主格(如 I、they 等),如:

The teacher is just as sensitive as they are.

这位老师和他们一样敏感。

as...as...这一结构可用于任何否定句中,如:

316

They aren't as clever as they appear to be.

他们可不像他们看上去那么聪明。

He is not as quick in answering questions as his sister.

他回答问题不如他妹妹那样快。

有时在否定句中可用 so 替代第 1 个 as,如:

I had seldom seen him looking so pleased with himself as he was now.

我极少见到他像现在这样看上去对自己那么满意。

在 as...as...结构前可以加上 twice、three times 或 one fifth 这类的词或短语,用来比较两事物的大小与程度。如:

He didn't sell half as / so many videos as he thought he would.

他售出的录像带还不到他设想的一半。

Water is eight hundred times as dense as air.

水的密度是空气密度的 800 倍。

如果所比较的人或事物十分明确,第 2 个 as 以及其后的名词(短语)或从句均可省略,如:

This fish is twice as big.

这种鱼是那种鱼的两倍大。

📁 词汇学习 Word study

1. enter

(1) *vt.*,*vi.* 进入,穿入(房间、场所等):

The police entered (the building) through / by the side door.

警察从旁门进入(这座楼房)。

Knock before you enter.

进门前先敲门。

注:1) enter 是个较正式的词,一般进入房间或某建筑物时多用 go into/in 或 come into/in,如:

He shut the door behind me as I went in.

我一进屋他就将门关上了。

2) 进入汽车、火车、轮船或飞机绝不能用 enter,而用 get in/into 或 get on/board,如:

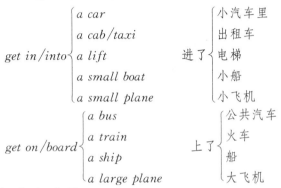

$$get\ in/into\begin{cases} a\ car \\ a\ cab/taxi \\ a\ lift \\ a\ small\ boat \\ a\ small\ plane \end{cases}\quad 进了\begin{cases} 小汽车里 \\ 出租车 \\ 电梯 \\ 小船 \\ 小飞机 \end{cases}$$

$$get\ on/board\begin{cases} a\ bus \\ a\ train \\ a\ ship \\ a\ large\ plane \end{cases}\quad 上了\begin{cases} 公共汽车 \\ 火车 \\ 船 \\ 大飞机 \end{cases}$$

(2) *vt.,vi.* 参加,加入,参予:

Several of the world's finest runners have entered the race.

几名世界最佳跑步运动员已报名参加这次比赛。

He entered politics after a career in banking.

他在银行工作了一段时间后进入了政界。

(3) *vt.* 录入:

We've hired him to enter all the new data into the computer.

我们已雇他将所有的新数据录入到计算机里。

2. fill

(1) *vt.* 注入,注满,灌满:

I filled the bucket with water.

我给桶里装满了水。

318

The wind filled the sails.

风将帆吹得鼓鼓的。

(2) *vt.* 充任,派人充任:

> *There is no one who can fill the office of president with as much credibility as our candidate.*
>
> 没有谁能像我们的候选人那么可靠而胜任总统的职位。
>
> *John's the best person to fill this vacancy.*
>
> 约翰是充任这一空缺的最佳人选。

(3) *n.* 充分,足够:

> *He took only a few minutes to eat his fill.*
>
> 他只用了几分钟就吃了个饱。
>
> *I've had my fill of commuting everyday.*
>
> 我对每天乘公交车上下班烦透了。

✍ 练习答案 Key to written exercises

1.关键句型、难点练习答案

1 I had *no sooner* opened the door *than* the telephone began to ring.

   He had *no sooner* finished his speech *than* everyone began to clap.

2 She is *as old as* I am.

   She is *not as tall as* I am.

3 *While I was working in the garden*, my brother was sitting in the sun.

   I was just going into the shop when I met an old friend.

4 *It takes* me an hour to get to college in the mornings.

   It has taken me two hours to get here today.

5 This car was *made in* Germany.

It was *made by* Germans.

The World Cup is *made of* gold.

Glass is *made from* sand and lime.

6　*Up till now* I have been to the UK three times.

So far I have seen that film five times.

2．多项选择题答案

1	b	2	c	3	b	4	d	5	c	6	a
7	d	8	c	9	c	10	b	11	b	12	a

Lesson 29
Funny or not?
是否可笑?

📖 **课文详注** **Further notes on the text**

1. Whether we find a joke funny or not largely depends on where we have been brought up.

(1) whether we find a joke funny or not 为一名词性从句,在句子中作主语。虽然从属连词 whether 和 if 意义相同,但它们在名词性从句的使用中,有较严格的使用界限:

1) 当引导的名词性从句在句中作主语时,必须使用 whether,而不能使用 if,如:

Whether he has signed the contract (or not) doesn't matter.

他是否在合同上签了字都无关紧要。

Whether they can stay with their mother is another matter.

他们是否能同他们的母亲住在一起则是另一回事。

2) 当引导的名词性从句在动词 be 后作补语或在介词后作宾语时,必须使用 whether,而不能使用 if,如:

The question is whether he has signed the contract.

问题是他是否在合同上签了字。

I'm concerned about whether he has signed the contract (or not).

我很关心他是否在合同上签了字。

在上述例子中,whether 不可用 if 代替。

(2) where we have been brought up 为疑问词引导的名词性从句，在句中作宾语。

2. **The sense of humour is mysteriously bound up with national characteristics.**

be bound up with 与/同……(紧密地)联系在一起,如：

People's living standard is bound up with the prosperity of the country.

人民的生活水平同该国的繁荣昌盛息息相关。

The future of a country is bound up with the education of the young.

一个国家的未来同年轻人所受教育密不可分。

3. **A Frenchman, for instance, might find it hard to laugh at a Russian joke.**

laugh at ... 因……发笑,如：

The audience laughed at every word the comedian said.

小丑说的每句话都使观众们发笑。

What are you laughing at?

你们在笑什么？

此外,laugh at 还常用来表示"嘲笑"、"对……一笑置之/嗤之以鼻"之意,如：

He who laughs at crooked men should need walk very straight.

(谚语)笑别人背驼就得自己挺胸走路。

He was laughed at by his friends for being so foolish.

他因为愚蠢的举动而受到朋友们的嘲笑。

She laughed at the difficulties.

她蔑视这些困难。

4. **In the same way, a Russian might fail to see anything amusing in a joke which could make an Englishman laugh to tears.**

322

（1）in the same way 此处为"同样"之意。

（2）amusing 为现在分词,作 anything 的定语,置后修饰 anything。这样的置后修饰方法,主要由不定代词 anything 所决定。当形容词或分词被用来修饰一不定代词（something、anything、somebody、anybody、nothing、anywhere 等）时,均需将形容词或分词置于该不定代词之后,如：

Have you read anything interesting lately ?
近来你读到过什么有趣的东西吗？

Have you anything important to tell us ?
你有什么重要的事情告诉我们吗？

（3）laugh to tears 意为"笑出泪来"。

5．Most funny stories are based on comic situations．

base...on... 以……作为……的根据/基础,如：

He based his statements on newspaper reports .
他的发言是以报纸的报道为根据的。

These charges are based on misunderstanding .
这些指控出自误解。

6．No matter where you live，you would find it difficult not to laught at，say，Charlie Chaplin's early films．

（1）no matter 无论,不管,引导一让步状语从句。

（2）say 为插入语,可译为"比如说"。

7．However，a new type of humour，which stems largely from the U.S.，has recently come into fashion．

（1）which 在此为关系代词,引导一非限制性定语从句。当定语从句中表示的语义同先行词的关系比较松散时,通常使用非限定性定语从句形式表达。

（2）stem from 起源于,引发于,如：

His leg trouble stems from an old gun injury .
他腿上的毛病是由一处旧枪伤引起的。

Correct decisions stem from correct judgement.

正确的决定来源于正确的判断。

（3）come/grow into fashion 开始流行,时兴起来,成为时髦,如：

This style of writing came into fashion at the end of last century.

这种文风盛行于上个世纪末。

Don't throw your old clothes away, they might come back into fashion in a few years.

不要把你的旧衣服扔掉,说不定过几年它们的样式还会再时兴起来。

8. Comedians base their jokes on tragic situations like violent death or serious accidents.

like violent death or serious accidents 为介词 like 构成的介词短语,修饰 situations,意即"喜剧演员根据悲剧情节诸如暴死、重大事故来编造笑话"。

9. From the moment he arrived there, he kept on pestering his doctor to tell him when he would be able to go home.

keep on doing sth. 同 28 课课文注释 14 中的 to keep doing sth. 一样,可用来表示在较短的一段时间内"不断或总是做某事"之意。就语法而言,虽然 keep doing sth. 中的 doing 为现在分词,而 keep on doing sth. 中的 doing 为动名词,但在表达上述语义时通常可以换用,如：

Alice kept on waving to us.

艾丽丝不断向我们招手。

People kept on coming to the hospital to see him.

人们不断到医院来看望他。

但在表达较长一段时间里不断重复的动作或持续的状态时,如第 28 课课文注释 14 中有关 keep doing sth. 中的最后一例中那样,通常用 keep doing sth.,而不用 keep on doing sth.。

324

10. He dreaded having to spend Christmas in hospital.

在动词 dread 后可使用名词、动词不定式、动名词(短语)等作宾语,表示"厌恶/害怕/担心(做)某事"之意,如:

She had begun to dread these excursions.

她已开始对这些旅行感到厌恶。

Everything you dread doing you must do straight away.

你必须马上做你不愿做的每件事情。

I dread to see him fail.

我不愿看到他失败。

11. He spent a miserable day in bed thinking of all the fun he was missing.

thinking of all the fun he was missing 为现在分词短语,在句中作方式状语,修饰动词 spent。he was missing 为定语从句,省略了关系代词 that。全句意即"他郁郁不乐地在床上躺了一天,想着他错过的种种欢乐"。

12. ... the doctor consoled him by telling him that his chances of being able to leave hospital in time for New Year celebrations were good.

by telling...good 为介词短语,作方式状语,修饰 consoled。在此介词短语中包含一个由 that 引导的名词性从句,作 telling 的直接宾语。此宾语从句中的主语较长(从 his chances of... celebration),were good 为该主语的谓语动词及其补语部分。

13. The man took heart and, sure enough, ...

(1) take heart 振作起来,受到鼓舞。表示从何处受到鼓舞时,其后需用介词 from 构成的介词短语。该短语的反义词为 lose heart,如:

It was impossible not to take heart in company of such a man like Tom.

跟汤姆这样的人在一起,精神不可能不振作。

He had taken heart at the little glimpse of hope.

看到一线希望后,他重新振作起来。

(2) sure enough 为插入语,为"果然"、"果真"之意。

14. To compensate for his unpleasant experiences in hospital, the man drank a little more than was good for him.

(1) compensate for ... in hospital 为动词不定式短语,在句中作目的状语,可译为"为了补偿……"。compensate for ... 与 compensate...for...虽然都具有"补偿"的含义,但前者中的 compensate 为不及物动词,与介词 for 一起作及物动词。其主体常指事物,是补偿的对象,for 后是补偿的原因,如:

Nothing can compensate for the loss of one's health.

没有什么能补偿失去健康。

No other qualities, however brilliant, can compensate for the absense of a correct understanding of things.

不管其他方面的才能技巧如何突出,也无法弥补缺少对事物的正确理解。

而 compensate...for... 中的 compensate 则为及物动词,其主体通常为人,是补偿的发起者,其后为被补偿对象,介词 for 后为补偿的原因,如:

We must in some way compensate him for his pains.

我们必须以某种方式,对他的劳苦给予补偿。

(2) a little more than was good for him 中 than 后省略了主语 what。be good for ... 对……有用/有益,如:

This medicine will be good for you.

这药对你有效。

This book is good for children.

这本书适于小孩读。

在口语中,有时在介词 for 后直接接钱款数额,表示"价值为",如:

That is a bike good for four hundred yuan.

那是一辆价值 400 元的自行车。

语法　Grammar in use

it 的先行用法

1. it 作先行主语

当句子中的主语为动词不定式、动名词或名词性从句时,往往由 it 开头,而将上述主语置后。此时 it 为先行主语。逻辑主语是被置于句后的动词不定式、动名词或名词性从句,如:

It's pleasant to lie in the sun. (*i. e. To lie in the sun is pleasant.*)

躺着晒太阳很舒服。

It's pleasant lying in the sun. (*i. e. Lying in the sun is pleasant.*)

躺着晒太阳很舒服。

It doesn't matter when we arrive. (*i. e. When we arrive doesn't matter.*)

我们什么时候到达无关紧要。

it 作先行主语时经常与下列各词类连用:

(1) 形容词如 difficult、easy、important、vital、necessary、obvious、advisable、odd 等,如:

It is obvious (*that*) *money doesn't grow on trees.*

显而易见,金钱总不会从树上长出来。

It is easy (*for me*) *to make mistakes.*

(我)很容易犯错。

(2) 名词如 fun、pity、pleasure、shame 等,如:

It's a pleasure (*for us*) *to be here.*

(我们)在这里很愉快。

327

（3）动词如 appear、happen、look、seem 等，如：

It appears that he forgot to sign the letter.

他似乎忘记在信上署名了。

It now looks certain that the fire was caused by a cigarette end.

现在似乎可以肯定火灾是由一个烟头引起的。

此外，有些动词如 agree、arrange、decide、say、believe、suggest、fear 等，在 it 后面用被动语态，引导一个 that 从句，如：

It's said that there is plenty of oil off our coast.

据说我国沿海有大量的石油。

It is feared that many lives have been lost in the train crash.

在这次列车碰撞事故中，恐怕有不少人丧生。

2．it 作先行宾语

"it + 形容词"可用在像 find、enjoy、hate、think 一类动词之后再接动词不定式或 that 引导的从句。此时 it 为先行宾语，其后的动词不定式或 that 从句为逻辑宾语，如：

I think it best to go.

我想最好走。

He considered it wrong that she should have to wait.

他认为她不得不等待是错的。

📁 **词汇学习 Word study**

1．depend *vi.*

（1）（on, upon）视……而定，取决于：

The price of the shares will depend on the number of people who want to buy them.

股票的价格将依购买这些股票的人数而定。

328

Whether or not we go to Spain for our holiday depends on the cost.

我们是否能去西班牙度假主要取决于费用的多少。

(2)(on, upon)依靠,依赖:

We in the United Kingdom have depended heavily on coal both for industrial and domestic uses.

我们在英国一直主要依赖煤炭供工业与家庭使用。

The old man depends on his daughter.

那位老人靠他的女儿养活。

(3)(on, upon)信赖,相信:

You can't depend on John—he nearly always arrives late.

你可别信约翰的,他几乎总是迟到。

2．laugh

(1)*vi.* 笑,发笑:

They all laughed when she fell over.

她摔倒时他们都笑了。

He laughed nervously when the police asked him where he had been on that evening.

警察问他那天晚上他去哪儿时,他不自然地笑了。

(2)*vi.*(at)因……而笑;嘲笑;不以为然;藐视:

They'll just laugh at you if you can't think of a better excuse than that.

你要是想不出一个比这个好的借口,他们就会笑话你的。

She laughs at the idea of danger.

她全不把危险当回事。

(3)*n.* 笑,笑声,引人发笑的事:

She gave a happy laugh.

她发出愉快的笑声。

329

3. keep (kept, kept)

(1) *vt.* 保留,保存;存放;饲养:

> *We keep the medicines in a locked cupboard.*
> 我们把药品存放在一个锁着的橱柜里。
>
> *The old couple keep a pig in their backyard.*
> 这对老夫妇在他们的后院养了一头猪。

(2) *vt.* (使)留在某处,(使)保持某种状态:

> *The illness kept her in hospital for six weeks.*
> 这个病让她在医院里呆了 6 个星期。
>
> *This coat will keep you warm.*
> 这件外衣会使你暖和。
>
> *They've got to hunt for food to keep alive.*
> 他们不得不寻找食物以活下去。
>
> *Keep left when you get to the end of the street.*
> 到了街尽头一直沿左侧往前走。

(3) *vi.* (on)继续下去,不停地做:

> *I wish you wouldn't keep (on) interrupting.*
> 我希望你别老打扰我。
>
> *The children keep (on) pestering me to take them to the zoo.*
> 孩子们不停地缠着我,让我带他们去动物园。

✍ 练习答案 Key to written exercises

1. 关键句型、难点练习答案

1 operate on, differ from, smell of, encourage... in, lean on, approve of, delight in, suffer from, assure of, escape from, interested in, concentrate on, include in

2 *He found it* difficult to walk after his operation.

330

She considered it sensible to forget what they had said to her.

He thought it silly to make a fuss.

3 When he heard the joke, he *laughed*.

He *laughed at* the joke.

4 *amusing* (*l* . 5) = funny：

The man *amused* us with some jokes.

I *enjoyed* his jokes.

He *entertained* the people by playing the piano for about an hour.

5 See text.

6 Please *keep off* the grass.

Don't run so fast. I can't *keep up with* you.

There was a notice on his door which said '*Keep out*'.

7 I *could* swim very well when I was younger.

I *was able to* solve the problem after an hour.

2．多项选择题答案

1	c	2	b	3	a	4	a	5	a	6	a
7	b	8	c	9	d	10	d	11	c	12	b

Lesson 30
The death of a ghost
幽灵之死

📖 **课文详注 Further notes on the text**

1. For years, villagers believed that Endley Farm was haunted.

(1) for years 为时间状语,正常情况下置于句尾,现提前,起到对此时间状语的强调作用。

(2) be haunted 常用来表示"鬼魂常出没的",有时也用来表示"(思想、精神等)受到困扰的"之意。在表示这两种意思时,haunt 通常用于被动语态形式,如:

> *The old castle is said to be haunted.*
> 人们说那座古老的城堡常有鬼魂出没。

> *The thief is constantly haunted by fear of discovery.*
> 那个小偷总担心被人发现。

2. Every time a worker gave up his job, he told the same story.

every time 每次,每当。相当于 whenever,在句中作从属连词,引导一时间状语从句,说明主句谓语动词动作所做的时间,如:

> *Every time I call on him, he is out.*
> 每次我去拜访他,他总是不在。

> *Every time he spelt the word, he made the same mistake.*
> 每次他拼写这个词,总是犯相同的错误。

3. Farm labourers said that they always woke up to find that work had been done overnight.

(1) that they...overnight 中的 that 为连词,引导一宾语从句。

(2) to find...overnight 为动词不定式短语,作结果状语。有关用法参见第 10 课课文注释 7。

4．**A farm worker, who stayed up all night, claimed to have seen a figure cutting corn in the moonlight.**

(1) who stayed up all night 中的 who 为关系代词, 引导一非限制性定语从句, 对 a farm worker 作进一步说明。stay up 为"熬夜"、"不睡觉"之意, 如:

I stayed up reading until midnight.

我看书一直看到半夜。

Tell her to stay up till I get home.

告诉她等我回来再睡。

(2) to have seen ... in the moonlight 为完成时态的动词不定式短语, 作动词 claimed 的宾语, 表明该动词不定式短语中的动作发生在该主句谓语动词 claimed 动作之前。

5．**In time, it became an accepted fact that .. ghost that did ...**

(1) in time 在此作"经过一定时间之后"、"久而久之"之意, 如:

In time you'll learn everything.

经过一段时间之后, 你一切都会明白的(即总有一天你一切都会明白的)。

(2) an accepted fact that... 中的 that 为连词, 引导一同位语从句, 指 fact 的具体内容。

(3) ... ghost that did ... 中的 that 为关系代词, 引导一定语从句, 修饰先行词 ghost。在定语从句中, 最常用的关系代词是 who、whom、which 和 that。who 和 whom 用来指人; which 用来指物; that 常用来代替 whom 或 which, 更常用的是代替 who, 如:

She's the only person that understands me.

她是惟一了解我的人。

6．**... , villagers were astonished to learn that the ... died.**

to learn that ... died 为动词不定式短语, 在句中作原因状语,说明产生 astonished 的原因。作原因状语的动词不定式(短语)常用于作主语补语的形容词/过去分词之后。

7. ..., for the 'ghost' was none other than Eric Cox, a third brother who ... died as a young man.

(1) none other than 不是别人而正是……,如:

> *The murderer was none other than the victim's husband.*
> 杀人犯不是别人,正是受害人的丈夫。
>
> *The new arrival was none other than the President.*
> 刚到达的正是总统本人。

(2) as a young man 作"在年轻时"解。

8. ...,Joe and Bob revealed a secret which they had kept for over fifty years.

(1) reveal a secret 透露/揭示一秘密。

(2) which 为关系代词,引导一限定性定语从句。由于从句中的动词 keep 的动作发生在过去所做出的主句谓语动词 reveal 动作之前,因此使用过去完成时态。

(3) keep a /the secret 保守秘密。

9. Eric had been the eldest son of the family,very much older than his two brothers.

(1) 形容词 old 有两个比较级和两个最高级形式,即:

> *old—older—oldest*
>
> *old—elder—eldest*

其用法如下:old、older 和 oldest 既可用来指人的实际年龄的大小,也可用来表示物的新旧及一些其他引申意义,如:

> *John is three years older than Mary.*
> 约翰比玛丽大 3 岁。
>
> *This is an older city.*
> 这是一座较古老的城市。

elder 和 eldest 通常仅限于某些特定的用法,指人的长幼,一般

只用在表示亲属的名词前作定语,如:

> *The elder brother is called Tom .*
>
> 哥哥名叫汤姆。
>
> *The girl standing at the gate is the eldest daughter of his family .*
>
> 站在大门口的那个女孩是他家的长女。

但在现代美语中,常用 older 和 oldest 分别代替 elder 和 eldest,如:

> *He was the oldest of the three children .*
>
> 他是 3 个孩子中最大的一个。
>
> *She was my older sister .*
>
> 她是我姐姐。

(2) 形容词短语有时被置于一名词或代词之后,作用接近于同位语,相当于一个非限定性定语从句(如 very much older than his two brothers 相当于 who was very much older than his two brothers),如:

> *During these struggles , many policemen , faithful to their duties , shed their last drop of blood .*
>
> 在这些斗争中,许多警察忠于职守,直到生命的最后一息。

这类形容词短语有时甚至被放在句首,如:

> *Conscientious and eager , she took down what was said , careful not to miss a word .*
>
> 她认真热情,把说的话一字不漏地记了下来。

形容词短语起状语作用,参见第 16 课课文注释 8。

10. He had been obliged to join the army during the Second World War.

(1) be obliged to do sth. 为"不得不做某事"之意。oblige 一词虽可用来表示强迫之意,但更多用来表示"必要性",如:

I was obliged to reprimend him for the sake of discipline .

为了维持纪律,我不得不说他几句。

You're not obliged to believe everything he said .

对他的话你不必都言听计从。

(2) join 作及物动词使用时(如文中),其后通常跟团体、组织等名词,表示"参加"、"加入"之意,如:

She joined the Party soon after she came to our unit .

她刚来我们部门不久就入了党。

有时后面也可直接跟表示人的名词或代词,表示"加入其中"之意,如:

May I join you ?

我可以和你们一道去吗?

但在表达"参加"群众性活动、会议等时,不用 join,而使用 take part in 或 attend 等,如:

He took an active part in a research into the cause of heart disease .

他积极参与心脏病起因的研究工作。

They attended the meeting yesterday .

他们参加了昨天的会议。

11. His father told everything that . . . in action .

in action 在此为"在战斗中"之意,如:

He was killed in action in France .

他在法国阵亡。

The soldier was unfortunate enough to have lost one of his legs in action .

这个士兵很不幸,他在战斗中失去了一条腿。

12. He used to sleep . . . ,quite unware of the fact that . . .

(1) used to do sth.用来表示"过去经常性/习惯性做某事"之意。

(2) quite unware of . . . the ghost of Endley 为形容词短语,在句中

336

作结果状语。

(3) ... the fact that... 中的 that 为关系连词,引导一同位语从句。

📖 语法 Grammar in use

suppose,say,believe 等动词的被动语态

1. 有时为了把话说得谨慎些,可以用被动结构,如:

> *Muriel pays less income tax than she should.*
> 缪里尔少交了所得税。

我们对事实确有把握时可以这样说,但出于谨慎,比较"保险"的说法是:

> *Muriel is said to pay less income tax than she should.*
> 据说缪里尔少交了所得税。

2. 常用的被动结构如下:

(1) It + 动词(被动语态结构) + that 引导的从句

常用于此结构的动词有 agree、allege、arrange、assume、believe、consider、decide、declare、discover、expect、fear、feel、find、hope、image、know、observe、presume、prove、report、say、show、suggest、suppose、think、understand 等,如:

> *It is said that there is plenty of oil off our coast.*
> 据说我国沿海有大量的石油。

(2) There + 动词(被动语态结构) + to be + 补足语

只有有限的动词可用于此结构,如 acknowledge、allege、believe、consider、fear、feel、know、presume、report、say、suppose、think、understand 等,如:

> *There is supposed to be a train at 12:37.*
> 想必 12 点 37 分有一列火车。

(3) 除 it 以外的主语 + 动词(被动语态结构) + 带 to 的动词不

定式

只有少数动词可用于此结构,如 acknowledge、allege、believe、consider、declare、know、recognize、report、say、suppose、think、understand 等,如:

> *Turner was considered to be a genius even in his lifetime.*
> 特纳生前已被看成是个天才。

> *Homeopathic remedies are believed to be very effective.*
> 人们认为顺势疗法很有疗效。

动词不定式中除 be 外,也可以用其他动词,如:

> *Jane is said to know all there is to know about chimpanzees.*
> 据说简了解有关黑猩猩的一切情况。

注意下句中 suppose 有两种不同的意义:

> *He is supposed to be at work at the moment.*
> 人们认为他正在工作或他应该在工作。

📁 词汇学习 Word study

1. own

(1) *vt.* 拥有,有(不用于进行时态):

> *Who owns this house?*
> 谁拥有这所房子?

> *Many underdeveloped countries own their natural resources.*
> 许多不发达国家都拥有自然资源。

(2) *adj.* 自己的,属于自己的(用于所有格之后加强语气):

> *I took no notice till I heard my own name mentioned.*
> 在我自己的名字被提到之前,我根本没注意听。

> *She was younger than my own two daughters.*

338

她比我自己的两个女儿要小。(注:数词放在 *own* 之后)

Accountants have their very own language.

会计师们有他们自己的专业语言。(注:可以用 *very* 修饰 *own* 以加强语气)

(3) *pron*. 属于自己的东西或人(用于所有格之后):

They treated the child as if she were their own.

他们对待那个孩子如同自己的一样。

(4) (all) on one's own 独自:

We can't solve this problem on our own.

我们无法自己解决这个问题。

2. suppose *vt*.

(1) 认为,以为:

She was commonly supposed (to be) extremely rich.

她被认为非常富有。

The hill was supposed to be haunted by a ghost.

人们认为这座山里闹鬼。

(2) 猜想,料定;假定:

As she's not here, I suppose she must have gone home.

她不在这儿,我想她一定是回家去了。

⎧ *He must have missed the train, then.*

⎪ 他肯定误了火车。

⎨

⎪ *Yes, I suppose so.*

⎩ 对,我也这么猜想。

用 I suppose so 表示赞同对方的说法,但也表示出并非十分肯定。表示赞同一个否定说法可以用"I suppose not",如:

That's not a good idea .

那不是个好主意。

No , I suppose not .

对,我也这么想。

但是对一个肯定的说法表示不赞成应说"I don't suppose so",如:

Will they have arrived by now ?

他们这会儿该到了吗?

I don't suppose so .

我想不会。

如果认为某件事不是事实,通常说"I don't suppose that it is...",而不说"I suppose that it is not...",如:

I don't suppose you would be prepared to stay in Edinburgh ?

我想你不会打算呆在爱丁堡吧?

I don't suppose she'll agree .

我没想到她会同意。

(3) be supposed to 认为必须,认为必要,有责任/义务去做:

The children are supposed to be at school by 8:45 a . m .

孩子们应该8点45分以前到校。

You are supposed to report it to the police as soon as possible .

你应该尽快向警察报告此事。

3. remain *vi* . (不用于进行时态)

(1) 留下,逗留,停留:

She remained at home to look after the children when her husband went out .

她丈夫外出时,她留在家里照看孩子们。

The doctor ordered him to remain in bed for a few days .

医生命令他卧床几天。

注:remain 与 stay 词义相同,但是 remain 更正式一些。此外,临时住在一个城镇、饭店、房子时只能用 stay,而不用 remain,如:

How long can you stay in Brussels ?

你能在布鲁塞尔呆多久?

(2) 保持不变(系动词):

It remains a secret .

那件事一直是个秘密。

The situation remains unchanged .

状况仍毫未改变。

(3) 剩余,余留:

After the flood , nothing remained of the village .

洪水过后村子荡然无存。

He was cut off from what remained of his family .

他已被断决了与他家庭现存人员的来往。

✍ 练习答案　Key to written exercises

1. 关键句型、难点练习答案

1　*gave up* = stopped doing

You must *give in* your homework on Friday.

I didn't need my bicycle any more so I *gave it away* to someone who couldn't afford one.

Eric didn't want to *give himself up* to the authorities because he had deserted.

2　I can't *tell a lie* .

We really must *say godbye* now.

I can never *tell the difference* between their cat and ours.

If that's what you think, *say so*.

Excuse me. Can you *tell me the time*?

3   I'd like you to *make a speech* at the wedding.

He'll *do his best* to win.

Can you *do me a favour*?

He never *makes a mistake*.

4   *I suppose* this house is very old.

He is supposed to speak English very well.

He was supposed to meet me at the station, but he didn't come.

5   See text.

6   *He used to work* here when he was younger.

He was working in the garden when I saw him.

2. 多项选择题答案

1	d	2	a	3	d	4	b	5	c	6	b
7	a	8	a	9	c	10	b	11	d	12	a

Lesson 31
A lovable eccentric
可爱的怪人

📖 **课文详注** **Further notes on the text**

1. True eccentrics never deliberately set out to draw attention to themselves.

（1）set out 在此表示"打算",后接动词不定式,表示"打算做"之意,如:

> *She could be very eloquent when she set out to be so.*
> 她要真讲起来是会滔滔不绝的。

（2）draw attention to 把注意力吸引到,如:

> *Our attention has been drawn to a spectacular display of fireworks.*
> 我们的注意力已被吸引到烟火奇观上。

2. They disregard social conventions without being conscious that they are doing anything extraordinary.

without ... extraordinary 为介词短语,作状语,意即"意识不到他们正做着与众不同的事情",表示伴随主动词一同发生的情况。

3. This invariably wins them the love and respect of others, for they add colour to the dull routine of everyday life.

（1）win 可用作双宾语动词,即如句中将代词 them 同名词 love and respect 作它的宾语。them 为间接宾语,love and respect 为直接宾语,这里表示"赢得其他人的爱戴和尊敬",再如:

> *She has a nature that quickly won her the friendship of*

her colleagues.

她具有一种天性,可以很快获得同事们的友谊。

此外,win 也可作为单宾语动词使用,如:

Mayakovsky's poems won high praise from both Lenin and Stalin.

玛雅可夫斯基的诗歌博得了列宁和斯大林的高度赞扬。

由于 win 的本义为"赢得",而非"打败"之意,因而其后可用诸如 war(战争)、battle(战役)、victory(胜利)等作宾语,而不能用诸如 enemy(敌人)、opponent(对手)、difficulty(困难)等作宾语,此时应用其他动词,如:

They defeated their enemy.

他们打败了敌人。(不能用 *won*)

We've triumphed over / overcome various obstacles and achieved success.

我们已克服了种种障碍,获得了成功。(不能用 *won over*)

(2) add ... to ... 中的 add 是及物动词,表示"把……添加到……"之意,如:

Would the program be too long if we added two new items to it?

我们若在此之上再加上两项,节目会不会太长了?

He added some wood to the fire.

他给火添了些木柴。

当 add 作不及物动词时,其后也用"to + 宾语"结构,表示"起到添加的作用"的含义,如:

The newly-published book has added to his reputation.

这部新出版的书使他的名声更大了。

4. Up to the time of his death, ...

up to 这里表示"直到"之意,可用来表示"时间"、"空间"上的延

344

伸,如:

> *Up to the war she had never lived alone.*
>
> 直到战争前,她从未单身生活过。
>
> *She went straight up to the door.*
>
> 她径直走到门口。

5. He was known to us all as Dickie and ...

be known to 为……所知,闻名于。其后一般接人或表示地方的名词,如:

> *The writer is known to the world.*
>
> 这位作家闻名于全世界。
>
> *Your neighbour is known to the police, so you'd better lock your door.*
>
> 你的邻居是警察熟知的人物,所以你最好把门锁上。

应注意,就结构而言,在由及物动词 know 的主动句变为被动句时,通常使用这一结构。比较:

> *We've all known him long.*
>
> 我们都认识他很久了。
>
> *He has long been known to us all.*
>
> 他早为我们大家所知。

6. ... he hardly ever used it, preferring always to go on foot.

preferring always to go on foot 在句中为现在分词短语,作原因状语。作原因状语的分词短语通常用于句首,但由于该主句前为由从属连词 though 引导的一个让步状语从句,因此,出于修辞需要,将其置于句末。

7. Even when it was raining heavily, he ...

even 即使,尽管,甚至。为副词,不可误当连词使用,因此本句中的 when 不可省略。

8. One day, he walked into an expensive shop after having been caught in a particularly heavy shower.

句中的 after 为介词,因此其后的 having been caught in...为完成时被动语态形式的动名词短语。由于 be caught in...动作发生在过去发生的主动词动作(walked)之前,因此需将其构成完成时态形式。

be caught in ... 突然遇上/碰上,如:

> *On their way home , they were nearly caught in a shower .*
> 在回家的路上,他们差点挨雨淋。

> *We were late because we had got caught in a rain / hurricane / storm / traffic jam , etc .*
> 我们因为遇上了雨/飓风/暴风雨/交通阻塞等才来迟了。

9. ... but he was in such a bedraggled condition that ...

such ... that ... 如此……以致……连词 that 后引导一结果状语从句。由于 such 为一形容词,因此其后需使用一名词或名词性短语。

10. Recognizing who the customer was, the manager was most apologetic and ...

most 在这里起到加强语气的作用,相当于 very。most 前没有定冠词,因此不应视其为形容词 apologetic 的最高级形式。

11. It contained ₤ 300 in pennies.

in pennies 为介词短语,作定语修饰 ₤ 300,意即"一便士一便士的 300 镑钱币"。

12. He insisted on the assistant's counting the money before he left—30,000 pennies in all!

(1) insist on (doing)... 坚持(做)……在短语动词 insist on/upon 后需用名词或名词性短语,其后若用动词时,需用该动词的动名词形式,或由该动词构成的动名词短语形式,如:

> *That's what the manager always insisted on .*
> 这正是该经理一贯强调的。

> *She insisted on the importance of being punctual .*

她强调守时的重要性。

They insisted on helping us in the kitchen.

他们坚持要为我们帮厨。

当这样的动名词(短语)有其逻辑主语,且该逻辑主语为代词时,可以使用其所有格形式;为名词时,通常需将其构成名词所有格形式(如文中的 assistant's),再如:

We ought to have insisted on your taking a thorough rest before going back to work.

我们本应该让你彻底休息好后再回去上班。

有关用法参见本课语法部分。

(2) in all 在此为"总共"、"合计"之意,如:

There were 100 people in all.

总共有 100 人。

用时还可用其表示"总之"、"简言之"之意,如:

In all, this is an interesting story book.

总之,这是一本有趣的故事书。

13. ... for though the pictures were supposed to be the work of famous artists, ...

(1) for 为一并列连词,用以表示因果关系,它通常被用于引导一事后想到的原因,或追加说明的原因,更类似于置于括号内的说明性文字。

(2) be supposed to do 被料想为,被预想为。常用来表示预想/期待发生的事,如:

Lucy was supposed to come to lunch. What's happened?

露西应该来吃午饭。出什么事了?

如课文中那样,它常被用来表明应该发生的事与实际发生的事的对比,如:

Cats are supposed to be afraid of dogs, but our Tibby has just chased Mr. Clidewell's bulldog right down the road.

猫本应怕狗,但我们的梯比把克莱德威尔先生的叭儿狗赶得往马路那头跑去。

That's a lovely picture,but what's if supposed to be?
那是幅很好的画,但不知它想说明什么?

📋 语法　Grammar in use

有一些可带动词-ing 形式的动词,其间可插入一个名词或代词。这个词有时必须是宾格(如宾语代词 me,him,或人名 John 等);有时则必须是一个所有格(即所有格代词或名词所有格,如 my,John's 等);有时则可为两者中的任何一个。该宾格为动词-ing的逻辑主语。

1.动词 + 宾格 + 动词-ing 形式

　有些动词后可以使用动词-ing 形式,还可在动词与该动词-ing形式间插入一个宾格(如 me、John,等)。这些动词有 catch、feel、find、hear、imagine、keep、leave、notice、observe、see、send、stop、watch 等,如:

　　When are you going to start him working?
　　你打算什么时候让他开始工作?

　　I'd better not catch you doing that again!
　　我可不想再抓住你干那事了!

2.动词 + 所有格 + 动词-ing 形式

　有些动词之后只跟动词-ing 形式或跟所有格(如 my、John's,等) + 动词-ing 形式。该动词-ing 形式相当于名词,因此其前可使用一所有格形式(指人而不指物)。这些动词有appreciate、avoid、consider(通常用于疑问句或否定句里)、defer、delay、deny、enjoy、postpone、risk、suggest 等,如:

　　He tried to avoid answering my questions.
　　他企图回避我的问题。

348

I don't think the children enjoy your/his/John's teasing.

我认为孩子们不喜欢你的/他的/约翰的嘲讽。

3．动词＋宾格或所有格＋动词-ing 形式

有些动词后,可以只跟动词-ing 形式,也可以跟宾格或所有格＋动词-ing 形式,如 anticipate、detest、dislike、dispute、endure、escape、excuse、face、fancy、forgive、hate、hinder、imagine、like、love、mention、mind、miss、pardon、prevent、understand 等,如:

Do you mind me smoking?

你介意我抽烟吗?

Are you trying to prevent me speaking?

你想阻止我说话吗?

I can't understand John/John's making such a fuss.

我不理解约翰为什么这么小题大做。

I can't imagine Frank and Mabel paying so much for a piano.

我不能想像弗兰克和梅布尔竟花这么多钱买钢琴。

注:动词-ing 形式前如有一个以上的名字时,一般不用-'s 形式,如上最后一例。

📂　词汇学习　Word study

1．hardly *adv.*

(1) 不十分,刚……就……:

I hardly know the people I work with.

我不大认识和我一起工作的人们。

Hardly had we started when the car got a flat tyre.

我们刚启动,一只车胎就没气了。

(2) 几乎不(常用 can 或 could 连用,置于 can 或 could 之后):

I can hardly wait to hear the news.

我迫不及待地想要知道那条消息。

I could hardly move.

我几乎一动也不能动。

(3) 不,从不:

We've hardly any money left.

我们没钱了。

I have hardly ever spoken to him.

我从未跟他说过话。

2．refuse

(1) *vt．,vi．*拒绝,回绝;拒绝接受:

He asked her to marry him but she refused.

他请求她嫁给他,但是她拒绝了。

I know he is in trouble but he's refused all my offers of help.

我知道他遇到了麻烦,可是他拒绝我的任何帮助。

(2) *vt．*（＋双宾语）拒绝给予;不允许:

We were refused entry permission to enter.

我们被拒绝入内。

The city council refused him permission to build an extra bedroom.

市政厅不允许他再建一间卧室。

(3) *vt．*（＋带 to 的动词不定式）拒不,不肯,不愿:

On cold mornings the car always refuses to start.

在寒冷的早晨,这辆车总是打不着火。

He refused to accept their advice.

他拒绝接受他们的忠告。

用法:refuse、decline、reject 和 turn down 均表示拒绝做某事或拒绝接受之意。一般可以说:

refuse/decline an invitation 谢绝（*decline* 较婉转,且口气不

350

那么坚决)

refuse permission 不允许

decline/reject/turn down a suggestion 拒绝某一建议

refuse/decline/reject/turn down an offer 拒绝接受(帮助)

reject/turn down a plan/proposal 否决某一计划/建议

此外,decline 必须指以语言谢绝,如:

> *I'm afraid I must decline your invitation.*
>
> 恐怕我得谢绝你的邀请。

而 refuse 和 reject 则无需以语言,如:

> *The horse refused to jump the fence.*
>
> 那匹马拒绝跳跃那个篱笆。

3. present

(1) *vt.* 赠送;授予;呈献:

> *He is going to present the town with a new hospital in memory of his mother.*
>
> 为纪念他的母亲,他准备赠送给这个城镇一所新医院。
>
> *When Mr. Brown left the firm, the manager presented a gold watch to him.*
>
> 布朗先生离开这个公司时,公司经理赠给他一块金表。

(2) *vt.* 提供;递交;提出:

> *When will the project team present their report?*
>
> 什么时候项目组提交他们的报告?
>
> *The flood presented the province with severe problems.*
>
> 洪水使该省面临种种严重问题。

(3) *adj.* 出席的,在场的;存在的(作表语,后常跟 at 引导的介词短语):

> *He had been present at the conference.*
>
> 开会时他一直在场。
>
> *There was a photographer present.*

有一名摄影师在场。

(4) *adj.* 现在的；目前的(作定语)：

Economic planning cannot succeed in present conditions.

经济规划在目前情况下不可能成功。

The present chairperson is a woman.

现在的主席是位妇女。

(5) *n.* 礼品，赠品：

They unwrapped their Christmas present.

他们打开了他们的圣诞礼物。

They gave me theatre tickets as a present.

他们将戏票作为礼物送给我。

✍ 练习答案　Key to written exercises

1. 关键句型、难点练习答案

1　I walked there *instead of* going by bus.

Apart from cleaning the windows, he hasn't done much all day.

I'm not really *interested in* fishing.

2　See text.

3　He walked *into* the hotel through the front door, and went *out of* the hotel by the back door.

He went *into* the restaurant at *6:00* and stayed *in* the restaurant till midnight!

4　Please *pay attention to* your teacher.

I *don't care* what she does!

Can you please take *care of* the apartment while we're away?

5　*I don't know who* he's talking about.

Ask him why he has never left England.

She asked if I could phone her.

6 *Would you mind my* opening the window?

   Imagine her wearing a dress like that!

7 At the beginning, the team did very well, but *in the end* they
   lost the match.

   He always owes money to people: he's always *in debt*.

   They never went far out to sea: land was always *in sight*.

   I gave her the bad news as gently as I could, but she was *in
   tears* when I left.

2．多项选择题答案

1 b	2 b	3 d	4 b	5 b	6 a
7 a	8 a	9 d	10 d	11 c	12 d

Lesson 32
A lost ship
一艘沉船

📖 **课文详注 Further notes on the text**

1. The small ship *Elkor*, which had been searching the Barents Sea for weeks, was on its way home.

(1) which 为关系代词,在此引导一非限制性定语从句,对 Elkor 号小船作进一步说明。因为 search 为发生在表示过去状态的主动词 was 之前,但仍是在进行的动作,因此使用了过去完成进行时态进行表述。

(2) on one's way (to...) 在(去……的)路上。由于句中 home 为副词,因此可直接作定语修饰 way。但当所去的地方为一名词时,需在 way 与该名词间使用介词 to,如:

   On my way to school, I met my old friend.
   在去学校的路上,我遇到了我的一位老朋友。

2. A radio message from the mainland had been received by the ship's captain instructing him to give up the search.

(1) from the mainland 这一介词短语在句中作定语,修饰 message,意即"大陆上发来的电报"。由于要表明的动作 receive 发生在过去状态 was on its way home 之前,因此需使用过去完成时态。

(2) instructing him... search 为现在分词短语作定语,修饰 message,意即"大陆上发来的指示让他放弃搜索的电报"。正常结构是将其放在 from the mainland 之后,但由于那样会使主语太长,使全句显得虎头蛇尾。出于修辞目的,将其置于句末,以使句子显得平衡。

3. **Despite the message, the captain of ...**

despite 尽管,不顾,介词。引导一让步状语。正因为是介词(而非连词),因此其后只能用名词、代词或名词性短语(而非从句)。

4. **The sea bed was scoured with powerful nets and ...**

with powerful nets 为介词短语,作方式状语,说明 scour 的方式。

5. **Though the crew were at first under the impression that the lost ship had been found, the contents of the chest proved them wrong.**

(1) be under the impression that 认为,以为。相当于 have the impression that..., 如:

> *We were under the impression that they were brothers.*
> 我们以为他们是兄弟。
>
> *I was under the impression that she was a journalist.*
> 我以为她是个记者。

(2) proved them wrong 中的 wrong 为宾语 them 的补足语,them 指 crew。

6. **What they had in fact found was a ship which had been sunk many years before.**

what 为关系代词,在此引导一主语从句。以 what 引导的名词性从句相当于一先行词(如 The thing) + 关系代词(which 或 that)引导的定语从句。但这两种结构在用法上并非总能互换,也有一定的限制条件。有关用法参见第 16 课课文注释 3。

7. **Nothing of value was found, but the numerous items which were brought to the surface proved to be of great interest.**

句中 of value 和 of great interest 均使用了同一种修辞结构,即"介词 of + 抽象名词"这样的结构。这一结构实际表达出的语义相当于该抽象名词的形容词所表达的语义。如 nothing of value = nothing valuable,而 of great interest = very interesting 之意。再如:

> *a matter of significance = a significant matter* 具有重大意义的事情
>
> *a man of great importance = a very important man* 一位要员

"of + 抽象名词"这样的结构多用于正式文体之中,而在口语中更常使用其形容词的形式表达。

8. **...the captain realized that the ship must have been a cruiser.**

"must + 完成时"结构表示对过去一件事情的肯定推测,即"……认为那艘船肯定是一艘巡洋舰",但是对过去事情的疑问推测或否定推测,通常需使用"can 或 can't + 完成时"结构来表达。有关用法参见第 1 课课文注释 12。

9. **From this the captain was able to piece together all the information that had come to light.**

(1) piece together 拼凑,如:

> *She pieced together odds and ends of cloth and turned them into a beautiful table-cloth.*
>
> 她把零布头拼成一整块,做成了一块漂亮的桌布。
>
> *He has written out a story book with the information he had pieced together during his visit to that native tribe.*
>
> 他用访问那一土著部落期间收集的材料写成了一本故事书。

(2) come to light 显露,暴露,为人周知,如:

> *When the old woman died, it came to light that she was actually very rich.*
>
> 那位老太婆死后,人们才发现她实际上非常富有。
>
> *He's anxious to keep his misdeeds from coming to light.*

他急于掩盖自己的不端行为。

10. This was later confirmed by a naval official at the Ministry of Defence.

confirm 用来指"证实(已知的事实或原有的想法)",如:

His conduct confirms a suspicion I have long held against him.

他的行为证实了我许久以来对他的怀疑。

The news has not yet been officially confirmed.

消息尚未得到官方证实。

在 confirm 之后,通常可使用诸如 statement(陈述)、suspicion(疑心)、appointment(任命)这类的词作直接宾语。该词后通常不能使用 that 引导的名词性从句,但 that 引导的名词性从句却可用于诸如 It has been confirmed that...这样的结构中,如:

It has been confirmed that he was appointed, a few days ago, the chief manager of the company.

已证实他于几日前就被任命为公司的总经理。

📑 语法 Grammar in use

1. 过去完成进行时

(1) 过去完成进行时由 had been + 现在分词构成,即:

I had /I'd

You had/You'd

He had/He'd

She had/Shs'd

It had/It'd   been waiting...

We had/We'd

You had/You'd

They had/They'd

(2) 过去完成进行时的用法

357

1) 过去完成进行时强调在过去更早的一段时间内一直在进行的动作,且该动作对过去某一时刻产生结果。动作是停止了还是继续进行要视上下文而定。句中常用 all + 表示时间的词,如 all day 等,如:

She was very tired; *she had been typing letters all day*.

她很累。她整天都在打信件。(她仍在打字还是刚停下来,要视上下文而定)

"延续性动词"如 learn、lie、live、wait、sit、sleep、stand、study、rain、work 等常与带 since 或 for 的表示时间的状语,或以 How long 引导的疑问句同时用于过去完成进行时,如:

When she arrived I had been waiting for three hours.

她到达时我已经等了 3 个小时。

I realized that I'd been overworking, *so I decided to take a couple of days off*.

我意识到自己一直在超负荷工作,因此我决定休几天假。

"延续性动词"往往既可以用一般时形式,也可以用进行时形式。过去完成时和过去完成进行时的区别是后者更强调动作的延续性。

2) 过去完成进行时常用来表示过去经常重复的动作,如:

Jenny was annoyed, *Jim had been phoning her every night for a whole week*.

詹妮生气了,整整一个星期,吉姆天天晚上都给她打电话。

3) 过去完成进行时表示根据直接或间接的证据而得出结论:

Her eyes were red, *it was obvious she had been crying*.

她的眼睛红了,显然她刚哭过。

(3) 过去完成时与过去完成进行时的比较

358

根据上下文和所使用的动词形式,可以判断出一件事仍在进行还是已经完成。在这种情况下,两种形式不能互换:

When I got home, I found that Jill had been painting her room.

当我回到家时,我看到吉尔还在油漆她的房间。

When I got home, I found that Jill had painted her room.

当我回到家时,我发现吉尔已漆完了她的房间。

在前一个例句中,当时工作尚未完成;在后一个例句中,这项工作在当时肯定已经结束。

2. 被动语态用以表示强调

当说话人认为所发生的事件对他来说比由什么人或什么东西造成该事件更为重要时,往往用被动语态,将说话的重点放在事件上。如:

Our roof was damaged in last night's storm.

在昨夜的暴风雨中,我家的房顶遭到了破坏。

Thousand of beaches are polluted.

几千处海滩被污染了。

Charles I was beheaded in 1649.

查理一世于 1649 年被处死。

📂 词汇学习 Word study

1. receive *vt.*

(1) 收到,接到;得到:

We've received a lot of complaints about the new radio programme.

我们收到许多对这一新的广播节目的不满意见。

注:用于此义时与 get 一词相同,只是 receive 较正式些,多用

359

于书面。比较：

I got a call from the President.

我接到总统的一个电话。

(2) 接受；经受；遭受：

He is receiving special medical treatment at a private clinic.

他正在一所私人诊所接受专门治疗。

The peasant woman wants her two daughters to receive good education.

这位农妇想让她的两个女儿接受良好的教育。

(3) 接纳；采纳；接收：

How did they receive your suggestion?

他们如何对待你的建议？

The prime minister's speech was warmly received by the conference delegates.

首相的讲话引起与会代表的热烈反响。

2. bring (brought, brought)

(1) *vt.* 带来，拿来，取来：

She brought some toys for the children.

她给孩子们带来一些玩具。

Bring me that knife, would you?

帮我把那把刀子拿来，好吗？

(2) *vt.* 导致；使发生：

The flood brought great hardship for the farmers.

洪水给农民带来了巨大的困难。

Her presence has brought so much happiness to us.

她的出席令我们欢喜异常。

(3) bring up 抚养，教养，教育：

When their parents died, an aunt brought them up.

360

他们的父母去世后,一位姨妈将他们抚养成人。

She was brought up to believe that money is the most important thing in life.

她所受的教育使她相信金钱是生活中最重要的东西。

3. realize *vt.*

(1) 认识;知道;体会:

He didn't realize his own mistake.

他没认识自己的错误。

I hope you realize that you're making a big mistake.

我希望你知道你正在犯一个大错误。

realize 与 understand 这两个词都可以表示"了解"、"知道"、"明白":

Everybody realizes/I understand how vital it is to have clean drinking water.

人人都知道享有清洁饮用水是多么重要。

understand 指"理解含义"、"懂某人的话":

I don't think I understand the meaning of the sentence.

我认为我不懂这个句子的意思。

They are listening to stories that are hard to understand.

他们正在听很难懂的故事。

realize 指"意识到"、"认识到":

Until he stopped working he hadn't realized how late it was.

他停下工作后才意识到已经很晚了。

As soon as I saw him, I realized that I'd seen him before.

我一看到他就知道我以前曾见到过他。

(2) 实现,使发生:

She realized her ambition of becoming an actress.

她实现了成为一名女演员的报负。

Ten years later her worst fears were realized .

10 年后她最害怕的事情发生了。

✍ 练习答案 Key to written exercises

1. 关键句型、难点练习答案

1 She *had been doing* the job for three years before she gave up.

 She *had been working* in the office for three years before she resigned.

2 Yesterday I *received* a letter from my brother in Australia.

 This morning I *took* it to my mother for her to read.

3 See text.

4 *the contents of the chest*

5 I've just cleaned the windows with a new *cloth* .

 She has just bought some new *clothes* from the shop in the square.

 We should give away all this old *clothing* .

6 She *has* just *brought* me some books from the library.

 She *took* some books back when she left.

 Can you *fetch* my glasses from my bedroom please?

7 We quickly *realized* that the old lady was mad.

 She didn't *understand* my friend because he only speaks German.

2. 多项选择题答案

1 a	2 b	3 a	4 c	5 b	6 d
7 c	8 c	9 d	10 b	11 c	12 a

Lesson 33

A day to remember

难忘的一天

   📖   **课文详注　Further notes on the text**

1. A day to remember

to remember 为动词不定式,作定语。有关用法参见第 11 课课
文注释 1。本课题目可视为 There is a day to remember 的省略
形式。a day 为中心词,是动词 remember 动作的承受者。一般
情况下,如果中心词为动词不定式动作的承受者时,其后的动
词不定式通常用被动语态形式表达,如:

    He has told me the subjects to be discussed at the next
    meeting.

    他已告诉我下次会议上将要讨论的题目。

    It is said that the country to be visited is several thousand
    miles away.

    听说要去访问的国家有几千英里之遥。

但是,当中心词为动词 have、want 等动词的宾语,且其后的动
词不定式的动作也由 have、want 等动词的主语做出时,该动
词不定式通常用主动语态表示,如:

    She has something important to tell you.

    她有件重要的事要告诉你。

    I just want something to drink.

    我只想喝些什么。

此外,当该中心词为 there be 结构的主语时,其后作定语的动
词不定式既可用主动语态,也可用被动语态形式,如:

There must be a lot to be said（*to say*）*about his journey in that country.*

对他在那一国家的旅行肯定有不少要说的。

2. ...but suddenly everything seems to get out of control.

get out of control 变得无法控制,如:

The plane got out of control and crashed.

飞机失去了控制并坠毁了。

The children got out of control.

孩子们无法无天了。

3. What invariably happens is that a great number of things choose to go wrong at...

（1）choose 通常用来指人做出的动作。这里用来指事物做出的动作,为拟人手法,使文字显得更为生动。

（2）go wrong 为"出岔子"、"出问题"之意。

4. It is as if single unimportant event set up a chain of reactions.

（1）as if 为从属连词,引导一方式状语从句。从句中的 set up 为过去式,表明使用了虚拟语气。

（2）a chain of 一连串的,如:

a chain of events / accidents / thoughts / misfortunes, etc.

一连串的事件/事故/想法/灾祸等

5. Let us suppose that...and keeping an eye on the baby...

（1）let us suppose...在这里是一个表示建议的祈使句型。

（2）keep an eye on 照看,照料;注意,监视,如:

Please keep an eye on my suitcase.

请照看一下我的箱子。

You'd better keep an eye on that fellow; I don't trust him.

你得留心那个家伙,我可不信任他。

6. ...and this marks the prelude to an unforeseen series of

364

catastrophes.

prelude 序幕,前奏。在此名词后,通常使用 to + 名词(名词性短语)的结构形式作其定语,如:

The discussions were a prelude to the treaty.

这些讨论是签订该条约的前奏。

I'm afraid that this border raid is the prelude to more serious attacks.

我担心,这次边界袭击是更为严厉进攻的序幕。

7. **While you are on the phone, the baby pulls the tablecloth off the table, smashing half your best crockery and cutting himself in the process.**

(1) be on the phone 在接电话。

(2) smashing...and cutting... 为两个分词短语,作结果状语,说明做出 pull 动作后所造成的后果。

8. **...and attend to baby, crockery, etc.**

and attend to ...意即"去料理孩子、收拾餐具"等。句中的 and 在意义上相当于 to,即 attend to 相当于作目的状语的动词不定式。这种结构在口语中很常用。

attend to 处理,料理,如:

He offered to go and attend to the matter.

他主动提出来处理这件事。

All the formalities have been attended to.

所有手续都办好了。

attend to 或 attend on 还可用来表示"照料"、"服侍"之意,后者更常使用,如:

The patient has been attended to/on by nurses night and day since the operation.

自手术以来,这位病人一直由护士日夜护理。

9. **As if this were not enough to reduce you to tears, your husband**

arrives, unexpectedly bringing three guests to dinner.

(1) as if 与本课课文注释 4 中的 as if 一样,为从属连词,引导一方式状语从句,其后的 this were 表明该句使用了虚拟语气。

(2) reduce you to tears 使你流泪。这里 reduce 表明"迫使"之意。在表达此义时,该动词之后总是使用"to + 名词(名词性短语)"结构,如:

The impact of the movie reduces people to tears.

这部影片很感人,催人泪下。

The class was reduced to order.

全班同学恢复了秩序。

10. Things can go wrong on a big scale, as a number of people recently discovered...

(1) on a big/large/vast scale 大规模地。

(2) as 在此为关系代词,相当于关系代词 which 引导的一个非限定性定语从句。as 作从句中的动词 discovered 的宾语,指 things can go wrong on a big scale 这一事实。as 的这一用法在英语中很常见,如:

He was an Englishman, as they perceived by his accent.

他是英国人,这是他们从他的口音中听出来的。

The night had turned cold, as is usual around here.

夜晚已变得很冷,这在此一带经常如此。

11. The woman immediately behind the two cars happened to be a learner.

immediately behind the two cars 作定语,修饰 the woman。副词 immediately 修饰其后的介词短语,意即"紧跟在这两辆车后的妇女"。

12. She suddenly got into a panic and...

get into a panic 变得惊慌失措。

13. This made the driver following her brake hard.

366

(1) following her 为现在分词短语,作定语修饰 the driver。

(2) 动词 made 之后为复合结构,补足语的动词 brake 的逻辑主语为 the driver。

14. As she was thrown forward, the cake went right through the ...

(1) as 在此为一从属连词,引导一时间状语,表示"正当……的时候"、"正值……之际"之意。

(2) went right...中的 right 为副词,表示"刚好"、"正好"之意,再如:

> *I turned around to find him right behind me.*
> 我转过身来,发现他就在我身后。
> *Don't stand right in the middle of the road.*
> 别站在路的正当中。

15. Seeing a cake flying through the air, a lorry driver who was drawing up alongside the car, pulled up all of a sudden.

(1) Seeing...the air 为分词短语,在句中作原因状语,表示"由于/因为看到……"之意。flying through the air 作 seeing 的宾语补足语,为动词 see...doing sth.的用法。

(2) pull up 停住,停车:

> *The policeman pulled up the motorist and asked to see his licence.*
> 警察叫开车人停下,要检查他的驾照。
> *He pulled up at a fashionable restaurant for lunch.*
> 他把车停在了一家时髦的饭店前去吃饭。

(3) all of a sudden 突然:

> *All of a sudden, I found myself surrounded by a group of people.*
> 突然,我发现被一群人围了起来。

16. The lorry was loaded with empty... slid off the back of the

367

vehicle and on to the road.

off...和 on to...为两个介词短语,作状语修饰动词 slid。

17．This led to yet another angry argument.

（1）lead to 导致。

（2）yet another 再一次,再一个,如:

> *They had to send yet another telegram.*
> 他们不得不再发一份电报。
>
> *Play the tape yet another time.*
> 把磁带再放一遍。

18．Meanwhile，the traffic piled up behind.

pile up 积聚,越积越多,如:

> *The evidence piled up against him.*
> 对他不利的证据越来越多。
>
> *Work has piled up during his absence.*
> 在他离开期间工作积压起来了。

19．...to get the traffic on the move again.

在 get（...）on the move 这一结构中,get 作及物动词,表示"使……开始移动"、"使……开始走动"之意,如:

> *It was dawn before the scientific group could get on the move over this difficult, unfamiliar terrain.*
> 直到天亮,这个科学小组才能在那崎岖生疏的地带活动。
>
> *In the autumn many wild birds get on the move and fly south for the winter.*
> 许多野鸟在秋天就开始迁移,飞往南方去过冬。

20．Only two stray dogs benefited from all this confusion, for they greedily devoured what was left of the cake.

benefit from 从……中获益,得益于,如:

> *They will benefit from the new way of doing the business.*
> 他们会从新的经营方式中获益。

He's just the man who's never benefited from experience .

他就是那种从不吸取经验教训的人。

📖 语法 Grammar in use

复合句中的分词结构

1. 复合句的构成

在英语中,特别是书面语中有很多复合句。复合句由两个或多个简单句构成。但它与并列句不同的是复合句中的各个组成部分并非同等重要,其中有一个独立子句(或称"主句")和一个或若干个从属子句(或称"从句"),主句往往可以独立存在。复合句的两种构成方法为:

(1) 用连词或关系代词将从句与主句连接起来,如:

He told me that the match had been concelled .

他告诉我比赛取消了。(名词性从句)

Holiday resorts which are very crowded are not very pleasant .

那些拥挤的度假场所令人感到不很愉快。(定语从句)

However hard I try , I can't remember people's names .

不管我怎样用心,还是记不住人们的名字。(状语从句)

(2) 用动词不定式或分词结构。这种结构组成的是短语而不是从句,但是它们构成复合句(而非简单句)的一部分,这是因为它们可以用从句的形式来表现,如:

To get into university you have to pass a number of examinations .

要进入大学,你必须通过一系列考试。(= *If you want to get into university* …如果你想上大学的话……)

Seeing the door open , the stranger entered the house .

那个陌生人看见门开着就进了房间。(= *When he saw*

the door open . . . 当他看见门开着……)

2．复合句中的分词结构

（1）分词的形式

	现在式	完成式
主动语态	finding	having found
被动语态	being found	having been found

（2）现在分词结构代替从句

1）现在分词结构代替时间状语从句

现在分词可用于 before、after、since、when 和 while 之后；但不用于 as、as soon as、directly、until 等之后，如：

Since phoning you (= Since I phoned you) this morning , I have changed my plans .

自今天早上给你打电话之后，我就改变了计划。

还可用于 on 和 in 之后，如：

On finding the front door open (= When I found . . .) , I became suspicous .

当发现大门开着，我就起了疑心。

In/While trying to open the can (= During the time when I was trying . . .) , I cut my hand .

在试图打开罐头时，我划破了手。

2）现在分词结构代替条件状语从句

现在分词用于 if 和 unless 之后，如：

If travelling north (= If you are travelling . . .) , you must change at Leeds .

如果到北方旅行，你必须到利兹换车。

Unless paying by credit card (= Unless you pay . . .) , please pay in cash .

除非使用信用卡，否则请付现金。

3）现在分词结构代替让步状语从句

370

现在分词用于连词 although、even though、though 和 while
之后,如:

> *While admitting that he received the stolen jewellery*
> (= *While he admitted that . . .*), *he denied having*
> *taken part in the robbery.*
>
> 尽管承认收受了盗窃的珠宝,但他否认参与了抢劫
> 案。

4) 现在分词结构代替原因状语从句

> *Being anxious to please him* (= *As I was anxious to*
> . . .), *I bought him a nice present.*
>
> 由于急于讨好他,我给他买了一份精美礼品。

5) 现在分词结构代替定语从句

现在分词可以代替其动词为一般现在时或现在进行时的
定语从句,如:

> *The train arriving at platform 8* (= *The train which*
> *is arriving . . .*), *is the 17 : 50 train from Crewe.*
>
> 即将进 8 号站台的列车是 17:50 从克鲁开来的。

(3) 过去分词结构代替从句

此用法在正式及文学体裁中比在口语中更为常见。

1) 过去分词代替状语从句,如:

> *Viewed from a distance* (= *When it was viewed . . .*)
> *the island looked like a cloud.*
>
> 从远处眺望,这个岛就像一朵云。
>
> *Although built before the war* (= *Although it was*
> *built . . .*), *the engine is still in perfect order.*
>
> 虽然这台发动机是战前造的,但仍然工作良好。
>
> *If accepted for the post* (= *If you are accepted . . .*),
> *you will be informed by May 1st.*
>
> 如果同意你任此职,5 月 1 日前将通知你。

注:在 after、before、since、on 和 in 之后不能直接跟过去分词,而需用"being + 过去分词",如:

After / On being informed the flight would be delayed (After / When we were informed ...), we made other arrangements.

得知飞行要推迟之后,我们另做了安排。

2) 过去分词结构代替限制性定语从句,如:

The system used in this school (= The system which is used ...), is very successful.

这所学校实行的制度非常成功。

注:无论现在分词还是过去分词,在上述用法中使用时,其逻辑主语必须与谓语动词的主语相一致,否则不成立。

📁 词汇学习 Word study

1. experience

(1) *n*. (可数) 经历,阅历:

Our journey by camel was quite an experience!
我们骑骆驼旅行的确是一次不寻常的经历!

I had a strange experience the other day.
那天我们经历了一件奇怪的事。

(2) *n*. (不可数)经验,体验,感受:

The best way to learn is by experience.
学习的最佳途径是从经验中学习。

I know from experience Tony never keeps his promise.
我从经验中得知托尼从不守信誉。

(3) *vt*. 经历,体验:

Our country has experienced great changes in the last 20 years.

我们国家在最近 20 年中经历了巨大的变化。

I experienced great difficulties in getting a visa to the United States.

在办理赴美签证时,我经历了很多困难。

New companies often experience a loss in their first few years.

新公司在头几年总是要有赔钱的经历。

2. enough

(1) *adj.* 足够的:

Have we got enough food?

我们有足够的食物吗?

We have enough seats for everyone.

我们有足够的座位让大家坐。

I was fool enough to believe her.

我相信她真是太愚蠢了。

enough 修饰名词时常放在复数名词前或不可数名词前,但也可放在不可数名词之后(不常用),如:

There would never be room enough for everything.

永远不会有足够的地方放所有的东西。

(2) *n.* 足够(的数量或数目):

I've eaten more than enough.

我吃得超量了。

Enough has been said about this already.

此事已谈论得够多的了。

(3) *adv.* 足够地;充分地(置于形容词或副词之后):

The water is warm enough to swim in.

水温足可以游泳。

The student isn't trying hard enough.

这个学生未尽全力去做。

3．besides

（1）*adv*. 而且；再说；此外：

> *Would these figures prove anything ? And besides , who keeps such statistics ?*
>
> 这些数字能证明什么吗？而且是谁拥有这些数据？
>
> *She has so much else to do besides .*
>
> 此外她还有许多其他的事情要做。

（2）*prep*. 除……之外：

> *There are a lot of people at the party besides us .*
>
> 除我们之外，晚会上还有许多人。
>
> *Besides being a professional pianist , he is also a keen amateur singer .*
>
> 他不仅是名专业琴师，还是个热情的业余歌手。

besides 和 beside 这两个词虽都是介词，但意义完全不同。beside 是指"在……旁边"，如：

> *Come and sit beside me .*
>
> 来坐到我旁边来。

besides 表示"除包括……之外"、"还包括……"；而 except 则表示"除……之外其他都……"，如：

> *Ten of us passed the exam besides John .*
>
> 除约翰外，我们中还有 10 人通过了考试。（约翰也通过了）
>
> *All of us passed the exam except John .*
>
> 除约翰外，我们都通过了考试。（但是约翰没有）

✍ 练习答案　Key to written exercises

1．关键句型、难点练习答案

1 For the first time in his life he *experienced* real fear.

374

She has *a lot of experience* in teaching young children.

2   This work is just not *good enough* .

I never seem to have *enough money* to do everything I want to.

He's a *fairly* tall person.

3   See text.

4   For years they said that Columbus *discovered* America.

I read somewhere the other day that the Chinese *invented* ice cream.

5   He came and sat down *beside* me.

I've got plenty of other books *besides* these.

6   *drawing up* = here, moving, travelling

He *drew back* when he saw the man with the gun.

The taxi waited a few minutes and then *drew off* .

7   He *had to take* an exam to qualify as an engineer.

I *should have taken* John's book back to him last week, but I forgot.

2. 多项选择题答案

1	c	2	b	3	a	4	b	5	d	6	a
7	a	8	c	9	c	10	b	11	a	12	d

Lesson 34
A happy discovery
幸运的发现

📖 **课文详注 Further notes on the text**

1. Antique shops exert a peculiar fascination on a great many people.

exert ... on ... 对……施加……,如:

He's been exerting a lot of pressure on me to change my mind.

他一直在给我施加种种压力,要我改变主意。

2. The more expensive kind of ... where rare objects are beautifully ... to keep them free from dust is ...

(1) where 在此为关系副词,引导一个定语从句,修饰 shop。

(2) to keep them free from dust,动词不定式短语,在 where 引导的定语从句中作目的状语,意即"为了使其免沾灰尘",修饰从句中的 are beautifully displayed in glass cases。free from dust 作动词 keep 的宾语补足语。

3. But no one has to muster up courage to enter a less pretentious antique shop.

muster (up) 鼓起(勇气等);奋(力),激起(感情等),如:

Muster (up) your courage and the difficulty will soon be overcome.

鼓起勇气,困难很快就会被克服。

He evidently wants more time to muster (up) support for himself.

显然他需要更多的时间来赢得人们对他的支持。

4．There is always hope that in its labyrinth of ... a real rarity ... that litter the floors．

in its labyrinth ... rooms 为同位语从句中的地点状语,倒装使用除表明对该状语的强调外,也可使句子显得更为紧凑和语义更为明了。在该地点状语中使用了修饰性暗喻,即把 rooms 比作 labyrinth,它们的关系为修饰与被修饰的关系,在这两部分间用介词 of 连接,意即"像迷宫般的……房间"。

5．No one discovers a rarity by chance．

by chance 碰巧,偶然,意外地,如:

> *I met him on my way home by chance.*
> 我在回家的路上偶然碰到了他。
>
> *It happened quite by chance.*
> 这完全是偶然发生的。

6．A study ... must have patience，and above all，the ability to recognize the worth of something when he sees it．

（1）above all 最重要地,首要地,尤其, 如:

> *Children need many things，but above all，they need love.*
> 孩子们需要很多东西,但他们尤其需要爱。
>
> *Relax，and above all，don't panic.*
> 放松,最重要的是不要惊慌。

（2）the ability 与 patience 并列作 have 的宾语。动词不定式短语 to recognize ... 作 ability 的定语。

7．To do this，he must be at least as ...

at least,介词短语,往往由于在句子中不同的位置而具有不同的含义:

（1）在数量词之前或之后修饰该词时,通常有"至少"含义,如:

> *He wolfed down at least three bowls of rice.*

他狼吞虎咽,至少吃了 3 碗米饭。

The repairs will cost twenty pounds at least.

修理费用至少 20 英镑。

(2)在动词或句子前修饰该动词或该句时,通常为"怎么也得"、"起码"、"至少"之意,如:

You might at least have told us.

你起码也得告诉我们。

She might at least be polite when she speaks to people.

她跟别人说话时至少应该有点礼貌。

(3)在一个陈述句的末尾,作附加说明使语气不太肯定时,通常为"无论如何"、"不管怎样"之意,如:

All these cheap foreign goods should not be allowed to enter the country, at least, that's my opinion.

所有这些廉价外国货都不准许进口,不管怎样,这是我的看法。

8. Like a scientist bent on making a discovery, he must cherish the hope that one day he will be amply rewarded.

(1) bent on making a discovery 为过去分词短语,作定语修饰 scientist。be bent on ... 决心要……,如:

You're bent on doing me some mischief, you rascal!

你成心想害我,你这个混蛋!

Mary, bent on becoming a musician, practises the piano hard day and night.

玛丽一心想成为一个音乐家,从早到晚苦练钢琴。

(2) one day,副词短语,做时间状语,通常用在过去时或将来时的句子中,表示"(过去的)某一天"或"(将来的)总有一天"之意,如:

One day he took us a long way over the mountains to visit a farm.

378

一天,他带我们翻山越岭走了老远的路参观了一个牧场。

I'll come and see you one day.

总有一天我会来看你。

9. He has often described to me how he picked up a masterpiece for a mere ￡50.

（1）how 为连接副词,引导宾语从句。

（2）pick up 在此句中作"偶然获得/得到"讲,如:

He picked up a few words about his girl friend when he entered the room.

他进屋时偶然听到几句有关他女友的话。

有关用法参见第 20 课课文注释 5。

（3）mere 为边缘形容词(peripheral adjective,即只能作为定语或补足语使用的形容词),不能作为中心形容词(central adjective,即既可作为定语又可作为补足语使用的形容词)来使用。在句子中只能作定语,以强化所修饰名词的含义,如:

Some experts say that was a mere coincidence.

一些专家认为那只不过是个巧合。

A nervous boss can become hysterical at the mere mention of money.

只要一提到钱,神经质的老板就会变得异常激动。

10. As he had never been ... a great deal to interest him.

a great deal 为名词性短语,意为"许多东西",其后的 to interest him 为动词不定式短语,作定语,修饰 a great deal。

11. ... and Frank was about to leave when he noticed a large packing case lying on the floor.

（1）be about to do 即将做,就要做,打算做。可用来表示"马上的将来要做……"。因其自身已包含"即将"、"就要"等含义,因此不能再与 immediately、very soon、at once 等连用。

（2）lying on the floor 为现在分词短语,在从句中作宾语补足语。

12. ... but that he could not be bothered to open it.

that he could ... 同前面 that 从句一样,均作动词 told 的直接宾语,意即"……他不想费事把它打开"。

13. Frank begged him to do so ... prised it open.

为避免文字上的重复,这里 to do so 代替 to open it。prised it open 中 open 为 it 的补足语。

14. Apart from ... much of it broken.

(1) apart from... 除……以外。作为一种话语标志,在话语结构中表明"例外"之意,即表明要说(写)的话与已说(写)过的话语之间的"例外"关系,如:

> *The children hardly see anyone, apart from their parents.*
>
> 除了他们的父母,这些孩子们几乎谁都见不到。
>
> *He lives apart from other people.*
>
> 他离群索居。

(2) much of it broken 可视为一个插入语,对 crockery 作进一步补充说明。由于语义明确,在 it 与 broken 之间省略了动词 was。

15. As its composition and line reminded him of ... he knew well, ...

remind sb. of 在使用时,往往表示下述含义:

(1)如文中那样,表示"使某人想起"。在表达此意义时,其主语通常为事物,如:

> *It reminded me of the mistakes I had made before.*
>
> 这使我想起了我从前犯过的一些错误。
>
> *What he said reminded me of the days I spent in the countryside.*
>
> 他说的话使我想起了我在农村度过的那些日子。

(2)表示"提醒某人记起……",在表示此意义时,其主语只能为表示人的名词或代词,如:

If you hadn't reminded me of the matter, I would have forgotten.

如果你不提醒我那件事,我就会忘了。

She reminded him of the pledge he had made a few days before.

她提醒他几天前他的保证。

16. Glancing at it briefly, the dealer told him that it was worth £ 50.

glancing at it briefly 为现在分词短语,作时间状语。be worth 价值。

17. ... by Correggio ...

(1) 这里的介词 by 表示"由"、"被"之意。

(2) Correggio 柯勒乔,意大利著名画家,真名为安托尼奥·阿来里。

语法 Grammar in use

1. 时间状语从句中的时态

当时间状语从句表示将来时,从句中不用一般将来时,而通常用一般现在时;不用将来完成时,而用现在完成时,而且这两种时态在时间连词后常常可以互换。如:

The Owens will move to a new flat when their baby is/has been born.

孩子出生后,欧文斯一家将搬到一套新房子里住。

We always have to wait till/until the last customer has left.

我们总得等到最后一位顾客离去。

现在完成时常常用于 once 和 now that 之后:

Once we have decorated the house, we can move in.

一旦我们把房间装饰好就能搬进去。

Now that we have decorated the house we can move in.

既然我们把房间装饰好了,我们可以搬进去了。

2. 条件状语从句中的时态

在条件状语从句中,表示将来的动作一般不用将来时态,而用现在时态:

If it rains, we'll stay at home.

如果下雨,我们就呆在家里。

If he is standing in the rain, he will catch cold.

如果他站在雨里,他会感冒的。

If she has arrived at the station, she'll be here soon.

如果她已经到了车站,她很快就会到这儿。

3. must 表示必须与推测

(1)must 表示必须时,通常可与 have(got) to 互换。

I must leave fairly soon.

我得尽快离开。

You have to find some compromise.

你必须得找出妥协的办法。

We've got to get up early tomorrow.

明天我们得早起。

但是如果要表示某人不得不经常性地做某事,只能用 have to,而不用 must。

She has to do the housework while her brother reads.

她哥哥看书时她得做家务。

1)如果要表示某人在某种特定情况下必须做某事,一般用 have got to:

I've got to report to the police.

我必须向警察报告。

We've got to get in touch with the builders.

我们得与建筑商取得联系。

2)在正式文体中,must 用来表示某人依法或规章必须做某事:

People who qualify must apply within six months.

符合要求的人必须在 6 个月内提出申请。

3)表示过去或将来必须怎样时用 had to 或 will have to:

We had to keep still for about four minutes.

我们不得不一动不动地呆了约四分钟。

He'll have to attend the meeting this afternoon.

他必须得出席今天下午的会。

4)表示绝对禁止,而且根本没有选择余地时用 must not 或 mustn't:

You must not accept it.

你可不能接受它。

We mustn't forget our past.

我们绝不能忘记我们的过去。

5)表示没必要做某事用 don't have to、haven't got to 或 don't need to 或 needn't:

I don't have to do it any longer.

我不必再做这件事了。

I didn't need to say anything at all.

我根本不需要说什么。

It's all right if you haven't got to work.

如果你不必工作,也行。

(2)must 表示推测,推论。

Jane's light is on. She must be at home. She can't be out.

简的房间里开着灯。她一定在家。她不会出去的。

There must be some mistakes.

一定出了点差错。

1) have to 与 have got to 也可以表示推测或推论,但主语不能是 you:

This has to be / has got to be the most stupid film I have ever seen.

这准是我看过的最乏味的影片了。

Money has got to be the reason.

金钱准是问题的所在。

2）must 后面可跟 be 或 be doing，但不能跟不定式，如不能说：

He isn't in his office. He must work at home.

而应说：

He isn't in his office. He must be working at home.

他没在办公室。他肯定在家里工作呢。

She must be exaggerating.

她肯定在夸大其词。

3）如果表示你认为某事不是事实或推测某事不是真的，不能用 must not be 或 have not to 而用 cannot 或 can't：

He can't be thirsty.

他不会口渴的。

The two messages cannot both be true.

这两条消息不可能都是真的。

📁　**词汇学习　Word study**

1. bent　*adj.*

（1）被弯曲的；弯曲的：

His back is bent from years of toil.

多年的劳累压弯了他的腰。

He only found a piece of bent wire.

他只发现了一节弯曲的电线。

（2）（on）决意的，一心一意的：

She's bent on becoming an actress.

384

她决意要当一个演员。

She became bent on revenge after the gunman was found innocent in court.

自从那个枪手在法庭上被认定无罪之后,她就决心要报仇。

2. pick up

(1) 拿起,捡起,拾起:

I picked up a magazine that was lying on the table.

我拿起桌子上放着的一本杂志。

The boy picked up a stone and threw it at the streetlight.

那个男孩捡起一块石头朝街灯砸去。

(2) (尤指偶然地、无意地、容易地)获得,找到;买到;学到:

Where did you pick up such ideas?

你从哪儿弄来这些点子?

The system looks difficult at first, but you'll soon pick them up.

这个系统初看上去难懂,但是很快你就会学会。

(3) 带走;取走;搭乘:

I'll pick you up at the hotel.

我在旅店接你。

I'm going to pick up my coat from the cleaner's.

我要到洗衣店取我的衣服。

3. come in

(1) 进入;进来:

The door opened and a policeman came in.

门开了,一个警察走了进来。

(2) 到来;收到:

Reports are coming in of a major earthquake in Mexico.

传来墨西哥发生大地震的报告。

Some more letters of complaint have just come in.

刚刚又收到一些抱怨的信。

（3）开始被采用;流行起来;上市:

When did the short skirt first come in?

短裙是什么时候最先流行的?

The new crop of tobacco will be coming in soon.

不久新烟草就下来了。

✍ 练习答案 Key to written exercises

1．关键句型、难点练习答案

1 I'll phone you *the moment he arrives.*

I'll wait here *until he comes.*

I'll speak to you again *before you leave.*

2 *He must be ...* = He has to be, He needs to be ...

You must be very tired ... = I assume that you are very tired ...

3 ～, an, a, The, ～, a, the, The, ～, the, The, an, the, ～ (See also text.)

4 Did you *notice* what she was wearing?

'It's a beautiful day,' he *remarked.*

2．多项选择练习答案

1	b	2	b	3	c	4	b	5	d	6	c
7	a	8	d	9	c	10	b	11	a	12	c

Lesson 35
Justice was done
伸张正义

📖 **课文详注　Further notes on the text**

1 . . . . when a man's innocence or guilt has been proved beyond doubt.

(1) when 为从属连词,引导时间状语从句,说明主句谓语动词 might say 发生的时间。

(2) beyond doubt 毫无疑问。作状语,修饰 proved。为加强语气, 可在 doubt 前用 all 进行修饰,如:

The authenticity of the news is beyond doubt.
这条消息的真实性不容置疑。

What he said is absolutely true; it is beyond all doubt.
他所讲的绝对真实,勿容置疑。

2 . Those who seek it undertake an arduous journey and can never be sure that they will find it.

who 为关系代词,引导定语从句,修饰 those。句中的两个 it 均指 justice。those 为 undertake 与 can be 的主语。

3 . Judges, however wise or eminent, are human and can make mistakes.

however 无论怎样,无论如何。从属连词,引导让步状语从句, 该从句中在 wise or eminent 后省略了 they are。由 however 引导的让步状语从句,其构成方法如下:

(1)当 however 直接修饰从句中的动词时,其词序为:however + 主语 + 动词,如:

However you travel, it'll take you at least two days.

无论你怎么走,至少都得花两天的时间。

(2)当 however 修饰形容词或副词时,其词序为:however + 形容词/副词 + 主语 + 动词,如:

However rich people are, they always want more.

人们不管多么有钱,他们总是想要更多的钱。

However much he eats, he never gets fat.

无论他吃得多么多,却总也长不胖。

注意:在使用中,不可将作为从属连词的 however 与作副词的 however 相混淆。有关作副词时的用法参见第 1 课课文注释 3。

4. **There are rare instances when justice almost ceases to be an abstract concept.**

cease to do ... 不再…… 动词 cease 多用于表示状态、存在的缓慢、逐渐地停止。因 cease 一词较为陈旧,因此现多用 stop 替代。在 cease 后使用动词不定式表示"不再"含义时多带书卷气,且多用于较正式的场合,如:

The dying man soon ceased to breathe.

那个垂死的人不久停止了呼吸。

The feudal moral code has ceased to be operative.

封建道德准则已无任何效力。

5. **Reward or punishment are meted out quite independent of human interference.**

(1) mete out ... 把……给予,把……分配,如:

The local government has meted out relief to the people in the flooded area.

当地政府已经把救济物资分发给了水灾地区的人们。

It's said that a judge who metes out justice with a firm hand is going to try the case.

据说一位执法如山的法官准备审理这桩案子。

(2) independent of ... 不受……,不依赖……这里 independent of 是形容词短语,在句子中作方式状语。形容词 independent 通常与介词 of 连用(此点与 dependent 不同,dependent 通常与介词 on 连用),如:

A wife can have property independent of her husband.
妻子可以拥有不受丈夫支配的财产。

They went camping so as to be independent of hotels.
他们去露营免得住旅店。

6. At such times, justice acts like a living force.

这里将 justice 比作 a living force,是一种修辞手段,称为明喻(simile)。通常是将两个本质不同的事物相比。常用的比喻词是 like, as... as ... 或 as, 如:

She sings like a nightingale.
她唱起歌来像夜莺一样。

She sings as beautifully as a nightingale.
她唱起歌来像夜莺一样好听。

7. ... we are, in part, admitting that a certain set of circumstances has enabled justice to act of its own accord.

(1) in part 在某种程度上,部分地。有时为了加强语气,可在 part 前使用表示程度的形容词 large 或 great,即 in large/great part (在很大程度上;大部分地),如:

His success is in part owing to her help.
他的成功在某种程度上要归功于她的帮助。

The responsibility was in large part mine.
我要负大部分责任。

(2) a certain set of 这里为"某些特定的"之意。

(3) of one's own accord 自愿地,自动地。介词短语,作状语,如:
He did it of his own accord.

他自愿做好这件事。

They gave generously of their own accord.

他们自愿慷慨解囊。

8. **When a thief was caught on the premises of a large jewellery store one morning, the shop assistants must have found it impossible to resist the temptation to say 'it serves him right'.**

(1) on the premises 在店/室/楼内,如:

He retails wine and beer to be consumed on the premises.

他零售的酒和啤酒只限在店内饮用。

(2) 名词 temptation 后的动词不定式短语 to say . . . 为 temptation 的定语。文中 impossible to resist the temptation to say 意即"禁不住要说"。

(3) serve one right 罪有应得;活该,如:

This punishment served him right.

他得到这样的惩罚罪有应得。

9. **As the cry repeated several times, she ran to tell the manager who . . .**

(1) as 为连词,引导原因状语从句,表示"由于"、"因为"。

(2) to tell . . . 动词不定式短语在句子中作目的状语,表示做出 ran 动作的目的。

10. **They located the right chimney by tapping at the walls and listening for the man's cries.**

by . . . cries 为介词短语,作方式状语,修饰动词 located。

11. **. . . figure that emerged, . . . to break into the shop . . . but had got stuck in the chimney.**

break into . . . 闯入,破门而入。动词词组,其后直接使用名词或名词性短语,如:

The thief broke into my house and stole my wife's fur coat.

小偷潜入我的住宅,偷走了我太太的裘皮大衣。

We had to break into the house as we had lost the key.

我们丢失了钥匙,不得不破门而入。

除了上述意思之外,有时还用来表示某行为的突然开始,如:

As the President's car appeared, the people waiting outside broke into loud cheers.

总统的轿车刚一出现,等候在外面的人群就爆发出响亮的欢呼声。

12. ... the man was handed over to the police.

hand over 移交,交出,如:

The offender was handed over to the police.

那个罪犯已被送交警方。

He's decided to hand over his business to his son.

他已经决定将公司交给儿子经营。

语法　Grammar in use

间接引语中的引述动词

1. 在间接引语中常用的引述动词有:say、tell、ask 及它们的过去式形式。

   say 和 tell + (that) 可以引导间接陈述句:

   He says/tells me (that) he's read Tony's book but doesn't understand it.

   他说/告诉我他读了托尼的书,但是不懂。

   He said (that)/told me (that) his life was in danger.

   他说/告诉我他有生命危险。

2. ask 可以转述疑问句。

   一般疑问句:

> "*Do you want anything ?*" *she asked me*.
> "你想要点儿什么吗?"她问我道。
> *She asked（me）if/whether I wanted anything*.
> 她问(我)是否想要点儿什么。

特殊疑问句:

> "*What do you want ?*" *she asked me*.
> "你想要什么?"她问我。
> *She asked（me）what I wanted*.
> 她问我想要什么。

3. 除 ask 之外 want to know、see、say、tell、wonder、inquire 也常用来转述疑问句。但是,inquire 一词较为正式,使用时后面不跟人称宾语。

一般疑问句:

> *She inquired if/whether I had passed my exam*.
> 她问我是否通过了考试。

> *He wants to know whether or not we want dinner*.
> 他想知道我们是否想用晚餐。

注:whether 多用于有选择的情况下:

> *I was asked whether I wanted to stay at a hotel or at his house*.
> 我被问到我想住在饭店还是住在他家里。

> *I wonder if/whether they've heard the news yet*.
> 我不知道他们是否已经听到了这个消息。

特殊疑问句:

> *She inquired why I was so late*.
> 她问我为什么迟到了这么久。

> *He didn't tell me how he did it*.
> 他没有告诉我他是怎么做的。

> *I'm wondering where they are going*.

392

我在想他们要去哪儿。

She doesn't know what we were talking about.

她不知道我们在谈论什么。

英语中还有一些动词可以用来转述直接引语的表达方式或态度等:

'*You really must let me pay the bill*,' *Andrew said.*

安德鲁说:"你一定要让我来付账。"

Andrew insisted on paying the bill.

安德鲁坚持要付账。

'*Why don't we go sailing?*' *Diana said.*

戴安娜说:"为什么我们不乘船游览呢?"

Diana suggested they should go sailing.

戴安娜建议他们应该乘船游览。

其他常用的还有:

She explained that a friend of her husband's had been arrested.

她解释说她丈夫的一个朋友被捕了。

She admitted she was very much in love with you once.

她承认她曾经深爱过你。

He claims he knows more about the business now.

他自称他现在对这宗生意更了解了。

📁 词汇学习 Word study

1. associate

(1) *vt.* (with) 联合;交往;使有联系:

The military regime dealt ruthlessly with anyone who was associated with the former government.

这个军事政权凶残地对待任何与前政府有联系的人。

I don't want my children associating with drug addicts and alcoholics.

我不让我的孩子们同吸毒者和酗酒者有任何来往。

(2) *vt.*(在思想上、记忆中、想像中)把……联系在一起:

I'd rather not associate myself with extremist political statements.

我可不愿意使自己与极端主义的政治宣言有什么瓜葛。

It's hard for me to associate those two ideas.

我很难将这两种概念联系在一起。

(3) *n.*伙伴,同事;合伙人:

She has invited all her business associates to her party.

她邀请了她所有的商业伙伴出席她的晚会。

A close associate of the author denied reports that she had cancer.

这位作家的一位亲密伙伴否定了她患癌症的报道。

(4) *adj.*副的;非正式的:

He is now an associate professor at New York University.

他现在是纽约大学的一名副教授。

After two years study at a junior college he got an associate degree.

在一所专科学校里学习了两年之后他获得了专科学位。

2.prove

(1) *vt.*证实;证明:

This receipt proves that I bought those goods here.

这张收据证明我是在这里买的那些商品。

This video tape proves he was a thief.

这盘录像带证明他是个小偷。

(2) *vt.*显示,表明:

During the rescue she proved herself（to be）a highly

competent climber.

在救援过程中,她证明她自己是个能力很强的登山运动员。

He proved himself(*to be*)*an amusing companion.*

他表现出他是个有趣的伙伴。

(3) *v.* 证明是,原来是;结果是(作系动词):

We've been trying to sell our house, but it's proving very difficult.

我们一直想把我们的房子卖掉,可是结果表明很困难。

The operation on his broken leg proved a complete success.

对他断腿所做的手术结果表明非常成功。

3. admit

(1) *vt.*, *vi.* (to) 承认;供认:

Sally admits(*to*)*using your computer.*

萨莉承认用过你的计算机。

Sally admits that she used your computer.

萨莉承认她用过你的计算机。

He admitted his guilt to the police.

他向警察供认了他的罪行。

(2) *vt.* 准许进入,(into, to) 容纳:

Spain was admitted to the European Community in 1986.

西班牙于 1986 年被纳入欧共体。

She was admitted to hospital suffering from a traffic accident.

车祸后她被送进了医院。

This hall admits 400 people.

这个大厅可容纳 400 人。

(3) *vt.*, *vi.* (of) 给……留有余地:

The facts admit（of）no other explanation.

事实确凿,无需其他任何解释。

The present schedule does not admit of modification.

现在的这个安排不需要做任何修改。

✍ 练习答案 Key to written exercises

1. 关键句型、难点练习答案

1 He says that *he has been very busy.*

He wants to know *if he can do the job now.*

He believes that *he has made a mistake.*

2 *The moment he has arrived*, I'll let you know.

Now that you have finished, you can go home.

3 See text.

4 chimneys, valleys, babies, days, hobbies, armies, moneys 或
monies, victories, turkeys, storeys

5 admitted, had tried, had got, had been, had been done（Also
see text.）

2. 多项选择题答案

1	c	2	b	3	b	4	d	5	c	6	d
7	c	8	c	9	a	10	d	11	b	12	d

Lesson 36
A chance in a million
百万分之一的机遇

📖 **课文详注** **Further notes on the text**

1. A chance in a million

A chance in a million 中的介词短语作定语,修饰 a chance。由于语义明确在 million 后面省略 chances。此处的 a million 在修辞学中为夸张(hyperbole)手法,即为增强表达效果,对所言事物的形象、特征、数量或作用等事实的夸大描述,如:

I'm so tired that I think I could sleep a year.

我太累了,我觉得我能睡上一年。

Herbert uttered a single piercing scream that must have been audible in Peru.

赫伯特发出一声刺耳的尖叫,这声尖叫肯定在秘鲁都能听到。

2. ... would bring his story to a conclusion by presenting his readers with a series of coincidences—most of them wildly improbable.

(1) bring ... to a conclusion 使……结束/完成,如:

They had made so wonderful a plan that the work was brought to a good conclusion.

他们制定出了完美的计划,因而使该项工作得以顺利完成。

(2) 介词 by 引导的介词短语在句子中作方式状语。

(3) a series of ... 一系列的……

（4）most . . . improbable 为插入语,对 a series of coincidences 作进一步说明。在 most of them 与 wildly improbable 之间省略了系动词 were。

3．. . . accepted the fact that . . . And so on.

that 为关系连词,在此引导一个同位语从句,说明 fact 的内容,为叙述方便,作者将后面两个实际均为 that 同位语从句内容的句子,即 A long-lost. . . the hero's downfall 和 And so on 从 that 从句中分出进行叙述,这样使叙述显得更为明快。

4．A long-lost brother，who was presumed dead，was really alive all the time and wickedly plotting to bring about . . .

（1）who 为关系代词,引导一个非限定性定语从句,该从句中 dead 作从句主语 who 的补足语。

（2）plotting 为现在分词,与前文中的 really alive all the time 共用 was,表示正在进行时态。虽然与其使用同一个 was,但就词性而言,was really alive. . . 中的 was 为谓语动词,而在 was plotting . . . 中的 was 为助动词。

（3）bring about 造成,导致,引起,如:

Gambling has brought about his ruin .

赌博把他给毁了。

It failed to bring about the desired effect .

它未能产生预期的效果。

5．. . . circumstances do sometimes conspire to bring about coincidences which anyone but a nineteenth century novelist would find incredible.

（1）do 为助动词,用来加强语气,意即"确实"。

（2）but 为介词,意即"除……之外"。本句中由其构成的介词短语作定语,修饰 anyone,如:

There is nothing but scrap-paper on the desk .

桌子上只有一些废纸。

> *What I am going to tell you is nothing but the unvarnished truth.*
>
> 我要告诉你的只是不加任何粉饰的事实。

在表示此意时,与介词 except 的意义相近,但是它更强调意义上的近乎完整性,而 except 则更着重后面的例外,比较:

> *I have written all my letters but one.*
>
> 我只差一封信就全写完了。
>
> *I have written all my letters except one.*
>
> 我还差一封信没写。

(3) incredible 作动词 find 的宾语补足语,引导定语从句的关系代词 which 在该从句中作宾语。

6. ... found a brother who was thought to have been killed twenty years before.

该从句中的动词不定式短语 to have ... before 作主语 who 的补足语。此外,句子中 before 不可用 ago 替代。因为 ago 用于表示"从此刻起若干时间以前"的概念,而 before 则用于表示"从过去某时起若干时间以前"的概念。

7. While on a walking tour with his wife, he stopped to talk to a workman.

(1) while 与 on a walking... wife 之间省略了 he was。在表示时间、地点、让步等状语从句中,如果从句中的主语与主句中的主语相同,且以 be 为谓语动词,或从句中的谓语部分包含助动词 be 时,常可将从句中的主语和谓语动词 be 或谓语部分的助动词 be 省略,如:

> *While on he way home, he met an old friend of his.*
>
> 在他回家的路上,他遇到了一个老朋友。(时间状语)
>
> *She hurriedly left the room as though angry.*
>
> 她急匆匆地走出房间,好像很生气的样子。(方式状语)

(2) 在动词 stop 后既可以使用动词不定式形式(stop to do sth.)也

可以使用动名词形式(stop doing sth.),但所表示的概念不同。在 stop to do sth. 中,stop 为不及物动词,表示"停下来(在做的事)去做某事",而 stop doing sth. 则表示"停止(在做的)事",比较:

> *The bus stopped to take up passengers.*
> 这辆公共汽车停下来搭载乘客。
> *The bus stopped taking up passengers.*
> 这辆公共汽车停止了搭载乘客。

> *He stopped to talk to John.*
> 他停下来,同约翰谈话。
> *He stopped talking to John.*
> 他停止了同约翰谈话。

8. After they had gone on, Mrs. Bussman commented on the workman's close resemblance to her husband and even suggested that he might be his brother.

(1) go on 继续往前走。

(2) comment on ... 对……进行评论,如:

> *The manager commented favourably on her ability.*
> 经理对她的能力加以称赞。

(3) resemblance to ... 与……相像。表示此意时,其后通常使用介词 to,如:

> *At that place, you may find some stones bearing curious resemblance to animal forms.*
> 在那里,你可以发现形状与动物形体奇妙相似的石头。
> *The girl in the picture bears some distant resemblance to her.*
> 图片中的这个女孩多少与她有些相似。

(4) suggest 认为;表明。之后的 that 从句中应使用正常时态和语气(如文中那样);表示"建议"、"提议"时,that 从句中通常用

400

(should) + 动词原形这样的虚拟语气结构。有关用法参见第22课课文注释6。

9．Franz poured scorn on the idea，pointing out that his brother had been killed in action during the war.

（1）pour scorn on 对……嘲笑，如：

Don't pour bitter scorn on those in miserable conditions.
不要恶意嘲弄那些境况窘迫的人。

He poured scorn on people who buy books for show.
他鄙视那些买书来摆样子的人。

（2）pointing out that ...为现在分词短语，在句子中作伴随状语，修饰动词 poured。

（3）in action 在战斗中。

10．Though Mrs. Bussman was fully acquainted with this story，... a chance in million that she might be right.

be acquainted with ... 知道……虽然 acquaint 为及物动词，表示"通知"、"使……知道"，但该词极少用于主动语态之中，将其用于被动语态结构中，过去分词 acquainted 已失去动作意义，相当于一个形容词，如：

I'm acquainted with all the facts.
我知道全部事实。

Are you acquainted with him?
你认识他吗？

由于 acquainted 已具有形容词特征表示状态，因此在用其表示动作的句子中，要特别注意动词同 acquainted 的搭配形式，如句子"我是去年认识他的"不能译作：

* *I acquainted him last year.*

* *I was acquainted with him last year.*

而需将上述句子改为：

I got/became acquainted with him last year.

401

I made his acquaintance last year.

11. Needless to say, ...

needless to say 作插入语,意即"不用说",对后面的句子起说明作用。

12. ... Hans explained how it was that he was still alive.

在此 how 引导的宾语从句中,that 从句为该宾语从句中的逻辑主语,而 it 为形式主语。

13. ...towards the end of the war, ...

towards the end of the war 战争临近结束时。

14. ... and Hans had made his way back into ...

make one's way 去,前往;前进,如:

The boys and girls made their way into the woods.
那些男孩和女孩们走进了树林。

15. ... knew what had become of the inhabitants.

become of 为用法比较特殊的动介型短语动词,表示"变得"、"结果是"。使用时,其主语只能用 what、whatever 或 whatever,来询问某事物的发展结果,如:

What has become of my notebook?
我的笔记本到哪儿去了?

No one seemed to care what had become of him.
似乎没人关心他发生了什么。

16. Assuming that ... in a village fifty miles away, where ...

assuming that ... 为现在分词短语,作原因状语,意即"由于认为……"。

语法 Grammar in use

used to 与 would

1. used to 与 would 都可表示过去的习惯,且现在此习惯已不存

402

在,如:

> *I used to smoke, but I don't any more.*
>
> 我过去常吸烟,但我现在已不吸烟了。
>
> *We would normally spend the winter in Miami.*
>
> 我们过去一般在迈阿密过冬。

2. used to 可以用来描述过去的状态,但是 would 则不行,如:

> *I'm not quite as sure as I used to be.*
>
> 我不再像以前那么自信了。
>
> *I used to be a ballet dancer, but now I'm a movie star.*
>
> 我曾经是个芭蕾舞演员,可是现在我是个电影明星。

3. used to 仅用于一般过去时,其疑问句和否定句形式为:

> *Did he use to live in London?*
> 他过去在伦敦住吗?
> *Yes, he did / used to.*
> 是的。

> *He didn't use to live in London.*
>
> 他过去不住在伦敦。
>
> *Fred never used to be so difficult.*
>
> 弗雷德从前从不这么别扭。

> *You used to smoke, didn't you?*
> 你过去常抽烟,不是吗?
> *No, I didn't.*
> 不,我过去不常抽烟。

📂 词汇学习 Word study

1. accept *vt.*

(1) 接受;领受;收受:

> *She offered me some clothes her children had grown out of*

and I accepted them .

她给我一些她的孩子们已穿不上了的衣服,我收了下来。

Do you accept credit card ?

你们收信用卡吗?

(2) 同意;承认;答应:

I don't accept（= *agree with*）*your opinion that we can't control inflation .*

我不同意你关于我们无法控制通货膨胀的观点。

试比较:

They invited me to their wedding and I've agreed to go .

他们邀请我参加他们的婚礼,我已经答应参加。(可以说: *I accepted their invitation .* 但是不可以说: * *I've accepted to go .*)

It is generally accepted that smoking causes bad health .

人们普遍承认吸烟有害健康。

(3) 接纳:

His fellow workers refused to accept him .

他的同事们不同意接纳他。

2．explain

(1)*vt .，vi .*解释;说明,讲解:

If there's anything you don't understand , I'll be happy to explain .

如果你们有什么不懂的话,我很乐意给予解释。

Can you explain the rules to the children ?

你能给孩子们讲解一下这些规矩吗?

Can you explain what this word means ?

你能解释一下这个词的含义吗?

(2)*vt .* 说明……原因(或理由):

I explained that I was trying to write a book .

我解释说我正在努力写一本书。

No one has been able to explain the accident.

没人能说出这场事故的原因。

(3) explain oneself 阐明自己的意思;解释自己的行为:

I don't understand what you're talking about. Would you explain yourself further?

我不懂你在说什么。你能说得更明白些吗?

Sam's mother asked him to explain himself why he didn't go to school.

萨姆的母亲让他解释一下他为什么没去上学。

(4) explain away 为……辩解;以解释而开脱:

The government will find it difficult to explain away the latest unemployment figures.

政府将很难对最近的失业数字作出辩解。

3. assume

(1) *vt.* 假设;假定;想当然地认为:

We can't assume the suspects (to be) guilty simply because they've decided to remain silent.

我们不能仅仅因为嫌疑人决定保持沉默而假定他们有罪。

I'm assuming our new assistant can write French as well as speak it.

我认为我们的新助手法语写得和说得一样好。

suppose 与 assume 的区别如下所示:如果用 I suppose ... 表示你认为某事有可能是那么回事儿;用 I assume ... 则表示你对某事比较肯定。如:

I suppose he left fairly recently.

我想他可能不久前刚离开。

I assumed that he had started working as soon as he left.

我敢说他刚离开就开始工作了。

(2) *vt.* 控制;夺取;担任:

The army assumed control of the government.

军队控制了政府。

The new President assumes office at midnight tonight.

新总统今晚午夜就职。

(3) *vt.* 假装,装出:

He assumed a well-informed manner but in fact he knows very little.

他装出一副见多识广的样子,但是实际上他却孤陋寡闻。

Tom assumed a look of indifference when he heard Mary was getting married, but we all knew he was upset.

汤姆听说玛丽要结婚时装出一副不以为然的样子,可是我们都知道他十分难过。

(4) *conj.* 假定:

Even assuming (that) smokers do see the health warnings, I doubt they'll take any notice.

即使假定吸烟人的确注意到了吸烟有害健康的警告,我也怀疑他们是否会理会。

Assuming (that) you are right about this, what shall we do?

假定这件事你是对的,我们该怎么办?

✍ 练习答案 Key to written exercises

1. 关键句型、难点练习答案

1 used to, used to, would

2 We'd like you to *accept* this present from the class.

 I *agreed* to go immediately.

3   *George's umbrella , that woman's handbag , Keats' poetry ,*
    the children's clothes , the soldiers' uniforms , in six
    hours' time , a hundred pounds' worth

4   *After having been* discovered, he gave himself up to
    the police.

    After having been told the way, we found the place with no
    problem.

2. 多项选择题答案

1   d   2   c   3   c   4   b   5   d   6   a
7   b   8   b   9   a   10 c   11 a   12 d

Lesson 37
The Westhaven Express
开往威斯特海温的快车

📖 **课文详注 Further notes on the text**

1 . . . . most of us have developed an unshakable faith in . . .

faith in . . . 为名词词组,faith 后常使用介词 in 表示"对……的信念"之意,如:

> *This does not increase one's faith in human nature.*
> 这不会增强人们对人性的信念。
>
> *I advise you not to put your faith in such a remedy.*
> 我奉劝你不要相信这种药。

2 . It is all too easy to blame the railway authorities when something does go wrong.

(1) 句子中 it 为先行词,在句子中作形式主语,to blame . . . 这一动词不定式短语在句子中作逻辑主语。不要将本句看作是"too + 形容词/副词 + to do . . ."结构表达"太……以致不能做……"的句子;这里 all too easy 表示 very easy 的含义,但语气要比 very easy 强得多。

(2) does 为助动词,这里表示强调,意即"真的"、"的确"。

3 . The truth is that when mistakes occur, they are more likely to be *ours* than *theirs*.

(1) when 为从属连词,在 that 引导的从句中引导一个时间状语从句。

(2) 课文中 ours 和 theirs 均为斜体表示强调,应重读。ours = our mistakes, theirs = the mistakes of the railway authorities。

4. After consulting my railway timetable, I noted with satisfaction that...

(1) 在 after 之后,可以直接使用分词短语,在句子中作时间状语,如:

> *After talking to you I always feel better.*
> 跟你谈过之后,我总觉得舒服一些。
>
> *After having annoyed everybody he went home.*
> 把所有人惹恼之后,他就回家了。

(2) with satisfaction 满意地。为介词"with + 抽象名词"构成的短语结构,作状语,修饰 noted。句中 that 为关系连词,引导 noted 后的宾语从句。

5. ... I could not help noticing that a great many local people got on as well.

(1) can not help (doing) ... 禁不住(做)……多用于口语中,其后接名词、代词或动名词,如:

> *Many people can't help admiring the picture when they look at it.*
> 许多人看到这幅画时都禁不住要赞美它。
>
> *We couldn't help being touched by their sincerity.*
> 他们诚恳的态度使我们不得不受感动。

(2) a great many 也可写作 a good many,比 many 语气要强得多,用法也与 many 相同,既可作形容词,也可作代词,如:

> *A good / great many new books were published last month.*
> 上个月出版了许多新书。(形容词)
>
> *A good many are in favour of my proposal.*
> 很多人赞成我的提议。(代词)

此外,由 a great/good many 修饰的名词和谓语动词均用复数形式。

（3）as well 也,同样地。副词短语,相当于 too 的含义。表示此义时,通常用于句末,间或也可用于主语之后,如:

> *Air is necessary for animals，it is necessary for plants as well.*

> 空气对动物必不可少,对植物也同样。

> *I as well will do what I can for you.*

> 我也要尽可能为你做些什么。

此外,在具有情态助动词 may 或 might 的句子中,as well 用于其后,表示"还是……好"之意,如:

> *We may as well finish the job，now we've got so far with it.*

> 既然我们把工作已经做了这么多,还是把它做完为好。

6．At the time, this did not strike me as odd.

strike me as odd 使我感到奇怪。动词 strike 在此表示"给人……印象"的含义。as 作介词,可将 as odd 视为 as being odd 的省略。介词短语 as odd 在句子中作主语 this 的补足语,如:

> *Your plan struck me as rather impractical.*

> 我觉得你的计划有点不切实际。

> *The idea at first struck me as stupid，but now I think it is a good one.*

> 起初我觉得这个主意很愚蠢,但现在我认为这是个好主意。

7．I reflected that there must be a great many people besides myself who wishes to take advantage of this excellent service.

（1）besides,介词,表示"除包括……之外还包括"之意。该介词短语作定语,修饰 people。

（2）take advantage of 利用。在使用这个短语时,在介词 of 后可以是人,也可是物作其宾语,但所表示的语义往往不同。当以人为宾语时,往往含贬义,主要指利用某人的弱点而占某人的便

宜,因此常表示"欺骗"、"捉弄"的含义,如:

Don't try to take advantage of me; I know fully well what you are up to.

别想捉弄我,你想干什么我都知道。

但是当以物为宾语时,既可用于褒义又可用于贬义。作褒义表示"利用";作贬义表示"乘机利用",往往指利用别人的不幸或不利等攻击或打击别人,以达到自己的目的,如:

I should like to take advantage of this opportunity to express my thanks for your help.

我想借此机会对你们的帮助表示感谢。

He always takes full advantage of the mistakes made by his rivals.

他总是充分利用对手所犯的错误。

8. Neither was I surprised when the train stopped at Widley, a tiny station a few miles along the line.

(1) 当要说明某人、某事或某种情况与前面提到的相同且均为否定含义时,可以使用 neither 引导这个句子,但这样的结构(如本句)需使用倒装语序,如:

The union does not want a strike, and neither does the management.

工会不希望罢工,管理部门也不希望。

I admit I have made a mistake, neither do I deny the serious consequences it may have.

我承认我犯了错误,我也不否认这错误可能产生的严重后果。

(2) a tiny station a few miles along the line 作 Widley 的同位语,对其作进一步说明。其中 a few miles along the line 作 station 的定语,意即"沿线几英里以外的一个小站"。

411

9. Even a mighty express train can be held up by signals.

hold up 使停顿,使耽搁,如:

> *Neither rain nor snow could hold up the laying of the foundations.*
>
> 无论风还是雪都不能阻滞奠基。
>
> *Pretty soon we were held up for lack of material.*
>
> 很快,我们就由于缺乏材料而无法进行下去了。

10. But when the train dawdled ...

dawdle 慢吞吞地干/做。通常用来形容人动作缓慢或闲散,如:

> *He dawdled over his coffee.*
>
> 他慢慢地喝着咖啡。
>
> *Don't dawdled over your work.*
>
> 不要磨洋工。

这里用拟人手法形容火车开得很慢。

11. It suddenly dawned on me that this express was not roaring down the line ... but barely chugging along at thirty.

(1) dawn on/upon 使……渐渐明白,如:

> *The idea suddenly dawned on/upon me.*
>
> 那个念头突然出现在我的脑海中。
>
> *Has it never dawned on you that his story may have been a fabrication?*
>
> 你从未想到他的故事是捏造的吗?

(2) 句子中 roar(发出隆隆声)和 chug(发出嘎嘎声)均为拟声词 (onomatopoeia),down 为介词,alone 为副词。句子中借助这两个拟声词及后面所用的介词 down 与副词 along 生动形象地表示出火车"隆隆轰鸣而过"和"咔咔蠕动而行"的情景。

(3) at thirty 后省略了 miles an hour,这样使句子简练和避免单词的重复使用。

412

12. ... and we had not even covered half the distance.

half 既可作形容词,又可作名词,但是在使用中需用不同结构。如文中那样,作形容词使用时,必须将修饰名词的冠词置于 half 与该名词之间,如:

Half the cloth is worm-eaten.

一半料子都让虫蛀了。

但作名词使用时,其后需用介词 of,如:

Half of it is pure rubbish.

有一半纯粹是废话。

作形容词时,既可用其修饰单数名词,也可用其修饰复数名词,如:

Half the peaches are good.

这些桃子中有一半是好的。

Half the peach is good.

这个桃子有一半是好的。

使用 half of 时,强调所占部分,使用 half the 时,则强调量。

13. ... when I told him that it was there in black and white.

(1) 代词 it 指 the train's existence。

(2) in black and white (用)白纸黑字。这里的 black 指写字用的墨水,white 则指写字用的纸。这里用写字材料的具体颜色代替写出的字,是明喻的一种用法。

语法 Grammar in use

1. too 和 enough + 形容词 + 动词不定式结构

too 放在形容词之前往往具有"过分"的意思,与 very 不同。very 用来加强形容词的语势。而 too 在含有不定式的句型里常具有否定的含义,表示不可能。如:

He is too weak to go to work today.

他太虚弱了,今天不能去上班。

She was too tired to stay up longer.

她太累了,不能再熬夜了。

This book is too boring to read.

这本书乏味得读不下去。

在这一结构中,主要动词的主语可以是不定式的主语,也可以是不定式的宾语,如:

He is too weak to lift the box.

他太虚弱了,举不起这只箱子。(*He* 既是主要动词 *is* 的主语,也是不定式 *to lift* 的主语)

The box is too heavy(for him)to lift.

这只箱子太沉了,他举不起来。(*The box* 是主要动词 *is* 的主语,也是不定式 *to lift* 的宾语)

注:在这种结构中,for 短语可以省略。

而 enough 放在形容词之后表示达到某种程度,如:

Do you think the water is warm enough(for us)to go swimming?

你认为水温达到(我们)可以游泳的程度了吗?

Would you be kind enough to open a window?

劳驾打开一个窗户好吗?

在这一结构中,主要动词的主语可以是不定式的主语,也可以是不定式的宾语,如:

He isn't strong enough to lift the box.

他没有足以举起这只箱子的力气。(*He* 既是主要动词 *is* 的主语,也是不定式 *to lift* 的主语)

The pear is ripe enough(for me)to eat.

这只梨熟得能吃了。(*The pear* 是主要动词 *is* 的主语,是不定式 *to eat* 的宾语)

注:在这种结构中,for 短语可以省略。

2. 否定副词后句子的倒装

具有否定含义的副词出现在句首时,句子往往倒装。这种倒装主要用来加强语气,常用于正式的讲话或书面语中。常见的否定副词有 never、seldom、hardly、scarcely、rarely、little、on no account、no sooner、neither、nor 等。

Never/Seldom has there been so much protest against the Bomb.

如此强烈的反对原子弹的抗议活动从未/很少有过。

Little does he realize how important this meeting is.

他对这个会议的重要性不甚了了。

On no account must you accept any money if he offers it.

如果他给你钱,你可绝不能接受。

此外,与 only 或 not only 构成的词组出现在句首时句子往往也要倒装:

Only then did I realize how dangerous the situation had been.

到那时我才意识到情况有多么危险。

Not only did we lose all our money, but we also came close to losing our lives.

我们不但把钱丢了,还几乎丢了性命。

📁 词汇学习 Word study

1. occur

(1) *vi.* 发生:

Mrs. Green had been in the milking shed when the explosion occurred.

爆炸发生时,格林太太在奶牛棚里。

The tragedy occurred only minutes after take-off.

起飞几分钟后灾难就发生了。

happen、occur、take place 这 3 个词（组）均表示"发生"；happen、occur 表示偶然发生的事,occur 较为正式,口语中常用 happen,如：

You might have noticed what happened on Tuesday.

你可能已经注意到了上星期二发生的事。

Mistakes are bound to occur.

错误再所难免。

take place 指计划或安排的事情发生,如：

The first meeting of this committee took place on 9 January.

这个委员会的第 1 次会议于 1 月 9 日召开。

表示某事发生在某人身上用 happen to 而不用 occur to,如：

I'm wondering what's happened to Jane. She is two hours late.

我在想简发生了什么事。她已经晚了两个小时了。

(2) *vi.* 存在：

Violence of some sort seems to occur in every society.

某种类型的暴力行为似乎存在于任何社会。

(3)（to）（观点、想法等）出现在脑海中,突然想到：

The idea had never even occurred to him before.

他以前从未有过这种想法。

It suddenly occurred to me that we could use a computer to do the job.

我突然想到可以用电脑做这项工作。

2. deny *vt.*

(1) 否认：

The accursed women denied all the charges brought against them.

被指控的那些女人否认对她们的所有指控。

He denied that he was involved.

他否认与此有关。

Tom denied doing anything illegal.

汤姆否认干过任何非法的事情。

（2）拒绝给予；不允许：

I was denied the chance of going to university when my parents' business collapsed and they lost everything they owned.

当我父母的生意失败，失掉所有一切时，我也就失去了上大学的机会。

He denied her nothing.

他对她有求必应。

No one should be denied a good education.

不能剥夺任何人接受良好教育的机会。

（3）抛弃；断绝关系：

He has denied his country and his principles.

他已经抛弃了他的国家和他的原则。

3. borrow *vt.*

（1）借，借入：

Can I borrow your pen for a moment?

我能借用一下你的钢笔吗？

They borrowed heavily from the bank to start their new business.

他们从银行借了大笔资金启动他们的新公司。

比较：borrow 为借入，lend 为借出，如：

I often lend her money.

我常借给她钱。

Could I borrow your car?

417

我能借用一下你的车吗？

一般只能用 borrow 或 lend 借入或借出能移动的东西,而不能用于不能移动的东西,不能说:

Can I borrow your garage next week?

而应说:

Can I use your garage next week?

下周我能用一下你的车库吗?

不能说:

He lent me his office.

而应说:

He let me use his office.

他让我使用他的办公室。

(2) 借用,采用:

English has borrowed words from many languages.

英语从许多语言中借用单词。

He borrowed a theory from Marxism to support his economic reform.

他借用一条马克思主义理论支持他的经济改革。

✍ 练习答案 **Key to written exercises**

1. 关键句型、难点练习答案

1 The wall is *too high (for me) to climb*.

   The wall is *low enough (for me) to climb*.

2 *I* can't stand *queueing at the cinema*.

   I don't mind *helping you*.

3 *Never* had I seen anything like it before.

   Hardly had I started when they told me to stop.

   Little did she know that she was being watched.

4 Two minutes *passed* before anything happened.

The time is exactly two minutes *past* twelve.

5 My friend *refused* to lend me any money.

He *denied* that he had stolen the money.

6 I *borrowed* three books from the public library.

Then I *lent* one of them to a friend.

2. 多项选择题答案

| 1 | b | 2 | c | 3 | a | 4 | b | 5 | c | 6 | a |
| 7 | d | 8 | c | 9 | d | 10 | d | 11 | b | 12 | a |

Lesson 38
The first calender
最早的日历

📖 **课文详注 Further notes on the text**

1. What is more, they will not have to rely solely on ...

（1）what is more 而且。作插入语,用新的附加信息对前文所述做进一步强调。为固定结构,无时态变化。

（2）rely on 依赖,依靠,如:

Aren't you relying too much on appearances ?
你是不是太注重外表了?

The town relies on seasonal tourist industry for jobs.
这个镇子依靠季节性旅游业提供就业机会。

2. They will be able, as it were, to see and hear us in action.

（1）as it were 可以说,好像,打个比方说。为虚拟语气的状语从句,可视为 as if it were so 的省略形式,可用于各种时态的句子中。通常作独立成分的插入语使用,位于句中,前后用逗号分开。其作用是表示所指的那个词或那句话是个比喻说法,如:

The sky is covered , as it were , with a black curtain.
天空好像被黑幕遮住似的。

A good dictionary is a useful tool and , as it were , a constant friend to a student of language.
一部好词典不仅是有用的工具,而且对学语言的人来说,可以说是个忠实的朋友。

注意:在使用中,勿将 as it were 同 as it is(按现在的情况,事实

420

上)和 as it was(按当时的情况,事实上)相混淆,后者均为一般的陈述语气。

(2) in action 在活动中,在进行中。作动词 see 和 hear 的宾语补足语,再如:

> *He's a very good table tennis player; you really ought to see him in action.*

> 他是个出色的乒乓球运动员,你确实应该去看看他打球。

注意本课 in action 与第 30 课中的 in action(在战斗中)的语义不同。

3. But the historian attempting to reconstruct the distant past is always faced with a difficult task.

(1) attempting ... past 为现在分词短语,作定语,修饰 historian,即"企图重现遥远过去的历史学家……"。

(2) be faced with ... 面临……,面对着……表示一种状态,而且往往不是出于主语的意愿,如:

> *He was faced with many difficulties which, with the help of his friends, he successfully overcame.*

> 他遭遇到许多困难,但是在朋友们的帮助下,都一一顺利地克服了。

> *Faced with this new turn of events, he decided to revise his original plan.*

> 面对事件的这一新的变化,他决定修改原计划。

然而,在使用 face ...(面对……,遇到……)时后要有直接宾语;此时句子表现出强烈的动作和意愿性,如:

> *They've learned to face all obstacles with resolution and courage.*

> 他们学会了以果断勇敢的精神正视一切障碍。

4. He has to deduce what he can from the few scanty clues available.

（1）在关系代词 what 引导的宾语从句中，为避免重复，he can 后省略了 deduce。

（2）deduce ... from ... 从……推断……表示此义时，deduce 后需使用介词 from，如：

> *deduce the development of a culture from archaeological remains* 根据古迹追溯一种文化的发展
>
> *deduce a conclusion from premises* 从前提推出结论

5．Even seemingly insignificant remains can shed interesting light on the history of early man.

（1）shed light on ... 照亮，使……清楚地显现出来，阐明，如：

> *The investigation shed new light on the mystery.*
> 这项调查使人们对这个疑案有了新的了解。
>
> *His explanation shed broad light on the subject.*
> 他的解释很好地阐明了这个主题。

（2）early man 早期人类。

6．... historians have assumed that calendars came into being with the advent of agriculture，... a real need to understand ...

（1）come into being 产生，形成，建立，如：

> *The European Common Market came into being in 1958.*
> 欧洲共同市场诞生于 1958 年。

（2）with the advent of agriculture 随着农业的产生。介词短语作状语，修饰 came into being。介词 with 在这里表示"随着"。

7．By correlating markings made in various parts of the world，...

by ... world 作方式状语，修饰 have been able to read。此介词短语中的 made in ... world 为过去分词短语，作定语，修饰 markings。

8．It has long been known that the hunting scenes depicted on walls were not ...

422

代词 it 作形式主语,其后由关系连词引导的从句为逻辑主语。

that 从句中的 depicted on walls 为过去分词短语,作定语,修饰 scenes。

9. . . . for they were as near as early man could get to writing.

(1) 代词 they 指 hunting scenes。

(2) be near to writing 接近书写形式。为使句子简练和避免不必要单词的使用,在 get 后面省略了 near。

(3) as early man could get 为方式状语,修饰 near。意即"它们(狩猎图像)是早期人类最接近的书写形式"。

10. . . . was making a real effort to understand . . . than has been supposed.

than has been supposed 中的 than 与 has 之间省略了 it(指时间)。

语法 Grammar in use

among 与 between

1.表示位置

1) among 表示在一群人或物中间,如:

James wandered among his guests.

詹姆斯在他的客人中间走来走去.

Among his baggage was a medicine chest.

他的行李中有一个药箱。

2) between 表示在两人或两件物品之间,如:

The island of Santa Catarina is roughly midway between Sao Paulo and Porto Alegre.

圣卡塔琳娜岛几乎正位于圣保罗与阿雷格里港之间。

She puts the cigarette between her lips.

她将香烟放在双唇之间。

2.表示在……中间(分配)

among 可用来表示在一群人中间分配某物,如:

> *He divided his estate among his brothers and sisters.*
>
> 他将他的财产分给他的兄弟姊妹。

如果动词 share、divide 后面跟的是几个单数名词则也可用 between。

> *I divided his money between/among his five sons.*
>
> 他将钱分给他的 5 个儿子。

3.表示区别、差异

只能用 between ,而不能用 among:

不能说:

> ** I couldn't see any difference among the three chairs.*

而应说:

> *I couldn't see any difference between the three chairs.*
>
> 我看不出这 3 把椅子有什么区别。

> *I asked him whether there was much difference between British and European laws.*
>
> 我问他英国和欧洲的法律之间是否有很多不同。

4.表示选择

只能用 between,不能用 among, 如:

> *It was difficult to choose between Paris and London for our holiday.*
>
> 是在巴黎还是在伦敦度假,很难作出选择。

📁 **词汇学习　Word study**

1.select

(1) *vt*.选择,挑选,选拔:

> *They select books that seem to them important.*

424

他们选择对他们似乎重要的书。

She selected a diamond ring from the collection.

她从中挑选了一只钻戒。

The methods used to select people for promotion were explained to every employee.

已经向所有雇员说明选拔晋升人员的方法。

choose、select、pick 这 3 个词都表示选择,挑选等意。select 比 choose、pick 较正式,一般口语中不用,多用 choose 与 pick,如:

Next time, let's pick somebody who can fight.

下一次我们选个会打架的。

I chose a yellow dress.

我选了身黄色的衣服。

表示选择做某事不能用 select to do 或 pick to do,只能用 choose to do:

The way we choose to bring up children is vitally important.

我们所选择的抚养孩子的方法至关重要。

(2) *adj.* 精选的,优等的,杰出的:

A select group were invited to the reception.

一些精心挑选的人被邀请参加招待会。

This is a very select area; you have to be rich to live here.

这是个上层居住区,要想住在这儿你必须得十分富有。

2. rely *vi.*

(1)(on, upon) 信赖,相信,指望:

We are relying on you to get us out of this mess.

我们全靠你使我们摆脱这个麻烦。

British weather can never be relied upon. It's always changing.

可别相信英国的天气。它总是变化无常。

Don't rely on the bank lending you the money.

别指望银行会借给你这笔钱。

(2)（on，upon）依靠，依赖：

They have to rely on rain for their water.

他们全仗着下雨以获取他们所需的水。

I'm relying on the garage to fix the car by tomorrow.

我全靠修车店在明天之前修好那辆车。

3.suppose

(1) *vt.* 猜想，认为，以为：

⌈*Will he phone when he arrives?*

⌊他到了之后会打电话来吗？

⌈*I suppose so.*

⌊我想会的。

⌈*It won't matter much if we're late.*

⌊如果我们迟到不会有多大的关系。

⌈*I suppose not./I don't suppose so.*

⌊我想不会的。

I don't suppose you would be prepared to stay in Edinburgh?

我想你没准备呆在爱丁堡吧？

(2) be supposed to 认为……必要，期望，认为应该：

He is supposed to be at work today.

他今天应该工作。

The train's supposed to arrive at 9:10.

火车应该9点10分到达。

(3) *conj.* 假使（也可用 supposing），用于提出某项建议：

Supposing something should go wrong, what would you do then?

假如出点什么差错,你该怎么办?

Suppose we wait a while?

我们等一会儿怎么样?

✍ 练习答案 Key to written exercises

1. 关键句型、难点练习答案

1 have assumed, came, was faced, seems, is, have *long* been puzzled, have been engraved, made, lived, began, ended (See also text.)

2 agree with, account for, mistake ... for, cope with, correspond with, apologize for, blame ... for, reason with, satisfied with, quarrel with, wait for, search for

3 What's the difference *between* this and that?

When I was with them, I always knew I was *among* friends.

2. 多项选择题答案

1	b	2	d	3	a	4	d	5	c	6	b
7	c	8	b	9	a	10	a	11	c	12	a

Lesson 39
Nothing to worry about
不必担心

📖 **课文详注　Further notes on the text**

1. Nothing to worry about

to worry about,动词不定式短语,作定语修饰 nothing。worry
作及物动词使用,表示"使担心/发愁"时,其主语多为事物,宾
语多为人,如:

> *His prolonged absence worries me very much.*
> 他长期缺席使我很担心。
>
> *There must be something worrying her.*
> 肯定有什么事令她不安。

作不及物动词使用表示"担心"时,其主语多为人,宾语可为人
也可为物,后面通常使用介词 about 或 over,如:

> *Don't worry about/over such trifles.*
> 不要为这样的小事犯愁。
>
> *In those days he always worried about / over being
> unemployed.*
> 那时候他经常为失业发愁。

因为 nothing 为"担心"的逻辑宾语,因此使用 worry about。

**2. . . . became so bad that we tried to get Bruce . . . the village we
had come from.**

（1）so . . . that . . . 太……以至于……为关联连词,引导一个结果
状语从句。这里的动词 get 为"劝说"之意。

（2）we had come from 在句子中为定语从句。由于先行词 village

在从句中作介词 from 的宾语,因此在 village 与从句间省略了关系代词 that/which。注意在此句中不应用关系副词 where 连接先行词和此定语从句。

3.Even though the road was littered with boulders and pitted with holes, Bruce was not in the least perturbed.

(1) even though,从属连词,引导一个让步状语从句。就语义而言,虽然 even 和 even though/if 均具有"即使"之意,但 even 为副词,不能用来引导一个从句,通常用于两个并列意思中对第 2 个意思的强调,如:

> *Some historians often misinterpret or even distort historical facts.*
>
> 有些历史学家往往曲解甚至歪曲事实。

有时用于比较的一层意思是默认的或是省略的,并不在字面反映出来,如:

> *In the south even children can swim.*
>
> 在南方就连孩子们也会游泳。

该句暗示出 not to say the grown-up people(不必说成年人)的含义。

此外 even though/if 与 though 相比较,前者较后者语气要强,通常用来表达退一步设想,其意义并非为真实的,但 though 引导的句子往往陈述一个事实。

(2) was littered with ... 布满……;was pitted with ... 因……而坑坑洼洼。它们共用一个主语 the road,这样为使句子简洁,省略了 was pitted with ... 中的 was。

(3) in the least 一点,丝毫。相当于 at all,通常用于否定句,疑问句或条件句中,如:

> *Is his sister in the least interested in becoming a nurse?*
>
> 她妹妹对当护士有点兴趣吗?
>
> *Most of the students don't understand in the least what*

429

this author is trying to say.

大多数学生根本不明白这位作家想说些什么。

4. It was not that Bruce always underestimated difficulties.

not that ... 并不是说……,并非……多用于口语,有时作插入语使用,对所述情况作进一步说明,如:

We were allowed at last to rest, not that much of the night remained.

我们终于获准可以休息了,但天也快亮了。

If he said so—not that he ever did—he lied.

即使他这样说过——并不是说他真的这样说过——他也是在撒谎。

有时用 not that ... but (that) ... 表示"不是……而是……",如:

It was not that Bruce always underestimated difficulties, but (that) he simply had no sense of danger at all.

并不是说布鲁斯总是低估困难,而是他压根儿没有一点危险感。

5. No matter what the conditions were, he believed that...

no matter what ... 无论……,不管……为从属连词,引导一个让步状语从句。注意其后所跟随的应为名词,这一点同 no matter how 不同,后者应跟随形容词或副词。

6. We felt sure that sooner or later...

sooner or later 迟早。作时间状语,如:

If you drive like that, sooner or later you'll have an accident.

你如果那样开车,迟早会出事的。

Don't worry about our safety, they'll come to help us sooner or later.

别为我们的安全担心,他们迟早会来救我们的。

7. ... we kept looking back, wondering if ...

wondering if ...,现在分词短语,作目的状语,修饰 kept looking back,意即"想知道……"、"想弄明白……"。

8. What a relief ..., giving way to a stretch of plain where ...

(1) giving way to ...,现在分词短语,作结果状语。give way to 让位给,转变为,如:

> *As winter gave way to spring, the days began to lengthen.*
>
> 随着冬春的交替,白天开始变长了。
>
> *Radio has given way to television in popularity.*
>
> 电视机越来越普及,逐渐取代了收音机。

(2) a stretch of ... 一大片……翻译中需根据其后的名词确定其量词的使用,如:

> *a beautiful stretch of wooded country* 一大片美丽的林地
>
> *a diabolical stretch of weather* 一段时间的坏天气
>
> *There is a stretch of hills near the village.*
>
> 村子附近有连绵的山丘。

有时根据其"延伸"、"扩展"之意,引申用于:

> *a stretch of authority* 超越权限
>
> *a stretch of imagination* 想入非非
>
> *a stretch of the law* 滥用法律

9. But there was worse to come.

这里 worse 为名词,指"更糟的事情"。to come,动词不定式作定语,修饰 worse。

10. Just ahead of us there was a huge fissure.

ahead of... 在……前面。短语介词,作地点状语,但也可用来表示"领先"的地位或表示时间"早于"、"先于"的意思,如:

> *The company commander is walking a few feet ahead of the soldiers.*

连长走在士兵前几英尺远。

Betty finished her test ahead of the others.

贝蒂比其他人先做完测验题。

11. **In response to renewed pleadings ...**

in response to renewed pleadings 意即"为回答我们的一再请求"。in response to 为短语介词,表示"应……"、"响应……"之意,如:

In response to an invitation we attended the meeting.

我们应邀参加了这个会议。

In response to your appeal, we've made following changes in the schedule.

应贵方要求,我们对日程作了如下修改。

12. **... and drove at a terrifying speed, keeping the front wheels astride the crack as ...**

(1) at a terrifying speed 以令人害怕的速度。这里的 terrifying 为夸张用法。

(2) keeping ... course,现在分词短语,作方式状语,修饰 drove,其中的介词短语 astride the crack 作定语 the front wheels 的补足语。

13. **Before we had time to ...**

注意,当用 before 表示"在……没有……之前"或"在未来得及……之前"之意时,before 只能用于肯定式中来表达否定含义,而不可将其用于否定式之中,如:

She ran out of the room before they could stop her.

他们还没来得及阻拦她,她已经跑出了屋子。

但不可说:

* Before they could not stop her, she ran out of the room.

14. **Bruce charged at it, but ...**

charge at ... 向……冲去,如:

432

He charged at me with his head down and both fists flying.

他低着头,挥舞着双拳向我扑来。

Suddenly the wild animal charged at us.

那只野兽突然向我们扑来。

15. **A yellow light on the dashboard flashed angrily and Bruce cheerfully announced that ...!**

句子中用 angrily 形容灯的 flash,是一种拟人用法,angrily 与 cheerfully 以对比的方式出现,形成修辞格——对照法(antithesis),即将相反或相对的两个意思或两个词以对等的结构安排在句子中,形成对照,以增强表达效果,如:

Speech is silver, silence is golden.

雄辩是银,沉默是金。

在此例中,speech 与 silence,silver 与 golden 在两个对等的句子结构中形成对照,使要表达的后者意义更为鲜明。

📄 **语法 Grammar in use**

1. **get sb. to do sth. 与 make sb. do sth.**

get ＋宾语＋带 to 的不定式表示"说服"、"设法"等意,如:

Get him to tell you what happened.

设法让他告诉你发生了什么事。

Nobody can get him to move away from his old house.

没人能说服他搬出他的老房子。

make sb. do sth. 表示"强迫",如:

You've got to make him listen.

你必须让他听讲。

He meant to make them sit still.

他企图让他们一动不动地坐着。

在主动句中 make 后面跟不带 to 的动词不定式；而在被动句中不定式必须带 to，如：

He is made to pay back the debt .

他被迫偿还债务。

2. 动词 suggest、insist、command 与 recommend

英语中表示希望某事发生、想让发生或以为要发生时，在美国英语中往往用虚拟语气。常见的有这类用法的动词有 suggest、insist、command、recommend、request、ask、advise、propose 等。句子结构为"动词＋that＋动词的虚拟语气"（即无论现在时还是过去时都用动词原形），如：

They insist that a meeting be held as soon as possible .

他们坚持要尽早召开一个会议。

To save time , I suggest we meet at the restaurant .

为了节约时间，我建议咱们在餐厅会面。

英语中有些表示"重要"、"必要"等的形容词用法与上述动词相同。这些形容词有 important、vital、essential、necessary、desirable 等，如：

It is essential that every child have the same educational opportunities .

重要的是每个孩子都有同样的教育机会。

Was it necessary that my uncle be informed ?

有必要通知我叔叔吗？

上述这种结构常用于正式文体。在英国英语中 that 从句中多用"should＋动词不定式"，如：

They insist that a meeting should be held as soon as possible .

他们坚持要尽早召开一个会议。

It is essential that every child should have the same educational opportunities .

重要的是每个孩子都有同样的教育机会。

It is vital that we should control the spread of malaria .

对我们来说控制疟疾的传播非常重要。

3．say 与 tell

say 说

（1）用于直接引用某人的话，如：

'*You haven't got much time ,*' *he said*（*to me*）．

"你的时间可不多了，"他（对我）说。

（2）与 so 连用，如：

Why didn't you say so earlier ?

你怎么不早说？

It is all quite unnecessary , but nobody dare say so , of course .

根本就没必要，可是当然谁也不敢这么说。

（3）后面接 that 从句或动词不定式，如：

He said that he was going to retire .

他说他就要退休了。

It is said that there is plenty of oil off our coast .

据说我国沿海有许多石油。

There is said to be plenty of oil off our coast .

据说我国沿海有许多石油。

Mandy is said to be some kind of secret agent .

据说曼迪是个特工。

（4）一些固定说法，如：

say a few words 说几句话

say goodnight 说晚安

say no more 不再说什么

say nothing 什么都不说

say your prayer 祈祷

435

say something 说点什么

tell 告诉

（1）后面跟"人称代词宾格＋that 从句或动词不定式"，如：

He told me that he had once studied chemistry.

他告诉我他曾学过化学。

She told me to be careful.

她让我小心点儿。

I was told to sit on the front bench.

我被告知坐在前排。

（2）一些固定说法，如：

tell jokes 讲笑话

tell lies 撒谎

tell stories 讲故事

注：say 可直接引用别人的话而 tell 不能，如：

He said , ' Open the door.'

tell 可以用于命令而 say 不能，如：

He told me to open the door.

📁 词汇学习 Word study

1. drive *vt. , vi.* (drove, driven)

（1）驾驶，驾驭：

She drives a red sports car.

她开着一辆红色的跑车。

（2）驱赶，驱使，迫使：

The dog drove the sheep into one corner of the field.

狗将羊群驱赶到牧场的一个角落。

The bad weather has driven the tourists away.

糟糕的天气已使游客离去。

436

（3）驾车送某人：

> *Can you drive me to the station ?*
> 你能开车送我去车站吗？
> *I drove my daughter to school .*
> 我开车送女儿上学。

  用法：drive a car 开车

   pilot a ship 驾船

   ride a bicycle 骑自行车

   掌握汽车方向盘,掌舵或握自行车把用 steer：

> *She steered the car carefully through the narrow*
> *gap .*
> 她小心翼翼地使车通过那个狭窄的通道。

   但是驾驶或掌握飞行航向均用 fly/pilot a plane。

2. inform *vt .*

（1）通知,告知,报告：

> *I wasn't informed of the decision until too late .*
> 我获悉这一决定已经太迟了。
>
> *We wish to inform passengers that flight departures may*
> *be delayed .*
> 我们想通知乘客航班起飞时间可能要推迟。
>
> *Could you inform me how to go about contacting a*
> *lawyer ?*
> 你能告诉我如何同一个律师联系吗？

（2）（against, on）告发,检举：

> *I'm amazed to hear that she was the one who informed on*
> *her husband .*
> 听说是她告发了她丈夫,真令我吃惊。

3. wonder *vi ., vt .*

（1）（about, if, whether, how, what, why, etc .）对……感到好

奇,想知道:

> *I keep wondering and worrying about what you said.*
> 我一直在想你说过的话,也感到不安。

> *I wonder/I'm wondering if we've made a mistake here.*
> 我想知道我们在这儿是不是犯了个错误。

> *Does she know we're here?*
> 她知道我们在这儿吗?
> *I'm just wondering.*
> 我不知道。

(2)(about, if, whether) 疑惑,怀疑:

> *He says such stupid things that sometimes I wonder if/whether he's got any brains at all!*
> 他常说蠢话,我有时都在怀疑他是否长着脑子!

(3)(at, that) 对……感到吃惊,对……感到诧异:

> *The fact that she left home is not to be wondered at.*
> 她离家出走不足为奇。

> *I wonder he dares to show his face here again after the way he behaved!*
> 我真不敢想像他那样行事之后还敢在这儿露面!

✍ 练习答案　Key to written exercises

1. 关键句型、难点练习答案

1　I *got* him to tell me the truth.

　He *got* me to translate the article into English.

2　*He suggested that* I should go with him.

　He insisted that I should stay to lunch.

3　Can he wait a few minutes longer? I wonder if *he can wait a few minutes longer*?

438

When will he arrive? I wonder when *he will arrive*.

4 What a wonderful garden!

What a terrible day!

5 How *are* you *getting on* in your new job?

She *has* just *got over* a serious illness.

Did she *get through* her exams all right?

6 He *said* that the village wasn't very far away.

He *told* us that the village was 15 miles away.

2．多项选择题答案

1	c	2	a	3	a	4	d	5	a	6	d
7	b	8	c	9	a	10	c	11	b	12	c

Lesson 40
Who's who
真假难辨

1. It has never been explained why university students ...

why 为连接副词,引导的从句在句中作逻辑主语,代词 it 为形式主语。在这样的结构中,it 没有具体意义,仅起到代替主语从句,将该主语从句移至句子后部,使句子显得平衡的作用。这样的从句除可用连词 that 引导外,也可用连接代词或连接副词引导,如:

Has it been found out who set the record ?

搞清楚这项记录是谁创造的了吗?

It hasn't been made clear when the new road is open to traffic .

还没有明确宣布这条新路何时通车。

有关用法参见第 1 课课文注释 13。

2. Students specialize in a particular type of ...

specialize in... 专门从事……,如:

Many students specialize in engineering .

许多学生专攻工程学。

The cinema specializes in Italian films .

这家电影院专门放映意大利电影。

3. Inviting the fire brigade to put out a nonexistent fire is ... indulge in.

indulge in ... 沉迷/沉溺于……,放任于……,如:

440

Many old people indulge in reminiscences of their youth.

许多上岁数的人都沉溺于追忆年轻时的往事。

Fishing, swimming, and dancing can be indulged in there.

在那里可以尽情地钓鱼、游泳和跳舞。

4. ...except the victims.

victims 在这里指恶作剧的受害者。

5. ... they were not to take him seriously.

be to do sth. 这个结构主要用来表示按计划或安排而将要做的事情或打算要做的事情。根据上下文的不同,be to 常常具有 should、can、may、must 等多种含义,因此在理解与运用中,要注意其情态意义的准确性,如:

They are to send more people to help us.

他们打算派更多的人来帮助我们。

We are not to be cowed or deceived.

我们是吓不倒也骗不了的。

The letter is to be handed to him in person.

这封信必须要交给他本人。

6. Both the police and the workmen were grateful to the student for his ...

be grateful for ... 因为……而感激/感谢。介词 for 构成的介词短语表示原因,如:

I'm very grateful for the help you've given me.

对您给予的帮助,我非常感谢。

be grateful to ... 对……表示感谢。介词 to (有时也可为 towards)后需使用表示人、组织、团体等的名词,如:

They felt deeply grateful to/towards their benefactors.

他们对他们的恩人深感谢意。

有时如课文中那样,可将这两个词组结合使用,构成 be grateful

to sb. for (doing) sth., 表示"因为(做)某事而感谢(激)某人"的意思,如:

His parents were very grateful to us for informing them of his safe return.

他的父母非常感谢我们告诉他们他平安归来的消息。

7. ... he threatened to remove them by force.

by force 用暴力,用武力,用强制手段,强迫地。介词短语,表示以暴力作为一种手段,作状语,如:

If they cannot do it by persuasion, they'll have to do it by force.

如果他们无法通过说服做到这一点,他们将不得不采取强制手段。

有时可使用 by force of ... 短语形式,表示"以……的暴力手段"之意,如:

They could not exist unless they defended their country by force of arms.

他们只有用武力保卫他们的国家,否则他们就无法存在。

8. The workmen told him to do as he pleased and ...

as he pleased 随他的便。为方式状语从句,其后省略了 to do。

as one please 常用来表示"随某人的便"之意,如:

You may go around and have free talks with them as you please.

你可以随便四处走走,同他们随便聊聊。

9. ... and remonstrated with the workmen.

remonstrate with ... 规劝…… 其后跟随表示人的名词。如表示"就……而规劝某人"时,通常使用 remonstrate with sb. about/regarding/upon/on sth. 这个结构形式,如:

His parents remonstrated with him about his bad habits.

他父母规劝他改掉他的恶习。

442

10. **... as the men were already under arrest.**

be under arrest 被拘留,被逮捕。

11. **Pretending to speak seriously, ... before being taken to the station.**

在 before being taken... 中,before 为介词,being taken ... 为动名词 taking 的被动语态形式。be taken to the station 意即"被带到警察局"。

12. **Only when he saw ... did he realize that ...**

only when 直到……才……,只有当时候……才。only 为副词,起强调作用。只有当 only + 状语(课文中为从属连词 when 引导的时间状语从句)这样的结构用于句首时,句子(或主句)的谓语部分方需使用部分倒装的语序;这类结构未用于句首时,使用正常的语序,比较:

(1) *Only if you've been through such agony will you believe it.*

只有你经受过这样的痛苦,你才会相信。

The sort of fuel can be burned only if it is vaporized and mixed with oxygen.

这种燃料只有在它蒸发并与氧气混合时才能燃烧。

(2) *Only when something went wrong with the machine did they turn off the switch.*

直到机器发生了故障,他们才拉下开关。

From a scientific point of view, work is done only when the applied force produces motion.

从科学的观点来看,只有当作用力产生运动时,才算是做了功。

在上述(1)、(2)两组示例中,每组的第 1 个例句均将"only + 状语"(第 1 组中,only 后为从属连词 if 引导的条件状语从句;第 2 组中,only 后为从属连词 when 引导的时间状语从句)这一结构形式用于句首,因此其主句中的谓语应构成部分倒装的语序,即第 1 组第 1 例中的 will you believe...和第 2 组第 1 例中的 did they turn off ...。由于每组第 2 例中的"only + 状语"的结构形式用于句尾,因此它们均使用正常的语序。

语法 Grammar in use

except 的用法

1. 后面跟名词或代词

Anything , except water , is likely to block a sink .
除了水,任何东西都有可能堵塞水池。

There's nobody that I really trust , except him .
除了他之外我不相信任何人。

在 all 或者以 every-或 any-打头的词的后面可以用 but 代替 except,如:

He enjoyed everything but maths .
他什么课程都喜欢只是不喜欢数学。

2. 后面跟动词不定式

He demanded nothing of her except to be there .
他只要求她在那儿。

She seldom goes out except to go to mass .
除了做弥撒她很少出去。

在动词 do 后面,except 可以跟不带 to 的不定式,如:

There was little I could do except wait .
我只能静等。

3. 后面跟从句

I know nothing about him except that he lives next door .
我对他一点都不了解,只知道他住在隔壁。

I can scarcely remember what we ate , except that it was

444

plentiful and simple.

我记不起我们吃过什么,只记得吃了不少简单食物。

4.后面跟介词短语

I can take my holiday at any time except in August.

除了 8 月份我什么时候都可以休假。

You can't get credit except by making special arrangements with the management.

除非你同管理部门作出专门的安排否则你得不到信贷。

📁 词汇学习 Word study

1.put out

(1) 扑灭,熄灭:

It took them 10 hours to put the fire out.

他们用了 10 个小时才将火扑灭。

(2) 使不快,使恼怒,使不安,使不便:

She was so put out by his rudeness that she didn't know what to say.

他的无理使她气得都不知道说什么了。

Would it put you out if we came tomorrow instead of today?

如果我们今天不来明天来,不会给你带来不便吧?

(3) 公布,发表:

The government has put out a statement denying these rumours.

政府发表了一项否认这些谣言的声明。

2.dress

(1) *vi.*, *vt.* 给……穿衣, 穿衣,更衣:

Could you dress the baby for me?

你能替我给孩子穿衣服吗？

I must get up and dress.

我得起床穿衣服了。

注：在口语中常用 get dressed 或 put on clothes，dress 较为正式，常用于书面语，如：

Please hurry up and get dressed, Morris.

请快点儿，穿好衣服，莫里斯。

I got up and put on my clothes.

我起床穿好衣服。

(2) dress up 穿上盛装，穿上礼服，精心打扮，穿戴成，装扮成：

Is everyone required to dress up for this party?

要求参加晚会的每个人都身着盛装吗？

I'm going to dress up as Napoleon.

我要装扮成拿破仑。

(3) be dressed in 穿……衣服：

He was dressed in a black suit.

他身穿一套黑色西装。

He saw people coming towards him dancing, dressed in colourful clothes and feathers.

他看见人们跳着舞向他走来，身着色彩鲜艳的服装和羽毛。

3. temper *n.*

(1) 心情，情绪，性情，脾气：

Don't ask your father for money just now. He's in a very bad temper.

现在可别向你父亲要钱。他现在心情不好。

Sometimes I lose my temper.

有时我发脾气。

(2) 生气，动怒：

446

She flies into a temper if you contradict her.

如果你反驳她,她就会大发雷霆。

✍ 练习答案 Key to written exercises

1. 关键句型、难点练习答案

1 We *put up* our tent in the corner of the field.

   Could you *put* us *up* for a couple of nights?

   We can't *put up with* her bad behaviour any longer.

   They have *put off* the game until next week.

2 Everyone found it funny *except* me.

   Except for/Apart from this one mistake, your composition is excellent.

3 We all got up, washed, *dressed* and left the house early.

   Most children like *dressing up*.

4 I *watched* the whole procession from where I stood.

   Her eyes *followed* him wherever he went.

5 I'm surprised you're *in* such *a good temper*.

   She is always *in a good mood*.

   Don't speak to her. She's *in a very bad temper*.

   I'm not *in the mood* to play games.

2. 多项选择题答案

1 a	2 c	3 c	4 d	5 a	6 d
7 c	8 c	9 b	10 a	11 d	12 a

Lesson 41
Illusions of pastoral peace
宁静田园生活的遐想

📖 **课文详注 Further notes on the text**

1．City born and city bred, ... something you look at ..., or something you occasionally visit ...

（1）city born 和 city bred 是两个由"名词＋过去分词"构成的合成词，做形容词使用，可视为在 city born 前省略了现在分词 being，作原因状语。在英语中，将形容词或形容词短语用作状语的情况很多。

（2）you look at ... 和 you occasionally visit ... 均为定语从句，分别修饰其前的 something。在 something 与两个定语从句间分别省略了关系连词 that。

2．... yet they always go into raptures at the mere mention of the country.

（1）go into raptures 变得极其喜爱，变得欣喜若狂。如表示"对……极其喜爱"、"对……欣喜若狂"时，其后通常使用介词 over 或 about，如：

They went into raptures at the good news.
听到这个好消息后，他们欣喜若狂。

She went into raptures over the dresses they showed her.
看到他们展示给她的那些服装她欣喜若狂。

（2）at the mere mention of ... 仅仅提到……这里的介词 at 为"一经"之意。

3．... under the illusion that country life is somehow superior to

448

town life.

（1）be under the illusion 有这样的错觉/幻觉。其后 that 引导一个同位语从句,如：

> *He is under the illusion that he is always right.*
>
> 他错以为他总是对的。

（2）be superior to ... 比……优越,胜过。含比较之意,用于两人或两个事物之间的比较,如：

> *Many critics consider Browning superior to Tennyson as a poet.*
>
> 许多评论家认为,作为诗人,勃朗宁胜过丁尼生。

（3）be superior to 还可引申为"不为……所影响"、"拒绝"等意,用于此意时,介词可用 above 替换,如：

> *He's superior to/above bribery.*
>
> 他拒收贿赂。

当表示"在……方面胜过……"时,通常使用 be superior in ... to ... 或 be superior to ... in ...这一结构,如：

> *He felt superior in mathematics to John.*
>
> 他觉得自己的数学比约翰强。

4. He is forever talking about the friendly people, ...

这里的副词 forever 与正在进行时态的一同使用,表示出作者的不满、不快这样的感情色彩。always、forever、constantly 和 continually 等副词同进行时态的一同使用,除表示某事经常发生外,往往还表示说话人对发生的此类事情的不满、厌烦等。

5. Nothing can be compared, he maintains, with the first cockcrow, ..., the sight of the rising sun glinting on the trees and pastures.

（1）compare ... with ... 将……同……相比。用于两者间的比较,以发现其异同之处,如：

> *Compare this article with that one, and you'll see which*

is better.

把这篇文章同那篇文章进行比较,你就会看出哪一篇文章更好些。

(2) he maintains 他坚持认为。在句子中作插入成分。

(3) glinting on the trees and pastures 为现在分词短语,在句子中做介词宾语 the rising sun 的补足语。分词短语的这一用法,常用于某些介词宾语之后,如:

Here is a picture of our manager talking intimately with one of our staff.

这是一张我们的经理同我们的一位工作人员亲切交谈的相片。

6. ...the long and friendless winter evenings in front of the TV — virtually the only form of entertainment.

此处形容词 friendless 的使用为暗喻的一种修辞手法,即使用修饰人的形容词(friendless)来修饰事物(因为 winter evenings 不可能 friendless)。这样来使用的形容词为转类形容词(transferred epithet)。这种用法不仅使文字显得更为生动,而且更为简洁,比较:

They have spent on the project several nights during which they did not sleep.

They spent several sleepless nights on the project.

他们为了这个项目度过了好几个不眠之夜。

7. Why people are prepared to tolerate ... is beyond me.

(1) why, 连接副词,在本句中引导一个主语从句。

(2) be prepared to do ... 愿意做……,准备好做……文中表示"甘愿"的含义。其后为名词时,通常构成 be prepared for ...,如:

We must be prepared for twists and turns.

我们必须准备好经受挫折。

(3) beyond me 我所无法理解的。

450

8. **They could be saved so much misery and expense if they chose to live...**

本句使用了与现在事实不符的虚拟语气结构,可译作"如果他们选择……,他们本可省掉诸多苦楚与开支"(事实是他们未做此选择,因此只能忍受……)。在动词 save 后面可以使用双宾语结构。将此句改为主动语态后为:To live in the city could save them so much misery and expense. 如文中那样,本主动语态句子中的间接宾语 them 提前作了主语,而直接宾语 misery and expense 作为保留宾语留在了句子中。

9. **If you can do without the few ... with the best that life can offer.**

do without 没有……也行,如:

> *People can do without a lot of things , but they cannot do without food .*
>
> 有许多东西人们没有也能过得去,但是没有食物则不行。

有时用来表达"用不着"之意,如:

> *We can do without your criticisms , thank you .*
>
> 我们用不着你的批评,多谢了。

10. **Some of my acquaintances in the country come up to town once or twice a year to visit the theatre as a special treat.**

come up to town 中 up 为副词,其反义词为 down:

> *The tourists went up/down the hill .*
>
> 旅游者上/下了山。
>
> *The prices have gone up/down .*
>
> 物价上涨/下降了。

还主要用来表示:

(1)去城市用 up,去乡下用 down,如:

> *He went up to the city .*
>
> 他进城了。

He went down to the country.

他下乡了。

(2)向北用 up,向南用 down,如:

The swallow flies up north in spring and down south in autumn.

燕子春天往北飞,秋天往南飞。

(3)入校用 up,离校用 down,如:

He went up to Beijing University last year.

他去年进了北京大学。

Shelley was sent down from Oxford.

雪莱被牛津大学开除过。

11. For them this is a major operation which involves considerable planning.

major operation、considerable planning 与前句中的 special treat 这些用词均具有夸张的色彩,产生诙谐效果,与结果(即下一句内容)一起,更强调在农村生活的不便。

12. As the play draws to its close, . . .

draw to a close 临近结束。这里 its 指"戏的",如:

The summer vacation is drawing to a close.

暑假即将结束。

13. The city dweller never experiences anxieties of this sort.

anxieties of this sort 这种焦虑。一般情况下,在 this sort . . .、this kind of . . . 和 this type of . . . 这类的结构中,介词 of 后的名词多用单数形式,如:

this kind of cigarette 这种烟

this kind of car 这种汽车

this type of sentence 这种句子类型

当名词为复数时,如文中那样,常常将 sort、kind、type 等放置在介词 of 之后。

14. ... are only a short bus ride away.

a short bus ride away 乘公共汽车一会儿就到。

15. There is so much variety that you never have to make do with second best.

(1) make do with 以……将就,以……勉强应对,如:

The armchairs haven't yet arrived so we have to make do with these stools.

扶手椅还未到,我们只得用凳子将就了。

(2) second best 第二好的东西,仅次于最好的东西。

16. Nor is the city without its moments of beauty.

nor 并非,也不。为否定词,用于句首时,句子的主语与谓语动词要倒装。

17. There is something comforting about the warm glow shed by ...

comforting 令人慰藉的。为形容词,由于 something 为不定代词,因此需将其置于 something 之后修饰该词。

18. Few things could be more impressive than the peace that ... when the thousands that travel to work ...

(1) few things 没有什么东西。few 用于表示基本否定的含义,意即"没有什么能比……更令人难忘"。

(2) 两个 that 均为关系代词,和关系副词 when 都用来引导定语从句,分别修饰 peace、weekends 和 the thousands。句子中的 the thousands 指成千上万的人。

19. It has always been a mystery to me why city dwellers, who appreciate all these things, obstinately pretend that they would...

it 为先行词,作形式主语。连接副词 why 引导的从句作句子的逻辑主语。who 关系代词,引导一个非限制性定语从句,修饰 city dwellers,起到对其进一步说明的作用。

📑 语法 Grammar in use

过去分词的用法

1.构成完成时态

> *I haven't seen him this morning.*
> 我今天上午没见过他。

2.构成被动语态

> *Smithers has been sent to California for a year.*
> 史密瑟斯已被派到加利福尼亚 1 年了。

3.作形容词

> *We cannot refuse to teach children the required subjects.*
> 我们无法拒绝教授孩子们那些必修课程。

4.书面语中引导具有被动含义的过去分词结构(也称非限定性从句),作状语表示原因、时间、伴随、方式、让步等

> *Saddened by their betrayal, she resigned.*
> 他们的背叛令她伤心,因此她辞职了。
>
> *Viewed from a distance, the island of Nepenthe looked like a cloud.*
> 从远处眺望,尼彭西岛就像一朵云。

过去分词前面可以有从属连词,如:

> *Although built before the war, the engine is still in perfect order.*
> 虽然这台发动机是战前制造的,但仍然工作良好。
>
> *If accepted for this post, you will be informed by May 1st.*
> 如果同意你就任此职,你会在 5 月 1 日得到通知。

在 after、before、since、on 和 in 之后不能直接跟过去分词,而需要用"being ＋过去分词"或"having been ＋过去分词",如:

> *After/On being informed the flight would be delayed, we*

454

made other arrangement.

在我们得知飞机要推迟起飞后,我们另作了安排。

注意:过去分词结构的逻辑主语应该与主句的主语一致。

5. 可以置于名词之后构成过去分词结构以代替关系从句

It doesn't have to be someone appointed by the government.

不见得非得是政府指定的人选。

Many of those questioned in the poll agreed with the party's policy on defence.

在这项民意测验中,被问及的人们中,有许多人赞成这个党派在防卫方面的政策。

📂 词汇学习 **Word study**

1. **beyond**

(1) *prep.*(空间)在……那一边,远处:

In the distance, beyond the river, was a small town.

远处,河的那一边,是个小镇。

(2) *prep.*(时间)迟于,晚于:

Don't stay there beyond midnight.

不要在那儿呆到半夜。

The new law extends this ban beyond 2000.

这项新法律将这一项禁令延长到了 2000 年。

(3) *prep.*(数量或限度)大于,超过:

Beyond a certain level of tiredness, it is impossible to work productively.

疲劳程度超过一定限度,就不可能有效地工作。

(4) *prep.*(能力、可能性、理解力等)超出,非……可及:

Tonight's performance has been cancelled due to circumstances beyond our control.

由于某些我们无法控制的情况,今天晚上的演出予以取消了。

The keyhole on the gate was beyond the girl's reach.

大门上的锁孔那个女孩够不着。

(5) *adv.* 在更远处,再往后:

This train goes to London and all stations beyond.

这列火车驶往伦敦及以远的各站。

2. breed (bred, bred)

(1) *vi., vt.* 产仔,繁殖:

Some animals will not breed if they are kept in cages.

有些动物关在笼子内就不产仔。

(2) *vt.* 培育,培养,养育:

He breeds tropical fish.

他培育热带鱼。

He was bred to be a gentleman.

他被培养成一个绅士。

(3) *vt.* 酿成,产生,惹起:

Flies and dirt breed disease.

苍蝇和灰尘引起疾病。

All this uncertainty breeds insecurity.

所有这些不确定因素导致不稳定。

3. pretend

(1) *vi., vt.* 假装,伪装(后加宾语/ that 从句/不定式):

He often pretends deafness when you ask him an awkward question!

每当你问他难以回答的问题时他就经常装聋。

She pretended (that) she didn't know me when we met in the street.

我们在大街上相遇时她假装不认识我。

456

Don't pretend to know what you don't know.

不懂不要装懂。

（2）*vt*. 扮作，假设(后加 that 从句/不定式)：

The children pretended（that）they were dinosaurs.

这些孩子们扮做恐龙。

Let's pretend to be on the moon.

让我们假装在月球上。

（3）*vt*. 自称，声称(常用于否定句和疑问句,后加不定式)：

He doesn't pretend to be a scholar.

他不自命是个学者。

✍ 练习答案 Key to written exercises

1. 关键句型、难点练习答案

See text.

2. 多项选择题答案

1 d	2 b	3 a	4 c	5 a	6 c
7 b	8 b	9 a	10 b	11 b	12 a

Lesson 42
Modern cavemen
现代洞穴人

📖 **课文详注** **Further notes on the text**

1. Cave exploration, ..., as it has come to be known, is ...

as ... known 是由从属连词引导的方式状语从句,课文中作插入语,表示"正如人们已开始知道的那样"。代词 it 指 cave exploration 或 pot-holing。as 除可用来引导时间、原因、让步等状语从句外,还可用来引导方式状语从句,表示"正如"之意,如:

We'd better leave the things as they are.

我们最好让这些东西保持其原来的样子。

2. Perhaps it is the desire for solitude or the chance of making an unexpected discovery that lures people ...

(1) 本句中 it is ... that ...结构为强调句式,由其正常结构 The desire for solitude or the chance of making an unexpected discovery lures people ... 变化而来。被强调的部分是正常结构中的主语,即 the desire for ...or the chance of ..., lures 为句子中的谓语动词。这种结构常常被译作"正是……"。有关强调 it 的用法参见第 21 课课文注释 12。

(2) 动词 lure 通常用来表示以强有力的或无法抗拒的方式"吸引"、"诱惑"之意,如:

The scent lured the hound on.

气味吸引猎犬前进。

Lured by the lust of gold, the pioneers pushed onward.

458

在黄金欲的诱惑下,开拓者们奋力向前。

3. **For him, caves have the same peculiar fascination which high mountains have for the climber.**

(1) for him 对他来说。这里的 him 泛指洞穴探险者。

(2) the same 不仅可以与 as、that 搭配使用,而且还可以同 who、which(较少用)为 where 等搭配使用,均表达"与……一样"之意,如:

> *He's the same man who/that was here yesterday.*
> 他就是昨天在这里的那个人。
>
> *I was born in the same room where my brother was born.*
> 我们弟兄二人都出生在这间屋子里。

但是,如果后面为省略句,即一个名词或代词(作从句主语)时,通常使用 as,如:

> *I read the same book as you.*
> 我与你读同样的书。
>
> *Her hair's the same colour as her mother's.*
> 她头发的颜色跟她母亲的一样。

上述两例中 as 不能用 that 等替代。

4. **It can take as long as eight days to rig up rope ladders and to establish supply bases before a descent can be made into a very deep cave.**

(1) as long as eight days 长达 8 天的时间。这里用 as...as...结构强调所用天数之多。it 在句子中为先行词 it 的使用方法,其后的两个动词不定式短语 to rig up ... 和 to establish ... 为逻辑主语。

(2) rig up 临时/草草搭起,架起,如:

> *Some of the soldiers had rigged up tents for the night.*
> 其中一些士兵已经搭起了过夜的帐篷。

(3) make a descent into ... 下降进入……,如:

459

They made a descent into the mine.

他们下了矿井。

Finally they discovered the crater and made a descent into it.

他们终于发现了火山口并走了进去。

在该句的从句中用的是被动语态结构，即将该短语结构中的宾语 a descent 提前作了主语。

5．As it is only six feet across, ...

as 为从属连词，引导一个原因状语从句，即"由于它(指洞口)仅 6 英尺宽……"。

6．The cave might never have been discovered had not the entrance been spotted ...

"might ＋完成时态"结构用来表示过去可能发生而没有发生的事情，如：

You were stupid to try climbing up there. You might have killed yourself.

你试图在那里攀登是愚蠢的。你也许会摔死的。

使用这一结构时，往往含有批评或责备的意味。这个结构同后面的 had not ...构成虚拟语气结构。had not ...为非真实性条件状语从句，省略了 if。正常的结构为：if the entrance had not been spotted by ...非真实性条件状语从句中 if 的省略多用于较正式的文体之中，并且该从句中的主语后通常为 were 或 had，或情态助动词 should。省略 if 的非真实性条件状语从句，需使用倒装结构形式，如：

Had I realized what you intended I should not have wasted my time trying to explain matters to you.

如果我本来了解你的意图，我就不会浪费时间向你作解释了。

Should you change your mind, let us know.

460

你如果改变主意,就告诉我们。

7. ... it has become a sort of pot-holers' Everest.

句子中的 it 指 Gouffre Berger 洞,把它比作 Everest 是暗喻手法。

8. ... much of it still remains to be explored.

remains to be explored 有待于进一步勘探。句子中的 it 指 Gouffre Berger 洞,much of it 意即"这个洞中的许多东西"。

9. They had to edge their way along this, sometimes wading ..., or swimming ...

edge their way 侧身缓缓……向前移动。sometimes wading across... 与 or swimming across ...为两个现在分词短语,在句子中作方式状语,修饰 edge。

10. They plunged into the lake, and after loading ..., let the ...

plunged ... 和 let ...在句子中并列作谓语。and after loading ...在句子中作插入语,说明动作 let 发生的时间。

11. To protect themselves from the icy water, they had to ...

protect ... from ... 保护……以免……有关动词 protect 的用法,见本课词汇部分。文中 To protect themselves from the icy water 为动词不定式,作目的状语。将作目的状语的动词不定式置于句首较将其置于句后更为正式,语气较重。

12. At the far end of the lake, ...

at the far end of the lake 在湖的顶那头/尽头。介词短语,在句子中作地点状语。根据其后所随内容的不同,短语介词 at the end of ...可表示"在……底(时间状语)"、"在……结尾(尽头,为地点状语)"和"达……限度(程度状语)",如:

They went to Beijing at the end of last year.
他们去年年底去了北京。

You'll find an index at the end of this book.
书后有索引备查。

She was at the end of her patience.

她已经忍无可忍了。

13. ... an insistent booming sound which they found was caused by a small waterspout shooting down ...

...which was caused by ... of the cave 为定语从句,修饰 sound。They found 为插入语,对其前面的成分作进一步的追加说明。除 find 外,常见用于此类插入语的动词还有 think, hope, guess, believe, suppose, wonder, see, know 等,如:

This, I suppose, will give you some idea of our stand on the issue.

这个,我想,可以帮助你们对我们在此问题上的立场有所了解。

The book he lent you, I think, was both interesting and instructive.

他借给你的那本书我觉得既有趣又有教育意义。

14. Squeezing through a cleft in the rocks, ..., the size of a huge concert hall.

Squeezing ... the rocks,现在分词短语,在句子中作时间状语,说明动作 arrived at 发生的时间。the size of a huge concert hall,同位语,对 cavern 做进一步的补充说明。

15. After switching on powerful arc lights, they saw great stalagmites—some of them over forty feet high—rising up like tree-trunks to meet the stalactites suspended from the roof.

switch on ... 打开……,拧开……some of ... feet high 前后用破折号隔开,为插入语,对 stalagmites 作进一步说明。rising up like ... roof 为现在分词短语,在句子中作宾语 stalagmites 的补足语。to meet ... the roof 动词不定式短语,在句子中作结果状语。suspended ... the roof,过去分词短语,作定语,修饰 stalactites。like tree-trunks 像树干似地。介

462

词短语作状语,修饰 rising up。这里使用了比喻词 like,为明喻手法。

16. **Round about, piles of ... glistened in all the colours of the rainbow.**

round about 周围,四周。作地点状语,修饰 glisten。in all the colours of the rainbow,直译为"以彩虹中的各种颜色",意即"像彩虹一样"。

17. **In the eerie silence of the cavern, ...**

in the ... cavern 为状语,提至句首使用,主要是为了使句子结构更为紧凑和对该状语部分进行强调。比较:

The only sound that could be heard in the eerie silence of the cavern was made by water which dripped continuously from the high dome above them.

📖 **语法 Grammar in use**

现在分词的用法

1. 构成动词进行时态

Cathy has been looking at the results.

凯茜一直在看那些结果。

2. 作形容词

Gloria was quite enchanting to be with.

葛洛里亚非常迷人。

3. 引导现在分词结构作状语表示时间、原因、条件、让步等

(1) 作时间状语时可以用于时间连词 after, before, since, when 和 while 之后,也可用于介词 on 和 in 之后,但不能用于像 as、as soon as、directly、until 等连词之后,如:

Since phoning you this morning, I have changed my plans.

从今天早上给你打电话之后,我就改变了计划。

如果表示同一个人几乎在同一时刻做两件事,在分词前可以不用任何时间连词,此分词结构置于主句之前,如果主语非常明确也可以置于主句之后,如:

Walking down Newbury Street, they spotted the same man again.

沿纽伯利街前行,他们又看见了那个人。

He looked at me, suddenly realizing that he was talking to a stranger.

他望着我,突然意识到他在同一个陌生人谈话。

也可用现在分词结构表示做完一件事紧接着做另一件事,如:

Leaping out of bed, he dressed so quickly that he put his boots on the wrong feet.

他从床上一跃而起,匆忙地穿戴起来,以致于穿错了靴子。

(2) 作原因状语,如:

Having forgotten his fear, Amy had become bored and restless.

由于忘记了恐惧,艾米已变得烦躁不安。

(3) 现在分词结构可以用于 if 和 unless 之后,作条件状语,如:

Unless paying by credit card, please pay in cash.

请付现金,除非使用信用卡。

(4) 现在分词可以用于连词 although、even though、though 和 while 之后,作让步状语从句,如:

While admitting that he received the stolen jewellery, he denied having taken part in the robbery.

尽管承认收受了盗窃的珠宝,但是他否认参与了抢劫。

4. being/having been + 过去分词(现在分词的被动形式)表示被动

Having been left fatherless in early childhood he was

464

brought up by his uncle .

由于他幼年时期就失去了父亲,所以他是由他的叔父抚养成人的。

注意:分词与谓语动词必须同用一个主语,如:

Reading my newspaper , I heard the doorbell ring . (= I was reading my newspaper and I heard the doorbell ring .)

读报纸时,我听到门铃响了。

当分词结构跟在宾语之后时,它必须与宾语相关联。这样句子才能成立,如:

I found him lying on the floor . (= He was lying on the floor .)

我发现他躺在地板上。

但是上述规则不适用于一些包含无关联分词的固定词组,如:broadly/generally/strictly speaking(广义地/一般地/严格地说)、considering (考虑到)、judging (从……判断)等,如:

Strictly speaking , you ought to sign the visitors' book before entering the club .

严格地说,在你进入俱乐部之前应该在来客登记簿上签名。

5. 书面语中与主语连用表示某一事实或情形与主句所述相关或与主句为因果关系

此种结构也称之为独立主格结构,如:

The subject having been opened , he had to go on with it .

这个主题已经展开,他不得不继续。

有时这一结构前用 with,但此时现在分词不能是 being 或 having,如:

The old man stood up with tears running down his face .

那位老人站起来,泪流满面。

6. 现在分词结构代替关系从句作定语

She is now a British citizen working for the Medical Research Council.

她现在是为医学研究委员会工作的英国公民。

Anyone following this advice could find himself in trouble.

任何遵循这一忠告的人都会遇到麻烦。

📁 词汇学习 Word study

1. require *vt*.

(1) 需要,有赖于(后跟宾语/动词-ing 形式/that 从句):

> *Is there anything you require?*
>
> 你需要什么吗?
>
> *Universities require a lot more money for research.*
>
> 大学需要更多的资金进行研究工作。

注意:此词较为正式,在口语中常用 need 或 want。

(2) 要求,命令,规定(后跟宾语 + 不定式/that 从句):

> *Candidates are required to present themselves fifteen minutes before the examination begins.*
>
> 按规定考生在考试开始前 15 分钟到场。
>
> *The regulations require that all students shall attend at least 90 percent of the lectures.*
>
> 这些规定要求所有的学生至少听 90% 的讲座。

2. protect *vt*.

(1) (against, from) 保护,防护:

> *Surely the function of the law is to protect everyone's rights.*
>
> 当然法律的作用就在于保护每一个人的权利。
>
> *He raised his arm to protect his face from the blow.*
>
> 他抬起胳膊不让面部受到击打。

466

> *The fence along the middle of the road is intended to protect vehicles against crashing into each other.*
>
> 公路中间的隔离栏是用来防止车辆相撞的。

（2）为……保险：

> *The insurance policy protect you against theft.*
>
> 你如果遭窃,保险单保证偿还损失。

3.switch

（1）switch on 打开(电器开关)：

> *Please switch the light on; it's getting dark.*
>
> 请打开灯,天黑了。
>
> *With this special instrument, you can set the cooker to switch on by itself while you're out.*
>
> 用这个特殊的装置,在你出门前你可以设定电饭锅自行开启。

（2）switch off 关闭(电器开关)：

> *Switch it off when you've finished using the electric typewriter.*
>
> 用毕,请将电动打字机关闭。

（3）switch over 改变电流,彻底改变,改变频道：

> *The power machine will be switched over at midnight.*
>
> 这台发电机在午夜时会改变电流。
>
> *I'm tired of this programme; switch (it) over to another channel.*
>
> 我对这个节目烦透了,换到另一个频道。

✍ 练习答案　Key to written exercises

1.关键句型、难点练习答案

See text.

2．多项选择题答案

1	d	2	a	3	b	4	c	5	c	6	b
7	d	8	b	9	c	10	a	11	d	12	b

Lesson 43
Fully insured
全保险

📖 **课文详注 Further notes on the text**

1 . ... to insure yourself in the event of bad weather .

in the event of 万一,倘若,如:

> *In the event of fire , ring the alarm bell .*
> 如果着火,就按警铃。
>
> *In the event of rain , the party will be held indoors .*
> 如果下雨,聚会在室内举行。

2 . Needless to say , the bigger the risk an insurance company takes , the higher the premium you will have to pay .

(1) needless to say 不用说。作插入语成分。

(2) the bigger . . . , the higher . . . 为 the + 形容词比较级结构,用来表达两个变化的同时发生。汉语通常译为"越……越……"。前面的 the + 形容词的比较级为主句,后面的为从句。有关用法参见第 9 课课文注释 9。

(3) take a risk 冒险,承担风险,如:

> *She's too sensible to take a risk when she's driving .*
> 她开车时很理智,不冒风险。
>
> *They took grave risks to save persons in peril .*
> 他们冒着极大的危险营救危难之中的人们。

3 . It is not uncommon to hear that a shipping company has made a claim for ...

(1) not uncommon 构成双重否定结构,uncommon 为含否定意义的词。双重否定句通常由否定形式的谓语动词＋含有否定意义的词(否定词)构成。

（2）make a claim for 要求得到,如:

> They've made a claim for compensation according to the seriousness of the accident.

他们已经根据事故的严重性,提出了赔偿要求。

4. But the claim made by a local authority to recover the cost of salvaging a sunken pie dish must surely be unique.

made by a local authority,过去分词短语,作定语,修饰 claim。

to recover ... pie dish,动词不定式短语,作定语,修饰 claim。

5. ... the best way to transport the dish would be by canal, so they insured it for the trip.

to transport the dish,动词不定式短语,作定语,修饰 way。by canal 以运河水运方式。代词 it 指 dish,这里的 trip 指 to transport the dish。

6. At the same time, a number of teenagers climbed ...

介词短语 at the same time 可以用来表达两种意义:(1)同时(如文中例句),一齐;(2)但是,然而。用于前一种情况时表示两者以上的动作同时开始或进行;用于后一种情况时,主要表示语义转折,对刚才所提及情况从另一方面加以说明,如:

> He's answering a phone call, jotting down something at the same time.

他一边听电话一边记下些东西。

> This is a difficult problem, at the same time, it is very interesting.

这个问题很难,但是很有趣。

> The boy is naughty, at the same time, he is hard at his studies.

这个男孩调皮,但是学习很用功。

470

a number of 若干,不少,很多。用于表示不确定的数量概念,作前置定语使用,后需用可数名词的复数形式,如:

> *A treaty usually consists of a number of articles and sections.*
>
> 条约通常包括许多条款。

名词 number 前可用 large、great、quite、small 等修饰,但用 quite 修饰时,quite 必须置于不定冠词 a 之前。

7. **Shivering in their wet clothes, the teenagers looked on while ...**

shivering in their wet clothes, 现在分词短语,作方式状语,修饰 looked on,意即"那些孩子们穿着湿漉漉的衣服颤抖着在一旁观看"。

8. **They had little difficulty in finding it，...**

在表示"在……方面有困难"时,have difficulty 后要使用介词 with + 名词/代词这样的结构,如:

> *She has great difficulty with her maths homework.*
>
> 她做数学作业有很大困难。

在表示"做……有困难"时,have difficulty 后要使用介词 in + 动名词或直接使用动名词的结构形式,如:

> *You won't have much difficulty（in）getting to know people in Italy.*
>
> 在了解意大利人方面,你不会有太大困难。

在 difficulty 之后不可使用动词不定式形式,如不能说:

> * *You won't have much difficulty to get to know people in Italy.*

9. **Eventually chains were fixed to one end of the dish and a powerful winch was put into operation.**

（1）fix ... to ... 把……固定在……,如:

> *He fixed the mirror to the wall.*
>
> 他把镜子固定在墙上。

(2) put ... into operation 使……开始工作/运转,使……生效,如:

> *The newly-introduced machine has been set up and put into operation.*
>
> 新引进的机器已经安装好并且已经投入使用。

10. **... because one edge was resting against the side of the canal.**

rest (...) against ... (把……)靠在……,如:

> *The ladder rested against the wall.*
>
> 梯子靠在墙上。
>
> *Don't rest your head against my arm.*
>
> 不要把你的头枕在我的胳膊上。

11. **... and one of the men started up the truck.**

start up 启动,发动,如:

> *How do you start up this motor-cycle?*
>
> 你怎么发动这辆摩托车?

12. **There was a danger that the wave would rebound off the ... and send the dish plunging into the water again.**

that 为连词,引导同位语从句,作 danger 的同位语。plunging into the water again,现在分词短语,作 send 的宾语 dish 的补足语。

语法 Grammar in use

过去分词与现在分词作形容词的区别

大多数现在分词均可作形容词用,如 frightening stories(令人恐怖的故事)。许多动词的过去分词也能作形容词用,如 a broken window(= a window which has been broken 一扇打破了的窗户)、a frozen lake(= a lake which is frozen 一个冻了冰的湖泊)、a locked door (= a door which is locked 一扇锁了的门)。

过去分词作形容词常与人称主语连用,表示对某事物的感觉,如:

I was very interested in the lesson.

我对这一课非常感兴趣。

I didn't enjoy the party because I was bored.

我觉得这次聚会没意思,我都厌烦了。

现在分词作形容词则常与非人主语连用,形容使我们产生某种感觉的人或事物,如:

The story is exciting.

这个故事激动人心。

Sheila's party was pretty boring.

希拉的那个聚会使人厌烦。

试比较:

If a story is exciting, you are excited when you read it.

如果一个故事令人兴奋,你读的时候就会感到兴奋。

You may be worried if you have a worrying problem.

假如你有一个令人担忧的问题,你可能感到担忧。

After a tiring day, you feel tired.

在度过使人劳累的一天之后,你会感到很累。

📁 词汇学习 Word study

1. insure *vt.*

(1) 保证,担保,保证获得(英国英语常用 ensure,后跟 that 从句或 + 间接宾语 + 直接宾语):

I shall try to insure that your stay here is a pleasant one.

我将保证你在这儿会很开心。

This medicine will ensure you a good night's sleep.

这种药能保证你睡个好觉。

(2) (against) 为……投保,为……上保险 (用于此义时英、美拼写

473

相同）：

> *My house is insured against fire.*
> 我的房子上了火险。

> *I lost my camera on holiday and I wasn't insured for it.*
> 在度假期间我把照相机丢了,而且我也没为它上保险。

2. purchase

（1）*vt*. 买,购买,购置（较正式,一般用 buy）：

> *He sold the house he had purchased only two years before.*
> 他卖掉了他两年前刚买的房子。

> *The purchasing power of the dollar has declined.*
> 美元的购买力已经下跌。

（2）*vt*.（以努力、受苦或牺牲等）换得：

> *They purchased life at the expense of honour.*
> 他们以荣誉换取生命。

> *The slaves purchased freedom with their blood.*
> 那些奴隶们以鲜血换取自由。

（3）*n*. 购买,购置(常用于正式文体中),购买的东西(较旧,现常用 shopping)：

> *We need to know the exact day of purchase.*
> 我们需要知道确切的购买日期。

> *Among his purchases were several tins of beans.*
> 他买的东西中有几听豌豆。

> *She made several purchases in the dress shop.*
> 她在服装店买了几件衣服。

3. oblige

（1）*vt*. 强使,迫使(常用被动语态)：

> *Falling profits obliged them to close the factory.*
> 利润下跌迫使他们关闭了工厂。

> *He looked at me so blankly that I felt obliged to explain.*

他不解地看着我,我觉得有必要给他做一番解释。

(2) *vt.*,*vi.* 帮······的忙,施恩惠于,帮忙,施恩惠:

*Could you oblige me with a pen and a piece of paper,
please?*

请你给我一枝笔和一张纸,好吗?

(3) *vt.* 使感激(常用于被动语态):

We're obliged to you for dinner.

我们感谢你请我们吃饭。

Here's the information.

这就是那些信息。

Oh, much obliged（to you）.

噢,非常感谢。

✍ 练习答案 Key to written exercises

1. 关键句型、难点练习答案

See text.

2. 多项选择题答案

1	b	2	c	3	c	4	b	5	b	6	a
7	d	8	c	9	c	10	a	11	d	12	b

Lesson 44
Speed and comfort
又快捷又舒适

📖 **课文详注 Further notes on the text**

1. **It is almost impossible to take your mind off the journey.**

   take one's mind off ... 不想……,将注意力从……上移开,如:

   Then she had already taken her mind off him and his wealth.

   那会儿她早已不再想他和他的财富了。

2. **... for the monotonous rhythm of the wheels clicking on the rails soon lulls you to sleep.**

   lull someone to sleep 哄某人入睡,如:

   It took us all night to lull the baby to sleep, singing to him and walking up and down with him.

   为了哄他入睡,我们一整夜又是给他唱歌又是抱着他踱来踱去。

3. **During the day, sleep comes in snatches.**

   in snatches 断断续续地。也可使用介词 by 代替 in,如:

   He did the work in/by snatches.

   他断断续续地做这件工作。

   Since then she often sleeps in snatches, waking up in horror suddenly.

   自那以来,她的睡眠经常断断续续,会突然惊恐地醒来。

4. **If you are lucky enough to get a sleeper, you spend half the night staring at ... of fumbling to find ...**

476

（1）to get a sleeper，动词不定式短语，在句子中作结果状语。作结果状语的动词不定式短语前通常可以用副词 only 加强其语气，使其句子成分的作用更加明显，如：

> *What you have said was only to make him angrier.*
> 你说的话只会使他更生气。

当句子中带有 too 或 enough 这样的词时，其后的动词不定式通常为结果状语，如：

> *She was too young to understand all that.*
> 她太年轻了还不能理解所有这些事情。

> *We found the room not big enough to hold so many people.*
> 我们发现这个房间不够大，坐不下这么多人。

（2）spend some time（in）doing sth. 花费一定时间做某事。表示上述意义时，spend 后的动词应构成动词-ing 形式或构成介词 in + 动名词的形式，不能直接使用动词不定式。

5. **Inevitably you arrive at your destination almost exhausted.**

almost exhausted 在句子中作伴随状况状语。

6. **..., but more often than not, ...**

more often than not 往往，多半，如：

> *More often than not the patient recovers.*
> 这个病人多半能恢复健康。

> *More often than not she misses the bus.*
> 她往往误车。

7. **By comparison, ferry trips or cruises offer a...**

by comparison 相比而言，相形之下。也可为 in comparison。在使用时，无论用 by comparison 还是用 in comparison，句中的修饰语用原级，通常不用比较级，如：

> *This way of putting it makes the other way seem tame by/in comparison.*

和这种说法相比较,那个就显得软弱无力了。

The old method suffers by comparison.

老方法相形见绌。

在点明与之比较的事物时,一般用 in comparison with ...,如:

Our achievement is nothing in comparison with what they have done.

与他们所做的事情相比较,我们的成就算不了什么。

8. ...,always assuming, of course, that the sea is calm.

always ... calm 为插入语,对破折号前的内容进行条件上的补充说明。

9. If it is not, and you are likely to get seasick, no form of transport could be worse.

(1) 由于意义明确 if it is not 后面省略了 calm。

(2) 这里的连词 and 用来连接一个表示结果的句子,意即"那么"、"则"。and 的这一用法尤其在口语中很常见,如:

If you speak the truth, and you need have no shame.

如果你说真话,那么你就不必害臊。

10. But nothing can match them for speed and comfort.

for speed and comfort 就速度和舒适而言。这里的介词 for 作"就……而论/而言"讲。

11. Travelling at a height of 30,000 feet, far above the clouds, and at over 500 miles an hour is ...

句子中 at a height of 30,000 feet 和 at over 500 miles an hour 为两个并列的介词短语作状语,修饰动名词 travelling,并与其一同构成动名词短语,在句子中作主语。far above the clouds 作插入语,对 at a height of 30,000 feet 作补充说明。

12. ... there is plenty to keep you occupied.

to keep you occupied,动词不定式,在句子中作定语,修饰 plenty。occupied 为 keep 的宾语补足语。

478

13. **However you decide to spend your time, one thing is certain: ... fresh and uncrumpled.**

however 不管，无论。连接副词，引导让步主语从句。fresh and uncrumpled 精神焕发，毫无倦意。可视为伴随状况状语。冒号后的内容为 one thing 的同位语。

📖 语法 Grammar in use

短语动词

1．短语动词的定义

短语动词是一个动词和一个副词，一个动词和一个介词或者一个动词、一个副词和一个介词的组合，这一组合具有单独的意思。短语动词或是扩展动词的词义或是产生新的词义。

The pain gradually wore off.

疼痛逐渐消逝。

I had to look after the kids.

我得照看孩子们。

2．短语动词宾语的位置

如果短语动词包含一个及物动词和一个副词，宾语往往置于副词之前或之后，如：

Don't give the story away, silly!

别把这事说出去，真笨！

I wouldn't want to give away any secrets.

我可没想泄密。

然而，如果宾语是一个代词，则此代词必须放在副词前，如：

He cleaned it up.

他把它收拾干净了。

如果短语动词包含一个及物动词和一个介词，动词宾语放在动词后面，介词宾语放在介词后面，如：

479

The farmer threatened to set his dogs on them.

那个农民威胁说要让他的狗扑他们。

如果短语动词包含一个及物动词、一个副词和一个介词,动词宾语通常放在副词前,而不放在其后,如:

Multinational companies can play individual markets off against each other.

跨国公司能够挑起单个市场相互竞争。

📁 **词汇学习　Word study**

1. prefer (preferred, preferred) *vt*. 宁可,更喜欢(不用于进行式):

(1) +宾语(+to):

I prefer it to more expensive machines.
我喜欢它而不喜欢更贵的机器。

Would you like meat or fish?
你喜欢肉还是鱼?
I'd prefer fish, please.
请给我鱼。

(2) +动词-ing(+to):

I prefer singing to acting.
我喜欢唱歌不喜欢跳舞。

I prefer swimming rather than cycling.
我更喜欢游泳而不是骑车。

(3) +带 to 的动词不定式:

I prefer to swim rather than to cycle.
我喜欢游泳而不是骑车。

He chose Spain, but personally I'd prefer to go to Greece.
他选择了西班牙,可是就我个人来说我更喜欢去希腊。

480

(4) + 宾语 + 不定式：

Would you prefer me to dry the dishes ?

你愿意让我把碟子擦干吗？

I'd prefer you not to smoke .

我倒愿意你不吸烟。

(5) + that 从句：

Would you prefer that we reschedule the meeting for next week ?

你愿意我们将下周开的会议改一下时间吗？

2. manage

(1) *vt .* 管理,处理,经营：

Has she had any experience of managing large projects ?

她有管理大型项目的经验吗？

(2) *vt .* 设法得到,努力完成：

I'm afraid I can't manage the time to see you at the moment .

恐怕眼下我忙得没时间去看你。

The little boy had somehow managed to tie his shoelaces together .

不管怎样那个小男孩总算把鞋带系上了。

(3) *vt ., vi .* 驾驭,管住,应付：

She knows how to manage him when he's angry .

他生气时,她知道怎样对付他。

Don't worry about us , we'll manage .

别为我们担心,我们能应付。

(4) *vi .* (on) 勉强生活下去,勉强维持：

After she lost her job , they had to manage on his salary .

她失去工作之后,他们只得靠他的薪水勉强维持。

3．sacrifice

（1）*vt.,vi.* 献祭,以……为祭品：

It was the practice of these people to sacrifice to their gods when rain had not fallen.

当一直不下雨时,这些人们的做法是向他们的神献祭。

（2）*vt.* 牺牲,献出：

The people are prepared to sacrifice everything to achieve victory.

人民已准备好为赢得胜利而不惜牺牲一切。

It is the company's policy to sacrifice short-term profits for the sake of long-term growth.

这个公司的策略是为了长期的发展而牺牲短期的利润。

（3）*n.* 祭品,供品,牺牲：

Success in your job is not worth the sacrifice of your health.

为了工作上的成功而牺牲自己的健康不值得。

His parents made a lot of sacrifices to make sure he got a good education.

他的父母为了保证他能接受良好的教育而付出了很大的牺牲。

✍ 练习答案　Key to written exercises

1．关键句型、难点练习答案

See text.

2．多项选择题答案

1 d	2 c	3 c	4 d	5 b	6 a
7 c	8 d	9 b	10 a	11 c	12 b

Lesson 45
The power of the press
新闻报道的威力

1. In democratic countries any efforts to restrict the freedom of...

to restrict ... press, 动词不定式短语, 作定语, 修饰 any efforts, 即"任何限制新闻自由的企图"。

2. Though we may enjoy reading about the lives of others, it is extremely doubtful whether we would equally enjoy reading about ourselves.

read about 同 read of, 读到, 获悉。在一般情况下可以互换使用, 但就意义而言, read about 通常指"通过阅读了解到有关的详情", 而 read of 通常指"通过阅读一种出版物而获悉一般的情况或消息"。在用法上, read about 可用于进行时形式, 且 read 后用 all、much、a little 等词修饰, 而 read of 则很少用于进行形式, 且 read 后不能用 all、much 等词修饰, 如:

I remember reading about it in English newspaper.

我记得是在一张英文报纸上读到对此事的报道。

I have of course read of the achievements you've made these years.

当然我已从书报中读到过你们这些年来所取得的成就。

3. Acting on the contention that facts are sacred, reporters can cause untold suffering to individuals by publishing details about their private lives.

Acting on ... sacred, 现在分词短语, 作条件状语, 修饰主动词

cause。act on . . . 根据……行动,对……起作用。连词 that 引导的从句为同位语从句,对 contention 作进一步的说明。

4. **As the parents had five children, life was a perpetual struggle against poverty.**

(1) as 由于,因为。从属连词,引导一个原因状语从句。

(2) life was a perpetual struggle against poverty 生活成为了同贫困进行的无休止的斗争。句中将 life 比作 a perpetual struggle against poverty 是暗喻手法。

5. **If they had only had one more child, the fact would have passed unnoticed.**

(1) 从属连词 if 在句中引导一个非真实性条件状语从句,这样从句中所用的 had only had 和主句中所用的 would have passed 均为虚拟语气结构,表述与过去事实不符的假设情况。

(2) unnoticed 过去分词,在句中作方式状语,其作用与表示方式状语的形容词相同。

6. **They would have continued to struggle against economic odds and would have lived in obscurity.**

(1) 本句中 would have continued 与 would have lived 同上句中的 would have passed 一样,均为虚拟语气,用来表示与过去事实不符的假设情况。

(2) struggle against . . . 同……(展开)斗争。其后既可接表示人的名词,也可接表示事物的名词,如:

> *They had to struggle against all kinds of difficulties.*
> 他们得同各种各样的困难做斗争。
>
> *Don't struggle against them.*
> 不要同他们斗了。

严格地讲,在表示"与……斗争"时,介词应该用 with。

(3) in obscurity 默默无闻地;在暗处,状语,如:

> *He lived with fame and wealth but died in obscurity.*

他活着时声名显赫,但死时却无声无息。

A dog hid in obscurity of the thick bushes.

一条狗藏在灌木丛中的阴暗处。

7. But they suddenly became the parents of quintuplets, four girls and a boy, an event which radically changed their lives.

four girls and a boy 作 quintuplets 的同位语。an event ... their lives 为 they became ... of quintuplets 的同位语。

8. ... an aeroplane arrived in Aberdeen bringing sixty reporters and photographers.

bringing ... photographers, 现在分词短语,作方式状语,修饰 arrived,即"一架飞机载着 60 名记者和摄影师抵达阿伯丁镇"。

9. Newspapers and magazines offered the family huge sums for the exclusive rights to publish stories and photographs.

(1) offered the family huge sums 给了这家人一大笔钱。动词 offer 后可使用双宾语结构。句中 the family 作间接宾语,huge sums 作直接宾语。

(2) sum 总数,总和,一笔钱(如文中之意)。使用该词时更着重于具体数量,而不像 amount 一词那样泛指"大量"。通常用 large、huge、vast 等词形容其量的大,用 small、trivial 等词形容其量的小。

10. Gifts poured in ...

pour in 涌入,倒进,如:

Crowds poured in all the morning.

整个上午人们不断地涌进来。

Orders for goods poured in.

订货单不断地涌来。

11. The old farmhouse the family lived in was to be replaced by...

was to be replaced by ... 即 be to do sth. 的被动形式, be to do sth. 结构表示"根据安排将要发生的事情",这里表示"将被

485

……取代"。

12. Reporters kept pressing for interviews so lawyers had to be employed to act as spokesmen ...

（1）press for 迫切要求,敦促,如：

> *They put forward a few problems pressing for solution.*
> 他们提出了几个亟待解决的问题。
>
> *They agreed to press for the conference to deal with the problem.*
> 他们同意敦促大会处理这个问题。

（2）so 因此,所以。并列连词,可用来表示因果关系,如：

> *My sister is expecting me, so I must be off now.*
> 姐姐在等我,我得走了。
>
> *It was already rather late, so we decided to go home.*
> 已经相当晚了,所以我们决定回家。

当 so 用于表达此义时,不要受汉语影响,将 so 同 because（因为）连用。在英语中,使用 because 则不能使用 so,使用 so 时则不能使用 because。

（3）act as 充当,扮演……的角色,如：

> *Many students acted as guides to the visitors.*
> 许多同学为来宾充当向导。
>
> *She acted as a woman teacher in the film.*
> 她在那部电影中扮演了一位女教师的角色。

📖 语法 Grammar in use

形容词的分类

1. 根据其词义

形容词依此可分为品质形容词、类别形容词、色彩形容词、强调形容词和特指形容词等。

（1）品质形容词

表示某人或某物具有某种特性,如 sad、pretty、happy、wise 等。

a sad story 一个伤心的故事

a small child 一个小孩子

a very pretty girl 一个非常美丽的姑娘

（2）类别形容词

表示某物属于某一类,如 financial help 中用形容词 financial (金融)区别是哪一类的帮助,因为有各种各样的帮助, financial help 只是其中之一。

my daily shower 我每天的淋浴

Victorian houses 维多利亚时期的房子

civil war 内战

（3）色彩形容词

表示某物是什么颜色。

a small blue car 一辆蓝色的小轿车

her black eyes 她那双黑眼睛

a bright green suit 一身艳绿色的套装

（4）强调形容词

用在名词前强调对某物的描述或强调程度,常用的这类形容词有 absolute、complete、entire、perfect、positive、pure、real、total、true、utter 等。

He made me feel like a complete idiot.

他使我觉得自己像个十足的傻瓜。

Some of it was absolute rubbish.

其中有一些纯粹是胡说八道。

（5）特指形容词

这类形容词不多,用来表示特指事物或人,其前要有限定词,其后可以跟任何形容词。这类形容词有 additional、first、 next、past、same、certain、following、last、other、existing、main、remaining、usual、previous 等。

the following brief description　下述简单的描述

He wore his usual old white coat.

他身着他常穿的那件白色的旧外套。

2．根据分级与否

(1) 形容词在下列情况下是可分级的：当我们可以想像形容词所指的品质有程度差别，因而可与像 very、too 和 enough 这样的词连用时，如 very good、too good、less good、not good enough等。

an extremely narrow road　一条特别窄的路

a rather clumsy person　一个非常笨手笨脚的人

可以用形容词构成比较级和最高级时，如：big, bigger, biggest; good, better, best 等。

(2) 形容词在下列情况下是不可分级的：当形容词不可加以修饰（即不可与 very、too 等词连用）时；当形容词不能构成比较级和最高级时，如 daily、dead、medical、unique 等。

3．根据所充当的句子成分

还可以分为定语形容词和补足语形容词。大部分形容词在语义不变的情况下，既可以作定语用也可以作补足语用。有一些则只可以作一种而不能作另一种。

an old ticket　一张旧票（定语）

This ticket is old.

这是一张旧票。（补足语）

the angry boy　生气的男孩（定语）

Your mother seems angry.

你妈妈好像生气了。（补足语）

以下形容词只能作补足语：afloat（漂浮）、afraid（害怕）、alight（照亮）、alike（相同）、alive（活着的）、alone（单独的）、ashamed（羞

488

愧)、asleep(睡着)、awake(醒着)。

The children were asleep at 7：00 , but now they're awake .

孩子们 7 点钟就睡着了,但现在他们醒了。

All the hostages on the plane are alive and well .

飞机上所有的人质都活着并且很好。

词汇学习 Word study

1.abuse *vt*.

(1)辱骂,诽谤:

The sergeant major abused the soldiers unmercifully .

那个军事长无情地辱骂士兵。

(2)滥用,妄用:

She is continually abusing her authority by getting other people to do things for her .

她总是不断地滥用她的职权,让他人为她做这个做那个。

He has abused the trust I placed in him .

他辜负了我对他的信任。

注意:abuse 不同于 misuse,后者常用来表示错用某物,如:

I hate to see him misusing my tools .

我讨厌看到他乱用我的工具。

而 abuse 很少用于物,如果用于物的话则暗含毁坏之意,如:

You must have been abusing the knife I lent you——the blade is completely ruined .

你肯定滥用了我借给你的刀子——刀刃全毁了。

(3)虐待,伤害:

He often abuses his wife and children .

他经常虐待他的妻子和孩子们。

489

The arrested man has been physically abused.

被逮捕的那个人身体受到伤害。

2. bring about

(1) 导致,招致,带来:

Major changes will have to be brought about in Chinese industry.

一定要给中国的工业带来大的变革。

Science has brought about many changes in our lives.

科学为我们的生活带来许多变化。

(2) 使(船、舰)掉头行驶:

If the wind changes you'll have to bring the boat about.

如果风向改变你就得将船掉头。

The captain brought the ship about and headed for shore.

船长掉转船头驶向岸边。

3. acquire *vt.*

(1) (尤指通过长期努力)取得,获得,学到,开始具有:

I managed to acquire three tickets for the New Year concert.

我设法搞到 3 张新年音乐会的票。

As our company is expanding, we've had to acquire more office space.

由于我们公司在扩大,我们得获得更多的办公面积。

The boy has acquired some very unpleasant habits recently.

那个男孩最近有一些非常不好的习惯。

(2) (利用探测仪器)捕获目标:

The pilot acquired a target by radar.

飞行员用雷达捕捉到一个目标。

490

✍ 练习答案 **Key to written exercises**

1. 关键句型、难点练习答案

See text.

2. 多项选择题答案

1	b	2	d	3	d	4	b	5	a	6	a
7	b	8	a	9	d	10	c	11	c	12	a

Lesson 46
Do it yourself
自己动手

📖 **课文详注 Further notes on the text**

1. So great is our passion for doing things for ourselves, that we are becoming increasingly less dependent on specialized labour.

(1) So great is our passion 为倒装结构,其正常语序为 Our passion for doing things for ourselves is so great ...以副词 so 开头的句子通常使用倒装结构。这里将 so great 提前是为了对 great 进行强调。全句使用的基本句型为 so ... that ... 太……以至于,引导的结果状语从句。

(2) become/be dependent on 依赖,依靠,如:

Despite technical progress, food production is still completely dependent on weather.

尽管技术进步,食物生产仍然完全依赖于气候。

2. No one can plead ignorance of a subject any longer, for there are countless do-it-yourself publications.

(1) plead ignorance of 以不知道……为借口,如:

She pleaded ignorance of the law.

她以不熟悉法律为借口。

(2) No one 构成了否定形式,因此应使用 any longer,不应使用 no longer。

(3) do-it-yourself 自己动手做的。为合成词,是将一个词组或句子中的每一个单词用连字符连接,作为一个单词来使用的构词形式。这类合成词多用作定语,如:

a can't-be-put-down book 一本爱不释手的书

a wait-and-see policy 一种观望态度

the do-what-you-can-and-take-what-you-need policy 各尽所能各取所需的政策

his nothing-can-be-done attitude 他的无所作为的态度

3．**Armed with the right tools and materials, newlyweds gaily embark on the …**

(1) Armed with … materials, 过去分词短语, 在句中作方式状语, 修饰 embark。

(2) embark on 开始, 如:

> *Mary embarked on her marriage with many hopes and fears.*
>
> 玛丽怀着许多希望与忧虑开始了婚后生活。

4．**Men, particularly, spend hours of their leisure time installing …, laying out …; building garages and making furniture.**

(1) spend 后的动词应构成动词-ing 的动名词形式。句中的 installing、laying out、building 和 making 均为 spend 后使用的动名词形式, 作宾语。

(2) lay out 布置, 设计, 花(钱), 如:

> *He works for a magazine and lays out pictures for it.*
>
> 他为一家杂志工作, 并为其设计图片的版面。
>
> *He laid out all his gains in purchasing land.*
>
> 他把全部所得都用来购置土地。

5．**Some really keen enthusiasts go so far as to build …**

so far as 直到……程度。这是该短语的一种借喻用法。在此意义时无论句子是肯定形式还是否定形式, 虽然 as far as 也可使用, 但多用 so far as, 且其后如用动词时, 均使用带 to 的动词不定式, 如:

> *He went so far as to declare himself infallible on all*

493

occasions.

他狂妄到宣称自己永远正确。

Tom went so far as to disregard the labour discipline.

汤姆竟然到了不遵守劳动纪律的地步。

除上述意义外,so far as 和 as far as 还可用于表示:

(1)直到……为止(指实际距离),如:

She accompanied me as far as the gate.

她一直陪我走到大门口。

用于表达此意义时,as far as 也可用于否定句中,但 so far as 不可用于肯定句中。

(2)就……而论。用于此义时,其后常用动词 know、go、concern 等,如:

As/So far as I know, he can speak only English.

就我所知,他只会讲英语。

6. Shops cater for ... not only by running ..., but by offering...

cater for ... 迎合……, 如:

This play centre caters for children of all ages.

这家游乐中心为各种年龄的儿童服务。

复合连词 not only ... but ... 连接的 by running ... novices 和 by offering ... home 在句子中作方式状语,修饰 cater for。

7. ... but unfortunately not all of us are born handymen.

are born handymen 生来就是能工巧匠。在 be born 后除了可以使用名词外,还可以使用形容词或动词不定式,如:

He was born rich.

他生来就富有。

He was born to succeed.

他命中注定要成功。

8. ... even men live under the delusion that they can do anything, ...

494

live/be/labour under a delusion 抱错误的想法,痴心妄想,如:

> *You are under a delusion in this matter.*
>
> 你对这事有误解。
>
> *Don't live under the delusion that you have the right to abuse privilege.*
>
> 不要总是妄想你有滥用特权的权利。

连词 that 引导的从句作 delusion 的同位语。

9. It is a question of pride as much as anything else.

as ... as anything (else) 不得了,了不得的。在句中作定语,修饰 pride。全句意为"这是个地道的自尊心问题"。再如:

> *It's as easy as anything (else).*
>
> 这事容易的不得了。
>
> *He saw as plainly as anything that they did not feel bound by those agreements.*
>
> 他看得极清楚,他们并不认为受到了那些协议的约束。

10. Last spring my wife suggested that I call in a man to look at our lawn mower.

(1) 动词 call 前省略了 should。在动词 suggest 后的宾语从句中要使用"主语 + should + 动词"或"主语 + 动词原形"这样的虚拟语气结构,如:

> *She has suggested that a meeting (should) be held to discuss our curriculum.*
>
> 她建议召开一次会来讨论我们的课程。

(2) call in ... 把……请来,把……找来,如:

> *Call in a doctor at once.*
>
> 立即请位医生来。
>
> *The librarian has called in all the books.*
>
> 图书管理员把全部图书都收了回去。

11. **... and though I promised to repair it, I had never got round to it.**

get round to ... 抽出时间(做……)。此短语中的副词 round 也可用 around 代替,前者多用于英国英语中,而后者多用于美国英语中。介词 to 后须用名词、代词或动名词形式,如:

Perhaps we'll get round to (doing) it some day.
说不定有一天我们会抽时间做这件事。

I should be able to get round to that job next week.
下周我会找时间去做那件事。

此外,此短语有时还用来表示"开始注意或考虑(做……)",用于此义时,常指"经过较长时间的耽搁后才开始注意或考虑(做……)",如:

After a long delay, he got round to writing the letter.
耽搁了许久之后,他才又开始考虑写信的事情。

12. **I would not hear of the suggestion and said that ...**

I would not hear ... 中 would 表示意愿,意即"我不愿听……"。句中的连词 and 用来表示结果,可译作"于是就说"。

13. **... it needed only a minor adjustment: a turn of a screw here, a little tightening up there, a drop of oil and it would be as good as new.**

(1) 句中 a turn of ...、a little tightening ...、a drop of ... 作 adjustment 的同位语,说明 adjustment 所包含的内容。

(2) as good as 除了可用于表示"如同……一样好"进行同级比较外,还可如课文中那样,作为固定词组使用,起副词作用,表示"和……几乎一样(= almost the same)"、"实际上"、"事实上(= practically)"的意义,如:

This place is as good as that one.
这个地方同那个地方一样好。

What he said has as good as shown his attitude.

他说的话实际上已经表明了他的态度。

14. The mower firmly refused to mow, so I ...

一般情况下,动词 refuse 的主语应为人,但文中用物体 mower 作其主语,是拟人用法,这样可以使文字显得更为生动。

15. The garden was soon littered with chunks of metal which ...

litter ... with ... 用……胡乱堆满……,如:

Thoughtless vacationers had littered the beach with cigarette packages and beer cans.

不顾及他人的度假者们在海滩上丢满了香烟盒和啤酒罐。

16. ... I was faced with the insurmountable task of putting the confusing jigsaw puzzle together again.

句中使用 insurmountable 和 confusing 两个较大的词分别修饰 task 和 jigsaw puzzle,具有夸张意味,并以暗喻手法,将 lawn-mower 比作 jigsaw puzzle(拼图游戏,七巧板)更有利于产生喜剧效果。

17. I was not surprised to find that the machine still refused to work after I had reassembled it, for the simple reason that I was left with several curiously shaped bits of metal which did not seem to fit anywhere.

(1)本句较长,为易于理解,在此作一简单的语法分析:

to find that ... 动词不定式短语,作原因状语,说明 not surprised 的原因。after 为从属连词,引导时间状语从句,修饰 was,说明 was not surprised 的时间。that 为连词,引导同位语从句,进一步说明 reason 的内容。which 为关系代词,引导定语从句,修饰 bits of metal。

(2) leave ... with ... 把……托付/交给/留给……,如:

Please leave word with him if you've anything important to do there.

如果你有什么要紧事儿要去那里做,请给他留个口信。

18. **When my wife nagged me to do something about it, ...**

nag sb. to do ... 唠唠叨叨责怪/数落某人或叫其做……也可为 nag sb. into (doing) sth. ...,如:

All the time my wife is nagging me to move to town.
我妻子总是唠唠叨叨,让我搬到城里去住。

His wife always nags him into doing what she wants.
他妻子老是唠叨不休地让他做她想要做的事情。

19. **Buried somewhere in deep grass there is a rusting lawn mower which ...**

Buried somewhere ...,过去分词短语,作定语,修饰 lawn mower。现置于句首位置,一是起到强调作用,此外,由于 lawn mower 后为 which 引导的定语从句,这样可使句子显得更为紧凑连贯。

语法 Grammar in use

形容词的词序(1)

1. 名词前有两个以上的形容词时的词序

品质形容词 + 色彩形容词 + 类别形容词:

a little white wooden house　一座白色的小木屋

rapid technological advance　高速的技术进步

a necklace of blue Venetian beads　一串蓝色的威尼斯珠子项链

然而,表示形状的不可分级形容词如 circular(环形的)、rectangular(长方形的),虽然它们是类别形容词,但常常用于色彩形容词之前,如:

the rectangular grey stones　长方形灰色石块

the circular yellow patch on the lawn　草坪上一片圆形的

498

黄色地带

2．品质形容词的词序

看法＋尺寸＋品质＋年龄＋形状：

We shall have a nice big garden with two apple trees.

我们会有一个有两棵苹果树的漂亮的大花园。

big, shiny beetles 闪闪发光的大甲壳虫

3．类别形容词的词序

如果不止有一个类别形容词修饰一个名词时,通常的词序如下：

年龄＋形状＋产地＋材料,如：

a rectangular plastic box 一个长方形的塑料盒子

an Italian silk jacket 一件意大利丝绸夹克

其他类型的类别形容词通常放在产地形容词之后：

a Chinese handmade cotton shirt 一件中国产的手工棉布衬衫

the American political system 美国的政治体制

4．比较级和最高级的词序

如果名词词组中包含比较级和最高级,通常放在其他形容词的前面,如：

These are the highest monthly figures on record.

这些是记录上月记录最高的数字。

5．名词作定语

当名词词组中既有形容词又有作定语用的名词时,形容词应放在这个名词前面,如：

He works in the French film industry.

他在法国电影业工作。

He receives a large monthly cash payment.

他领到高额的现金月薪。

1. lay out

(1) 安排,布置,筹划,设计:

> *The garden is laid out in a formal pattern.*
> 花园的布局被设计成规则的几何图形。

> *They are busy laying out an election campaign.*
> 他们正忙于筹划竞选活动。

(2) 摊开,摆开,展开(常用于被动语态):

> *She laid out the map on the table.*
> 她将地图摊在桌子上。

> *The goods for sale were laid out attractively.*
> 出售的商品摆放得十分吸引人。

(3) 击倒,击昏:

> *I laid him out with a blow to the head.*
> 我一拳打在他头上,将他击倒。

2. break down

(1) 损坏,坏掉,出毛病,不起作用:

> *My car broke down on my way back home, and I had to get a taxi.*
> 我的车在我回家的路上坏了,我不得不改乘出租车。

(2) 摧毁,捣碎,拆除:

> *The angry protesters broke all the shop windows down on their way to the city hall.*
> 愤怒的抗议者在他们去往市政厅的路上砸碎了所有商店的橱窗。

(3) 制服,击垮,垮掉:

> *The prisoner's opposition broke down under repeated questioning.*

那个犯人的对抗在一连串的质问下被击垮。

This agreement will break down the barriers to free trade.

这项协议将打破妨碍自由贸易的障碍。

3.fix *vt*.

（1）修理：

I must get my washing machine fixed.

我必须得把我的洗衣机送去修修。

（2）固定，钉牢，安装：

She fixed it to the wall with a nail.

她用一个钉子将它固定在了墙上。

Her heart was beating so violently that she could not fix her thought on anything.

她的心在狂跳使她无法想任何事。

（3）安排，确定（具体时间、地点、价格等）：

Let's fix（up）a time for our next meeting.

我们确定一下我们下次见面的时间吧。

📝 **练习答案 Key to written exercises**

1.关键句型、难点练习答案

See text.

2.多项选择题答案

1	c	2	d	3	d	4	c	5	d	6	a
7	b	8	c	9	b	10	a	11	c	12	b

Lesson 47
Too high a price?
代价太高?

📖 **课文详注 Further notes on the text**

1. Pollution is the price we pay for an overpopulated ...

句中 we pay for 为定语从句。由于 price 在此从句中起宾语作用,其间的关系代词 which / that 因此可以省略。

2. ... there are only four ways we can deal with rubbish: dump it, burn it, turn it into ..., attempt to ...

we can deal with rubbish 为定语从句,这里 only four ways 在从句中作方式状语。当先行词为 way 时,它与其后所接定语从句间的关系代词 that 常常省略,如:

I went out the same way I'd got in.

我顺着进来的路又原路走了出去。

冒号后的 4 个动词短语作同位语, 对 four ways 作具体说明。

3. ... but the sheer volume of rubbish we produce worldwide ...

sheer 纯粹的,完全的。定语形容词只能用于名词前对其进行语义强调。常见类似的词还有 mere、bloody 等,如:

It's sheer madness.

这完全是发疯。

He's a mere child.

他不过是个孩子。

You bloody fool.

你这个大笨蛋。

4. And if you think you'll abandon meat ... you have the choice of

502

very expensive organically-grown vegetables or a steady diet of pesticides every time you think you're eating ..., or just having...

(1) abandon 放弃,遗弃。及物动词,后接名词、代词或动名词。表示"放弃"时,其后常使用表示活动、思想、职业、习惯等方面的词;表示"遗弃"时,主要指遗弃妻子、儿女等,如:

> *I abandoned my research for lack of fund.*
> 由于缺乏资金,我放弃了研究。
> *The doctor advised me to abandon smoking.*
> 医生建议我戒烟。
> *The man shamelessly abandoned his wife and child for another woman.*
> 那个男人无耻地遗弃了妻儿,另寻新欢。

(2) have the choice of ... or ... 在……和……之间选择。表述此义时,choice 后也可使用 between ... and ... 这种结构,如:

> *You have the choice of A or B.*
> 你可以在 A 或 B 中挑选。
> *He has his choice between A and B.*
> 他可以在 A 和 B 中任选一个。

该句的完整形式为:... you have the choice of very expensive organically-grown vegetables or you have the choice of a steady diet of pesticides.

(3) 句中 every time you think ... water! 为时间状语从句,修饰连词以后省略了的动词 have,即如上所述,or you have the choice of a steady diet of pesticides 中的动词 have。

5．**Burglar alarms going off at any time of the day or night serve only to annoy passers-by and actually assist burglars to burgle.**
go off 有多种意义,本句中为"响起"之意,但更强调"响起"的突然性。

503

only to annoy ... burgle,动词不定式短语,作目的状语。副词
only（仅仅,只）用来强调此目的状语。

6. Car alarms constantly scream at us in the street and are a source of profound irritation.

be a source of ... 是……的源泉,成为……的原因,如:

Books are a source of knowledge.

书籍是知识的源泉。

Money is often a source of tension and disagreements in young married couples.

金钱常常是导致年轻的新婚夫妇关系紧张与不和的根源。

7. Lawn mowers whining on a summer's day, ... especially large container trucks thundering through quiet villages, planes and helicopters flying overhead, large radios carried round in public places and played at maximum volume.

从 lawn mowers 至 maximum volume 中包含 6 个短语,并非完整的句子。整个部分作前句中 a large number of sources of noise(大量噪音源）的同位语,对其进行具体说明。其中 especially large container trucks thundering through quiet villages 作 vehicles of all kinds 的同位语,对其进行追加说明。短语中分别使用 whining ...、thundering ...、flying ...、carried ... and played...等,这些现在分词和过去分词短语均作定语,分别修饰其前的 mowers, trucks, planes and helicopters 和 radios。

8. Now technology has also made its own contribution to noise.

make a/one's contribution to ... 对……作出贡献;对……发挥（其)作用,如:

In so doing you will make a substantial contribution to your college.

你这样做将会对你的学院作出巨大的贡献。

Every word makes its own contribution to the general

504

effect .

每个词都为达到总体效果发挥其各自的作用。

本句使用了反语(irony)以达到讥讽作用和加深读者的认识。

9. **A lot of people object to mobile phones，...**

object to 反对,不同意。该动词短语多着重于"个人嫌厌"和
"(由于与个人有关因此)提出不同意见"之意。其后如果不是
that 引导的从句时,多作不及物动词,同介词 to 连用,因此其后
只能接名词、代词或动名词,如:

I strongly object to this proposal .

我坚决不同意这个提议。

He objected to being treated as an outsider .

他对别人把他当作外人表示不满。

10. **It turned out to be snoring!**

turn out to 结果是,证明是。用 turn out 表达此义时,后应使
用动词不定式;其后为形容词时,可将该动词不定式省略,如:

Everything turned out（to be）satisfactory .

结果一切令人满意。

The beggar turned out to be a thief .

那个乞丐原来是个贼。

11. **It was revealed that 20% of men in their mid-thirties snore.**

句中 it 为先行词,作形式主语,其逻辑主语为 that ... snore
从句。

12. **Against these figures，it was found ...，while the rest ...**

(1) against these figures 与这些数字相比。介词 against 可用来表
示对比,如:

He was elected by a majority of 20 votes against 10 .

他以 20 比 10 票的多数当选了。

*Now the mill has 2,000 workers as against the 500 or so
then* .

这个厂现有 2,000 工人,而那时才有 500 人左右。

(2) while 而。并列连词,除课文中用法外,while 还可作从属连词,引导条件状语从句或让步状语从句,如:

In general, metals are good conductors, while nonmetals are insulators.

一般说来,金属是良好的导体,而非金属则是绝缘体。(并列连词)

While one finds company in himself and his pursuits, he cannot feel old, no matter what his years may be.

一个人只要在自己的生活中和在其工作中自得其乐,那么,不管他年龄多大,他都不会感觉到老。(从属连词,引导条件状语从句)

13. Whatever the source of noise, one thing is certain:...

whatever 不管,无论。连接代词,引导让步状语从句,如:

You must have your own view on such an important subject, whatever other people may say about it.

不管旁人说什么,对这样重要的问题你应该有自己的见解。

语法 Grammar in use

形容词的词序(2)

6. 形容词置于名词之后

通常形容词不置于名词之后。然而,在下述情况下形容词置于名词之后:

(1) 当形容词后面跟有介词短语或动词不定式时,如:

a warning to people eager for a quick cure 对急于想迅速治愈者的一个警告

the sort of weapons likely to be deployed against it 很可能

被用来进攻它的那种武器

(2) 当 alive 和 awake 前面有一个副词,如 first、last、only、every 或 any 等词时,如:

> *Is Phil Morgan the only man alive who knows all the words to that song ?*
>
> 费尔·摩根是惟一活着的知道这首歌完整歌词的人吗?
>
> *She sat at the window , until she was the last person awake .*
>
> 她坐在窗户旁,直到就剩下她一个人还醒着。

(3) 在一些"头衔"中,形容词需用于名词之后,如:

> *a minister designate* 已经被任命而尚未上任的部长
>
> *She was now the president elect .*
>
> 她当时是当选的总统。
>
> *Attorney General* 检查总长

7.可用在名词前面或后面的形容词

(1) 在名词前或后而意义不变的形容词不多,大部分以 -able、-ible 结尾之后而意义一般不变,如 available、eligible、imaginable、taxable:

> *I doubt whether we can complete our contract in the time available/in the available time .*
>
> 我怀疑我们是否能在现有的时间内完成我们的合同。

(2) 用在名词前或后但是意义有所改变的形容词如 concerned、elect、involved、present、proper、responsible:

> *The concerned (= worried) doctor rang for an ambulance .*
>
> 心情焦虑的医生打电话叫救护车。
>
> *The doctor concerned (= responsible) is on holiday .*
>
> 主管医师在休假。
>
> *The number of present employees (= those currently*

employed）*is 3,000.*

现有雇员 3,000 人。

Employees present（= *those here now*）*should vote on the issue.*

在场的雇员应该对这一问题进行表决。

Jenet is a responsible girl.（*i.e. She has a sense of duty.*）

珍妮特是一个有责任心的姑娘。

The girl responsible（= *who can be blamed*）*was expelled.*

负有责任的那个姑娘被开除了。

8．形容词用于度量时

置于名词之后,常用的有 deep、long、thick、high、tall、wide 等:

He was about six feet tall.

他大约 6 英尺高。

The island is only 29 miles long.

这座岛屿只有 29 英里长。

词汇学习　Word study

1．deal with

（1）处理,惩处,对付:

The government has to take effective measures to deal with drug smuggling.

政府必须采取有效的手段对付毒品走私。

Bank staff are to be given more training to help them deal with armed robbers.

银行职员要接受更多的帮助他们应付武装抢劫者的培训。

（2）论述,谈到:

He dealt with unemployment and financial crisis in the country these years.

他谈到这些年来这个国家的失业和金融危机。

Her new film deals with the relationship between a woman and her ill daughter.

她的新影片是关于一个妇女和她生病的女儿之间的关系。

(3) 做生意：

We only deal with companies which have a good credit record.

我们只同信誉好的公司做生意。

2. lead to

(1) 导致，致使：

The scandal led to his resignation.

那桩丑闻使他辞职。

Disobeying the school regulation will lead to trouble.

违反校规会带来麻烦。

(2) 引导，引路：

The new information led the police to a house near the harbour.

那条新线索引导着警察来到码头旁边的一座房子跟前。

The distant lights led me to the village.

远处的灯光引导着我到了那个村庄。

(3) 通往，通向：

This path leads directly to the lake.

这条小路直接通往那个湖。

3. abandon *vt.*

(1) 抛弃，遗弃，离弃，丢弃：

He abandoned his wife and his two children.

他抛弃了他的妻子和两个孩子。

The thief abandoned the stolen car and ran into the woods.

那个小偷丢弃了那辆偷来的车,跑进了树林。

(2)放弃:

Living in an English speaking country, he had to abandon his native language.

由于住在一个说英语的国家,他不得不放弃说他的母语。

The bad weather forced them to abandon their search.

恶劣的天气迫使他们放弃了寻找。

(3)(oneself)放纵,使沉溺于:

He abandoned himself to his emotions.

他受自己情感的驱使。

She abandoned herself to the serene landscape.

她沉浸在景色的宁静之中。

✍ 练习答案 Key to written exercises

1.关键句型、难点练习答案

See text.

2.多项选择题答案

1	c	2	b	3	a	4	c	5	a	6	c
7	a	8	a	9	c	10	c	11	a	12	b

Lesson 48
The silent village
沉默的村庄

📖 **课文详注** Further notes on the text

1. ... there are still thousands of places which are inaccessible to tourists.

be inaccessible to ... 是……难于达到的,是……难于接近的,如:

She kept the medicine at the place inaccessible to children.
她把药放在孩子们拿不到的地方。

2. But people who are cut off not only from ...

cut ... off from ... 把……同……隔开/切断,如:

The flood cut the townspeople off from the rest of the world.

洪水切断了该镇居民与外界的联系。

They cut themselves off entirely from the pleasures and enjoyments of the world.

他们完全摒弃了尘世间的欢乐和享受。

3. Visits to really remote villages are seldom enjoyable—as my wife and I discovered during a tour through the Balkans.

(1) to really remote village 作名词 visits 的定语,意即"到名副其实的偏僻村庄去游览"。

(2) 句中 as 为关系代词,指代 visits to really remote village are seldom enjoyable, 作动词 discovered 的宾语。有关用法参见第 33 课课文注释 10。

4. ... and visited a number of old churches in the vicinity.

in the vicinity 在……附近,邻近。此介词短语在句中作定语修饰 churches,意即"附近的许多古老的教堂",如:

There are two schools in our vicinity.

我们附近有两所学校。

The workers' residential district is in close vicinity to the factory.

工人住宅区靠近工厂。

使用 in the vicinity of 时,除可以表示"在……附近"外,还可表示出"在……上下"和"在……左右"之意,如:

The cost of the coat is in the vicinity of twenty dollars.

这件外衣约值 20 美元。

5. ... for they were not only of great architectural interest, ...

be of + 抽象名词,在此结构中,介词 of 同其后的抽象名词实际相当于该抽象名词的形容词,即 interesting。

6. ... several bus loads of tourists descended on the town.

descend (up)on 突然访问,突然袭击,如:

The whole family descended on us at Christmas.

他们全家突然在圣诞节来拜访我们。

The plague descended on the province.

瘟疫袭击了该省。

文中使用这个词组颇为贴切,正好同前文形成呼应。

7. This was more than we could bear, ...

当 more than 同其后含有 can/could 一词的从句连用时,more than 的作用相当于一个连词,常用来表示"难以"的含义,如:

The beauty of the place is more than I can describe.

此地之美我难以形容。

more than 用于连接一个从句时,起到将前后两个句子中所用的某一成分进行比较的作用,即"比……多"的含义,如:

512

You should sleep more than you do.

你应当比现在睡的要多一些。

一般情况下,more than 起副词的作用,加强被修饰词的分量或含义。其后接数词时,常表示"……以上"、"超过……"之意,如:

He is more than twenty years old.

他二十多岁了。

接形容词或副词时,往往表示"非常"、"很"、"简直"之意,如:

She said that she was more than surprised to see him.

她说她见到了他简直吃惊极了。

而后接名词时,则常常含有"不只"、"不仅仅"之意,如:

A science is more than a large amount of information on some subject.

一门科学不只是有关某门学科的大量资料。

8. ... but we found that it traced its way through the trees.

it ... trees 它蜿蜒穿过树林,trace a way through ... 沿路穿过,trees 树林。

9. ... but we had no idea how we could get across the stream.

(1) how 为连接副词,引导的从句作 idea 的同位语。

(2) get (...) across ... (使)通过、穿过,从一边到另一边。有时引申用于表达"(使)……被理解"之意,如:

The bridge was destroyed so we couldn't get across.

桥被破坏了,所以我们无法过河。

He found it difficult to get his Chinese humor across to an English audience.

他发现自己中国式的幽默很难为英国听众们理解。

10. In it there was a boatman fast asleep.

In it 为地点状语,本句将此状语提前,使同上文连接更为紧密。fast asleep 熟睡，睡得很沉。

11．The path led to a tiny village perched on the steep sides of a mountain.

perched on ... a mountain 坐落在陡峭山坡上的。过去分词短语，作定语，修饰 village。perch 原为"禽鸟的栖木"，引申为"坐落在高处"。在句中表达该义时，通常使用(be ＋)该词的过去分词形式，如：

Over there you could see a pagoda perched on a cliff.
在那边，你可以看到耸立在悬崖上的宝塔。

The fortress is perched（up）on a mountain difficult of access.
堡垒位于一座难于攀登的山上。

12．... the only sign of life being an ugly-looking black goat on a short length of rope tied to a tree in a field nearby.

the only ... nearby 作状语，其中 sign of life 作 being ... nearby 的逻辑主语，说明 seemed deserted。这样的由"逻辑主语＋分词短语"构成的结构为独立主格结构中的一种，在句子中可起到多种状语的作用，如：

He rushed into the room, his face covered with sweat.
他满脸是汗地跑进屋来。（伴随状况状语）

The shower being over, we continued to march.
阵雨之后，我们继续行进。（时间状语）

Her eyes dimmed with tears, she did not see him enter.
泪水模糊了她的双眼，因此她没看到他进来。（原因状语）

All things considered, her paper is of greater value than yours.
从各方面考虑，她的论文比你的论文有价值。（条件状语）

514

tied to ... nearby 为过去分词短语,作定语,修饰 goat,意即
"拴在附近田里一棵树上的山羊"。其中 nearby 为副词,作定
语,修饰 a field。

13. All at once, I noticed that ...

all at once 突然,猛然,如:

All at once, we heard a loud noise.

猛然间我们听到了一声巨响。

14. Looking up I saw ... by children in rags who ...

Looking up 为现在分词短语,作时间状语,修饰 saw。in rags
为介词短语,作定语,修饰 children,意即"穿着破衣烂衫的孩
子们"。

15. I concluded that they were simply shy of strangers.

be shy of ... 羞于……,畏缩于……,如:

His eye trouble made him shy of sight.

眼疾使他怕光。

This made him shy of trying it again.

这使他不敢再试了。

在美国英语中还用来表示"对……感到不足"或"缺少……"之
意,如:

They are shy of funds.

他们资金不足。

16. ...immediately came to life.

come to life 苏醒过来,恢复生气,如:

A drooping plant comes to life in water.

凋萎的植物在水里又活了过来。

17. Men in shirt sleeves stood ...

in shirt sleeves 只穿衬衫未穿外衣的。介词短语,固定搭配形
式,在句中作定语,修饰 men。

18. Turning back down the main street ... and made our way

rapidly towards the stream where we hoped the boatman was waiting.

（1）这里的 down 为介词，意即"沿着"。

（2）make one's way to/towards ... 向……走去，如：

> *In the evening we made our way towards the appointed meeting place.*
>
> 到了晚上，我们就向约定会面的地方走去。
>
> *The survivors made their way towards the jungle.*
>
> 幸存者们向丛林走去。

（3）we hoped 在句中作插入语。

语法 Grammar in use

缩略语

缩略语为省略了单词、复合词、短语等的一些字母或只是使用其首字母的一种简短形式。缩略语的构成须遵循一定的规则。如果单词的首字母为大写字母则其缩略语也应为大写字母。下面是缩略语的 5 种基本形式：

1.由单词的首字母构成，按完整的单词发音，如：

> *m = metre* 米
>
> *p. = page* 页
>
> *F = Fahrenheit* 华氏
>
> *N = North* 北方

2.由单词的前几个字母组成，通常按完整的单词发音，如：

> *cont. = continued* 待续
>
> *usu. = usually* 通常
>
> *vol. = volume* 卷
>
> *Brit. = British* 不列颠
>
> *Hon. = Honourable* 尊敬的

Thurs . = *Thursday*　　星期四

3. 省略了单词的某些字母,按完整的单词发音,如:

　　asst . = *assistant*　　助手

　　dept . = *department*　　系

　　jct = *junction*　　交叉口

　　km = *kilometre*　　公里

　　tbsp . = *tablespoonful*　　一大汤匙的量

　　Sgt = *sergeant*　　中士

　　HQ = *headquarters*　　司令部

　　TV = *television*　　电视

　　KW = *kilowatt*　　千瓦

4. 由一组词中各主要词的首字母组成,分别发出各字母的读音,
　　主重音落在最后一个字母上。这类缩略语前应根据第一个字
　　母的读音选择不定冠词 a 或 an ,如:MP 前应该用 an 而不是用
　　a,因为 M 的读音为/em/,如:

　　MP = *Member of Parliament*　　议员

　　CD = *compact disc*　　光盘

　　HRH = *His/Her Royal Highness*　　殿下

　　USA = *United States of America*　　美国

　　VIP = *very important person*　　大人物

　　rpm = *revolutions per minute*　　每分钟转数,转/分

5. 由一组词中各主要词的首字母缩合成一个新词,称之为首字母
　　缩拼词(acronym)。这类词要读成一个单词,而不能分别发出各
　　字母的读音。大多数这类词都用大写字母,如果用小写字母则
　　表示其已被视为普通名词,如:

　　laser = *light amplification by stimulated emission of*
　　radiation　　激光

　　BASIC = *Beginner's All-purpose Symbolic Instruction*
　　Code　　初学者通用符号指令码

517

OPEC = Organization of Petroleum-Exporting Countries
石油输出国组织

TEFL /tefl/ = *teaching English as a foreign language*
作为外语的英语教学

前4种缩略语各字母后面可以用句号,但现在常不用句号,特别是在英国英语中。第5种缩略语一般不用句号。另外,缩略语可以有复数形式,s要小写,如:hr, hrs; MP, MPs; UFO, UFOs。但是表示度量的缩略语单复数一样,如:millilitre 和 millitres 的缩略语都是 ml。此外还有个别词例外,如:page 的缩略语为 p, pages 的缩略语是 pp; Saint 的缩略语是 St, Saints 的缩略语是 SS。

📂 词汇学习 Word study

1.cut off

(1) 使与……隔绝,使分开:

> *The army was cut off from its supplies.*
> 那支队伍的给养被切断了。
>
> *That old woman has cut herself off from the society.*
> 那位老妇人使自己与社会隔绝。

(2) 切断,砍掉:

> *Her little finger was cut off in an accident at the factory.*
> 她的小手指在工厂的一次事故中被切断了。

(3) 打断,终止:

> *The President decided to cut off foreign aid to these countries.*
> 总统决定终止对这些国家的对外援助。

2.bear *vt*.

(1) 忍受,容忍(后跟宾语/+动词-ing/+不定式):

518

She bore the pain with great courage.

她以巨大的勇气忍受疼痛。

This place is so untidy. I don't know how you can bear living in it.

这个地方这么乱,我不知道你是如何忍受住在这儿的。

I couldn't bear to listen any longer, so I left the room.

我实在听不下去了,于是我离开了房间。

bear、stand、endure、tolerate 都可以表示此义,且都可以与 can、can't 连用。但是当 endure 与 can't 连用时,往往用于谈论严肃的话题,试比较:

I can't endure talking to people who are racists.

我无法忍受与种族主义者交谈。

I can't bear/stand black coffee.

我受不了苦咖啡。

bear、endure、stand 还可以用以表达身体上的痛苦,用于此义时,endure 主要表达忍受长期的痛苦,试比较:

He bore/stood the pain as long as he could.

他尽可能久地忍受疼痛。

She had endured great pain for a number of years.

她已经经受了多年的巨痛。

tolerate 只用于表示对人或行为的容忍,而不能用以表示忍受痛苦,如:

I won't tolerate your rudeness.

我不会容忍你的无理。

(2) 支撑,承担:

The chair, too fragile to bear her weight, collapsed.

那把椅子,太不结实了,支撑不起她的体重,垮了。

The captain of the ship bears a heavy responsibility.

船长承担着重任。

(3) 生产,产仔,结果实,长出(花、叶等):

The tree is bearing a lot of apples this year.

那棵树今年结了很多苹果。

Most animals bear their young in the spring.

大多数动物都在春季产仔。

Eventually her efforts bore fruit and she got the job she wanted.

她的努力最终获得了成功,她得到了她想得到的那份工作。

3. trace *vt.*

(1) 追踪,跟踪,查出,找到:

The police are trying to trace the mother of a new-born baby found abandoned outside a hospital.

警察正在企图查找被遗弃在一所医院外面的一个新生儿的母亲。

(2) 追溯,追究,探索:

Many explorers tried to trace the river to its source but failed.

许多探险家都尝试过追溯那条河流的源头,但是都失败了。

No one has yet been able to trace the source of the rumour.

尚没有人能够追究出谣言的根源。

✐ 练习答案 **Key to written exercises**

1. 关键句型、难点练习答案

See text.

2. 多项选择题答案

1	a	2	b	3	c	4	d	5	a	6	a
7	c	8	d	9	b	10	c	11	b	12	a

520

Lesson 49
The ideal servant
理想的仆人

  📖 **课文详注** **Further notes on the text**

1. If she were alive today she would not be able to air her views on her favorite topic of conversation: domestic servants.

(1) if she were ... she would not be able ...为非真实性条件状语从句。因为所陈述的内容为对现在情况的假设,因此使用 were 和 would not be 这样的动词形式。

(2) air one's views (on/about/to) (对……)公开发表意见,如:

    He's always airing his views about politics.

    他总是发表有关政治的看法。

    He spoke on the radio, airing his views to the nation.

    他在广播电台演讲,向全国公开阐明他的观点。

(3) domestic servants 为 topic of conversation 的同位语。

2. She was sentimentally attached to this house, for even though it was far too big for her needs, she persisted in living there long after her husband's death.

(1) be attached to 喜爱,依恋。

(2) it was too big for her needs 她用不了这么大的房子。

(3) persist in (doing) 坚持/执意(做),一般用于"坚持/执意于某行为"。多用来表示不顾困难阻碍,也可用来表示顽固而不听开导或劝告,后应使用介词"in + 名词或动名词"形式,如:

    He persisted in carrying on his work in spite of great fatigue.

虽然他疲倦极了,但是他仍然坚持工作。

He persisted in his opinion .

他固执己见。

而 insist on(doing)多用来表示"坚持意见或主张"等。

3.The parquet floors shone like mirrors; highly polished silver was displayed in gleaming glass cabinets; even my uncle's huge collection of books was kept miraculously free from dust.

shone like mirrors 中 like 为比喻词,用于明喻。句中 shone like mirrors、highly polished、gleaming 以及 miraculously 均具有夸张色彩,以形容房子的洁净。

4.Aunt Harriet presided over an invisible army of servants that continuously scrubbed, cleaned, and polished.

(1)preside over 管理……,主持……有时也用来表示"(担任要职时)无可奈何地目睹",如:

The city council is presided over by the mayor .

市政会议市长主持。

Successive post-war governments have presided over the gradual dissolution of the British Empire .

战后的英国历届政府眼巴巴地看着英帝国逐步解体。

(2)invisible 无形的,看不见的。由于哈丽特姑妈对众多仆人的不断解雇和再雇用,因而使其难于固定,这样就形成了无形的队伍。而句中所使用的 preside over, army, continuously 等词都具有夸张的意味。

5.Though my aunt pursued what was, in those days, an enlightened policy, in that ... she was extremely difficult to please.

(1)what was an enlightened policy 算得上是一项开明政策。what 为代词,引导名词性从句,该从句作动词 pursued 的宾语。what 相当于 the thing which,即定语从句中一个先行词同关

522

系代词 which 的关系。

(2) in that 因为,就在于,既然。复合连词,引导原因状语从句,从狭隘的一面或几面来说明原因或理由,含有"推论条件"的意味,多用于书面语,通常置于主句后,偶尔置于主句前,如:

> *The book is unsatisfactory in that it lacks a good index.*
> 这本书不能令人满意,因为缺少一个完善的索引。
>
> *I could understand his point of view, in that I'd been in a similar position myself.*
> 我能理解他的观点,因为我自己也有过类似的处境。
>
> *In that he killed Abel, he was a murderer.*
> 既然他把艾贝尔杀了,他就是一个凶手。

(3) to please 作状语,修饰 difficult。she 与 to please 有逻辑上的动宾关系。

6. While she always criticized ... to the end of her days, ...

(1) while 虽然,尽管。这里作从属连词使用,引导让步状语从句。有关 while 的并列连词和从属连词的使用,见本册第 47 课课文注释 12。

(2) to the end 到底;直到死。通常用于表示极点或程度,如:

> *They'll fight to the end.*
> 他们将战斗到底。
>
> *A true friend is faithful to the end.*
> 一个忠诚的朋友是忠实到底的。

7. ... she so gained my aunt's confidence, that she was put in charge of the domestic staff.

in charge of 主管,负责,如:

> *Professor Smith is in charge of the experiment in physics.*
> 史密斯教授负责这项物理实验。
>
> *The doctor in charge of this ward has just gone out.*
> 主管此病房的大夫刚出去。

句中 was put in charge of 意为"被放到负责……的位置上"。

8. In addition to all her other qualifications, ...

in addition to ... 除……以外还,短语介词,后接名词、动名词等,并与之一起作状语。往往用来表示对所陈述事情首先肯定后再加以补充,如:

> *In addition to books, the delegate presented our university with other valuable gifts.*
>
> 除书籍外,那位代表还赠送给我校其他一些珍贵礼品。

9. After being absent from The Gables for a week, ...

be absent from 不在,缺席。absent from 为形容词短语,常与 be 动词连用,其后为 class、meeting 等名词时,通常表示"缺席",后为表示地点的名词时,通常表示"不在……"的意思,如:

> *You shouldn't be absent from class.*
>
> 你不应该旷课。
>
> *When they came to see me, I was absent from Shanghai.*
>
> 他们来看我时,我不在上海。

10. She bumped into the furniture ...

bump into 撞到。有时也用来表示"意外碰到",如:

> *The man slipped and bumped into a little girl.*
>
> 那人滑了一下,撞到一个小女孩身上。
>
> *He bumped into an old friend yesterday.*
>
> 他昨天意外地碰到了一个老朋友。

11. She reluctantly came to the conclusion that Bessie was drunk.

come to the conclusion 得出这样的结论。其后的 that 从句为 conclusion 的同位语,说明 conclusion 的内容。

12. ... realized this from the moment Bessie opened the door for them and, long before the final catastrophe, had had a difficult time trying to conceal their amusement.

(1) 在英语中,the moment 可作连词,表示"一……就……",即 as

524

soon as 之意,如:

> *Tell me the moment you get the results.*
>
> 你一得到结果就立刻告诉我。

除此以外,immediately、the minute、the instant、the second 等也可以这样使用,如:

> *Tell me immediately you have any news.*
>
> 一有消息,你就立刻告诉我。
>
> *I loved you the instant I saw you.*
>
> 一见到你我就爱上了你。

(2) 这里 the final catastrophe 指最后的灾难。指 When she came in with ... with considerable force 这件事。

(3) have a difficult/hard, etc. time doing ... 费很大的力气做……如:

> *Poor Susan had a time trying to get the children to go to bed.*
>
> 可怜的苏珊费了很大的力气才使孩子们上床睡觉。

13. They had mysteriously found their way there from the wine cellar!

find one's way ... 找到……的路。句中 had mysteriously found their way ...为拟人用法,如:

> *In those days many precious art objects found their way across the Atlantic.*
>
> 那时许多珍贵艺术品被运到了大西洋彼岸。
>
> *The word has found its way into some diplomatic documents.*
>
> 这个词已在一些外交文件中使用。

📄 语法 Grammar in use

子句

子句也称为分句或小句。子句是包含一个动词的一组词,一个简单句有一个子句,如:

Stephen apologized at once.

斯蒂芬马上道了歉。

She married a young engineer.

她嫁给了一个年轻的工程师。

子句可分为 3 种:主句、从句和非限定性从句。

1. 主句

在并列句中有两个或两个以上的主句,各主句由 and, but, or 等连词连接,各主句所分别表达的动作、情形等同样重要,没有主次之分,如:

Stephen realized his mistake and (he) apologized at once.

斯蒂芬认识到了他的错误,于是马上道了歉。

We fished all day, but (we) didn't catch a thing.

我们钓了一天的鱼,但是一条也未钓到。

如果各句的主语相同,后面句中的主语可以省略。但在复合句中包含至少一个主句和一个从句,主句和从句并非同等重要,如:

When he realized his mistake, Stephen apologized at once.

当斯蒂芬认识到自己的错误,就马上道了歉。

If you're not good at figures, it is pointless to apply for a job in a bank.

如果你不擅于计算,向银行求职就没有意义。

To get into a university you have to pass a number of examinations.

要想进入大学你必须通过一系列的考试。

2. 从句

在复合句中包含至少一个主句和一个从句,从句提供有关主句更多的信息并由从属连词或关系代词引导。从句可以出现在主句前面、后面或中间:

When he stopped , no one said anything .(时间状语从句)

他停下来时,没人说什么。

I said that I should like to come .(宾语从句)

我说我愿意来。

The man who came into the room was small .(定语从句)

走进房间的那个男人是个小个子。

3. 非限定性从句

非限定性从句由非限定动词——动词不定式或分词短语构成。它们构成复合句的一部分:

Seeing the door open , the stranger entered the house .

那个陌生人看到门开着就进了屋子。

She was the first woman to be elected to the council .

她是第一个经选举进入这个委员会的妇女。

📂 词汇学习 Word study

1. air

(1) *vi .* , *vt .* 晾晒(衣物等),(使)通风:

Leave the clothes out on the washing-line to air .

把这些衣服留在晾衣绳上晾着。

We aired the room by opening the windows .

我们打开窗户给房间通风。

(2) *vt .* 公开(观点、不满等):

He'll air his views on the economic reform whether people want to listen or not .

527

不管人们想不想听他都要公开谈一下他对经济改革的看法。

（3）*vi.*，*vt.* 广播：

The interview with the President will air tomorrow morning.

对总统的采访将于明晨播出。

The game will be aired on Channel 5, CCTV at 8：00 tonight.

这场比赛将由中央电视台的第5套节目于今晚8时播出。

2.persist

（1）*vi.*（in, with）坚持不懈，执意：

If you persist in causing trouble, the company may be forced to dismiss you.

如果你继续不断地捣乱，公司可能会被迫解雇你。

The government is persisting with its ambitious public works programme, despite the massive costs involved.

尽管费用极高，政府仍在坚持它雄心勃勃的公共设施规划。

（2）*vi.* 持续存在：

The CCTV weather forecast predicted that the cold weather would persist throughout the week.

中央电视台天气预报预测寒冷的天气还会持续整整一周。

Despite official denials, the rumours persisted.

尽管官方予以否认，但是谣言仍在流传。

3.pursue *vt.*

（1）追赶，追捕，追杀：

The tourists were pursued by beggars.

游客被乞丐追赶着。

He was wondering why bad luck had pursued him all

528

through the year.

他在纳冈为什么厄运在一年里总追随着他。

(2) 进行,实行,从事,继续:

We need to decide soon what marketing strategy we should pursue for these new products.

我们需要尽快决定我们应该为这些新产品奉行什么样的市场策略。

The government is pursuing a policy of mutual benefit and non-intervention.

这个政府奉行互惠和互不干涉的政策。

(3) 追求,寻求:

She is ruthless in pursuing her goals.

她不顾一切地追求她的目标。

The development of industry must not be pursued at the expense of environmental pollution.

不能以环境污染为代价而一味地追求工业的发展。

✍ 练习答案 Key to written exercises

1. 关键句型、难点练习答案

See text.

2. 多项选择题答案

1 b	2 d	3 d	4 c	5 d	6 c
7 c	8 a	9 c	10 d	11 d	12 c

Lesson 50
New Year resolutions
新年的决心

📖 **课文详注** **Further notes on the text**

1. Mentally, at least, most of us could compile formidable lists of 'dos' and 'don'ts'.

dos and don'ts 为名词 do 或 don't 的复数形式,意即"要做的事和不要做的事"。

2. ... recur year in year out with ...

year in year out 年复一年。作时间状语,修饰 recur,如:

There she lay year in year out, unable to move, and with no hope of recovery.

她年复一年地躺在那里,不能挪动,没有恢复的希望。

3. We resolve to ... do a thousand and one jobs ...

a thousand and one 许许多多的,如:

He made a thousand and one excuses, trying to justify himself.

他提出了许许多多的借口,企图为自己辩护。

4. Past experience has taught us that certain accomplishments are beyond attainment.

beyond attainment 达不到的,做不到的。为介词短语,常作补语,如:

Such a lofty object is beyond attainment.

这么高的目标是无法达到的。

5. ... so often experienced the frustration that results from

failure.

that results from failure 由于失败而产生的。作定语。result from 由……产生。result 前的主语为结果,而介词 from 后的宾语为起因,如:

His success results from hard work.

他的成功是艰苦工作的结果。

His death resulted from an overdose of drugs.

他因过量吸毒而丧生。

6．**Most of us fail in our efforts at self-improvement …**

fail in 在……方面失败。后接名词、代词或动名词,如:

He failed in everything he tried.

他想的一切办法都没成功。

She failed in persuading me.

她没能说服我。

7．**… to everybody so that we look even more foolish when we slip back into our bad old ways.**

slip back 滑回,退回,如:

Your work has been slipping back recently, so you must make more effort.

近来你的工作在倒退,你必须再努力一点。

The pack of wolves slipped back into the jungle after they had had their wonderful feast.

那群狼在饱餐了一顿后,悄悄溜回到丛林地区。

8．**Aware of these pitfalls, this year I attempted to keep my resolutions to myself.**

(1) Aware of these pitfalls 由于知道这些易犯的错误。形容词短语,在句子中作结果状语,修饰 attempted。

(2) keep … to oneself 把……秘藏心底,如:

Keep your remarks to yourself.

我不要听你的评论。

Don't keep the news to yourself. Let's all share it.

不要把这个消息藏着。让我们都来分享一下。

9. I limited myself to two modest ambitions: to do physical exercises every morning and to read more of an evening.

(1) limit . . . to . . . 把……限定在……,如:

I shall limit myself to three aspects of the subject.

我只准备讨论这个问题的 3 个方面。

Limit your answer to yes or no.

你只要回答"是"或"不是"。

(2) of an evening 相当于 in the evenings,类似的表达法如:

of a Sunday = on Sundays

of a night = at nights

10. . . . but on the second, I applied myself assiduously to the task.

(1) on the second 后承上省略了 day of the year。

(2) apply oneself to . . . 全力以赴于……,致力于……用动词 apply 表达此义时,其后需要使用反身代词,to 为介词,其后需使用名词、代词形式。该表示法不能用于被动语态,如:

You must apply yourself to the job you have to do.

你必须尽力做好你该做的工作。

He applied himself diligently to the Chinese classics.

他孜孜不倦地研究中国古典作品。

11. . . . and twisting the human frame into uncomfortable positions, . . .

twist (. . .) into . . . 使(……)扭曲成……,把(……)扭曲成……有时被引申用来表示"将(……)歪曲成……,把(……)歪曲成……",如:

Her face twisted into a picture of pain.

她面部扭曲,神情痛苦。

The police tried to twist his words into a confession of guilt.

警察企图把他的话曲解为供认有罪。

12. It was this that betrayed me.

强调句由 it 引导。被强调部分是指示代词 this,系指前文 I sat down at the breakfast table in an exhausted condition。

13. The next morning the whole family trooped in to watch the performance.

(1) trooped in 结队而入。

(2) to watch the performance 为动词不定式短语,作目的状语。这 里 performance 指 jumping about on the carpet and twisting the human frame into uncomfortable positions。句中的 trooped in 和 performance 均有夸张意味,以增强文章的幽默效果。

14. ... but I fended off the taunts and jibes of the family good-humouredly ...

(1) fend off ... 挡开……,回避……,制止……,如:

This soup will help you to fend off hunger for a time.

这汤可以暂时帮你解除饥饿。

This medicine is enough to fend off a chill and fever.

这药能退寒热。

(2) good-humouredly 心平气和地。作方式状语,修饰 fended off。

15. Little by little the eleven minutes fell to zero.

little by little 一点点地,逐渐地。表程度状语,如:

Little by little the flood water receded.

洪水渐渐退去。

After the operation, the old man was gaining in health little by little.

手术后,老人渐渐康复。

16. **...I was back to where I had started from.**

where I had started from 回到起始点。这里 where 连词引导
一个名词性从句,作介词 to 的宾语。除 where 外,名词性从句
还可由连词 what、whatever、whoever、whichever、wherever、
when、whenever 等引导。这样使用的连词相当于定语从句中
"先行词 + 关系代词/副词"的作用,如文中那样,当用于介词
之后时,介词不能省略,如:

I'll vote for whoever promises to reduce taxes.
谁答应减税,我就投谁的票。

I often think about when I was young.
我经常回想我年轻的时候。

17. **... I would keep my mind fresh for reading ...**

keep one's mind fresh for ... 保持头脑清醒地……,如:

*You'll keep your mind fresh for this complicated situation
if you have had the comprehensive knowledge of the facts.*
如果你对事实已有全面的了解,你就会头脑清醒地处理
这种复杂局面。

18. **Resisting the hypnotizing effect of television, I sat in my room
for a few evenings with my eyes glued to a book.**

Resisting ... television 为现在分词短语,在句中作目的状语。
with my eyes glued to a book 为带有介词 with 的独立主格结
构,my eyes 为分词短语 glued to a book 的逻辑主语。

19. **... for I soon got back to my old bad habit of dozing off in
front of that screen.**

(1) get back to 回到,恢复到,如:

His only desire is to be cured and to get back to work.
他惟一的希望是治好病,重新工作。

*Let's get back to what we were saying before we were
interrupted.*

534

我们还是回到刚才被打断的话题上吧。

(2) dose off 打瞌睡。

20. In fact，I have just bought a book entitled *How to Read a Thousand Words a Minute*.

entitled *How ... Minute* 为过去分词短语，作定语，修饰 book，意即"题为《一分钟读一千字的诀窍》"。

📑 语法 Grammar in use

perhaps 与 maybe

perhaps 与 maybe 均表示某事有可能，但是并不肯定。这两个词在词义上没有什么区别。只是 maybe 常用于非正式的口语中，不常用于正式文体中：

Maybe/Perhaps the weather will get better.

也许天气会晴好起来。

Julius Caesar is perhaps the greatest of Shakespeare's early plays.

《裘力斯·恺撒》也许是莎士比亚最伟大的早期戏剧。

通常 maybe 只用在句首，而 perhaps 可以用在句子中任何地方，如：

The Allies had better luck, perhaps, than they deserved.

盟军的运气也许太好了。

Ask him again. Perhaps he'll change his mind.

再请他一次。也许他会改变主意。

注意 maybe 是副词，不要将其与 may be(情态助动词 + be)相混淆，如：

Maybe Jane will stay at home tomorrow.

也许简明天呆在家里。

Jane may be at home tomorrow.

明天简可能在家。

英语中表示可能性和肯定性的词还有(从可能性最小列起):

possibly

perhaps，maybe

hopefully

probably

presumably

almost

certainly

no doubt，doubtless

definitely

📁 词汇学习　Word study

1. result

(1) *vi.* (from) (作为结果)产生,发生:

> *If these two substances are combined, an enormous explosion will result.*
>
> 如果将这两种物质混合在一起,会产生巨大的爆炸。
>
> *His blindness resulted from a childhood illness.*
>
> 他的失明是由小时候的一场疾病引起的。

(2) (in) 导致,结果是:

> *The traffic accident resulted in the death of two passengers.*
>
> 这场交通事故导致两名乘客的死亡。
>
> *Environmental pollution is resulting in the forests dying.*
>
> 环境污染正在导致森林的死亡。

(3) *n.* 结果,成果,比分,成绩:

> *She was late for school as a result of the snow.*

她上学迟到是因为下雪的缘故。

When will you get your examination results ?

你什么时候能得到考试成绩？

Your hard work is beginning to show results .

你辛勤的工作正在开始见成效。

2．carry out

（1）实行，执行，进行：

An investigation into the cause of the crash will be carried out by the Department of Transport .

一项有关这次坠机的调查将由运输公司进行。

Our planes carried out a bombing raid on enemy targets .

我们的飞机对敌人的目标进行了一次空袭。

（2）完成，实现（诺言、职责等）：

It is hoped that the kidnappers will not carry out their threat to kill the hostages .

希望绑架者不要履行他们杀害人质的威胁。

They have failed to carry out their orders .

他们没能完成他们的任务。

3．argue

（1）*vi .*（with, over, about）争执，争论，争吵：

They are always arguing about / over money .

他们总是在为钱而争吵。

I wish you wouldn't argue with me all the time .

我希望你不要总跟我争吵。

（2）*vi . , vt .*提出理由，提供理由：

The minister argued for making cuts in military spendings .

部长提出削减军费的理由。

I would argue that sending men to the moon is a waste of

money.

我会摆出理由说明送人上月球是浪费金钱。

（3）*vt*.说服：

She argued him into leaving his job.

她说服他放弃了他的工作。

He argued her out of her decision.

他说服她改变她的决定。

✍ 练习答案 Key to written exercises

1. 关键句型、难点练习答案

See text.

2. 多项选择题答案

| 1 | c | 2 | a | 3 | d | 4 | d | 5 | b | 6 | c |
| 7 | b | 8 | a | 9 | c | 10 | c | 11 | b | 12 | b |

Lesson 51
Predicting the future
预测未来

📖 **课文详注 Further notes on the text**

1. **Who could have imagined, in the mid 1970s, for example, ...**

could + have done(不定式完成式)表示过去没有实现的可能性:某事可能发生,但是却没有发生。

2. **Mainframe computers were very large indeed, often occupying ..., employing ... and run on specially-written software.**

句中现在分词短语 occupying ..., employing ... 和过去分词短语 run ... 均作定语,修饰 computers。正常情况下,分词短语作定语应直接置于所修饰词之后,即 computer 之后,但这里由于3个分词短语一起构成的定语很长,而谓语部分相对较短,为使句子平衡,如句中那样将整个作定语的分词短语置于全句的句后。这里现在分词 occupying 和 employing 表示当时的经常性动作和状态。

3. **... many of their functions have been taken over by small powerful personal computers, commonly known as PCs.**

(1) take over 接管,接任,控制,如:

When Mr. Green retired, his son took over the business from him.

格林先生退休后,由他的儿子接管了他的生意。

Larger companies are taking over smaller firms by buying their shares.

较大的公司通过购买较小商号的股份而控制它们。

539

（2）commonly known as PCs 为过去分词短语，作非限定性定语（相当于一个非限制性定语从句 which are commonly known as PCs），用来补充说明 computers，如非限定性定语从句那样，用作非限定性定语的分词短语与被修饰词之间需用逗号分开，再如：

> *In these years，many brilliant records have been scored，indicating very rapid progress.*
>
> 这些年创造了许多优秀成绩，说明进步是快的。
>
> *The substance，discovered almost by accident，has revolutionized medicine.*
>
> 这种物质几乎是偶然发现的，却使医学发生了革命性的变化。

4. ... and it pointed the way to the future.

point ... to ... 把……指向……，为……指出……，如：

> *A loaded gun was pointed to me.*
>
> 上满子弹的枪对着我。
>
> *Education is a matter of pointing the children to ways in which they can improve the world，and then leaving the job to themselves.*
>
> 教育就是：向孩子们指明他们能藉以改造世界的方法，然后将此项工作交给他们去做。

5. In the early 1980s，the computer giant，IBM produced ...

IBM 国际商用机器公司（International Business Machines）。

6. This ran on an 'operating system' called DOS，produced by a then small company named Microsoft.

（1）run (...) on ... 在……上跑，靠……运转（……），在……上进行（……）。此短语为动词加介词型短语，如：

> *This washing machine runs on very little electricity.*
>
> 这台洗衣机非常省电。

540

His mind ran on his own trouble.

他脑子里想着自己的烦恼。

(2) 句中 called . . .、produced . . . 和 named . . . 均为过去分词短语,作定语,分别修饰 system,DOS,和 company,但 called . . . 和 named . . . 为限定性定语,而 produced . . . 为非限定性定语。有关用法参见本课课文注释3。

7. . . . and multimedia machines which are in common use today.

in use 被用,正被使用。表示进行意义的介词短语,含被动含义,多作主语补语或后置定语,如:

The instruments are in use.

那些仪器正在使用中。

A series of short pulses were sent out by the transmitter in use.

一系列的短脉冲是由正在运转的发射机发送的。

8. Considering how recent these developments are, . . . as long ago as the 1960s, . . .

as long ago as . . . 早在……,如:

I knew him as long ago as 1960.

我早在 1960 年就认识他了。

9. Bagrit dismissed the idea that . . .

dismiss 对……置之不理,不考虑。为动词 dismiss 的借喻用法,如:

He dismissed my argument contemptuously as not worth refuting.

他把我的论证轻蔑地一笔抹杀,认为不值得一驳。

The possibility should not be lightly dismissed.

这种可能性不容忽视。

10. Bagrit foresaw a time when computers . . ., when they would . . ., when they would be used . . ., when they would

541

relieve...

time 后连续出现的 4 个 when 从句均为 time 的定语从句。

11. **... the Internet，the worldwide system that enables us to communicate instantly with anyone ...**

communicate with ... 与……联系,与……沟通,如：

It is always difficult to communicate with someone who speaks a foreign language.

与讲外语的人沟通一向很难。

The girl claims to be able to communicate with the dead.

那女孩声称她能同死人沟通。

12. **Computers have become smaller and smaller，more and more powerful and cheaper and cheaper.**

句中连续使用 3 次"形容词比较级 + and + (同一)形容词比较级",即 more and more 这一结构,为双重比较法,表示出"越……越……"这种持续不断的变化,如：

I'm getting fatter and fatter.

我越来越胖了。

We're going more and more slowly.

我们越走越慢。

在使用 more and more 这种结构时,应注意不能重复其后所用的形容词或副词。如上述后两例中不能使用 more nervous and more nervous 和 more slowly and more slowly。

13. **If he，or someone like him，were alive today，he might be able to ...**

句中从属连词 if 引导非真实性条件状语从句,从句中的 were 和主句中的 might be able 均为虚拟语气用法。

542

📄 语法 Grammar in use

副词的分类(1)

副词用来修饰动词,告诉我们某事是在何时、何地、何种情况下、如何发生的。副词主要用来表示方式、方面、观点、地点、时间、频度、持续时间、程度、强调、焦点以及可能性;此外还有用来表示子句间衔接的连接副词。

1.方式副词

用来表示做某事的方式或某事发生的方式。方式副词多由形容词 + -ly 构成,如 quiet, quietly; bad, badly; happy, happily;此外有些方式副词与形容词同形同义,如 fast、loud、slow、hard:

He reported accurately what they had said.

他准确地报告了他们所说的话。

I receive quarterly bills. I pay my bills quarterly.

我收到的是季度账单,我是按季度付清账单的。(第 1 个 *quarterly* 是形容词,第 2 个是副词)

I hope to catch an early train. I want to arrive early.

我希望赶上早班火车。我想早到。(第 1 个 *early* 是形容词,第 2 个是副词)

2.方面副词

用来表示谈论事情的哪个方面,常由类别形容词 + -ly 构成,如:economical, economically; social, socially; racial, racially:

We had a very bad year last year financially.

去年在金融方面我们很糟糕。

He's not a doctor, technically speaking.

他不是个医生,从技术上讲。

3.观点副词

用来表达说话人或作者对自己所说的话或对谈话或写作对象的看法、态度等。由于这类词修饰的是说话或写作内容,而不影响句子的语法结构,所以这类词也称为"句子"副词。这类副词也常以-ly 结尾,如:frankly、honestly、clearly、generally、surprisingly、incredibly:

Frankly，I am not satisfied with your work.
说实在的,我对你的工作并不满意。

Hopefully，I'll see you sometime tomorrow.
我希望明天什么时候能见到你。

4．地点副词

用来表示某事发生在什么地方或其去向:

A plane flew overhead.
一架飞机从头顶上飞过。

Indoors it was nice and warm. Outside it was snowing heavily.
屋内舒适温暖。屋外正下着大雪。

5．时间副词

用来表示某事发生在何时:

She will be here soon.
她很快就会到这儿。

I'll see you tomorrow.
我明天见你。

📁 词汇学习 Word study

1．imagine *vt*.

（1）想像:

She imagined herself sitting in her favourite armchair back home.
她想像自己已回到家里正坐在她最喜欢的扶手椅上。

Yon can imagine my surprise when they told me the

news .

你能想像得出当他们告诉我那条消息时我有多么吃惊。

(2) 猜测,猜想,认为：

He imagines that his wife doesn't love him , but she does .

他猜疑他的妻子不爱他,但是实际上她爱他。

I thought I heard something , but perhaps I was imagining it .

我以为我听到点声音,但是也许是我想像出来的。

(3) 想,料想,设想：

I imagine he'll be present .

我想他会出席的。

I imagine you'd like to rest after your long journey .

我想经过长途旅行,你想休息一下。

2. occupy *vt .*

(1) 占领,占据,侵占：

The workers occupied the factory and refused to leave .

工人们占据了工厂,拒绝离开。

(2) 占(空间/时间),占用,占有：

Writing occupies most of my free time .

写作占用了我大部分的空闲时间。

Is that seat occupied ?

那个座位有人吗?

(3) 使忙碌,使从事：

This game will keep the children occupied .

这个游戏会使孩子们忙了一阵子。

The people of that country are mainly occupied with agriculture .

那个国家的人民主要从事农业。

3. dismiss *vt*.

(1)（从头脑中）去除,不再考虑,不接受：

    We dismissed the idea of cycling to the Great Wall.

    我们放弃了骑自行车去长城的想法。

    The theories are dismissed by a number of economic authorities.

    这些理论被一些经济学权威所摒弃。

(2)解雇,开除：

    She was dismissed from her job for disobeying the company safety regulations.

    她因为违反公司的安全条例而被解雇。

(3)解散,让……离开：

    The teacher dismissed the class early because she had a meeting.

    老师因为有个会,所以就提前下课了。

    She was dismissed from the hospital when found free from leukaemia.

    当她查出没有得白血病时,就被允许出院了。

✍ 练习答案 Key to written exercises

1. 关键句型、难点练习答案

See text.

2. 多项选择题答案

1	c	2	b	3	d	4	b	5	c	6	a
7	a	8	a	9	a	10	b	11	a	12	a

Lesson 52
Mud is mud
实事求是

📖 **课文详注** **Further notes on the text**

1. **My cousin，Harry，keeps a large curiously-shaped bottle on permanent display in his study.**

   on display 陈列着，展览着。介词短语，在 keep ... on display 短语中作动词 keep 后所随宾语的补足语。该短语常用作句子的主语补语或后置定语，如：

   These pictures are on display in the shop windows.

   这些画片陈列在商店的橱窗里。

   They praised highly of the Chinese lacquer wares on display.

   他们对展出的中国漆器给予很高的评价。

2. **Despite the fact that the bottle is tinted a delicate shade of green，an observant visitor would soon notice that ...**

   (1) that，连词，引导同位语从句，对 fact 作具体说明。

   (2) a delicate shade of green 浅灰色。在句中作 that 从句主语 bottle 的补足语。

3. **If you were to ask Harry ...，he would tell you ...**

   if，从属连词，这里引导一个非真实性条件状语从句。从句中的 were 和主句中的 would tell 为虚拟语气用法。（下句中 if、expressed 与 would invite 也如此。）

4. **How Harry came into the possession of this outlandish stuff makes ...**

How... stuff 为连词 how 引导的名词性从句,在句中作主语。

come into the possession of ... (被……)占有/获得(……),
如:

> *The document came into the possession of the* Daily Mail.
>
> 《每日邮报》得到了这份文件。
>
> *Being the only child, he came into possession of a great deal of property when his father died.*
>
> 作为惟一的孩子,他父亲去世后,他获得了大笔财产。

5. **Furthermore, the acquisition of this bottle cured him of a bad habit he had been developing for years.**

cure sb. of ... 治愈某人的……纠正某人的……,如:

> *No medicine can cure a man of discontent.*
>
> 没有药物能消除一个人的不满。
>
> *Parents try to cure their children of bad habits.*
>
> 父母试图纠正孩子们的不良习惯。

6. **Harry used to consider it a great joke to go into expensive cosmetic shops and make outrageous requests ...**

句中 it 为先行词,作形式宾语,to go into ... 和 make ... 两个动词不定式作句子的逻辑宾语。

7. **He would invent fanciful names on the spot.**

(1) 这里的 would 表示过去习惯性动作,意即"总是"。

(2) on the spot 当场。作状语,修饰 invent。有时也可用来表示
"立刻",如:

> *The news of important events is often broadcast on the spot over television.*
>
> 重要新闻经常通过电视在现场播出。
>
> *I'll post that letter for you on the spot.*
>
> 我立刻就替你发那封信。

8. On entering a shop, he would ask for ...

On entering a shop 一走进商店。这里 on entering a shop 意即 as soon as he entered a shop。

9. ... he would pretend to be considerably put out.

put ... out 使……烦恼/不安/不高兴,如:

The traveller was much put out by the loss of his bag.

由于丢失了提包,这位旅游者极为烦恼。

10. ... was temporarily out of stock ... but of course he never did.

be out of stock 脱销,没现货,如:

The dictionary you wrote for is out of stock.

你来信要买的词典现在已经脱销了。

he never did 中的 did 代替 called again,以避免重复。

11. How Harry managed to keep a straight face during these performances is quite beyond me.

(1) How ... performances 为连词 how 引导的名词性从句,在句子中作主语。

(2) keep a/one's face straight 板着面孔,一本正经,如:

He has such a strange voice that it is difficult for us to keep a straight face when he is talking.

他的嗓音怪怪的,我们很难一本正经地听他说话。

(3) beyond one 超出某人(能力等),如:

This book is quite beyond me.

这本书太深奥,我实在看不懂。

He has gone far beyond me in learning.

他的学识已经大大地超过了我。

12. Harry does not need to be prompted to explain how ...

prompt sb. to do ... 促使/鼓励某人做……,如:

The incident prompted him to call a meeting of the staff.

那个事件促使他召开了一次全体人员会议。

13．... and Harry repeated the word, slowly stressing each syllable.

这里 slowly stressing each syllable 为现在分词短语,作方式状语,说明做出 repeated 动作的方式。

14．When the woman shook her head in bewilderment, Harry went on to explain ...

in bewilderment 为难地。作方式状语,修饰 shook。

15．This explanation evidently conveyed something to the woman ...

convey ... to ... 向……转达……,使……知道……,如:

The ambassador personally conveyed the President's message to the premier.

大使亲自向总理转交了总统的信件。

This picture will convey to you some idea of the beauty of the scenery.

这张图片将使你对那里风景之美有一定的了解。

16．When Harry put on his act of being mildly annoyed, ...

put on an act 装模做样,如:

John wasn't really angry, he was putting on an act.

约翰并没有真的生气,他是在装样子。

17．Intoxicated by his success, ...

Intoxicated ... success 为过去分词短语,作原因状语,意即"由于被胜利所陶醉"。

18．He expected the assistant to look at him in blank astonishment.

in blank astonishment 茫然发愣地。作方式状语,修饰 look at。

to look ... astonishment 为动词不定式短语,作宾语 assistant 的补足语。

550

19. ... and he beat a hasty retreat, clutching the precious bottle under his arm.

beat a hasty retreat 匆忙溜走,如:

They beat a hasty retreat when they saw they were too few.

见到自己的人数太少,他们匆忙溜掉了。

clutching ... his arm 为现在分词短语,作方式状语,修饰 beat a hasty retreat。

语法 Grammar in use

副词的分类(2)

6. 频度副词

用来表示事情发生的频率:

We often swam in the sea.

我们常在大海里游泳。

I was never very good at maths.

我的数学从来不好。

7. 持续时间副词

用来表示某事持续的时间,常用的表示持续时间的副词有 briefly、temporarily、long、indefinitely、always、permanently、forever 等:

She glanced briefly at Lucas.

她短暂地瞥了卢卡斯一眼。

I can't stay long.

我不能久呆。(long 通常只用于疑问句和否定句)

8. 程度副词

用来表示某种状态或行为的程度。常用的有 almost、altogether、barely、enough、fairly、hardly、nearly、quite、

rather、somewhat、too、largely、partially、completely、totally
等。

> *The news is quite amazing.*
> 这消息十分惊人。

> *The lecture was fairly good.*
> 这次讲座还好。

9. 强调副词

用来起进一步强调作用。常用的有 absolutely、just、quite、
simply、certainly、positively、really 等：

> *I really appreciate all you've done for me.*
> 我实在感谢你为我所做的一切。

> *I'm terribly confused by all this information.*
> 我被所有这些信息搞得十分糊涂。

10. 焦点副词

用来指出主要的事情，以使人对其集中注意，如 chiefly、
especially、mostly、just、only、simply 等：

> *Only Tom knows the answer.*
> 只有汤姆知道答案。

> *We want especially to thank the numerous friends who
> encouraged us.*
> 我们想特别感谢那些鼓励我们的无数朋友。

11. 可能性副词

用来表示你认为某事有多大的可能性。常用的有
conceivably、possibly、perhaps、maybe、hopefully、probably、
presumably、definitely 等：

> *I definitely saw her yesterday.*
> 我昨天肯定看到她了。

> *The driver probably knows the quickest route.*
> 司机可能知道最快捷的路。

12. 连接副词

这类副词具有补充、修饰或总结前面所说的话的作用。如果要在口头或书面上连贯地传达信息就必须用这种副词。这类副词有 moreover、also、besides、furthermore、too、again、so、hence、thereby 等：

> *The police were sure that Griffiths was lying. They had found his fingerprints everywhere. Furthermore, they knew for a fact that he hadn't been at his mother's at the time of the crime.*
>
> 警察肯定格里菲斯在说谎。他们已经发现到处都有他的指纹，而且认定出事的时候，他没有在他母亲家里。
>
> *Instead, he sank back in his chair, gasping for breath.*
>
> 他反而坐回到他的椅子上，大口地喘着气。

📁 词汇学习　Word study

1. contain *vt.*

(1) 包含，容纳：

> *This book contains all the information you need.*
> 本书有你所需的一切信息。
>
> *How much liquid do you think this bottle contains?*
> 你认为这个瓶子里能装多少液体？

(2) 控制，抑制(感情等)，克制：

> *Contain yourself! It's not that exciting.*
> 克制点！没那么令人激动。
>
> *More police were sent to the football ground in order to contain the violence.*
> 为控制暴力，更多的警察被派到了足球场。

2. put out

(1) 令……不安,令……不快,令……不适:

She never gets put out even by the most difficult matters.
即使最困难的事也不会令她不安。

She was so put out by his rudeness that she didn't know what to say.

他的无礼令她十分不快,她都不知道该说什么了。

(2) 熄灭,将火扑灭:

She put out all the lights when she left the building.
她离开大楼时将所有的灯都关了。

It took the firemen ten hours to put out the fire.
消防队员用了10个小时才将火扑灭。

(3) 使……不便,给……带来麻烦:

Are you sure it won't put you out if I stay to dinner?
你肯定我留下来吃晚饭不会给你带来不便吗?

She never puts herself out to help people.
她从不为帮助别人而自找麻烦。

(4) 发表,公布,广播:

The sinking ship put out a call for help over its radio.
那艘下沉的船通过无线电发出了求救信号。

The police has put out a statement denying these rumours.
警方已经公布了一项否定这些谣言的声明。

3. meet

(1) vi., vt. 遇见,相遇,偶遇,碰面:

The teacher met one of her pupils in the supermarket.
那个老师在超级市场碰见她的一个学生。

Let's meet for lunch.
我们一起去吃午饭。

(2) vt. 接,迎接:

554

I'll meet you at the airport.

我会到机场接你。

A bus meets every train.

每一辆火车到站都有汽车接。

(3) *vt.* 满足(要求/需要),达到(目标):

Does the hotel meet your expectations?

饭店与你期望的一样吗?

We haven't been able to find a house that meets our needs.

我们还没有找到满足我们需要的房子。

练习答案 Key to written exercises

1. 关键句型、难点练习答案

See text.

2. 多项选择题答案

1 a	2 c	3 d	4 b	5 c	6 d
7 b	8 a	9 c	10 d	11 a	12 d

Lesson 53
In the public interest
为了公众的利益

📖 **课文详注** **Further notes on the text**

1. In the public interest

in the interest(s) of ... 为了……利益,符合……的利益,如:

I'm speaking entirely in your own interests.

我说这番话完全是为了你好。

The names are arranged in alphabetical order in the interest of ready reference.

为了便于查阅,姓名按字母顺序排列。

2. The Scandinavian countries are much admired all over the world for their enlightened social policies.

admire sb. for ... 因为……而钦佩某人,如:

I admire her for her bravery.

我钦佩她的勇敢。

He is admired for what he has done.

他为他所做的事而受到人们的赞扬。

3. ... an excellent system for protecting the individual citizen from high-handed ...

protect ... from ... 使……不受……

4. ... or act over-zealously in the belief that they are serving the public.

in the belief that ... 自以为,相信,如:

He came to me in the belief that I could help him.

556

他来找我,是相信我能帮助他。

He bought the diamond ring in the full belief that it was genuine.

他买了这枚钻戒,深信它是真货。

在此短语中,that 引导的从句为 belief 的同位语。

5. ... the Swedish Parliament introduced a scheme to safeguard the interest of the individual.

to safeguard ... individual 为动词不定式短语,作 scheme 的定语,即"一个保护公民利益的制度"。

6. A parliamentary committee representing all political parties appoints a person who is suitably qualified to investigate private grievances against the State.

(1) representing ... parties 为现在分词短语,作 committee 的定语,意即"代表各政党的……"。

(2) be qualified to do ... 有资格做……,胜任做……,如:

He's the best/least qualified to do the work.

他最/没有资格做这项工作。

She is qualified by training and natural gifts to undertake the job.

她所受的训练及天赋使她有资格从事这项工作。

表达此义时,也可使用 be qualified in doing ... 这样的结构,如:

She's well qualified in teaching English.

她完全有资格教英语。

后为名词时,通常使用介词 for,即 be qualified for ...,如:

He is eminently/highly qualified for the task.

他非常适合担当那项工作。

在表达"使……有资格作/当……"时,通常使用 qualify sb. as... 这一结构,有时这一结构被引申为"认为……是……"的

557

含义,如:

> *They have qualified his proposal as practical.*
> 他们认为他的建议是切实可行的。

在表达"使有……资格"、"使能担当……"时,其后通常使用介词 for, 即 qualify sb. for sth., 如:

> *Her selfless spirit qualifies her for the task.*
> 她的无私精神使她适合担当这项任务。

(3) 句中 against the State 为介词短语,作定语,修饰 State。句中的 State 指 Sweden,因此需用大写。

7. **The Ombudsman is not subject to political pressure.**

be subject to ... 受……控制,视……而定,需经……,如:

> *We are all subject to the laws of nature.*
> 我们都受自然规律的支配。

> *Our plan may change subject to the weather.*
> 我们的计划可能因天气而改变。

> *The treaty is subject to ratification.*
> 本条约需经批准后方能生效。

8. **He investigates complaints large and small that come to him from all levels of society.**

large and small 程度不同的。作 complaints 的定语。两个意义相反的形容词并用时通常需置于被修饰词之后。

9. **As complaints must be made in writing, ...**

(1) as 由于。从属连词,引导原因状语从句。

(2) in writing 以书面/笔头形式地,如:

> *The evidence was put down in writing.*
> 此证据被记录在案。

10. **... and he examines every single letter in detail.**

in detail 详细地。作状语,在句中修饰动词 examine,如:

> *There isn't time to explain in detail.*

没有时间来详细解释了。

Tell me what happened in a few words ; don't go into details.

扼要地告诉我发生了什么事,用不着讲得太详细。

11. ... for his correspondence is open to public inspection.

be open to ... 对……开放/公开的,可接受(考虑)的,易受……的。短语中的 to 为介词,因此其后需用名词、代词等。

The clinic is open to outsiders as well as employees and their families.

这个诊所除了给雇员及其家属看病,还对外开放。

All careers are open to talents.

有才能的人到处可立业。

This book is open to misunderstanding/criticism.

这本书易被误解/受批评。

12. ... the Ombudsman will act on his behalf.

on one's behalf 代表某人,如:

My husband could not be here tonight, but I want to thank you on his behalf.

我丈夫今晚因故不能前来,我代表他向你们致谢。

She gave evidence on her own behalf.

她为自己提出证据。

13. ... or even suggest to parliament that a law be altered.

连词 that 为动词 suggest 引导的一宾语从句。在 law 与 be 之间可视为省略了 should。无论现结构还是加上 should,均为虚拟语气结构,这是由动词 suggest 的用法所决定的。有关用法参见第 46 课课文注释 10。

14. A foreigner living in a Swedish village wrote to the Ombudsman complaining that he had been ill-treated by the police, ...

complaining that ... foreigner 为现在分词短语,作目的状语,

559

修饰 wrote。

15. **The Ombudsman immediately wrote to the Chief of Police in the district asking him to send a record of the case.**

(1) the Chief of Police 警察局长。

(2) asking . . . the case 为现在分词短语,作目的状语。

16. **There was nothing in the record to show that . . . and the Chief of Police strongly denied the accusation.**

(1) to show that . . . justified 为动词不定式短语,作定语,修饰 nothing。

(2) 并列连词 and 后的 the Chief of Police . . . accusation 与 There was . . . justified 为两个并列的句子,而非连词 that 从句中的内容。

17. **The lawyer ascertained that a policeman had indeed dealt roughly with foreigners on several occasions.**

(1) deal with . . . 对待……,对付……,还可用来表示"处理"某事或"论述"某内容或课题等,如:

Deal with a man as he deals with you.
以其人之道,还治其人之身。

They have learnt to deal with various problems.
他们学会了处理各种问题。

(2) on several occasions 多次。on occasions 需在句中作状语,表示时间频率。occasion(s)前面不加修饰词时,表示"有时"、"间或"之意,如:

He visits the city on occasion.
他有时进城去。

We no longer keep up the close friendship of a few years ago, though we still visit each other on occasion(s).
我们已经不再保持几年前的亲密友谊了,虽然我们仍然偶尔互相拜访。

18. The fact that the policeman was prejudiced against foreigners could not be ...

(1) that the policeman ... foreigners 为 fact 的同位语。

(2) prejudice ... against ... 使……对……抱有偏见,使……对……反感,如:

> *His voice and manner prejudice his audience against him.*
> 他的声音和举止使听众反感。

> *One unfortunate experience prejudiced him against all lawyers.*
> 一次不幸的遭遇使他对所有的律师都抱有偏见。

句中 prejudiced (抱有偏见的) 作形容词,构成 be prejudiced against ...(对……抱有偏见)结构,如:

> *He's strongly prejudiced against me.*
> 他对我抱有强烈的偏见。

19. It was only possible for the Ombudsman to find this out by sending ...

句中 It 为形式主语,句子的逻辑主语为带介词 for 的动词不定式短语。

20. The policeman in question was ... if any further complaints were lodged against him, ...

(1) in question 上述的,当事的,讨论中的,如:

> *The book in question is out of print.*
> 所说的书已绝版。

> *Where's the man in question?*
> 我们谈到的那个人在哪里?

(2) lodge a complaint against ... 对……提出控诉/诉状,如:

> *He lodged a complaint against his neighbours with the authorities.*
> 他向当局控告他的邻居。

561

21. The Ombudsman's prompt action at once put an end to an unpleasant practice which might have gone unnoticed.

（1）put an end to . . . 结束,终止,消失。短语中 to 为介词,因此其后需用名词或代词,如:

> *We must put an end to this foolish behavior.*
> 我们必须终止这种愚蠢的行为。
>
> *Death put an end to his wicked career.*
> 死亡结束了他邪恶的一生。

（2）which 为关系代词,引导定语从句,修饰 practice。该从句中的 might ＋ have done(完成式结构)表示对过去可能发生的事情的一种推测,为虚拟语气结构。

（3）unnoticed 为过去分词,在这里作方式状语,修饰 gone。

语法　Grammar in use

副词在句子中的位置(1)

1. 方式副词、地点副词、时间副词

（1）通常用于主要动词之后。如果动词有宾语,则用在宾语之后,如:

> *She sang beautifully.*
> 她的歌唱得很美。
>
> *Thomas made his decision immediately.*
> 托玛斯立即作出了他的决定。

（2）如果在句子中这几种副词同时出现,通常的次序为方式副词、地点副词和时间副词,如:

> *She spoke very well at the village hall last night.*
> 她昨天晚上在村议事厅里演讲得非常出色。

方式副词可以用于主要动词前面。但是,如果动词是句子的最后一个词则很少用于动词前面,如:

562

He silently counted four, then put the receiver down.

他默默地数到 4,然后将听筒放下。

She listened carefully.

她仔细地听着。

(3) 如果动词词组包含一个或多个助动词,可以将方式副词用于主要动词之前或第一个助动词之后,特别是当其中是个情态助动词时,如:

She had carefully measured out his dose of medicine.

她曾经认真地测出他的用药剂量。

They might easily have been taken for brothers.

他们有可能轻易地被看成是兄弟。

(4) 大多数不以-ly 结尾的副词只用于动词或动词宾语后面,如:

I work hard and play hard.

我拼命工作也拼命玩。

The train goes fast.

火车跑得快。

(5) 在描述性文体中,为了强调,方式、时间和地点副词有时用于句首,如:

Recently, I went to Berlin. It was very interesting...

最近,我去了柏林,那地方很有趣……

She rang the bell for Sylvia. In came a girl she had not seen before.

她按铃叫西尔维亚。进来了一个她从未见过的姑娘。

(6) 不用于 be 动词之前,如:

I was recently in Berlin.

我最近在柏林。

2. 观点副词

常用于句首,然后稍微停顿一下,书面上则用逗号隔开,这样就起到了修饰后面句子的作用,如:

Surprisingly，most of my help came from the technicians.

令人吃惊的是对我的帮助大多来自那些技师们。

3.频度副词和可能性副词

（1）常用于第一个助动词后或主要动词之前,如：

I usually have cream in my coffee.

我常常在咖啡里放奶油。

They can probably afford another one.

他们可能能买得起另外一台。

（2）也可以用于句首,如：

Sometimes we get a lot of rain in August.

有时在 8 月份雨水很多。

Presumably they'd brought him home and he'd invited them in.

很有可能他们将他送回家,他邀请他们进屋。

（3）在没有助动词时需用于 be 动词之后,如：

Debbie is sometimes not responsible for what she does.

戴比有时对她所做的事不负责任。

He was definitely scared.

他一定是给吓坏了。

（4）用于 don't、won't 等否定简略式之前,如：

We usually don't get up before 9 on Sundays.

星期日我一般不在 9 点以前起床。

It probably won't be that bad.

可能还不那么糟。

📁　词汇学习　Word study

1.adopt

（1）*vt*.采用,采纳：

The new tax would force companies to adopt energy saving measures.

这项新税收会迫使公司采用节能措施。

This factory has adopted our production methods.

这家工厂已经采用了我们的生产方法。

(2) *vi.*, *vt.* 收养,领养:

Since she was so poor that she had her child adopted.

由于她非常贫困所以她让别人收养了她的孩子。

They have no children of their own, but they're hoping to adopt.

他们没有自己的孩子,但是他们希望收养一个。

(3) *vt.* 正式通过,批准:

The committee adopted my suggestion.

这个委员会批准了我的建议。

The House adopted the report.

众议院正式通过了这个报告。

2. refer to

(1) 提到,谈到,指称:

The scientist referred to the discovery as the most exciting new development in this field.

那位科学家称这一发现是这一领域最激动人心的新进展。

In his autobiography he often refers to his unhappy schooldays.

在他的自传中,他常常提到他那段不愉快的学校生活。

(2) 参考,查看,查阅:

Let me just refer to my notes to find the exact figure.

让我查看一下我的笔记,看一看准确的数字。

You'd better refer to a dictionary.

你最好查一下词典。

（3）与……有关,针对:

The new law does not refer to land used for farming.

这项新法律不适用于耕种的土地。

Does your remark refer to all of us?

你的话是针对我们大家的吗?

3.justify *vt.*

（1）给出正当的理由,给出满意的解释:

How can you justify spending so much money?

你怎么解释花了这么多钱?

The President will find it difficult to justify this decision to the public.

总统很难就这项决定给公众一个满意的解释。

（2）是……正当理由:

Nothing can justify such rudeness.

没有任何理由能解释这样的无礼。

The results of the study have certainly justified the money that was spent on it.

这项研究的结果当然就是这项研究所用费用的最好理由。

✍ **练习答案　Key to written exercises**

1.关键句型、难点练习答案

See text.

2.多项选择题答案

| 1 | c | 2 | d | 3 | c | 4 | b | 5 | a | 6 | c |
| 7 | a | 8 | a | 9 | c | 10 | a | 11 | b | 12 | b |

Lesson 54
Instinct or cleverness?
是本能还是机智？

📖 **课文详注** **Further notes on the text**

1. **We have been brought up to fear insects.**

   因为句子使用被动语态形式,因此句中的动词不定式 to fear insects 作主语 we 的补足语。(在主动语态中为宾语补足语。)

2. **We continually wage war on them,...**

   wage war on/against 对……开战,如:

   The police don't have the resources to wage war on/against crime.

   警察没有财力同罪犯斗争。

3. **... they fly uninvited into our rooms on ...**

   uninvited 为过去分词,作方式状语,修饰 fly。

4. **We live in dread not only of unpleasant insects like spiders or wasps, but of quite harmless ones like moths.**

   in dread of ... 在……恐惧之中,如:

   A criminal lives in constant dread of being arrested.

   一个犯罪的人总是担心被捕。

   He is in perpetual dread of exposure.

   他总是害怕暴露出来。

   在对等连词 not only...but 之后跟随的是对等的语句成分(本句中均为介词短语结构)。

5. **Reading about them increases our understanding without dispelling our fears.**

Reading about them，动名词短语，在句中作主语。

without...fears，介词短语，作方式状语，修饰 increases。

6．**Knowing that the industrious ant lives in ... when we find hordes of them crawling over... lunch.**

Knowing that... society 为动名词短语，作主语，that 从句中的 ant 前使用了定冠词，指蚂蚁这一类，而非指一只蚂蚁。定冠词用于可数名词单数前表示一类的概念，如：

The compass was invented in China four thousand years ago.

指南针是中国 4,000 年前发明的。

7．**No matter how much we like honey，or how much we have read about...，we have a horror of being stung.**

（1）No matter how ... honey 与 or how much we ... possess 均为让步状语从句，or 后的让步状语从句承前省略了 no matter。

（2）have a horror of（doing）害怕（做），厌恶（做），如：

He has a horror of being flattered.

他最怕别人奉承他。

Most of us have a horror of spiders.

我们大多数人都极厌恶蜘蛛。

8．**... but they are impossible to erase.**

这里 they 指 fears，与 to erase 有逻辑上的动宾关系，即 they 是 to erase 的逻辑宾语。

9．**... especially when we find that，like the praying mantis，they lead...**

动词 find 后有连词 that 引导的宾语从句 they ... lives 被 like the praying mantis 断开。这里 like 为介词，它所构成的短语在句中作方式状语，修饰 lead。这里把状语提前起强调作用。like（像……一样）为比喻词，用于明喻。在 praying mantis 中，是将螳螂把两只前腿合在一起比作人祷告时的姿势，为暗喻

568

用法。

10. We enjoy staring at them, entranced as they go about their business, unaware (we hope) of our presence.

(1) staring at them 为动名词短语,作宾语,由动词 enjoy 的用法所决定。

(2) entranced as they . . . business 为过去分词短语,作伴随状况状语,可视为 entranced 前省略了 being,用来修饰 staring。

(3) go about 从事,干,为动介短语,如:

She went about her work in a cold way.

她干工作很冷静。

It's high time that they went about their own business.

他们早该去干自己的事了。

(4) unaware of our presence 为形容词短语,也可视为其前省略了 being,作伴随状况状语,修饰 go about。

11. Who has not stood in awe at the sight of spider pouncing on a fly, or a column of ants triumphantly bearing home an enormous dead beetle.

(1) in awe (of . . .) (对……)敬畏地,畏惧地,如:

They gazed at her in awe.

他们害怕地注视着她。

The savages live in awe of nature.

未开化的人们对自然有敬畏感。

(2) pouncing on a fly 和 bearing home . . . beetle 均为动名词短语,作介词 of 的宾语。spider 和 a column of ants 分别作它们的逻辑主语。

12. Clusters of tiny insects called aphids were to be found on the underside of the leaves.

were to be found 为 to be to do . . . 用法,可表达多种情态含义。这里表示 could 的含义,但语气较 could 要强,再如:

Not a cloud was to (= could) be seen.

天上没有一丝云。

How are you to/can you keep it from us?

你怎么能瞒着我们?

13. I immediately embarked on an experiment which, even though it failed to get rid of the ants, kept me fascinated for twenty-four hours.

kept me fascinated 中 fascinated 作宾语 me 的补足语。which 为关系代词,引导定语从句,指代先行词 experiment。

14. ... making it impossible for the ants to reach the aphids.

making ... aphids 为现在分词短语,作目的状语,修饰 bound。

15. I got up early next morning hoping to find ... in despair.

hoping ... in despair 为现在分词短语,作原因状语,说明做出 got up 动作的原因。

16. ... and then on to the leaves of the tree.

这里的 on 为副词,修饰 climbing,含"继续"之意。

17. The ants had been quick to find an answer to my thoroughly unscientific methods!

(1) to find an answer ... methods 为动词不定式,作结果状语。

(2) to my thoroughly unscientific methods 为介词短语,作 answer 的定语,即"对付我那套完全不科学的办法"。

语法 Grammar in use

副词在句子中的位置(2)

4. 程度副词

(1) 某些程度副词一般用于主要动词之前,如果句子中有助动词,它们可以用于头一个助动词之后或用于主要动词之前。这些程度副词有 almost、quite、nearly、really、largely、rather 等:

570

He almost crashed into a lorry.

他差点儿撞上一辆卡车。

I quite enjoy mountain holidays.

我相当喜欢在山区度假。

(2) 有一些程度副词可以用于主要动词之前或之后,还可以用于宾语之后。这些程度副词有 badly、heavily、completely、greatly、little、seriously、strongly、totally 等:

I disagree completely with Mr. Green.

我完全不赞成格林先生的看法。

Mr. Brooke strongly criticized the Bank of England.

布鲁克先生严厉地批评了英格兰银行。

That argument doesn't convince me totally.

那个论点不能使我完全信服。

(3) 有一些程度副词总是用于动词或动词宾语后面。这些程度副词有 hard、immensely、terribly、remarkably、hugely、tremendously 等:

I missed you terribly.

我太想你了。

Annual budgets varied tremendously.

年度预算差别巨大。

5. 强调副词

强调副词通常用于主语、助动词或 be 之后,否定简略式 don't,won't 等之前:

I really appreciate all you've done for me.

我实在感谢你为我所做的一切。

Miss Hargreaves is extremely helpful.

哈格里夫斯小姐非常帮忙。

That simply isn't true.

完全不是那么回儿事。

6. 焦点副词

一般用于头一个助动词后面,主要动词或你想要对方集中注意的词前面,如果谓语动词是 be,且没有任何助动词时,应用于 be 之后:

I've written the letters. I should also have posted them.

我写了那些信,我本也应该把它们寄出去。

I play squash and I also play tennis.

我打壁球,也打网球。

Even Tom knows that 2 and 2 make 4.

连汤姆都知道 2 加 2 等于 4。

Economic development is primarily a question of getting more work done.

经济发展主要是做更多的工作。

7. 连接副词

通常用于句首,主语或头一个助动词的后面。有些连接副词也可以出现在句子中间,用逗号与句子的其他部分隔开:

It will never be possible to release these criminals. Moreover, as the years go by, there are bound to be other similar cases.

永远不可能释放这些罪犯。此外,随着岁月的流逝,肯定还会有其他类似的案件发生。

The effect on wild flowers, however, has been enormous.

然而对野花的作用却非常大。

注意:一般不能用副词将动词和其宾语分开,如不能说:

* I like very much English.

而应说:

I like English very much.

1. enjoy *vt*.

(1) 享受……乐趣,欣赏,喜爱:

I enjoyed my stay in the U.S.A. very much.

我在美国呆得非常愉快。

I enjoy skiing in winter.

我喜欢在冬天滑雪。

(2) 享有,享受:

He has always enjoyed very good health.

他总是非常健康。

The staff in this company enjoy a good income.

这个公司里的职员收入丰厚。

(3) (oneself)得到乐趣,过得快活:

I enjoyed myself during the holidays.

我假期过得很快活。

Did you enjoy yourself at the party?

聚会上你尽兴了吗?

2. go about

(1) 做,干:

It was a typical Monday morning and people were going about their work in the usual way.

那是个典型的星期一早上,人们像往常一样在工作。

In spite of last night's terrorist attack most people seem to be going about their business as if nothing had happened.

尽管昨晚上发生了恐怖分子的袭击,可是大多数的人们好像什么事都未发生一样在照常工作。

(2) 开始做,开始干:

That's not the best way to go about it.

那不是着手干这件事的最好方法。

How can we go about solving this problem ?

我们该如何着手解决这个问题？

（3）四处走动：

The quickest way to go about the city is by underground train .

逛这座城市的最快捷办法是乘地铁。

Why did you go about the park with such strange people ?

你为什么同那些怪人在公园里走来走去？

3. embark

（1）*vt . , vi .*（使）上船，装载：

We embarked at Liverpool for New York .

我们从利物浦上船去纽约。

The ship embarked passengers and wool at an Australian port .

那艘船在澳大利亚的一个码头装载了乘客和羊毛。

（2）*vt .*（upon，on）从事，着手（尤指新的或巨大、重要的事）：

We're embarking upon a new project later this year .

今年晚些时候我们要着手实施一项新的方案。

✍ 练习答案 **Key to written exercises**

1. 关键句型、难点练习答案

See text .

2. 多项选择题答案

1 b	2 d	3 a	4 c	5 c	6 a
7 c	8 d	9 b	10 b	11 b	12 c

Lesson 55
From the earth：Greetings
来自地球的问候

📖 **课文详注 Further notes on the text**

1. From the earth：Greetings

正常语序应为 Greetings from the earth，即以介词 from 构成的介词短语修饰 greetings。本文题目中将定语提前，并在冒号后将 Greetings 以首字母大写的形式写出，使这两个部分都得到强调。

2. Finding planets is ..., but finding life on them ...

句中的 Finding planets 和 finding life on them 均为动名词短语，在句中作主语。

3. The first question to answer is whether a planet can actually support life.

whether 为连词，引导一个名词性从句，在句中作主语补语。

4. Whether a planet can support life depends on the size and brightness of its star, that is its 'sun'.

(1) Whether a planet can support life 一颗行星是否能支持生命。是由连词 whether 引导的名词性从句，作句子的主语。

(2) that is 就是，即。经常作插入语，对句子中的某一成分进一步说明。

5. A planet would have to be a very long way from it to be capable of supporting life.

to be capable of supporting life 为动词不定式短语，作目的状语。

6. Alternatively，if the star were small，the life-supporting planet

would have to have . . .

if 为从属连词,这里引导一个非真实性条件状语从句,即对现在情况的一种假设,因此从句中的动词 were(用于单数名词 star 之后)和主句中的 would have to . . .(同前句中 A planet would have to be life 一样)均使用了虚拟语气结构。

7. But how would we find such a planet?

这里 would 为虚拟语气用法,这种用法用来提出问题,多用于口语中。使语气显得比较客气、委婉,如:

What would you advise me to do ?

你看我怎么办好呢?

8. At present, there is no telescope in existence that . . .

in existence 现存的,存在的,现有的。介词短语,在句中作定语,修饰 telescope,如:

This is the largest ship in existence .

这是世上现有的最大的一条船。

This is the oldest Chinese manuscript in existence .

这是现存的最早的汉语手稿。

9. It is important to look for . . . using earth-based telescopes.

using . . . telescopes 为现在分词短语,作方式状语,修饰 look for。

10. Even a telescope in orbit round the earth, . . .

in orbit 在轨道上的。介词短语,作定语,修饰 telescope。
round the earth 围绕地球的。介词短语,作定语,则修饰 orbit。

11. A telescope would have to be as far away as the planet Jupiter . . . , because the dust becomes thinner the further we travel towards the outer edges of our own solar system.

(1) as far as . . . 像……一样远。这里在 far 后使用了副词 away,作语义和语气上的强调,可理解为"远至……"。

(2) the dust becomes thinner the further we . . . system 为 the more

（形容词/副词比较级）...the more（形容词/副词比较级），即"越……越……"结构的变异。就正常语序而言,应为 the further we travel ... system the thinner the dust becomes。由于 thinner 未用于句首,且直接在动词 becomes 后作主语补足语,这样就省略了 the。

12. Once we detected a planet，we would have to find a way of blotting out the light from its star，so that we would be able to...

（1）once 一旦。连词。引导条件状语从句,强调只需"一次",就可给人不能忘的印象或达到某目的等,如:

You won't find it difficult once you have mastered the rudiments.

一旦掌握了基本东西,你就不会感觉困难了。

注意:使用连词 as soon as(一……就……)引导的时间状语从句,更强调主句与从句的两个动作在时间上的紧接状态,比较:

As soon as I met him，I was fascinated by him.

我一遇见他,就被他吸引住了。

Once you see him，you'll never forget him.

只要你见到他,你就会永远忘不了他。

（2）句中 detected, would have to 和 would be able to 均为虚拟语气表达形式,更强调一种假设情况。

（3）blot out ... 把……遮住/抹掉,如:

The sky is blotted out by the clouds.

乌云遮住了天空。

His sins are all blotted out.

他的罪恶被全部抹掉了。

13. In the first instance，we would be looking for plant life，rather than 'little green men'.

(1) in the first instance 起初,首先。介词短语,其反义表达为 in the last instance(最后),如:

> *I thought so too in the first instance.*
> 我起初也这样想。

(2) rather than 而不是,而非。连词,用于两者选择中被否定的部分。这种表达方式常常用于"平行结构"中,即其前后用词应为同一属类,可均为形容词、状语词组、代词、动词不定式或动词-ing形式,如:

> *I'd call her hair chestnut rather than brown.*
> 我宁愿说她的头发是栗色,而不是棕色。(两个形容词)
> *I'd prefer to go in August rather than in July.*
> 我愿 8 月去,不愿 7 月去。(两个作状语的介词词组)
> *It ought to be you rather than me that signs the letter.*
> 在信上署名的应该是你而不是我。(两个代词)
> *I always prefer starting early, rather than leaving everything to the last minute.*
> 我总是愿意早开始,而不愿意把所有事情都留到最后才做。(两个动词-*ing* 形式)
> *I decided to write rather than（to）telephone.*
> 我决定写信而不打电话。(两个动词不定式)

作动词不定式时,rather than 后的动词不定式既可带 to,也可不带 to。

14. The life forms most likely to develop on a planet …

to develop on a planet 为动词不定式短语,作定语,修饰 forms。likely 这里作为程度副词修饰其后的动词不定式。当 likely 作副词使用时,通常使用 very 或 most 对其进行修饰,如:

> *They'll very likely ask for an increase in the budget.*
> 他们很可能会要求增加预算。

15. It is bacteria that have generated the oxygen we breathe on

578

earth.

bacteria 细菌,复数名词。其单数为 bacterium。

16. **But this hope is always in the realms of science fiction.**

in the realm of ... 在……领域/界/方面,如:

> *The differences between the two groups are quite profound, both in the realm of ideology and in the realm of practical policy.*
>
> 这两个组织之间,无论在思想领域还是在现行政策方面,都存在着极大的分歧。
>
> *The story remains in the realms of fantasy but is presented as an adult dream.*
>
> 这个故事仍属于幻想故事,但是是以一个成年人的梦的形式讲述的。

17. **As Daniel Goldin of NASA observed, 'Finding life elsewhere would change everything. No human endeavour or thought would be unchanged by it.'**

(1) as 这里作关系代词,指代 Finding ... everything 和 No human... by it。作关系代词使用的 as 常用来指代整个句子或一件事,如:

> *As has been said before, grammar is not a set of dead rules.*
>
> 正如前文已经提到过的,语法不是一套死规则。(指代 *grammar ... rules* 全句)
>
> *Old Tom was driven out of the house and, as might be expected, died of hunger and cold.*
>
> 老汤姆被撵出了房门,正如所料,他因饥寒而死去。(指代 *he died of hunger and cold* 这一事实)

(2) No human endeavour or thought would be unchanged by it 为双重否定句,直译为"没有人类的任何努力或思想不会被改变"。

这里所使用的 would change、would be unchanged 以及前文中许多"would + 动词"的结构形式均为虚拟语气,用来表示委婉提出看法。在虚拟语气中,应对 would 的这一用法加以注意。

语法　Grammar in use

修饰语

修饰语是位于名词前的一个词或一组词,用来提供此名词所指事物更多的信息。修饰语可以是形容词、名词、地名、地点和方向副词以及表示时间的副词。

1.形容词修饰语

This is the main bedroom.

这是主卧室。

Tom is a heavy smoker.

汤姆烟抽得很厉害。

2.名词修饰语

英语中名词作修饰语很常见。名词修饰语一般为单数形式,但是也有个别以复数形式出现的名词作修饰语时保持其复数形式,如 arms、clothes、jeans、glasses、sunglasses 等:

It's a cotton dress.

那是件棉布衣裙。

He is a football player.

他是个足球运动员。

I'm going to a family dinner party.

我去参加一个家庭晚餐聚会。

arms control　武器控制

clothes pegs　衣服夹

3. 地名修饰语

a London hotel 一个伦敦饭店

Arctic explorers 北极探险家

4. 地点和方向副词修饰语

the downstairs television room 楼下的电视间

Gradually the underground caverns fill up with deposits.
渐渐地地下洞穴塞满了存储物。

5. 时间修饰语

表示钟点和一天中某个时段的词可以作修饰语：

Every morning he would set off right after the eight o'clock news.

每天早上他一听完8点钟新闻就起程。

morning coffee 早点咖啡

an evening dress 晚礼服

📂 词汇学习 Word study

1. detect *vt.*

（1）（当场）发现：

The policeman waited to detect the prisoner in a lie.
警察静静地等待以发现罪犯在撒谎。

The supervisor detected a candidate cheating.
监考发现一个考生在作弊。

（2）察觉,觉察,发现：

I detected a note of annoyance in his voice.
我从他的声音中觉察出他有点不满。

Financial experts have detected signs that the economy is beginning to improve.
金融专家已经觉察出经济即将开始复苏的迹象。

(3)（用专门仪器、设备）测出,侦察出:

Radar equipment is used to detect enemy aircraft.
雷达设备被用于侦察敌机。

Radioactive material has been detected in the atmosphere.
已经在空气中发现放射性物质。

2. capable *adj.*

(1) 有能力的,有才能的,有技能的:

Tom is a very capable driver.
汤姆是个非常能干的司机。

We need to get an assistant who's capable and efficient.
我们需要有一个既能干又有效率的助手。

(2) 有……能力/技能,有……本领:

He is not a man who is capable of intense concentration.
他可不是能专心致志的人。

A force 10 wind is capable of blowing the roofs off houses.
10 级风能将房顶掀掉。

(3) 能……的,有……可能的:

I think your plan is capable of being improved.
我认为你们的计划还可以改进。

His remark is capable of being misunderstood.
他的讲话可能会被误解。

3. observe *vt.*

(1) 看到,察觉到:

A good novelist observes everything and misses nothing.
一个好的小说家能注意到一切而不错过任何事。

I observed him climb the wall and enter the garden.
我看到他爬过墙,进到花园里。

I observed him climbing the wall and entering the

garden.

我看到他正在爬墙进入花园。

(2)监视,观察:

The role of scientists is to observe and describe the world, not to try to control it.

科学家们的作用是观察世界,描述世界,而不是企图去控制世界。

He spent a year in the jungle, observing how deforestation is affecting local tribes.

他在丛林里度过了一年的时间,观察森林的毁坏是如何影响当地部落的。

(3)说,评论,评述:

She observed that it would soon be time to stop for lunch.

她说很快就要到停下来吃午饭的时间了。

I observed nothing on this subject.

我对此问题没有发表任何看法。

✍ 练习答案 Key to written exercises

1. 关键句型、难点练习答案

See text.

2. 多项选择题答案

1 b	2 c	3 a	4 b	5 c	6 a
7 a	8 c	9 a	10 c	11 b	12 a

Lesson 56

Our neighbour, the river

河流,我们的邻居

📖 **课文详注** Further notes on the text

1. **The river which forms the eastern boundary of our farm has always played an important part in our lives.**

play a part in ... 在⋯⋯中起作用,在⋯⋯中扮演角色,如:

> *He played a very important part in the negotiations.*
>
> 他在那些谈判中担任很重要的角色。
>
> *Life is a great lottery, in which chance and opportunity play an enormous part.*
>
> 人生不可预测,机遇作用巨大。

2. **Without it we could not make a living.**

Without it 如果没有它。介词短语,起到非真实条件状语从句的作用。因此句中的 could not make 需使用虚拟语气结构形式。虚拟语气句并非必须由 if 引导出非真实性条件状语从句部分,主要依其真实性或非真实性的语义概念为标准。当某些介词短语起到非真实性状语从句作用时,句子就应以虚拟语气结构来表达,如:

> *We could have done better under more favourable conditions.*
>
> 在更为有利的情况下,我们可以做得更好。
>
> *We might have failed without your timely help.*
>
> 没有你的及时帮助,我们可能已经失败了。

3. **There is only enough spring water to supply the needs of the**

584

house, so we have to pump from the river for farm use.

the needs of the house 就字面意义,可译作"家庭需求",根据上下文所表达的意义,译作"家庭生活用水"。

4. **We know instinctively, just as beekeepers with their bees, that misfortune might overtake us if the important events of our lives were not related to it.**

(1) 在该宾语从句中,使用了由从属连词 if 引导的非真实性条件状语从句,因此使用了 might overtake 和 were not related 这样的虚拟语气结构的动词形式。

(2) just as beekeepers with their bees 正像养蜂人同蜜蜂的关系那样。作方式状语,修饰 know。这里,作者以比喻表述形式(just),把那条河与村民的关系比作养蜂人同蜜蜂之间的关系,因为就英、美某些地区的旧风俗,养蜂人把蜜蜂视为一家人,并把家庭秘密或死讯等大事情告诉蜜蜂,以使蜜蜂不会成群离去。

5. **... which a predecessor of ours at the farm built in the meadow hard by the deepest pool for swimming and diving.**

hard by ... 在……近旁,如:

Hard by the school stood a big bookstore.

学校旁边就有一家大书店。

6. **In a heat wave we choose ...**

in a heat wave 在大热天。heat wave(热浪)指气温较平常高得多的一段时间。这里用具体的"热浪"(heat wave)泛指"炎热的天气"(hot weather)。

7. **We welcome the seasons by the riverside, crowning ..., holding ..., giving ..., and throwing ...**

句中的 crowning ...、holding ...、giving ... 和 throwing ... 为 4 个并列的现在分词短语,均作方式状语,修饰动词 welcome,说明做出 welcome 动作的方式。

585

8．This is a rare occurrence as our climate seldom goes to extremes.

（1）a rare occurrence 罕见的情况。这里指 the river may overflow its bank。

（2）as 因为,由于。从属连词,引导原因状语从句。

（3）go to extremes 走极端,采取极端手段,如：

> *She goes to extremes in everything.*
>
> 她凡事都走极端。
>
> *I won't go to extremes.*
>
> 我不想采取极端手段。

go to extremes 也可用 to run to an extreme 形式表达。

9．We are lack in that ..., and flooding can sometimes spell disaster for their owners.

in that 因为,由于。复合连词,引导原因状语从句。有关用法参见第 49 课课文注释 5。and 为并列连词,这里用来表示结果,意即"因此/结果洪水有时会给农场带来灾难"。

10．All the cattle had been moved into stalls and we stood to lose little.

and we stood to lose little 结果我们没有造成什么损失。此句中并列连词 and 同上句中 and 那样表示结果。stand to do（因采取特定行动或作下特殊承诺而）必然会做,如：

> *A big percentage of the farmers stood to benefit by the redistribution.*
>
> 大部分农民会因为再分配而受益。
>
> *The growing population stands to slow the rate of the development of society.*
>
> 不断增长的人口一定会降低社会发展的速度。

11．As the flood had put the telephone out of order, ...

out of order（机器等）失灵,次序紊乱,有毛病,不合规定,如：

> *The railway traffic is out of order owing to floods.*

洪水使铁路交通中断。

My stomach is out of order.

我的胃不舒服。

All these papers are out of order.

这些文件都不合规定。

句中 put ... out of order 为"使……中断/失灵"之意。

12. ... we could get a sweeping view of the river ... and at the most critical juncture we took turns in ...

（1）get a sweeping view of 一览无余地看到，get a view of 看到，如：

> *If we stand at this window, we'll get a better view of the procession.*
>
> 如果站在这个窗口，我们就能更清楚地看到游行队伍。

（2）at the most critical juncture 在最紧急的时刻，at a ... juncture 在……关头，在……时刻，如：

> *at an important historical juncture* 在重大的历史关头
>
> *It was at this juncture that he arrived upon the scene.*
>
> 他正好在这个关头到达了现场。

（3）take turns 轮流，依次。其后既可使用动词不定式也可如文中那样，使用"介词 in/at ＋ 动名词短语"的形式，表示"轮流/依次做……"的含义，如：

> *The two boys took turns in/at digging the hole.*
>
> 这两个小男孩轮流挖洞。
>
> *All of them take turns to clean the classroom.*
>
> 他们所有人都轮流打扫教室。

13. The first sign of disaster was a dead sheep floating down.

floating down 顺流漂下的。现在分词短语，作定语，修饰 sheep。

14. Next came a horse, swimming bravely, but ...

Next came a horse 为倒装句,正常语序为 A horse came next。在表达动作的简短句子里,为使句子表达生动和同前文更为紧凑,通常将"主语 + 动词 + 副词"这样的自然语序用倒装形式,即"副词 + 动词 + 主语"表示出来,如:

In came the teacher and the lesson began.

老师走了进来,接着开始上课。

Out rushed the boy.

那男孩冲了出去。

在口语中,也常使用这类倒装结构的语句,但往往是为了唤起注意,如:

There came the bus!

车来啦!

但当主语为人称代词时,需使用"副词 + 主语(人称代词) + 动词"这样的部分倒装的语序形式,如:

Away they hurried.

他们匆匆地走开了。

Out he rushed.

他冲了出去。

swimming bravely 为现在分词短语,作方式状语,修饰 came。

15. Suddenly a raft appeared, looking rather like Noah's ark, carrying the whole family...

(1) 句中 looking ... ark 和 carrying ... cage 均为现在分词短语,作 raft 的非限定性定语,对 raft 进行补充说明。

(2) Noah's ark 诺亚方舟。摘自《圣经·旧约》:上帝看到人世间充满了暴力和罪恶,决定用洪水把所造人和物统统消灭。但是由于不忍把一切都毁灭,他就决定让安分守己的诺亚等人活下来,并授意他和他的 3 个儿子造一只方舟,装载家人以及各种动物雄雌各一,以逃脱洪水浩劫。

16. We realized that they must have become unduly frightened by

588

the rising flood, for their house, which had sound foundations, would have stood stoutly even if it had been almost submerged.

even if 为复合连词,引导让步状语从句,使用 even if 后,句子通常用虚拟语气结构。文中 would have stood 和 had been submerged 即为虚拟语气的动词结构形式。

17. **... in the hope of being able to ...**

in the hope of 希望能。介词短语,作目的状语,修饰 waded down。其后如用动名词(如文中那样),或其后仅用名词时,也可使用 in hopes of ... 短语,如:

I am in the hope (in hopes) of succeeding this time.

我希望这次能成功。

He lives in hopes of better times.

他希望情况会好转。

语法 Grammar in use

as 的用法

1. 作从属连词引导时间状语从句

意即"当"、"一边……一边":

I pulled a muscle as I was lifting a heavy suitcase.

当我提一个重箱子时拉伤了肌肉。

Parts are replaced as they grow old.

零件老化时就要更换。

注意:as 不能用来表示在某一时间,如不能说:

∗ As I started work here, the pay was $4 an hour.

而应说:

When I started work here, the pay was $4 an hour.

我开始在那儿工作的时候,酬金是每小时 4 美元。

2．作从属连词引导原因状语从句

意即"因为"，与 because、since 相同：

As there was very little support, the strike was not successful.

由于得到的支持很少，罢工未获成功。

As the gorilla is so big and powerful, it has no real enemies.

由于大猩猩又大又厉害，它没有真正的敌人。

as 常用于句首，但是当表达某件事的某一特殊原因时，在 as 前面可以用 especially 或 particularly，此时 as 引导的原因状语从句放在主句后面，如：

I was frightened when I went to bed, especially as my room was so far up.

每当我睡觉时我都十分害怕，特别是因为我的房间在那么远的高处。

3．作从属连词引导方式状语从句

置于主语之后：

Type this again as I showed you a moment ago.
把这份文件照我刚才告诉你的那样再打一遍。

4．作从属连词引导比较状语从句

He looked over his shoulder as Jack had done.
他像杰克一样回头望了望。

He answers as quickly as his sister does.
他回答得和他妹妹一样快。

5．作副词

用于形容词前，意即"被认为"：

They regarded manual work as degrading.
他们认为体力劳动丢人。

Officials described him as brilliant.

590

官员们认为他英明。

6．作介词

意即"以……身份"、"作为"、"当作"、"像"：

He is greatly respected both as a person and as a politician.

无论作为一个人还是一位政治家他都受到人们的极大尊敬。

7．作介词

意即"像"：

The bread was as hard as a brick.

这面包像砖头一样硬。

注意：通常在将一件事或人同另一件事或人进行比较时，名词词组前不用 as 而用 like，如：

He swam like a fish.

他游泳像一条鱼。

Children , like animals , are noisy at meal times.

孩子们像动物似的，在吃饭时吵闹。

📂 词汇学习 Word study

1．overtake（overtook，overtaken）

（1）*vi.*，*vt.*追上，赶上，超过：

Don't overtake at a corner.

不要在拐弯处超车。

We overtook the slow lorry.

我们超过了那辆开得很慢的卡车。

By now no one can overtake his record.

到目前为止还没有人能超过这项记录。

（2）*vt.*（常用于不好的事）突然降临，突然发生（常用被动语态）：

The family was overtaken by tragedy several years ago ,

and they still haven't recovered.

几年以前悲剧降临到这个家庭，他们至今还未恢复过来。

She was overtaken by misfortune.

她突然遇到不幸。

2. make up

（1）组成，构成：

These three articles make up the whole book.

这 3 篇文章构成了这本书。

Road accident victims make up almost a quarter of the hospital's patients.

公路事故的受害人几乎占这所医院所有病人人数的1/4。

（2）补充，补足，补偿：

I'll make up the money to the amount you need.

我会补足你所需要的钱数。

We're hoping to make up time on the return journey by not stopping at night.

我们希望在回程中晚上不停下来，以把时间补回来。

（3）解决（争端），和解，言归于好：

It's time you made it up with your sister.

你该和你姐姐和好了。

They are quarrelling and making up by turns.

他们总是吵了好，好了又吵。

3. affect *vt.*

（1）影响：

Will the war affect the price of oil?

这场战争会影响石油的价格吗？

The divorce of his parents affected every aspect of his life.

他父母的离异影响到他生活的各个方面。

（2）（在感情上）打动，震动：

    She was much affected by the news of his death.

    他去世的消息使她受到很大的震动。

（3）（疾病）侵袭：

    The disease affected Jane's lungs.

    这个病使简的肺受到感染。

✍ 练习答案 Key to written exercises

1．关键句型、难点练习答案

See text.

2．多项选择题答案

1	b	2	a	3	c	4	c	5	d	6	c
7	b	8	c	9	a	10	d	11	c	12	a

Lesson 57
Back in the old country
重返故里

📖 **课文详注 Further notes on the text**

1. I stopped to let the car cool off and to study the map.

to let ... and to study ... 为两个并列的动词不定式短语。在句子中作目的状语。stop to do 表示"停下(原做的事)去做(另一件事)"之意,与 stop doing(停下在做的某件事)概念不同。

2. I had expected to be near my objective by now, but everything still seemed alien to me.

(1) expect to do ... 期望想做……在动词 expect 后可使用动词不定式作宾语;当构成 expect 的过去完成时(had expected)+一般动词不定式(to do)时,表示"过去想做而未做的事情",如:

I expect to start out early tomorrow morning.
我想明天一早就动身。

I had expected him to say 'Yes', but he said 'No' instead.
我原以为他会同意没想到他居然不同意。

(2) be alien to ... 对……陌生,与……不容,如:

Cruelty is quite alien to his nature.
残忍完全不合他的本性。

Orange trees are alien to Canada.
加拿大不生长桔树。

3. ... he did not quickly recover from the shock and loneliness.

recover from ... 从……恢复过来。通常用于健康或情绪方面

594

的"恢复",作借喻用法使用时,也可表示"力量、实力等受创后的恢复"。通常以当事人为主语,用于主动语态,如:

She has not yet recovered from the shock caused by the accident.

她在事故中受了惊吓,至今还未恢复过来。

It did not take them long to recover from the blow.

他们受到那次袭击后,很快就恢复过来。(借喻用法)

4. Everything around him was full of her presence, continually reopening the wound.

Everything ... presence 他身边的一切都有她的身影。continually reopening the wound,现在分词短语,作结果状语,意即"不断触痛他心头的创伤"。这里 wound 指"作者母亲的死给作者父亲心中造成的痛苦"。

5. In the new country he became absorbed in making a new life for the two of us, so that ...

be absorbed in (doing) ... 全神贯注/专心致志于(做)……,如:

No sooner had he finished his talk with them than he again became completely absorbed in his scientific work.

他一同他们谈完话,心思就又集中在他的科学工作上。

6. ... but I lacked for nothing ...

lack for 缺少,如:

They do not lack for funds.

他们不缺资金。

Space lacks for a detailed description of it.

篇幅有限,不能对此详述。

Money was lacking for the plan.

这项计划缺少经费。

7. He always meant to go back one day, but not to stay.

这里 mean 为"打算"、"想"之意,如:

> *I didn't mean to talk to her.*
>
> 我并没有打算要同她谈。
>
> *What do you mean by saying that?*
>
> 你那样说是什么意思?

not to stay,动词不定式 to stay 的否定形式,作目的状语,修饰 go back。这里的 stay 为"定居"之意。

8. ... **he made me promise to go on my own.**

on one's own 独自的/地。多用于口语,如:

> *I'm all on my own today.*
>
> 今天就我一个人。
>
> *You'd better tackle the problems on your own.*
>
> 你最好独立解决这些问题。

9. ... **a comprehensive book of maps,which I found most helpful...,but which I did not think I should need ...**

句中的两个 which 均作关系代词,引导非限制性定语从句,对 a comprehensive book of maps 作进一步说明。

10. It was not that ... But my father had described ... so that I was positive I should recognize it as familiar territory.

(1) 这两个句子在语义上是连贯的,实际使用了 not that ... but (that) ...(不是因为……而是因为……)这一完整的句型。有关用法参见第 39 课课文注释 4。

(2) 在 positive 与 I should ... territory 之间省略了连词 that。该从句为 was positive 的宾语从句,从句中的 should recognize 为虚拟语气结构,表示出说话者的情绪,往往使语气显得比较客气委婉。如果仅使用一般陈述语气,通常只着重叙述事实。

(3) recognize it as familiar territory 中,代词 it 指代 what we should see at every milestone 这一宾语从句。

11. Well,I had been wrong ...

596

well 为语气词,这里用来表示语气的转折,意即"可是"。

12. **... I should be looking at farms and cottages in a valley, with the spire of the church of our village showing in the far distance.**

这里 should be looking at 是虚拟语气结构,表明一种推测。with the spire ... in the far distance,带介词 with 的独立主格结构,the spire of the church of our village 相当于一个主语,而 showing 相当于其动词。这一独立主格结构在句中作状语,表明背景情况。

13. **I decided that I must have taken a wrong turning somewhere.**

take a wrong turning 拐错了弯。句中的"must + 动词完成时"结构表示对过去情况的推测。

14. **I felt as if I had stumbled into a nightmare country, as you sometimes do in dreams.**

as if,复合连词,引导方式状语从句,如课文中 had stumbled 那样,常使用虚拟语气结构。这里的代词 you 为泛指用法,其意义相当于 people,而非特指的第 2 人称单数。do 这里用于代替 stumble into a nightmare country, 以避免重复。

15. **... there was nobody in sight to help me.**

in sight 看得见,在视野内。to help me,动词不定式短语,作定语,修饰 nobody。

16. **... there appeared on the horizon a man on horseback, riding in my direction.**

there appeared on the horizon a man on horseback 为倒装语序。正常语序为:a man on horseback ... appeared there on the horizon。文中的句子构成了"副词 + 谓语动词 + 主语"这样的倒装句形式。有关此类倒装句的用法参见第 56 课课文注释 14。riding in my direction 向我骑来。现在分词短语,作定语,修饰 a man。

17. **The village no longer existed because it had been submerged，and all the valley too.**

all the valley too:承上在 all the valley 与 too 之间省略了整个谓语动词部分，即 had been submerged，意即"整个山谷也被淹没了。"

📁 词汇学习 Word study

no 的几种用法

1. 用作否定回答，如：

> *Can James play chess?*
> 詹姆斯会下象棋吗？
> *No, he can't.*
> 不，他不会。

no 也用作否定疑问句的否定回答，如：

> *You don't smoke, do you?*
> 你不抽烟，对吧？
> *No.*
> 对，我不抽。

2. 用于名词前作否定限定词，可以用在单数（可数和不可数）名词和复数名词前面，相当于 not any 或 not a。由于其本身就是一个限定词所以它不能和另一个限定词连用。如：

> *I have no complaints.*
> 我没什么好抱怨的。
>
> *No cigarette is completely harmless.*
> 没有无害的香烟。

3. 作副词，意即 not at all，可以同形容词和副词的比较级搭配使用，如：

> *The woman was no older than Kate.*

598

这个女人不比凯特年龄大。

Some people can eat what they like and get no fatter.

有些人想吃什么就吃什么，一点也不发胖。

4. 作副词，可以和 different、good、use 连用，如：

> *Is that book any good?*
> 那本书好吗？
> *It's no good at all.*
> 一点也不好。

It's no use crying over spilt milk.

事已至此，哭也没用。

The tasks which confront him are no different from those which faced his predecessor.

他所面临的任务与他前任的毫无区别。

5. no 可以和动词的 -ing 形式或名词搭配，表示不允许做某事。这个结构可以单独使用也可以用在 there is 后面，常用于公告等，如：

No smoking.

禁止吸烟。

No entry.

禁止入内。

No dogs.

狗不得入内。

📁 词汇学习 Word study

1. absorb *vt.*

(1) 吸收（液体或气体）：

Salt absorbs moisture from the air.

盐从空气中吸收水分。

The drug is quickly absorbed into the bloodstream.

药很快就被吸收到血液里了。

（2）掌握，理解：

So many new ideas! It's all rather too much for me to absorb all at once.

这么多的新观念！让我一下子全记下来真是太多了。

Have you absorbed all the details of the plan?

你把计划的全部细节都掌握了吗？

（3）吸引……注意力，使全神贯注，占去(时间、注意力等)：

I was absorbed in the computer games and didn't hear you call.

我的注意力全在电脑游戏上了，没听到你叫我。

She was absorbed in her thoughts.

她陷入沉思冥想中。

（4）把……并入，兼并，同化：

Our countryside is increasingly being absorbed by/into the large cities.

我们的农村正在日益不断地被大城市所吞并。

The company has gradually absorbed all its small rivals.

这家公司已经逐渐地将他所有的小型的竞争对手兼并了。

2. lack

（1）*vt*. 缺乏，没有，不足：

Their work is repetitive and lacks variety.

他们的工作是重复性的，缺乏变化。

We lack trained staff at the moment.

眼下我们缺少训练有素的职员。

（2）*n*. 缺乏，没有，不足：

There's a lack of trained engineers at the moment.

眼下缺少的是训练有素的工程师。

The plants died for lack of water.

这些植物死于缺水。

3. promise

(1) *vt., vi.* 允诺,答应,答应给予:

Promise (me) to be back before midnight.

答应(我)午夜前回来。

They promised (that) the work would all be finished by next week.

他们答应在下一周所有的工作都做完。

Her parents have promised her a new bike if she passes the exam.

她父母已经答应如果她通过考试就给她买一辆新自行车。

(2) *vt.* 有……可能,给人以……指望:

The clear sky promises fine weather.

晴朗的天空预示着好天气。

The men's final this afternoon promises to be a very exciting match.

今天下午举行的男子决赛可能非常令人激动。

She promises to be a fine dancer.

她有望成为一个优秀的舞蹈演员。

(3) *n.* 诺言,承诺,保证,(有)可能,(有)前途:

If you've made a promise you should keep it.

如果你作出了承诺你就得实现它。

Despite their promise to bring down inflation, prices have gone on rising.

尽管他们的承诺是降低通货膨胀,可是物价还是一直在上涨。

The news brings little promise of peace.

这个消息没有带来什么和平的希望。

✍ 练习答案 Key to written exercises

1. 关键句型、难点练习答案

See text.

2. 多项选择题答案

| 1 | d | 2 | d | 3 | b | 4 | a | 5 | c | 6 | b |
| 7 | c | 8 | d | 9 | a | 10 | c | 11 | c | 12 | b |

Lesson 58

A spot of bother

一点儿小麻烦

📖 **课文详注** **Further notes on the text**

1. ... and her basket had grown heavier with every step of the way home.

with every step of the way home 为介词短语,作状语,表示伴随情况。with 在这里表示"随着",意即"篮子随着回家的每一步越变越重"。

2. In the lift her thoughts were on lunch and a good rest; but when she got out at her own floor, both were forgotten in her sudden discovery that her front door was open.

(1) her thoughts were on ... 她只想到……

(2) got out 走出(电梯)。可理解为省略了 of the lift。

both,这里指她所想的 lunch 和 a good rest 这两件事。

(3) in her sudden discovery that ... 当她突然发现……discovery 后的连词 that 引导的从句为 discovery 的同位语。

3. She was thinking that she must reprimand her home help the next morning for such a monstrous piece of negligence, when ...

(1) reprimand sb. for ... 因为……而训斥某人,如:

The boss reprimanded him for insufficient control.
老板因其管理不善而训斥了他。

The secretary was severely reprimanded for leaking out some secret without permission.

603

这位秘书因未经允许泄露某项机密而遭严厉训斥。

(2) when 为从属连词,用来引导时间状语从句。但是这里使用了其倒置形式,即未将其置于逻辑上的时间状语之前,而使用在了主句之前。when 的这种倒置用法,常用于表示增强某动作的突发性效果。有关用法参见第20课课文注释4。

4.... yet following her regular practice she had shut ...

yet 为副词,意为"而"。following ... practice,现在分词短语,作方式状语,修饰 had shut。

5. It was as clear as daylight then that ...

as clear as daylight 像白天一样清楚,即"十分清楚"之意。这是一个明喻成语。其他常见的此类明喻成语有 as cold as ice(冰一样冷)、as white as snow(雪一般白)、as red as a rose(红如玫瑰)、as steady as rock(坚如磐石)、as swift as lightening(迅如闪电)、as strong as a horse(体壮如牛)等。

6. Her first impulse was to go round all the rooms looking for the thieves, but then she decided that at her age it might be more prudent to have someone with her ...

(1) looking for the thieves 为现在分词短语,作目的状语,修饰 go round。

(2) it 为先行代词,作形式主语,其逻辑主语为后面的动词不定式短语 to have someone with her。

7.... she was ready to set off with the porter's assistance to search for any intruders who might still be lurking in her flat.

with the porter's assistance 在看门人的协助下。介词短语,作方式状语,修饰 set off。注意"在……帮助下"应使用介词 with,如 with the help/assistance of ...。

8. They went through the rooms, being careful to touch nothing, as they did not want to hinder the police in their search for fingerprints.

（1）being careful to touch nothing 小心翼翼地不碰任何东西。现在分词短语,作方式状语,修饰 went through。

（2）hinder sb. in ... 在……方面妨碍某人,如:

> *Don't hinder him in his work.*
>
> 不要妨碍他的工作。
>
> *Her stubbornness hinders her in relationship with other people.*
>
> 她的倔强妨碍了她同他人的关系。

当用 hinder 来表示"妨碍/阻止某人做……"这一含义时,通常需使用介词"from ＋ 动名词"结构,即 hinder sb. from doing ...,如:

> *Nothing shall hinder me from accomplishing my purpose.*
>
> 什么也不能阻止我达到目的。

9. At least sorting out the things she should have discarded years ago was now being made easier for her.

sort out 把……加以分门别类,挑选,如:

> *Sort out the things you want to keep and throw everything else away.*
>
> 把你要保存的东西拣出来,其余的都扔掉。
>
> *You should have the ability to sort out the good from the evil.*
>
> 你应有区分善恶的能力。

由于句子为被动语态形式,因此形容词 easier 作句子主语的补足语。

10. ... thereby proving that ...

proving that ... the balcony,现在分词短语,作非限定性定语,修饰 that the front door locks had not been forced 这一事实。

11. ... which the old lady said was not hers.

the old lady said 作插入语,作进一步说明。

12. ... but since the porter agreed with him, she rang up her daughter and asked for her help in what she described as a little spot of bother.

in what she described as a little spot of bother 中的 what 为关系代词，作动词 described 的宾语。describe ... as ... 把……说成/描述成……as 后的名词性短语 a little spot of bother(一点小麻烦)为宾语补足语。

📑 语法 Grammar in use

祈使句

祈使句常用来告诉某人做某事或不做某事,一般没有主语。主要用于表示命令、建议、请求、告诫、指引、指导、禁令、劝告、邀请、提议等。

1. 祈使句的形式与一些普通用法

用动词原形,否定祈使句用 don't + 动词原形,在较正式的情况下用 do not + 动词原形,如:

Follow me.

跟着我。(命令)

Enjoy yourself.

玩个痛快。(建议)

Look out! There's a bus!

当心! 有辆公共汽车。(告诫)

Take the 2nd turning on the left and then turn right.

在第 2 个拐角处向左,然后再向右拐。(指引)

Use a moderate oven and bake for 20 minutes.

在中温烤箱里烘烤 20 分钟。(指导)

Keep off the grass!

请勿践踏草坪! (禁令)

Always answer when you're spoken to !

别人跟你说话时,你要回应!（劝告）

Come and have dinner with us soon .

一会儿来跟我们一起吃饭吧。（邀请）

Help yourself .

请自己动手。（提议）

2.祈使句的强调

（1）将 always 或 never 用于句首,如:

Always check that you have enough money first .

总要先检查一下你有足够的钱。

Never believe what he tells you .

永远不要相信他告诉你的任何事。

（2）用 do,如:

Do have another cup of coffee .

请再喝一杯咖啡。

Do help me with this math problem .

请帮助我解答这道数学题。

（3）用主语 you 可以引起我们说话对象的注意,也可以加强语气
或表达愤怒,如:

You wait here for a moment .

你在这儿等一会儿。

You get in the car this minute !

你马上进到车里去!

3.用 please 使语气更婉转

在句首或句尾用 please 使语气更婉转,如:

Please don't do that .

请别那么做。

Follow me , please .

请跟着我。

4.与附加疑问句连用表示请求、不耐烦等

Post that letter for me , will you ?

请你替我把那封信发了,好吗?

Hurry up , can't you ?

快点,行吗?

5.用 and 与 or 连接的祈使句

某些祈使句后面可以跟 and 和另一个祈使句,如:

Go and buy yourself a new pair of shoes .

去给自己买双鞋吧。

Wait and see .

等着瞧吧。

在美国英语中,有时 go 后面直接加动词原形,如:

Go fetch some water . (= Go and fetch . . .)

去拿点水来。

有时后面跟 and 或 or 具有条件状语从句的含义,如:

Say that again , and I'll hit you . (= If you say that again , I'll hit you .)

如果你再说一遍,我就揍你。

Hurry up , or you'll be late for school . (= If you don't hurry up , you'll be late for school .)

快点,要不你上学就迟到了。

📂 词汇学习 Word study

1.force

(1) *vt*.强迫,迫使:

He forced me to do it .

他强迫我做它。

His arguments forced them to admit he was right .

608

他的辩论迫使他们承认他是对的。

(2) *vt.* 用力：

> *They had to force their way through the crowd.*
> 他们必须得费力地从人群中穿过。
>
> *He tried to force the box through the tiny hole in the fence.*
> 他试图将那只箱子从篱笆上的一个小洞塞过去。

(3) *vt.*, *vi.* 勉强做出，牵强地使用(言辞)：

> *He had to force a smile as he said goodbye.*
> 当他说再见时不得不强装笑脸。
>
> *In his speech he forced a metaphor.*
> 在讲话中他牵强地使用了一个比喻。

2. force *n.*

(1) 力，力量：

> *The force of the wind was so great that roofs were blown off houses.*
> 巨大的风力将房顶掀掉了。
>
> *Sometimes the window gets stuck and you have to use a bit of force to get it open.*
> 有时窗户被卡住了，你不得不用点力气才能将它打开。

(2) 暴力，武力：

> *Teachers are not allowed to use force in controlling their pupils.*
> 在管理学生时不允许老师使用暴力。
>
> *They took back those islands by force.*
> 他们靠武力夺回了那些岛屿。

(3) 军事力量，部队，一群人：

> *Both land and sea forces were employed in the attack on the island.*

609

在进攻那个岛屿时陆军和海军都用上了。

A small force of doctors and nurses was rushed to the scene of the big fire.

一小队医生和护士被急速地派往大火现场。

3. possess *vt.*

(1) 具有(品质),拥有:

He possessed the qualities of a war leader.

他具有充当战时领导人的品质。

For hundreds of years London possessed only one bridge.

在上千年里伦敦只有一座桥。

(2) 控制,使受(感情或想法等的)支配:

I don't know what possessed him to drive so fast down that busy street.

我不知道什么使得他在那么繁忙的大街上把车开得那么快。

Whatever possessed you to act so foolishly?

究竟是什么使你干如此蠢事?

✎ 练习答案　**Key to written exercises**

1. 关键句型、难点练习答案

See text.

2. 多项选择题答案

1 c	2 b	3 d	4 a	5 a	6 a
7 c	8 a	9 b	10 b	11 d	12 d

Lesson 59
Collecting
收　藏

📖　**课文详注　Further notes on the text**

1 . . . . sometimes without being aware of doing so.

without . . . so，介词短语，作方式状语，修饰 amass。be aware of . . . 意识到……

2 . . . . become indiscriminate collectors of what can only be described as clutter.

关系代词 what 引导的从句作介词宾语的情况很常见，如：

This reminded me of what he had once told us .

这使我想起了他有一次给我们讲的话。

They were never satisfied with what they had achieved .

他们从不满足于他们已取得的成就。

本句中介词 of + what 从句作定语，修饰 collectors。to describe . . . as . . . 把……说成/描述为……。

3 . . . . in the belief that they may one day need just those very things.

(1) in the belief that . . . things 作伴随状况状语，修饰 leave。在 in the belief that . . . 中，that 引导的从句作 belief 的同位语。

(2) very 这里用来加强语气，意即"正是那个(些)"、"正是所要的"，如：

He is the very man the police want .

他正是警察要找的人。

She took it from me under my very nose !

她就在我鼻子底下把它拿走了。

4. ... for two other reasons, lack of physical and mental energy, both of which are essential in turning out and throwing away, and sentiment.

(1) lack of physical and mental energy 和句尾的 sentiment 为两个并列成分,作 two other reasons 的同位语,对其具体指明。both of which are essential in turning out and throwing away 中的 both of which 指 lack of physical and mental energy 和 sentiment,意即"这二者都是翻出来扔出去(即无用的东西)时所必不可少的"。整个这一部分作 physical and mental energy 的非限制性定语,对其作进一步说明。

(2) be essential in ... 在……方面十分重要,如:

He respected every opinion his friend held, which is essential in friendship.

他尊重他朋友的每一个意见,这对保持友谊十分重要。

Punctuality is essential in the business world.

守时在商界至关重要。

表示"为……所必需"时,介词常用 for,表示"对……所必不可少"时,介词常用 to,如:

Exercise, fresh air and sleep are essential for the preservation of health.

锻炼、新鲜空气和睡眠是保持健康所必需的。

Is wealth essential to happiness?

财富对于幸福是必不可少的吗?

5. Things owned for a long time are full of associations with the past ...

(1) be full of 充满。

(2) association 为动词 associate 派生的名词。使用动词 associate 时,其搭配形式为 associate ... with ...(把……同……联系

612

起来）。派生为名词 association 后,其意义和搭配都无变化,
即为 association with ...(与……有联系)。

6. **Some things are collected deliberately in the home in an attempt to avoid waste.**

in an attempt to do ... 为了做……,试图/企图做……介词短语,作目的状语,其中动词不定式作 attempt 的定语,如:

> *Her father sent her to the warm south in an attempt to restore her health.*
> 她父亲把她送往温暖的南方,希望使她恢复健康。
> *He was in a vain attempt to rob the house.*
> 他抢劫这所房子没有成功。

7. **... string and brown paper, kept by thrifty people when a parcel has been opened, to save buying these two requisites.**

(1) kept by ... requisites 为过去分词短语,作非限制性定语,修饰 string and brown paper。

(2) to save buying these two requisites 为动词不定式短语,作目的状语,修饰 kept,其中 save doing ... 意为"省去做……"。直接用于动词 save 后的动词通常需构成动名词形式,如:

> *If you walk to the office every morning, you'll save spending money on bus fares.*
> 如果你每天早上步行上班,就可省去买车票的钱。

8. **I know someone who always cuts sketches out from newspapers of model clothes that she would like to buy if she had the money.**

介词短语 of model clothes 作定语,修饰 sketches,作 cuts out 的宾语,即按正常语序应为 cuts sketches of model clothes out from newspapers。由于关系代词 that 引导的定语从句较长,且同 sketches of model clothes 关系较为密切,需直接置于其后对它进行修饰,这样就会使 from newspapers 置于全句末尾,从而使

613

全句头重尾轻,失去平衡。为使句子保持较好的平衡,这样把表示地点状语的介词短语 from newspapers 放在了 sketches 和 of model clothes 之间。

9. **... the chances that she will ever be able to afford such purchases are remote; but she is never sufficiently strong-minded to be able to stop the practice.**

that ... purchases 作 chances 的同位语,对其作具体说明。动词不定式 to be able ... the practice 作结果状语,修饰 sufficiently strong-minded; the practice 在这里指 cut out sketches of model clothes 这一做法,意即"她从来就没有足够的坚强意志停止这种做法"。此为夸张说法,以强调其着迷的程度。

10. **... to such an extent that every time she opens it, ...**

此介词短语在句子中作结果状语,其中 that 引导的从句作 extent 的同位语,如:

He was mad to such an extent that he beat his father.

他竟然疯到打起他父亲来了。

The car was damaged to such an extent that it could not be repaired.

这辆车毁得太厉害,根本就无法修了。

every time 每次,每当。作连词,相当于 whenever。

11. **Whatever it consists of, stamps, records, first editions of books, china, glass, antique furniture, pictures, model cars, stuffed birds, toy animals, there is always something to do in connection with it, from finding the right place for the latest addition, to verifying facts in reference books.**

(1) whatever 无论什么,不管什么。关系代词,引导让步状语从句。这里的代词 it 指代 collection。stamps ... toy animals 一系列表示具体事物的名词作关系代词 whatever 的同位语,对

614

其进行举例说明。

(2) in connection with 与······有关，与······相连，关于，如：

He asked many questions in connection with life in Britain.

他问了很多有关英国生活情况的问题。

Several people have been detained in connection with the robbery.

好几个人因与这起抢劫案有牵连而被拘留。

(3) 句中 in connection with 同其前面的动词不定式 to do 均作 something 的定语。from finding ...、to verifying facts ... 与 in connection with it 并列，作 something 的定语，因此用逗号将其分开。这里是 from ... to ...(从······到······)的搭配使用。由于 from 后所随内容较长，且直接连接使用(即 the latest addition to verifying ...)易于造成句子的误解，因此将此搭配结构间用逗号予以分开。

12. ... but also in general matters which have some bearing on it.

have bearing on ... 与······有关，如：

It has direct（immediate）bearing on the subject.

它和本题直接有关。

It has an important bearing on the relations between China and the United States.

这对于中美关系举足轻重。

13. One wants to meet like-minded collectors, ... to show off the latest find.

(1) 句中 wants 后连续使用的 5 个动词不定式短语并列作动词 wants 的宾语。这样使用时，应如文中那样，将其一一用逗号分开。

(2) show off 炫耀，如：

She loves showing off her new dress.

她喜欢炫耀自己的新衣。

He never shows off.

他从不卖弄自己。

14. Soon the hobby leads to travel, perhaps to a meeting in another town, ... for collectors are not confined to any one country.

(1) lead to 导致。短语中 to 为介词,因此所用 travel 为名词。to travel 与 to a meeting ... specimen 为两个并列的介词短语,作状语,修饰 lead。a meeting 与 possibly a trip ... specimen 为并列成分,作介词 to 的宾语。

(2) confine ... to 把……限制在,把……关闭在,如:

He is confined to his house by flu.

他因流感闭门不出。

She confines her remarks to scientific management.

她所讲的话仅限于科学管理问题。

15. In this way self-confidence grows, first from mastering a subject, then from being able to talk about it.

first from ... 和 then from ... 这两个介词短语并列作动词 grows 的状语。grow from ... 由……发展起来。

16. Collecting, by occupying spare time so constructively, makes a person contented, with no time for boredom.

by occupying spare time so constructively 为介词短语,作方式状语,说明 makes a person contented 的方式。正常语序为:Collecting makes a person contented with no time for boredom by occupying spare time so constructively. 句中将 by ... 这一方式状语提前,主要是为了强调和使句子显得更为紧凑。with no time for boredom 也为方式状语,修饰 makes a person contented。

📖 语法 Grammar in use

情态助动词 may 与 might

may 与 might 主要用来表示可能性,也可用于请求,或提出建议。当这两个词无意义区别时,may 比 might 更正式些。在口语中 might not 的简略式 mightn't 较常用,而 may not 的简略式 mayn't 则很少见。

1. 表示可能

(1) 表示现在和将来的可能性

> *This may be why women enjoy going back to work.*
> 这可能就是为什么妇女喜欢重新工作的原因。
> *They might be able to remember what he said.*
> 他们可能能记住他说了些什么。

可以用 might well 或 may well 表示某事相当有可能,如:

> *You might well be right.*
> 你很可能是对的。
> *I think that may well have been their intention.*
> 我认为那极可能原本就是他们的打算。

用 might not 或 may not 表示可能某件事不是那么回事,如:

> *He might not be in France at all.*
> 他可能根本不在法国。
> *That may not be true.*
> 那可能不是真的。

注意:不能用 might not 或 may not 表示不可能某件事是那么回事,而只能用 could not、can not 或 can't,如:

> *Kissinger can't know what the situation is in the country.*
> 基辛格不可能知道那个国家的情形如何。

注意:不能用 may 询问某事是否可能,而用 might 或 could,如:

Might / Could this be true ?

这会是真的吗?

(2) 表示过去的可能性

用 might 或 may + have + 过去分词表示可能某事在过去发生,但是不知道确实是否发生过,也可用 could,如:

His brother might / could have secretly married her classmate , Louise .

他弟弟可能秘密地同他的同班同学露易丝结婚了。

I may have seemed to be overreacting .

我可能看上去反应太过分了。

如果要表达过去可能发生而没有发生的事情,则只能用 might have 或 could have + 过去分词形式,不能用 may have + 过去分词形式,如:

A lot of men died who might have been saved .

很多人死了,他们原本可能被救活的。

用 might not + have 或 may not + have + 过去分词形式表示可能过去某件事不是那么回事或不曾发生,如:

They might not have considered me as their friend .

他们可能并不把我当成他们的朋友。

The parents may not have been ready for this pregnancy .

这对父母可能尚未对这次怀孕做好准备。

注意:不能用 might not + have 或 may not + have + 过去分词形式表示不可能过去某件事是那么回事或曾发生过,而只能用 could not + have 或 cannot + have + 过去分词形式,如:

The measurement couldn't have been wrong .

那个测量不可能错。

The girls cannot have been seriously affected by the system .

那些姑娘不可能受到那种体制的严重影响。

2．表示请求

may 和 might 可以用于请求或请求得到允许或给予允许,此为较正式的用法:

May/Might I have a sandwich ?

请问我可以要一份三明治吗?

You may speak .

你可以讲。

3．表示非常客气的提议

May I take your coat ?

我可以为您拿大衣吗?

You might like to comment on his latest proposal .

你可能想就他最新的建议谈点看法。

📁   词汇学习   Word study

1．tend   *vi* .

(1)易于,往往会:

Plants tend to die in hot weather if you don't water them .

如不浇水,植物在炎热的天气里容易枯死。

(2)(to, towards)走向,趋向:

Modern industry tends towards consolidation .

现代工业趋向合并。

(3)有助于:

These measures tend to improve（the improvement of）working conditions .

这些措施有助于改善工作条件。

2．describe   *vt* .

(1)(用文字)描写,描述:

In several of his novels Dickens describes the miserable

conditions of children in the early 19 th century.

狄更斯在好几部小说里都描写了 19 世纪早期儿童的困境。

(2) (as) 把……说成,把……称为:

She is always describing him as a genius.

她总是把他称作天才。

(3) 画出(图形),形成……形状:

His arm described a circle in the air.

他的手臂在空中划了个圈。

3. confine *v.*

(1) (to) 限制,使局限:

Their knowledge about agriculture has so far been exclusively confined to books.

他们的农业知识至今仍仅限于书本上的东西。

(2) (to) 使不外出,禁闭:

His parents confined him to his room for the weekend for failing to do his chores.

他父母周末不让他外出,因为他没做家务。

Since theft has become his habit, he should be confined.

偷盗既已成了他的习惯,就该把他关起来。

✍ 练习答案 Key to written exercises

1. 关键句型、难点练习答案

See text.

2. 多项选择题答案

1 a	2 d	3 a	4 d	5 b	6 d
7 d	8 b	9 b	10 a	11 d	12 b

Lesson 60
Too early and too late
太早和太晚

📖 **课文详注 Further notes on the text**

1. **Without it, nothing could ever be brought to a conclusion; everything would be in a state of chaos.**

在一些使用了介词 without 的句子中,常使用虚拟语气,如本句中 could be brought 和 would be 即为虚拟语气的动词结构形式,用来表示较委婉地陈述看法。

2. **Only in a sparsely-populated rural community is it possible to disregard it.**

only 用于句首或用于 only + 状语 + 句子其他成分的句子中时,其后的主语和谓语动词通常须构成倒装形式。

3. **The intellectual, who is working on some abstruse problem, has everything coordinated and organized for the matter in hand.**

(1) work on ... 从事于……,致力于……为动介短语,其后须使用名词,代词或动名词做宾语,多用于进行时态或完成进行时态,如:

> *They have been working on a design for a lighter plough.*
> 他们一直在设计一种比较轻的犁。

当 on 为副词时,即构成动词加副词短语时,除可表示上述意思外,还可表示"继续工作"之意,但其后不能使用宾语,如:

> *They'll work on until sunset.*
> 他们将继续工作到日落。

(2) for the matter in hand 为手中的事。作目的状语,其中介词短语 in hand 为定语,修饰 matter。

4. He is therefore forgiven if late for a dinner party.

if 如果。从属连词,引导条件状语从句。现从句省略了 he is。在以连词 when, though, if 等引导的从句中,如果其主语与主句主语相同,且其主语后为动词 be 时,从句中的主语和动词 be 往往可以省略。有关用法参见第 36 课课文注释 7。

5. But people are often reproached for unpunctuality when their only fault is cutting things fine.

(1) reproach sb. for (doing) ... 责备/指责某人(做)……。通常指以平等关系提出意见,这种意见可以是正确的,也可以是吹毛求疵的,如:

His wife reproached him for his spending too much.
他妻子指责他花钱太多。

They severely reproached the driver for his carelessness.
他们严厉指责那个司机粗心大意。

(2) cut things fine 把时间安排得不留余地。也可为 cut it fine,多用于口语中,如:

She arrived thirty minutes before her flight, so she was cutting it a bit fine.

航班起飞前 30 分钟她才到;她把时间安排得有点太紧了。

He always cuts things fine.
他总把时间安排得很紧。

6. ... so they are often tempted to finish a job before setting out to keep an appointment.

be tempted to do ... 忍不住做……,如:

I was tempted to stand up and refute him then and there.
我简直忍不住想要当场站起来驳斥他。

She was tempted to ring him up, but her pride would not

let her do this.

她忍不住想给他挂电话,但是她的自尊心阻止了她。

7. If no accidents occur on the way, like punctured tyres, diversions of traffic, sudden descent of fog, ...

like 为介词,它所构成的介词短语,即 like punctured tyres ...
fog 作定语,修饰 accidents,意即"如果没有像爆胎……之类的
事情发生的话"。

8. The over-punctual can be as much a trial to others as the unpunctual.

(1) over-punctual 和 unpunctual 为形容词,其前使用定冠词后,如
the rich、the poor 搭配那样,使之表示"……类的人"之意。

(2) as much as... 像/和……一样。这里将此短语用作同等程度
的比较,much 为副词,还可表示诸如"几乎等于……"、"差不
多"、"实际上"等意义。可将此句视为 The over-punctual can
be a trial to others as much as the unpunctual。用于表示同等
程度的比较时,此短语为状语,用来修饰句中的动词,如:

You hated him as much as I (did).

你恨他像我恨他一样深。

You as much as promised you would help me.

你实际上答应了要帮助我。

9. The only thing to do was ask them to come ...

to do 为动词不定式,作 thing 的定语,意即"惟一能做的事情"。
ask them to come ... quests 为动词不定式短语,作主语的补足
语。通常作主语补足语的动词不定式前需使用 to,但如果主
语全部或部分含有作主语补足语的动词不定式的意义时,即为
主语中所含"do"的意义的引申或为其内容时,该动词不定式的
to 可以省略,如:

All I did was turn off the tap.

我只不过把水龙头关上罢了。

The only thing you can do is wait and see.

你别无它法,只能观望。

10. ... than even a fraction of a minute too late.

a fraction of a minute 一分钟里的几秒,几秒钟。意即"……也比晚到哪怕几秒钟要好"。

11. ... this will be less than if you miss the train and have to wait an hour or more for the next one; and you avoid the frustration of arriving at the very moment when the train is drawing out of the station and being unable to get on it.

(1) 根据上文中,句中的 this 指 wasted time,因此使用了 little 的比较级 less。

(2) at the every moment when... 中,when 为关系副词,引导定语从句,修饰 moment。

(3) being unable to get on it,动名词短语,与 arriving ... station 并列作 frustration 后的介词 of 的宾语,勿将此作为 when 引导的定语从句中的内容。being unable to get on it 前的连词 and 表示结果。

12. ... the first time she was travelling alone.

the first time 为连词,引导时间状语从句,意即"她第一次单独旅行的时候"。

13. ... since her parents had impressed upon her that it would be unforgivable to miss it and cause the friends with whom she was going to stay to make two journeys to meet her.

(1) impress ... upon/on ... 把……铭刻在…… 即"要……牢记……",如:

They impressed on their children the virtue of always telling the truth.

他们要孩子牢记永远说老实话的美德。

(2) cause the friends ... to make two journeys to meet her 为 cause

624

sb. to do . . .（迫使某人做……）的用法。在此结构中，sb. 后的动词不定式 to do，即文中 to make two journeys to meet her，作宾语补足语。意即"赶不上火车，使得与她相聚的朋友来接她两次是不可原谅的"。

14. She felt in her handbag for the piece of paper on which . . .

feel 也可跟 after。feel for 更口语化，如：

He had to feel for the stairs in the dark.

在黑暗中，他不得不摸着找寻楼梯。

由于句中 for 后的宾语太长，为使句子更为紧凑，这样将正常语序中应置于句尾的地点状语 in her handbag 提到了现句中的位置。句中 felt . . . 和 gave it to the porter 并列作谓语。

15. He agreed that a train did come into the station . . . and that it did stop, but only to take on mail, not passengers.

句中的两个 did 均为 do 的强调用法。but only to take on mail, not passengers，动词不定式短语，作目的状语，修饰 stop。其中，在 not 与 passengers 之间，承上省略了 to take on，意即"但只是为了装邮件，而不是为了上客"。

16. The girl asked to see a timetable, feeling sure that . . . .

feeling sure that . . . mistake，现在分词短语，作原因状语，修饰 asked。

17. The girl, tears streaming down her face, begged . . .

tears streaming down her face，带分词短语的独立主格结构，作方式状语。

18. And she had to watch that train disappear towards her destination while she was left behind.

and 起承上启下的作用，以使上下文连接更为紧凑，表示"于是"；while 为连词，这里表示"而"。

语法 Grammar in use

间接引语中动词不定式的结构和用法

1. 引述动词 + 宾语 + to 动词不定式用来转述命令、请求、建议等。句子中的宾语是接受命令、请求、建议的人。常用的引述动词有 advise、ask、beg、command、instruct、invite、order、remind、tell、warn 等，如：

> "*Keep a record of your expenses*," *I said.*
> 我说："把你的花费记个账。"
> *I told him to keep a record of his expenses.*
> 我叫他把他的花费记个账。

> '*Remember to switch off all the lights*,' *she said.*
> 她说："记着把所有的灯关掉。"
> *She reminded me to switch off all the lights.*
> 她提醒我把所有的灯关掉。

在转述否定祈使句时，需将 not 放在带 to 的不定式之前，如：

> '*Don't make a mess in the kitchen.*' *she said to the boy.*
> "别把厨房搞得乱七八糟，"她对那个男孩说。
> *She told/asked/warned the boy not to make a mess in the kitchen.*
> 她叫/要求/警告那个男孩子别把厨房搞得乱七八糟。

2. 当说话人请求允许或提出请求时，可以用引述动词 + to 动词不定式转述，如：

> '*May I speak to the manager?*' *I asked.*
> "我可以同经理谈话吗？"我问道。
> *I asked to speak to the manager.*
> 我请求同经理谈话。

引述动词 ask 后面也可以跟被动不定式，如：

> *He asked to be kept informed about developments.*

626

他要求随时向他报告发展情况。

3. 表示建议和征询意见情况的一般疑问句和含有疑问词的征询等，除了用宾语从句转述外，还可以用疑问词 + to 动词不定式转述，如：

'Shall/Should I phone her?'
"我应该给她打电话吗?"

He wanted to know if/whether he should phone her.
(宾语从句)
他想知道他是否应该给她打电话。

He wanted to know whether to phone her.(疑问词 + to 动词不定式)
他想知道他是否应该给她打电话。

📁 词汇学习 Word study

1. forgive (forgave, forgiven) *vi.*, *vt.*

(1) 原谅, 宽恕:

This is an insult that will not be easily forgiven.
这个侮辱是不能轻易被宽恕的。

She has already forgiven him for his being rude.
她已经原谅了他的鲁莽。

(2) 免除:

I forgave him the whole amount he owed me.
我免除了他欠我的全部债款。

2. reproach *vt.*

(1) (多用于平等关系上的)责备, 指摘:

Don't reproach him with laziness; he has done his utmost.

不要指责他懒惰, 他已尽了最大努力。

627

He reproached his wife for spending too much.

他责怪妻子花钱太多。

(2) 引起对……的指摘,使蒙耻:

What you've said and done reproaches your character.

你的所说所为有损你的人格。

3. tempt *vt.*

(1) 引诱,诱惑:

His ambition tempted him into politics.

他的野心诱使他投身政界。

(2) 吸引,引起……的兴趣,使很想要(做):

The offer tempts me.

这个提议使我感兴趣。

She was tempted out by the pleasant weather yesterday.

昨天的好天气使她忍不住外出游玩。

Their unfriendliness tempted me to leave the party at once.

他们冷淡的态度使我很想立即离开聚会。

(3) 冒……风险:

He finally decided to tempt the hardships of that strange land.

他最终决定去冒那异地艰苦生活的风险。

✍ 练习答案 **Key to written exercises**

1. 关键句型、难点练习答案

See text.

2. 多项选择题答案

1	b	2	b	3	d	4	b	5	b	6	c
7	a	8	c	9	c	10	b	11	a	12	c

628

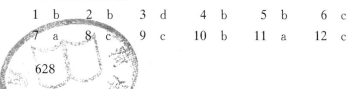